THE ISSEI

THE ISSEI

The World of the First Generation Japanese Immigrants, 1885–1924

Yuji Ichioka

THE FREE PRESS
A Division of Macmillan, Inc.
NEW YORK

Collier Macmillan Publishers
LONDON

The Free Press
A Division of Macmillan, Inc.
866 Third Avenue, New York, N. Y. 10022

Collier Macmillan Canada, Inc.

First Free Press Paperback Edition 1990

Printed in the United States of America

printing number

1 2 3 4 5 6 7 8 9 10

Library of Congress Cataloging-in-Publication Data
Ichioka, Yuji.
　　The Issei.

　　Bibliography: p.
　　Includes index.
　　1. Japanese—United States—History. 2. Japanese
Americans—History. 3. United States—Emigration
and immigration. 4. Japan—Emigration and immigra-
tion.
I. Title.
E184.J3142　　1988　　973'.04956　　88-3693
ISBN 0-02-932435-1

Grateful acknowledgment is made to the following journals for permission to reprint my previously published articles:

Agricultural History
"The Japanese Immigrant Response to the 1920 California Alien Land Law," 58:2 (1984), 157–78.

Amerasia Journal
"A Buried Past: Early Issei Socialists and the Japanese Community," 1:2 (1971), 1–25.

"*Ameyuki-san*: Japanese Prostitutes in Nineteenth Century America," 4:1 (1977), 1–21.

"The Early Japanese Immigrant Quest for Citizenship: The Background of the 1922 Ozawa Case," 4:2 (1977), 1–22.

"Asian Immigrant Coal Miners and the United Mine Workers of America: Race and Class at Rock Springs, Wyoming, 1907," 6:2 (1979), 1–23.

"An Instance of Private Diplomacy: Suzuki Bunji, Organized American Labor, and Japanese Immigrant Workers; 1915–1916," 10:1 (1983), 1–22.

Labor History
"Japanese Immigrant Contractors and the Northern Pacific and Great Northern Railroad Companies, 1898–1907," 21 (1980), 325–50.

Pacific Historical Review
"Japanese Associations and the Japanese Government: A Special Relationship, 1909–1926," 46 (1977), 409–37.

"*Amerika Nadeshiko:* Japanese Immigrant Women in the United States, 1900–1924," 48 (1980), 339–57.

"'Attorney for the Defense': Yamato Ichihashi and Japaneses Immigration," 55 (1986), 192–225.

To My Parents,
the Late Kunio Ichioka and Sei Ichioka,

and

To My In-Laws,
Gee Nay Ning and Hom Tiu-gok

Contents

Acknowledgments

I am indebted to many individuals and organizations in the course of researching and writing this book. A Ford Foundation grant, administered by the Institute of American Cultures at UCLA, provided some of the initial support. The past and present staff and students of the Asian American Studies Center at UCLA were continually supportive of my work, for which I am deeply grateful. Alexander Saxton, Norris Hundley, and Fred Notehelfer, all members of the UCLA History Department, and Emma Gee were unfailing in their warm encouragement and critical comments. Yasuo Sakata of the UCLA Japan Exchange and Research Program was of uncommon help throughout my research. He gave me indispensable advice on numerous occasions.

I received invaluable help from many scholars and friends in Japan as well. A 1981–82 Japan Foundation Professional Fellowship enabled me to spend six months in Japan. During this time, I became acquainted with recent Japanese studies of Japanese immigration history. Kachi Teruko, now professor emeritus at Tsuda Women's College, who then headed an immigration research group, was my academic sponsor. Ishikawa Tomonori, Kodama Masaaki, Tsurutani Hisashi, Shimaoka Hiroshi, and Togami Sōken all generously shared their research findings with me. I also received help from Shōji Keiichi, Ōtsuka Hideyuki, Iino Masako, Oshimoto Naomasa, Matsui Shichirō, Seki Hajime, Sodei Rinjirō, Yanagawa Keiichi, Sanada Takaaki, Nakajima Yoriko, Arai Katsuhiro, Matsubayashi Shun'ichi, Yamane Nobuyo, Yamaguchi Kōsaku, and the late Chiba Kō. Finally, I owe a special debt to Shibusawa Masahide and his wife, Chako.

Seizo Oka, head of the Japanese American History Library of San Francisco, supplied me with certain sources from his library. Jere Takahashi of the University of California at Berkeley and Jerry Surh of North Carolina State University critically read many of my early articles. Clifford Uyeda and Nikki Bridges of the Center for Japanese American Studies of San Francisco regularly invited me to give talks to share my preliminary research findings with their group. H. Mark Lai, Russell Leong, Jim Omura, and Karl Yoneda consistently encouraged me to write this book. A number of Issei women living in the Los Angeles Japanese Retirement Home kindly shared their life experience with me in a series of group discussions in 1978. Those who attended my classes in Japanese-American history in various local communities and at UCLA motivated me to complete the book. Their keen interest in the subject matter made me realize, in a very personal and concrete way, the dire need for a history of the Issei generation.

All historians are indebted to special library holdings. I would like to single out those libraries and their staffs which were especially important to this study: the National Diet Library and the Foreign Ministry Diplomatic Records Office in Japan; The Hoover Institution and University Archives, Stanford University; the Bancroft Library, University of California, Berkeley; the Minnesota Historical Society, St. Paul; the Colorado Historical Society, Denver; the California History Room, California State Library, Sacramento; the Western History Research Center, University of Wyoming, Laramie; and the Department of Special Collections, University Research Library, UCLA, Los Angeles, which holds the invaluable Japanese American Research Project Collection on Japanese immigration history.

Grant Ujifusa, senior editor of The Free Press, enthusiastically supported the publication of this book. I would like to thank him here and commend his staff for its fine job of editing. I alone, of course, bear responsibility for any factual error or misinterpretation.

CHAPTER

I

Introduction

The early history of Japanese immigrants in the United States, far from being a success story, is, above all, a history of a racial minority struggling to survive in a hostile land. Past studies of Japanese immigration have concentrated heavily on the anti-Japanese exclusion movement from 1900 to 1924, focusing on the excluders rather than the excluded, on the anti-Japanese racists rather than the Japanese immigrants. In 1790 Congress had enacted the first naturalization act which restricted the right of naturalization to an alien who was a "free white person." Subsequent enactments, legislated during the course of the nineteenth century, all included this racial condition. In 1870 Congress extended the right of naturalization to former slaves, making aliens of African birth and persons of African descent also eligible. Being neither white nor black, Japanese immigrants, along with other Asian immigrants, were classified as "aliens ineligible to citizenship," without the right of naturalization. This study, adopting the perspective of the excluded, narrates the history of Japanese immigrants as aliens ineligible to citizenship from 1885 to 1924.

Without the right of naturalization, Japanese immigrants stood outside the American body politic. Many European immigrants faced formidable obstacles upon their arrival in America. Italians, Poles, Greeks, Armenians, Jews, and others experienced great hardship adjusting and adapting to an alien and often hostile land. Japanese immigrants shared much in common with their European counterparts. Yet

1

every European immigrant group, regardless of national origin, had the right of naturalization. And precisely because they possessed it, no matter how beleaguered they were, they were able to enter the political arena to fight for their rights. Indeed, they were often able to elect someone from their own midst. By contrast, much of the legal discrimination Japanese immigrants encountered was based on their ineligible status. The alien land laws enacted by most western states prohibited aliens ineligible to citizenship from purchasing and leasing land. In fights against anti-Japanese racists, Japanese immigrants never had the option of entering the political arena to defend themselves. They had either to depend upon the diplomacy of Japanese government officials, seek redress of injustice through the court system, or appeal to an abstract American sense of fair play and justice. Excluded from the political process, Japanese immigrants were political pariahs who had no power of their own to exercise. This state of powerlessness is a central theme in Japanese immigrant history.

Japanese immigrant history is also labor history. During the rapid expansion of industrial capitalism after the Civil War, non-English-speaking immigrants, chiefly of eastern- and southern-European origin, filled the ranks of the unskilled labor force required by American industry. In the western United States, Japanese immigrants entered the urban service trades and the agricultural, railroad, mining, lumber, and fishing industries. With the exception of those who found employment in the urban service trades, they all started out as common laborers who worked under a labor-contracting system, replacing a declining and aging Chinese immigrant labor force. Within the contracting system, Japanese immigrant labor contractors served as intermediaries between the laborers and their employers. Flourishing during the peak of Japanese labor immigration, the contracting system enabled the contractors and employers to profit at the expense of the laborers. The life of hardship, struggle, and sacrifice of Japanese immigrant laborers under this contracting system represents the dark side of Japanese immigrant history and the untold Japanese side of western labor history.

The entry of Japanese immigrant laborers into the western labor market coincided with the ascendancy of the American Federation of Labor (AFL) in the American labor movement. The AFL, representing an aristocracy of labor, consisted overwhelmingly of craft unions of skilled, white workmen. As a leading proponent of Japanese exclusion, the AFL continually advocated the termination of all Japanese immigration to the United States. According to its public stance, Japanese immigrants worked for cheap wages and had a low standard of living, so that white workmen thrown into competition with the Japanese were degraded. Exclusion was thus held necessary to preserve American labor standards; the AFL ostensibly championed it solely for economic self-protection, not for racial reasons. Coupled with this surface justification, the AFL opposed Japanese immigration by fostering the myth that Japanese laborers were dominated completely by their labor bosses and would never make good union men.

The history of Japanese immigrant labor belies the AFL's position. Until the 1930s, the AFL adhered to a racist policy of assigning skilled minority workers to segregated locals or excluding them from union membership altogether. As for Japanese laborers, it refused flatly to admit any of them, even those who were skilled workmen. Thus Japanese immigrant laborers stood outside the structure of organized labor as well. Under the labor-contracting system, tensions between Japanese laborers and their contractors periodically erupted into open conflict. Many laborers, especially those with student backgrounds, were keenly interested in modern labor problems and solutions. They were knowledgeable about principles of trade unionism and aware of AFL racism. A few were attracted by the Industrial Workers of the World (IWW) because of its militant advocacy of industrial unionism and its rejection of AFL racism. Japanese laborers, moreover, notwithstanding AFL hostility, made significant efforts to organize themselves to eliminate the labor-contracting system and to establish genuine labor unions. All this, too, is an untold aspect of Japanese immigrant history.

The history of Japanese immigrants can be divided into two broad periods: 1885 to 1907, and 1908 to 1924. The first period was characterized by a pattern of *dekasegi* immigration. *Dekasegi* designates the practice of Japanese laborers leaving their native place temporarily to work elsewhere; a *dekaseginin* is any person who engages in this practice. *Dekasegi* always includes the ideal of returning home eventually. During Tokugawa times, that is, until 1868, the term was applied to internal migration only, but from the Meiji era it was broadened to encompass the practice of going abroad to work temporarily, known as *kaigai dekasegi*. The earliest instance of *kaigai dekasegi* was a handful of *yatoi-dohi*, or menial servants, who were hired in Japan by westerners and taken abroad; the first mass case was the nearly 30,000 government contract laborers who went to Hawaii between 1885 and 1894. Three common phrases embodied the *dekasegi* ideal: *toshu kūken*, meaning empty-handed, described the destitute state in which Japanese

immigrants landed on the Pacific Coast; *ikkaku senkin* expressed the
dream of striking it rich overnight; and *kin'i kikyō* meant to return
home wealthy, the dream of dreams. This *dekasegi* pattern of Japanese
immigration, it should be noted, in no way makes Japanese immigrants different from their European counterparts, because many European immigrants also started out as birds of passage or sojourners.

The Japanese government never envisioned permanent labor emigration to the United States or elsewhere. During the 1870s and
1880s, the Foreign Ministry was engrossed in seeking revisions in the
unequal treaties which had been imposed upon Japan by the Western
powers. It looked with disfavor on labor emigration, for fear that
uneducated laborers would make it harder to obtain such revisions by
reinforcing the western image of Japan as an uncivilized nation. The
short-term effect of this negative view was that the Japanese government began to exercise strict control over the departure of laborers.
The Foreign Ministry set two conditions for the issuance of passports
to *dekasegi* laborers: contractual terms of employment and wages had
to be spelled out clearly, and safe return passage to Japan had to be
guaranteed. In this way, it was believed, the danger of indigent laborers becoming stranded abroad could be averted. The long-term effect
was the limitation of labor emigration, particularly to the United
States and Canada, and its unilateral termination once the anti-Japanese
exclusion movement began at the turn of the century.

During the anti-Japanese exclusion movement, the Japanese government protested anti-Japanese acts and utterances. This has given rise
to the common belief that Japanese immigrants, unlike Chinese immigrants, benefited from the backing of a strong homeland government.
Contrary to this belief, however, the Japanese government regularly
sacrificed the welfare of the immigrants for the sake of what it perceived as diplomatic necessity. It gave in to American pressure time
and again. This ambivalent policy did not escape the attention of Japanese immigrant leaders. To describe the failure of their government
to come to their aid, they coined the term *kimin*, which means literally
"an abandoned people," suggesting that the government abandoned
them so that they had to fend for themselves in a hostile land.

From approximately 1908, Japanese immigrants began to shed their
dekasegi orientation, marking the beginning of the second period in
Japanese immigrant history. Many laborers started to settle on agricultural land to take up farming. Historically, this transition from laborer
to farmer occurred, not because of a sojourning mentality as some
have argued, but because of the influence of immigrant leaders. In

response to the exclusion movement, the leadership became convinced that their fellow immigrants, for their part, had to discard their *deka-segi* ideal and opt for permanent residency. But to make the shift from itinerant laborer to permanent resident, the leaders realized that the men had to have an economic stake in American society as an incentive to sink roots in American soil. That stake proved to be primarily in agriculture. Based on the belief that Japanese laborers were suited ideally for farming, immigrant leaders actively promoted agriculture as the economic foundation of permanent residency. Under their influence, many laborers took up farming, while some became proprietors of small businesses, which became their stake in American society.

Social factors buttressed the economic foundation. Many women entered immigrant society between 1910 and 1920. Japanese government regulations allowed farmers and businessmen, but not laborers, to summon wives from Japan. This difference served as an extra incentive for laborers to become farmers or businessmen. With the encouragement of immigrant leaders, many onetime laborers sent for wives as soon as they changed occupation. Wives enabled these men to enjoy a settled family life. In this way, the immigrant family unit emerged as the key social institution underlying permanent settlement. The birth of children, in turn, gave new meaning to their American residency. Japanese immigrants now had to consider the future of their children in the United States.

Concurrent with this shift in orientation, Japanese immigrants struggled against the anti-Japanese exclusion movement. Always sensitive to white criticism, immigrant leaders strove to eradicate what they considered the unsavory features of Japanese immigrant life. They established Japanese Associations as political organizations which exerted a powerful influence. In concert with religious and social bodies, these associations conducted periodic moral-reform campaigns to rid immigrant society of prostitution, gambling, and other vices. They tried to control the behavior of all immigrants in various ways and even cooperated with police authorities to have so-called undesirable elements deported. Externally, the associations conducted educational campaigns appealing to the understanding and goodwill of Americans. Believing that anti-Japanese sentiments were rooted in ignorance, they attempted to educate the American public about Japanese immigrants. The immigrants themselves adapted to American society in many other ways. They accepted the primacy of an American public school education for their children, assigning a secondary educational role to the private Japanese language schools which they themselves established. To solve the problem of the dual nationality of their children, they successfully lobbied for amendments to Japan's Nationality Act.

Fully aware of the American judicial process, they also sought justice through the court system. Besides ordinary civil and criminal cases, they brought two other types of cases to court: the naturalization and alien land law test cases. Japanese immigrants pursued the right of naturalization in the landmark Takao Ozawa case. In ruling on this case in 1922, the Supreme Court affirmed that the Japanese were ineligible under existing naturalization statutes. By this ruling, the high tribunal upheld the powerless political status of the Japanese and indirectly sanctioned the legal discrimination against them based on their ineligibility. In several key 1923 land law test cases, Japanese immigrants contested the constitutionality of the alien land laws of California and Washington. For them, these two alien land laws as well as those of other western states were a bread-and-butter issue since they threatened their very livelihood. To the utter disbelief and dismay of the immigrants, the high court upheld the constitutionality of the laws. This ruling, which ended the immigrant quest for justice, had a drastically adverse effect on the Japanese who were in agriculture.

The anti-Japanese exclusion movement climaxed with the passage of the 1924 Immigration Act. One provision of this Act prohibited the admission of aliens ineligible to citizenship as immigrants. The high court had already ruled that the Japanese were ineligible. Hence this provision, based on the assumption of the racial inferiority and undesirability of Asians, abruptly halted all Japanese immigration to the United States. All through the exclusion years, Japanese immigrants had adapted themselves to American society and had endured countless instances of racial hostility and discrimination. The Supreme Court had denied them naturalization rights and upheld the alien land laws. Now Congress closed the doors to Japanese immigration with the 1924 Immigration Act symbolizing, to the Japanese immigrants, their total rejection by the United States. From this point in time, it was difficult for the immigrants to conceive of any real future for themselves in this country. The only future they saw was that of their American-born children, the Nisei. The anti-Japanese exclusion movement left an enduring legacy of bitterness and resentment which rankled in the hearts of Japanese immigrants through the 1930s. Not a Horatio Alger saga, this early Japanese immigrant history, centered primarily in the state of California, opens with the arrival of the first student-laborers, prostitutes, and *dekasegi* laborers in the late nineteenth century.

CHAPTER

II

Early Japanese Immigration

Student-Laborers

Indigent students were among the first Japanese immigrants in the United States. Students who went abroad during the Meiji era were divided into two broad categories. On the one hand, there were government scholarship-holders, the elite among all students. Granted full stipends by the Meiji government, the majority of these students were sent to Europe. Those sent to the United States studied principally in New England and assumed high posts when they returned to Japan. On the other hand, there were private students who went abroad to study at their own expense. These students were divided into two subcategories: those with financial means, and those with few or no resources. In the first subcategory were students supported by well-to-do families or generous patrons. These students also studied mostly in the East and returned to Japan. As such, neither the government scholarship students nor the privileged private students can be considered as being among the pioneers of Japanese immigrant society.

The real forerunners were indigent private students. Known as *hinsei* or *kugakusei*, two terms which denoted their penurious state, the students in this subcategory, in contrast to their wealthier brethren, had to work their way through school. Like the laborers who would follow them, they were sojourners at first. They came to learn English and to acquire some kind of knowledge and/or skill with which to embark on a career in Japan. But because they were compelled to work, they were laborers of a kind, and known by another common term: *dekasegi-shosei,* or student-laborers. This designation set the indigent students apart from the government scholarship students and the privileged private students. For the student-laborers, labor was a means to an end. Their immediate aim was to learn English and acquire knowledge and/or a skill. Their ultimate goal was to achieve success in Japan by applying what they learned and acquired in the United States. Prepared to endure hardships, many of these students had high ambitions, drawing inspiration from the Meiji creed of *risshin shusse.* This embodied the belief that anyone could realize lofty goals with dedication, diligence, thrift, and perseverance.

Scores of indigent students landed in San Francisco from the mid-1880s. The U.S. Census of 1890 reported 2,039 Japanese residents in the United States, of whom 1,147 were in California. Between 1882 and 1890 the Japanese government issued 3,475 passports to persons leaving for the United States, of which 1,519 were issued to private students.[1] More numerous than any other category, the 1,519 private student passports accounted for 43.8 percent of all the passports issued during this period. The number of passports issued to private students in 1882 and 1883 was very small, but in 1884 it jumped sharply to 202 and averaged over 200 in successive years.[2] Of course, these figures cannot be equated with the actual number of private students who came to the United States. After all, every student who received a passport did not necessarily leave Japan, and an undetermined number of students landed without passports. The figures represent at best a rough estimate.

The majority of these private students were *dekasegi-shosei.* An 1886 guide to San Francisco for student-laborers noted the predominance of indigent students among an estimated 300 Japanese in the city in 1885.[3] Another guide to the city, also published in 1886, estimated the 1886 population as being 700, with the majority being "penniless, destitute students."[4] Of an estimated 1886 population of 800, an 1887 guide observed:

> the majority . . . are sons of small, middle-level businessmen and farmers between the ages of 15 and 25. Although insufficiently, they have been educated under the compulsory education law currently in force in Japan. After studying English and learning the customs and manners of Caucasians, they plan to return to Japan and obtain desirable positions.[5]

Ozaki Yukio, a former Japanese government official and journalist, visited San Francisco in 1888. Based upon conversations with local residents, he reported 2,000 Japanese in the city, with poor students numbering between 1,600 and 1,700.[6] In March 1890 the *Japan Weekly Mail* reported:

> The Japanese community in San Francisco . . . has been growing by leaps and bounds within the past few years, until it numbers over three thousand souls. . . . The rank and file are of the poor student class, youths who have rashly left their native shores. . . . Hundreds of such are landed every year, with miserably scant funds in their pockets. . . . Their object is to earn, with the labour of their hands, a pittance sufficient to enable them to pursue their studies in language, sociology, and politics.[7]

The estimate of 3,000 may be too high. Yet the 1890 U.S. Census count of 1,147 Japanese in California is probably too low. In all likelihood, the Japanese population in 1890 was in the neighborhood of 2,500, composed mainly of student-laborers concentrated heavily in San Francisco.

Indigent students continued to arrive through the 1890s and after. The Japanese government statistics again offer a rough estimate of numbers. The number of passports issued to private students from 1891 to 1900 was 2,764.[8] Except for a small drop during the Sino-Japanese War period, the number averaged over 200 in the early 1890s and rose slightly towards the end of the decade. In sum, the arrival of the *dekasegi-shosei*, beginning in the mid-1880s, preceded the arrival of large numbers of laborers. Lacking the wherewithal to travel east, the students settled down in San Francisco and its vicinity and constituted the majority of local Japanese residents until the late 1890s.

A popular vision of America attracted these students to the United States. As the foremost advocate of Western learning, Fukuzawa Yukichi played an influential role. A renowned scholar, prolific writer, and respected teacher, he wrote many books concerning the West. Prior to the 1880s his two most celebrated and widely read guides to the West were *Seiyō Jijō* (Western Conditions) in 1866, and *Seiyō Tabi Annai* (A Travel Guide to the West) in 1867.[9] In 1882 he launched the *Jiji Shimpō*, a Tokyo newspaper, in which he encouraged young men to go abroad.

In Fukuzawa's judgment, Japanese society was unable to absorb the growing number of educated youth who were coming out of the new Meiji educational system. Opportunities were far too few and narrow.

The world of commerce offered little in the way of satisfying employment to impatient, ambitious youth, and the government bureaucracy
offered even less. Fukuzawa exhorted such youth to strive for a career
abroad, particularly in America where, he believed, opportunities
abounded because the country was blessed with abundant natural resources and an enterprising population. Indeed, America had made
such giant strides that she was surpassing the accomplishments of Europe. The emigration of youth, in Fukuzawa's opinion, would benefit
Japan by expanding her contacts with foreign countries and generating
a demand for Japanese goods abroad.[10] Fukuzawa promoted his idea
of emigration, not only in the *Jiji Shimpō*, but also in public speeches
at Keiō Gijuku, the private academy he founded in 1858.

In 1887 he helped finance an overseas venture. Under Fukuzawa's
direct influence, Inoue Kakugorō, a former Keiō student, organized
a party of 30 persons to establish an agricultural colony in California.
Along with another person, Fukuzawa financed this expedition. According to Inoue, Fukuzawa thought as follows:

> Fukuzawa argued at length on the need for emigration. If one reads
> the *Jiji Shimpō* from its inception, and especially from 1885 to 1889,
> one will find editorials on the need for emigration on every third or
> fourth page. Japan is now quite civilized; the social order is established.
> No reason exists for Japan to remain a small, isolated island in the
> Orient. Japanese should go to foreign lands without hesitation and se-
> lect suitable places to live. They must not forget Japan, however, in
> normal or other times. They should consume Japanese products for
> daily necessities, and they should start businesses which will benefit the
> homeland. The more emigration flourishes, the further our national
> power will expand. These were the main points Fukuzawa advanced
> in promoting emigration. Fukuzawa said to me personally that people
> as a rule believe that one should never abandon one's birthplace. Then,
> he said that I should lead others and go abroad. He gave me money,
> and I immigrated to America.[11]

Landing in San Francisco in the summer of 1887, Inoue led his group
to Valley Springs, Calaveras County. There he started a short-lived
colony with the purchase of 20 acres of land.[12] Tsukamoto Matsuno-
suke, who became a prominent leader of the San Francisco Japanese
community, was among the members of this colony. Ushijima Kinji,
commonly known outside of Japanese immigrant society as George
Shima, the Potato King, came to the United States as an indirect result
of the establishment of this colony. In 1887, he read Inoue's accounts
of the settlement in the *Jiji Shimpō*, and it inspired him to leave Japan

in 1888 after he had failed the entrance examination for the Tokyo Higher Commercial School.[13]

In Wakayama Prefecture, Honda Waichirō, a former student of Fukuzawa who had studied at Keiō Gijuku, opened a small academy called the Kyōshū Gakusha.[14] This school was located in Honda's native village of Ikeda in Naga District. Influenced by Fukuzawa's thinking, Honda encouraged local youth to emigrate to the United States. One of the first to do so was Domoto Takanoshin who landed in San Francisco in 1884 as a student-laborer. He later became the successful proprietor of the North American Mercantile Company, a major import-export firm based in San Francisco, while his younger brothers became noted floriculturists in northern California. Honda's influence went beyond the district of Naga and extended to the neighboring district of Kaisō and the city of Wakayama, both of which also contributed many emigrants to the United States. Many young men from this area of Wakayama Prefecture relied upon those who preceded them in the 1880s for assistance to make the trans-Pacific crossing.

Guides to America were important sources of popular knowledge of this country. Three guides for student-laborers appeared in the 1880s: Akamine Seichirō, *Beikoku Ima Fushingi* (Mysterious America) (Tokyo, 1886); Tomita Gentarō and Ōwada Yakichi, *Beikoku-yuki Hitori Annai: Ichimei Sōkō Jijō* (How to Go to America Alone: A Guide to San Francisco) (Yokohama, 1886); and Ishida Kumatarō and Shūyū Sanjin, pseud., *Kitare, Nihonjin* (Come, Japanese!) (Tokyo, 1887). Written by student-laborers who had lived or were living in San Francisco, these guides presented, with typical Japanese thoroughness, facts about schools, employment, and living conditions, and projected a rosy picture of the city as a place where Japanese youth could work and study at the same time. And more often than not, hyperbole was used. The guide *Kitare, Nihonjin,* for example, projected this deceptively alluring image:

> Come, merchants! America is a veritable human paradise, the number one mine in the world. Gold, silver, and gems are scattered on her streets. If you can figure out a way of picking them up, you'll become rich instantly to the tune of ten million and be able to enjoy ultimate human pleasures. Come, artisans! Sculptors, lacquerers, carpenters, painters—anyone skilled in the least in the Japanese arts—can earn a lot of money by making fans, ceramics, and lacquerware. Come, students! Working during the daytime, you'll have time to attend night school in the evening. And if you earn your school expenses by persevering

for two to three years, it's not far-fetched to think of graduating from
a college.[15]

In 1889 the Ōsaka Mainichi published Beikoku Jijō (American Conditions) which also contained descriptions of student life in San Francisco.

An 1887 treatise actually espoused Japanese labor immigration to
California. Entitled Beikoku Ijūron (On Immigration to America), it
was authored by Mutō Sanji. Mutō had also been a Keiō student. He
left Japan in January 1885, aboard the City of Tokyo, the ship on
which the first contingent of Japanese contract laborers sailed for Honolulu to toil on Hawaiian sugar plantations. Mutō resided three years
in the San Francisco area as a student. He was fascinated by the presence of Chinese immigrants in Honolulu and on the West Coast. He
admired them for having left their homeland and for competing
economically with Americans. He believed that the western United
States was a vast, undeveloped area which only awaited an adequate
supply of labor to tap its rich natural resources. The Chinese had been
a major source of labor. The Chinese Exclusion Act of 1882, however,
halted all Chinese labor immigration. Seeing Japanese laborers as a
substitute for Chinese labor, Mutō argued that their shipment to California could be a profitable business undertaking.[16]

Popular knowledge of America filtered through personal contacts
as well. One of the first student arrivals was Miyama Kan'ichi who
landed in 1875. After residing ten years in San Francisco, he returned
temporarily to Japan in 1885. In public talks, he gave the impression
that Japanese youth could work and study in the city of San Francisco.
To assist prospective student-laborers, Miyama set up branches of the
Gospel Society, or Fukuinkai, the first Japanese immigrant group in
San Francisco, in Yokohama and Tokyo.[17] Personal contacts of course
were not limited to formal talks, but included informal conversations
between returnees and aspiring student-laborers. Letters were also a
source of information. Katayama Sen, the well-known Japanese Com-
munist, arrived in 1884. A close friend in San Francisco informed him
by letter that it was possible to work one's way through school,
which prompted him to cross the Pacific. More than anyone else, he
typified the student-laborer. He had to borrow money not only for
his steerage passage but also for a set of used western clothes. When
he landed, he had only a Mexican peso in his pocket, the equivalent
of sixty cents.[18]

One organization, the Rikkōkai, specifically assisted indigent students to go abroad. Founded in 1897 by Shimanuki Hyōdayū, the Rikkōkai was a Christian organization which extended a helping hand to poor students in the Tokyo area. Shimanuki toured the United States in the winter of 1897–98, and he came away convinced that he could help his students best by sending them to this country. In 1901 he published the first of several guides to America under the title *Seikō no Hiketsu* (The Secret of Success). In 1902 he wrote *Tobei Annai* (Guide to America), and in 1904 *Saishin Tobeisaku* (Recent Guide to America). In addition to facts on educational institutions, all of Shimanuki's guides contained information regarding employment opportunities and the nascent Japanese immigrant community. In 1907 he began publication of the *Tobei Shimpō,* a monthly devoted exclusively to disseminating news about America and how to cross the Pacific.[19]

Apart from the popular knowledge of America, changes in the Japanese conscription laws were a factor behind the emigration of student-laborers. According to the first law enacted in 1873, all males between the ages of seventeen to forty were subject to military service. Certain provisions allowed exceptions to this blanket rule, the most pertinent of which covered males who occupied unique positions in their households. In deference to the Japanese family system, these provisions granted exemptions to heads of families, sole sons and grandsons, adopted sons, and others. Another provision gave exemptions to the wealthy by permitting any person to pay a substitute fee of 270 yen in lieu of military service. Deferments were granted under special circumstances to various types of persons, among them students studying abroad. To make the terms of exemption and deferment stricter, this original law was amended in 1879 and again in 1883, but the exemptions in relation to the family system and the deferment for students studying abroad were retained. The 1883 amendment outlawed the substitute fee, eliminating the exemption based on wealth. Additional revisions, far more drastic in scope, were enacted in 1889, when the law was amended to remove all exemptions tied to the family system. Regardless of standing in a household, and independent of other considerations, every male became subject to conscription.[20]

These amendments altered the draft status of a sizable segment of the male population. Males who at one time were exempted found themselves suddenly eligible for conscription. If they did not want to serve in the military and perceived no other options, their new eligibility became an inducement to leave Japan. And if they left as students, they qualified for deferments which enabled them to legally avoid the

draft. While it is impossible to determine how many student-laborers
actually left Japan to avoid being conscripted, what can be said with
a degree of certainty is that the 1889 amendments became, at least to
some student-laborers, an added reason to emigrate. While the popular knowledge of America attracted them to this country, the changes
in the conscription law played a role in their decision to leave Japan.[21]

Among the student-laborers, there was a small group of political
exiles of about 30 young men who had participated in the so-called
People's Rights Movement in Japan. To understand their arrival in the
United States, it is essential to outline the People's Rights Movement.
During Tokugawa times, the samurai as a class had occupied a privileged position in feudal society. That position changed dramatically
with the Meiji Restoration in 1868. The new Meiji government
stripped the samurai class of the socio-economic prerogatives it had
enjoyed during Tokugawa times, thereby forcing all samurai to fend
for themselves. Dissident samurai of Kōchi Prefecture initiated a protest campaign in 1874. Drawing on eighteenth-century French doc-
trines of the natural rights of man and the equality of social classes,
they advocated the creation of a national elected assembly in the hope
of curbing the power of the central government. Besides being opposed to the centralization of government, they also advocated the
right of self-government and local autonomy, and instituted mutual-
aid programs to rehabilitate themselves economically.

Spreading outward from Kōchi Prefecture, this samurai class-based
local protest campaign developed into the People's Rights Movement.
Rallying around the objective of establishing a national assembly,
small political groups sprang up throughout the country from 1878.
Discontented samurai were not the only people with grievances.
Wealthy farmers and rural landowners resented the land tax imposed
upon them by the central government. Viewing a national assembly
as a means of reducing their taxes, many of them joined the movement
in the late 1870s. As a result of the broadening appeal of the movement, the Liberal Party was organized in October 1881. That year,
peasants were drawn into the movement as well. To curb a runaway
inflation, the Meiji government in 1881 adopted monetary measures
to force down agricultural prices. The result was a rural depression
which drove dispossessed peasants into the ranks of the new party.
From 1882 the peasants stressed economic issues at the local level, and
the movement, reflecting the full onslaught of the depression, turned
progressively violent, with armed uprisings, and even attempts to assassinate government leaders.

The movement ultimately collapsed under severe repression. In 1880 the Meiji government had promulgated regulations governing public meetings and political associations. Police authorities were granted the power of prohibiting political meetings if they deemed them "injurious to public peace." Sponsoring groups had to secure permits in advance by submitting not only membership rosters and by-laws but also lists of speakers and their topics. Military personnel, police officers, teachers, students, and others were barred from attending political meetings and enrolling in political associations. And all political groups were restricted in terms of advertisement and communication. These regulations, revised and strengthened in 1882, enabled the Meiji government, in a sweeping way, to control the content of political meetings, limit membership in political associations, and hinder the growth of the People's Rights Movement.

The government adopted even more repressive acts in 1887. The National Press Law was revised to muzzle the press completely. The amendments, requiring all publishers to obtain police permits, empowered the police to revoke the permit of any newspaper which published material deemed "prejudicial to public peace and order" or detrimental to "morals." The Peace Preservation Regulations became the most infamous measure. Banning all secret societies and assemblies, the regulations authorized police authorities to prohibit any meeting, regardless of content, "whenever they deem such a course necessary." In addition, they granted the police the power to order anyone near the Imperial Palace or Imperial Resort who was suspected of plotting disturbances to leave the area within a prescribed time period. As soon as the regulations became effective, the police rounded up more than 500 persons in Tokyo who had participated in the People's Rights Movement and summarily ordered them to vacate the city. The Liberal Party had been dissolved in October 1884 because the leadership realized that it was unable to control the rank and file, and that it was impossible to preserve the Party intact without the freedoms of speech, assembly, and press. The Peace Preservation Regulations sounded the death knell of the movement.[22]

The political exiles among the student-laborers came from this type of background. The first contingent landed in 1886 and included such figures as Sugawara Tsutau, Watari Tokuji, Yamato Masao, Ishizuka Masatsugu, Hinata Terutake, Hirota Zenrō, and Yamaguchi Yūya. A native of Wakayama Prefecture, Yamaguchi had served a jail term for violating the National Press Law. Sugawara, the group leader, was a native of Miyagi Prefecture. In common with their fellow student-laborers, these young men worked and studied in the San Francisco area. Unlike their counterparts, however, they did not come with this objective primarily in mind. Instead, they left Japan to escape political persecution. In keeping with this motive, on January 7, 1888, they established in San Francisco a political club called the Patriotic League. This club was located on the edge of Chinatown, at 314 O'Farrell Street. The Meiji government promulgated the Peace Preservation Regulations on December 26, 1887, so that the formation of the League at this time was significant. Even the name of the club harked back to the Patriotic Society formed in Ōsaka in 1875 as the People's Rights Movement spread beyond Kōchi Prefecture. The aims of the League were threefold: to sponsor talks and debates, to publish a newspaper, and to maintain contacts with movement leaders in Japan. Today, these aims seem so innocuous; yet they must have been precious to members of the Patriotic League, for in exile they were able to enjoy freedom of speech, assembly, and press, fundamental rights which had been abridged in Japan by the Meiji government.[23]

Origins of Immigrant Society

The origins of Japanese immigrant society can be traced to the student-laborers and political exiles. The roots of the society go back to the establishment of Christian institutions. As already noted, the first immigrant organization was the Fukuinkai or Gospel Society, which was composed of early student converts to Methodism and Congregationalism. Miyama Kan'ichi and Nonaka Kumatarō led the Methodists. Both had arrived in 1875 and had been baptized in 1877 by the Reverend Otis Gibson, superintendent of the Chinese Methodist Episcopal Mission in Chinatown. Miyama had come with a letter of introduction from Dr. George Cochran, a missionary in Tokyo, to Dr. Thomas Guard, pastor of the Howard Street Methodist Episcopal Church, who in turn had introduced him to the Reverend Gibson. Koyano Keizō and Nishimaki Toyosaku headed the Congregationalists. These two men had arrived in 1874 and had been baptized by a Congregational minister. These new Methodist and Congregationalist student converts and others founded the Gospel Society on October 6, 1877.

The society started under austere conditions. The members secured a room as a meeting place in the Chinese Methodist Episcopal Mission located at 916 Washington Street. Situated in the basement, the room had no windows and was so dark that lighting was necessary even during the day. The furniture consisted of a broken-down table and wooden crates which served as chairs. Candles, placed on nails driven into the table, provided the lighting. Here 35 members assembled every Saturday night for Bible study under the guidance of Reverend Gibson. Each member paid monthly dues of 35 cents, and the membership elected a president, treasurer, and secretary. Koyano Keizo served as the first president. Soon after the society was established, an adjoining room was secured as a residence where the members constructed wooden-tiered bunks, described as similar to those found on sea-going vessels, on which they slept, with bedding made of potato sacks stuffed with grass. Cold, dark, and damp, the facility left so much to be desired that it came to be dubbed an *ana kura*, which literally means a storage hole.[24]

Later Christian institutions evolved out of the Gospel Society. In 1881 the Congregational members withdrew and established another Gospel Society. Located first at 116 and later at 126 Tyler Street, it came to be known as the Golden Gate Gospel Society after Tyler Street was renamed Golden Gate Avenue. A second splinter group founded a third society in 1883. Unable to sustain itself, this group merged with the Golden Gate Gospel Society, which then had Akamine Seichiro, author of one of the first guides to San Francisco, as president. With 33 members drawn from the Golden Gate Gospel Society, the First Japanese Presbyterian Church of San Francisco was inaugurated in May 1885. Dr. Ernest A. Sturge appeared on the scene at this juncture. A former medical missionary to Siam, he had returned to San Francisco in the summer of 1885. In the following spring, the Reverend A. W. Loomis, Superintendent of the Chinese Presbyterian Mission, introduced Sturge to the members of the newly formed Japanese church and assigned him the task of building a Japanese mission. In August 1886 the Golden Gate Gospel Society was dissolved and a Japanese YMCA was organized in its stead. Headed by Sturge, both the YMCA and church then moved to larger quarters at 1163 Mission Street. By 1887 the infant mission had a membership of 66 persons.

The mission expanded in the 1890s. In August 1892 the mission, church, and YMCA relocated to 121 Haight Street. The building at this location had been the home of the San Francisco Theological Seminary, a Presbyterian school. When the seminary was transferred to San Anselmo in Marin County, Dr. Sturge obtained the use of the building. In 1894 another facility was created at 22 Prospect Place near

Chinatown—the Japanese Presbyterian Mission Home for Japanese women. Subsequently, Presbyterian churches were established in outlying areas, beginning with churches in Salinas, Watsonville, and Stockton in the late 1890s; all of these came under the jurisdiction of the Japanese Presbyterian Mission on the Pacific Coast, with Dr. Sturge as its superintendent.[25]

Methodist institutions were also founded. The original Gospel Society remained in the Chinese Methodist Episcopal Mission as an auxiliary of the mission. After the Congregationalists withdrew, the Society had only 12 members, but slowly increased membership under the leadership of Miyama Kan'ichi. At its thirty-third annual conference, the California Methodist Conference resolved to build a Japanese mission. In the preceding conference, it had been reported that "one of the most cheering facts . . . is the unusual success attending the work among the Japanese."[26] The Gospel Society ended its cellar days in the spring of 1886. Renting the second floor of a building at 920 Washington Street, it moved out of the basement of the Chinese mission. The Japanese mission was established formally in September 1886. Called the Japanese Methodist Episcopal Mission on the Pacific Coast, the first superintendent was the Reverend M. C. Harris, a former missionary to Japan. Later both the mission and the Gospel Society relocated to 531 Jessie Street, below Market Street and between 6th and 7th Streets, an area where many student-laborers rented rooms.

This mission grew spectacularly. Membership rose from 90 persons in 1887 to 165 by 1888.[27] In 1889 and 1890 a religious revival swept through the student community, and the mission gained many new converts. By 1891 it had 200 members and 70 probationers. Plans were drawn up to construct a new church with the purchase in 1892 of a plot located at 1329 Pine Street. The new church opened in 1894. A Japanese Women's Home was established in 1893, and other churches were founded in other locales—in Sacramento in 1892, Fresno in 1893, and San Jose and Watsonville in 1895. By 1894 the mission claimed 733 members and 650 probationers with 21 Japanese pastors and assistants. The uncommon growth of the mission caused the California Methodist Conference to report glowingly:

> In the work among the Japanese, God has given the people of California a great opportunity. Such an opening as rarely comes to Christian people is now presented, and such results from so small beginnings, in the same time, and on the same expenditure of money, have perhaps never been equalled by any work for God on this continent.[28]

Despite the growth of the mission, the Gospel Society was not disbanded. In 1889 the members left the mission and moved the Society to 118 Golden Gate Avenue in the belief that it should be kept as an autonomous student residence. Located at various addresses during the 1890s, it lasted until the Great Earthquake of 1906.

The Japanese Immigrant Press

The origins of the immigrant press can be traced to the members of the Patriotic League and the student-laborers. The first publication was entitled *Shinonome* (Dawn), a mimeographed sheet that appeared in 1886. The second publication was the *Shin Nippon* (New Japan), a mimeographed weekly published in Oakland from September 1887 to February 1888 by Yamaguchi Yūya, Hirota Zenrō, and others. Although no copies have been preserved, the measures adopted by the Meiji government imply that this weekly assailed the government in an unbridled manner. On February 6, 1888, the government banned the sale and distribution of the *Shin Nippon* in Japan. When Yamaguchi returned to Tokyo in March 1888, the police arrested him, and he, along with five persons in absentia, including Hirota, was charged with slandering cabinet ministers. Brought to trial and found guilty, Yamaguchi was sentenced to fifteen months imprisonment and a fine of 107 yen.[29]

The Patriotic League itself published a weekly from 1888 to 1893. Initially entitled *Dai-Jūkyū Seiki* (Nineteenth Century), the weekly was issued under various titles. As with the *Shin Nippon,* the Meiji government banned its sale and distribution. The League countered by changing the title to *Jiyū* (Liberty), which the government banned in turn. This cycle of banning and title changing occurred six times in all. The members of the League were political emigrés who were absorbed in homeland politics. They voiced their dissenting opinions in their weekly and tried to smuggle it into Japan.

The February 28, 1890, issue of the *Jiyū* carried the following editorial:

> What is the reason for the want of liberty in an aristocratic nation? None other than social inequality! To divide the nation, the aristocratic system creates several classes and several subclasses within a class. The condition is akin to several circles placed in a society to partition it. In both the large and small circles, there are upper and lower ranks of unequal standing. People form their own subgroupings within their

own classes and live within their confines. Since society is subdivided in this manner into classes, liberty does not exist in an aristocratic nation. Corresponding to levels of society, language, literature, customs, human feelings—all things—differ. Those who occupy the upper class are refined and cultivated. Those below are progressively coarse and conservative. The power of monarchy and royalty is immense. The power of the mean and poor is feeble. Thus an aristocratic nation can easily oppress the lower classes. Because it can oppress the lower classes, there is no liberty in an aristocratic nation.[30]

The advent of daily newspapers in the 1890s marks the real beginning of the immigrant press. Yamato Masao, Watari Tokuji, Sugawara Tsutau, and a few other members of the Patriotic League published the first one. Printed as a four-page lithographed newspaper from 1892 to 1897, this first daily had three separate titles during its lifespan. Starting as the *Sōkō Shimbun* (San Francisco News) in 1892, it was retitled *Sōkō Shimpō* (San Francisco Daily) in 1893 and *Sōkō Jiji* (San Francisco Times) in 1895. The Meiji government banned specific issues of this daily. The changes in title were made as the government placed its limited ban. The *Kimmon Nippō* (Golden Gate Daily) was the second daily. It was published as a lithographed newspaper from 1893 to 1895 by Nagai Gen and other student-laborers.

Two other dailies appeared at this time which eventually became the pillars of the immigrant press. The first was the *Shin Sekai* (New World) which commenced publication on May 25, 1894. Interesting circumstances surrounded the origins of this first typeset daily. Japanese residents of San Francisco commemorated the Meiji Emperor's birthday as early as 1877. In 1893 they assembled for this annual event, held on November 3. After the commemoration, Ishikawa Sadakuni, a member of the Haight YMCA, was overheard saying that the custom of bowing before the Emperor's portrait was a form of "idolatry." Rumors swiftly circulated through the student community, and Ishikawa and his fellow YMCA members came under scathing criticism. To defend themselves in print, they launched the *Shin Sekai* as the YMCA's house organ. In 1897 Soejima Hachirō, a founder and chief editor, moved the newspaper out of the YMCA over a disagreement with his associates.

Founded by Abiko Kyūtarō and others, the *Nichibei Shimbun* (Japanese American News) was the other daily. This paper combined two preexisting dailies: *Sōkō Nihon Shimbun* (San Francisco Japan News) and *Hokubei Nippō* (North American Daily). The former dated back to 1896 as the *Japan Herarudo* (Japan Herald) and became the *Sōkō*

Nihon Shimbun in 1897 when Abiko took over its management. The latter had been published by the Haight YMCA since November 3, 1898. Once Soejima turned the *Shin Sekai* into an independent newspaper, the YMCA members started the *Hokubei Nippō* as their new house organ. The *Sōkō Nihon Shimbun* and the *Hokubei Nippō* merged on April 3, 1899 to form the *Nichibei Shimbun*. The *Shin Sekai* became the oldest, continuously published Japanese immigrant language newspaper, while the *Nichibei Shimbun* evolved into the most influential one with the largest circulation.[31]

All of these daily newspapers stood on shaky foundations at the beginning. Circulation never exceeded 300 in the 1890s. The *Shin Sekai* printed only 80 copies in 1894 and 200 in 1897. And the readership was confined to the student-laborer population. A well-known Issei writer, Washizu Bunzō, was associated with the early immigrant press. Recalling his experience, he wrote:

> Among those who lived in San Francisco, the majority were students. Cobblers, laundrymen, and a few store operators had families who numbered less than fifty. Since those scattered in rural areas were either railroad laborers or other transients, they did not subscribe to newspapers. . . . The newspapers . . . were only read by the students in San Francisco. Because the Japanese community was not cohesive, they were distributed to people of like mind rather than read by all classes.[32]

With such a small readership, the newspapers were struggling enterprises. The monthly income of the *Sōkō Shimbun,* derived from subscriptions and advertisement, was a meager $60 or so around 1895. Publishers worked as lithographers or typesetters and even delivered the newspapers themselves. Newspaper offices served as living quarters where the staff cooked and ate. Washizu depicted the lot of newspapermen with a touch of humor:

> The life of newspapermen . . . was wretched. It was commonplace for publishers to be lithographers and delivery boys. Three meals a day were impossible. The *Sōkō Shimbun,* which took pride in being the oldest newspaper, had a broken-down stove in the kitchen (an old one worth five dollars). The staff ate biscuits as hard as rocks with no butter. The coffee had no milk and was like piss. If they weren't on the verge of starvation, the food was inedible.
>
> Biscuits (bisuketto) . . . were called stonecuits (ishiketto), and beefsteaks (bifusuteki) were dubbed stonesteaks (ishisuteki). The reality was more miserable. . . . [33]

Noguchi Yone, the famous poet who wrote in English, arrived in 1893 as a student-laborer with a letter of introduction to Sugawara Tsutau. He delivered the *Sōkō Shimbun*. Regarding his life with the newspaper, he wrote:

> The (Patriotic) League was then publishing a daily paper called the *Soko Shimbun* . . . , for which I was engaged as a carrier; the paper had only a circulation of not over two hundred. I did not enter into any talk about payment; I soon discovered it was perfectly useless when we hardly knew how to get dinner every day. You can imagine how difficult it was for five or six people to make a living out of a circulation of two hundred. . . . By turns, we used to get up and build a fire and prepare big pancakes . . . with no egg or milk, just with water.[34]

Early Student Life

The Christian institutions served several indispensable functions. First, every institution conducted English classes. Few student-laborers commanded passable English when they landed. In 1888 Ozaki Yukio observed disparagingly that the majority had not even studied English before their passage. Katayama Sen in fact did not possess even a rudimentary knowledge of the English alphabet. Although some persons had studied the language in Japan, their knowledge was woefully inadequate. Noguchi Yone was sure of his own abilities, but was dismayed to discover that he could not communicate. Length of residency did not always enhance fluency in every case. In 1888 Mutsu Munemitsu, newly appointed Japanese minister to the United States, observed that "those who came three years ago still cannot understand English adequately."[35] For the sake of daily survival, every student-laborer had to learn some English. To enroll in schools, they had to advance beyond an elementary knowledge. Thus the student-laborers flocked to the English classes offered by the Methodist and Presbyterian Missions.

Secondly, the Christian institutions provided room and board. New arrivals in the early 1880s, for example, lodged at the Golden Gate Gospel Society. For lodging, the Society charged 10 cents per night and $2 per month for members and 15 cents per night, $1 per week, and $3 per month for nonmembers. For members and nonmembers alike, the cost of board was 30 cents per day for three meals. These rates were cheap by prevailing standards. All residents had to obey strict rules. Everyone had to rise at 7:00 A.M. and clean up the facilities. No drinking or gambling was permitted.[36] Katayama Sen spent his first night in San Francisco at the original Gospel Society, which could accomodate up to 60 students during the time it was located at 531 Jessie Street. Thirdly, the institutions served as quasi-employment bureaus, operating as a job information clearinghouse for student-laborers and as an agency for American families who wanted to hire Japanese domestics. Finally, the institutions functioned as social havens for the student-laborers who struggled to survive in an alien land.

Shimada Jūsuke landed in 1881 at the age of eighteen and resided six years at the original Gospel Society. Reminiscing about those years, he assessed the worth of the society:

> We were all penniless *kugakusei*. . . . The Gospel Society was of immense value. . . . If it had not existed, many people no doubt would have been lost on the streets. . . . For those of us who were suffering from homesickness, it is impossible to measure the sense of gratitude we owe to the society.[37]

The same can be said for all of the Christian institutions. They helped many student-laborers to survive by teaching English, providing room and board, and rendering employment and other assistance.

Those student-laborers who lived apart from the Christian institutions clustered in one area of San Francisco. They rented dilapidated houses on Stevenson and Jessie Streets between 3rd and 7th Streets for ten to fifteen dollars a month. Washizu described these houses in the following manner:

> This entire area was a San Francisco slum. . . . All the houses were so small and dirty that one could not use them to store things now. . . .
>
> When I arrived in America, we didn't need addresses to visit Japanese homes. As long as we were told of such-and-such intersecting streets, we always found the houses. We had only to look for basements with sooty curtains to find them. There we invariably found Japanese living in cave-like dwellings.[38]

The interior was no better than the exterior:

> Corresponding to these dwellings, the kitchens were filthy and disorderly to the extreme. There were no stoves as the boardinghouses had. All cooking was done on one or two-burner oil stoves. We brewed coffee, toasted bread, and grilled smoked salmon on these oil stoves. Thick, black smoke darkened the rooms, and we were oblivious to the odor which assailed our nostrils.[39]

Labor was inseparable from the daily life of the student-laborers. In Japan some had worked as newspaper carriers, milk delivery boys, or rickshaw men, three common jobs for students; others had no work experience at all. In either case, the employment they found in America was new to everyone. The most readily available job was that of a so-called school-boy. This term designated a student-laborer who lived with an American family. In exchange for room and board, plus a nominal wage, he performed domestic service. A school-boy's job, ideally at least, allowed time for a student to attend school. Rising before everyone in the family, he kindled a fire, boiled water, and set the table for breakfast; depending on the household, he also made coffee and mush. After breakfast, he cleared the table and washed the dishes. He then attended school during the daytime. Returning to the house by 3:00 or 4:00 P.M., he helped to prepare the evening meal and set the table again. Then he cleaned up after supper. During the rest of the evening, he was free to devote himself to his studies. This routine applied to weekdays. On Saturday he had additional house-cleaning duties which occupied the entire day. Sunday was his day off.

All student-laborers did not adapt easily to this work. Being young men from Japan, many considered it beneath them. In Japan only lower class women worked as domestic servants. A school-boy's job was associated with the work of such women. When described in deprecating terms, the job was referred as *gejo hōkō* or maid-servant's work, which made it analogous to the tasks female domestics performed in Japan. Certain people went so far as to blame the job for the loss of self-respect by many student-laborers, and for the development of a subservient mentality among them. Indeed, Ozaki Yukio believed that the school-boys had developed "a maid-servant's servility" as a consequence of their lowly station. They were "a blot on Japan's national image" because Americans perceived them as "representatives of Japan." Ozaki waxed indignant at this state of affairs, and predicted that, if matters did not change, the Japanese in the United States would be excluded in the same manner as the Chinese had been.[40] Mutsu Munemitsu reached the same conclusions regarding the student-laborers employed as domestic servants. He called them "shiftless students" whom he likened to the "menial servants" hired by Europeans and Americans at the open-treaty ports of Yokohama and Kobe.[41] On a practical level, a school-boy's job was undesirable too. Everything was foreign to the novice—the assigned chores, no less than American family customs and practices, not to mention the dishes, utensils, appliances, and furnishings, all were new to him. And compounding the difficulty of doing strange new tasks was the inability to comprehend enough English to follow instructions.

The results were predictable, and frequently comic. Many novices were unable to hold their first job. One student-laborer was fired on his first day. His troubles began in setting the table. He neglected to place the coffee cups on saucers. As he started to wash the breakfast dishes, he scalded his hands in the hot rinse water. And when he swept the outside walkway, he inadvertently entered the neighbor's home. Whereupon, according to this student's confession, his employer dismissed him with the curt remark, "This Jap doesn't know anything at all."[42] Noguchi Yone captured the school-boy's ordeal in a humorous vein:

What a farce we enacted in our first encounter with an American family! Even a stove was a mystery to us. One of my friends endeavoured to make a fire by burning the kindling in the oven. Another one was on the point of blowing out the gaslight. One fellow terrified the lady when he began to take off his shoes, and even his trousers, before scrubbing the floor. It is true, however fantastic it may sound. It was natural enough for him, since he regarded his American clothes as a huge luxury. Poor fellow! He was afraid he might spoil them. I rushed into my Madam's toilet room without knocking. The American woman took it good-naturedly, as it happened. She pitied our ignorance, but without any touch of sarcasm. Japanese civilization, if it was born in America, certainly was born in her household—in some well-to-do San Francisco family, rather than in Yale or Harvard.[43]

In poor but understandable English, another student recorded his experience less humorously:

I was told there was one job as a "school-boy" in Sutter Street near Steiner Street. First thing I had to do was to buy a white coat and apron. Some Japanese lent me the money for that. Then he took me to the house. He settled my wages with the "ma'am"—one dollar and half a week.

Immediately the ma'am demanded me to scrub the kitchen floor. I took one hour to finish. Then I had to wash windows. That was very difficult job for me. Three windows for another hour! She said, "You are slow worker, but you do everything so neat. Never mind; you will learn by and by. I like you very much."

In the evening her husband, sons, and daughters came back. The whole family was eight in number. The ma'am taught me how to cook.

She asked me if my name was "Charlie." I said, "Yes, ma'am." At the dinner-table, she called, "Charlie, Charlie." But by that time I had quite forgotten that "Charlie" was my own name; so I did not answer. I was sitting on the kitchen chair and thinking what a change of life it was. The ma'am came into the kitchen and was so furious! It was such a hard work for me to wash up all dishes, pans, glasses, etc., after dinner. When I went into the diningroom to put all silvers on sideboard, I saw the reflection of myself on the lookingglass. In a white coat and apron! I could not control my feelings. The tears so freely flowed out from my eyes, and I buried my face with my both arms.[44]

This student was struck obviously by his abject appearance. Wearing a white coat and apron, he saw himself reduced to a Japanese maid-servant.

American families gave English names to the school-boys, often arbitrarily. Either they found Japanese names too hard to pronounce, or they never bothered to ask their help what their names were. Names like Frank or Joseph were neutral, but "Charlie" had strong condescending overtones. A reverse case had a humorous twist. A student on his first day at work was asked his name by the head of the household. Fumbling for the proper English words, he began his answer with the Japanese word, *danna,* meaning the household master he was addressing. Interpreting *danna* to be the student's name, the man and his family called him *danna* from that moment. They thus reversed the master-servant relationship in name by calling their own domestic help "master" in Japanese. Hence, whenever the student's friends visited the home and asked to see *danna,* they could scarcely restrain their laughter.[45]

This episode points up the language barrier that existed between the school-boys and American families, and the misunderstandings which arose from it. A typical English conversation lesson for the school-boys illustrates ordinary misunderstandings. The lesson covers an imaginary initial meeting between a student and a household mistress. As exactly printed in a guide, it reads:

JAPANESE:	Good-morning; Is this Mrs. Smith's house?
HOUSEHOLDHEAD:	Yes, where you come from?
JAPANESE:	I came from Japanese Mission, they told me that you want school boy.
HOUSEHOLDHEAD:	Yes, just come in and sit down there. Can you speak English?
JAPANESE:	Yes, Madam, I can talk some.
HOUSEHOLDHEAD:	Do you know how to work?
JAPANESE:	I understand house-work, but I don't know anything about cooking.
HOUSEHOLDHEAD:	O, that's very easy; only make coffee, cook mush, and peel potatoes, that's all.
JAPANESE:	Will you teach me?

HOUSEHOLDHEAD:	Yes, I will show you.
JAPANESE:	What time shall I get up?
HOUSEHOLDHEAD:	Six o'clock; then wash the front steps.
JAPANESE:	All right, madam.
HOUSEHOLDHEAD:	How much wages you want a week.
JAPANESE:	Let me see; and how many people in your family?
HOUSEHOLDHEAD:	Only three, and I have very nice room for you.
JAPANESE:	Will you, please, show me the room. Well, then give me a dollar and half a week, and I wish to go out at half past eight in the morning, and come home at four in the afternoon.
HOUSEHOLDHEAD:	Yes, and what is your name?
JAPANESE:	My name is Frank.
HOUSEHOLDHEAD:	All right, Frank, you work from to-day.
JAPANESE:	Yes, madam, I will come to-day at four o'clock in the after-noon. Good-day.[46]

This English lesson had four practical points. A school-boy had to ask what his precise duties were, had to examine his living quarters, had to seek guarantee of time-off to attend school, and had to settle on his wages. Because of the language barrier, many school-boys misinterpreted or failed to clarify these terms of employment. The lesson was designed to avert the most common misunderstandings. As the head of the original Gospel Society, Miyama Kan'ichi is said to have rescued many school-boys from predicaments caused by frequent misunderstandings. He no doubt had to grapple with the practical points covered by this lesson, and probably much more.

The student-laborers engaged in other forms of menial labor. A school-boy's job usually left time to attend school. Other jobs offered the promise, however remote, of saving money to enroll in schools later. A variant of a school-boy was a so-called day-worker who also performed domestic work but never lived in homes. Hiring himself out on a daily basis, a day-worker looked after his own room and board. The student-laborers also worked as general dishwashers, window-cleaners, janitors, and—higher on the wage scale,—as waiters and cooks. The latter job categories required experience and knowledge of English. New arrivals, or "greens" as they were labelled (short for greenhorns), rarely if ever became waiters or cooks overnight. In 1886 a school-boy earned $1 to $2 per week, a combined cook-servant $5 to $6 per week, and a cook-waiter with good English $30 to $40 per month.[47] Agriculture was a final source of employment. In the summer of 1888, a few student-laborers first entered the agricultural fields as harvest hands.

Despite their goal of seeking an education, few student-laborers actually graduated from schools. Most began by taking the English classes offered by the Christian institutions. Some managed to enroll in the San Francisco public schools, but the number was very small. In 1893 fewer than 50 Japanese students were enrolled.[48] Others entered the public schools in Oakland and Alameda. A few enrolled in two private boarding schools, the Belmont School near San Mateo and the Hopkins Academy in Oakland. Both institutions were preparatory academies whose graduates were able to matriculate into universities without examinations. The handful of Japanese who attended these two schools did so as subpreparatory students, as was the case with Katayama Sen who attended Hopkins Academy briefly. Only a rare few ever obtained diplomas. In the 1880s only 3 Japanese graduated from the Hopkins Academy, among whom was Nemoto Shō, a member of the Gospel Society, who received his diploma in 1885.[49] As for institutions of higher learning, only 7 students graduated from the University of California between 1887 and 1900, and 5 students from Stanford University from its inception in 1891 to 1900.[50] A few students attended the College of the Pacific, a Methodist school near Santa Clara, and the Pacific Theological Seminary in Oakland, but, again, the number of graduates was miniscule. The historical significance of the student-laborers lies, not with their limited educational achievements, but rather with the fact that they laid the initial foundations of Japanese immigrant society, and that a sizable number of them later became labor contractors and immigrant leaders.

Prostitutes

Prostitutes were also among the pioneers of Japanese immigrant society. American immigration statistics record 1,195 female arrivals between 1861 and 1900.[51] Japanese government statistics corroborate this low admission figure; only 2,036 passports were issued to women destined for the United States from 1868 to 1900, 800 of them to females classified as laborers.[52] According to the U.S. Census of 1900, there were only 985 females.[53] Japanese government population statistics record 1,130 females in the same year.[54] Discrepancies in the statistics of the two governments are minute. Both sets attest to the fact that few women came to the United States during the initial phase of

Japanese immigration. The small female population in 1900, in the neighborhood of a thousand, included many prostitutes who probably comprised the majority. No documented evidence on the first appearance of the prostitutes nor precise figures on their number and geographical distribution exist.

They appeared as an historical fact in the late 1880s. Consular reports bear out their arrival. In January 1890 the San Francisco consul reported that prostitutes had begun to land in the preceding years and estimated that 30 worked in the city.[55] By March 1891 the estimate rose to 50 prostitutes who worked in ten brothels described as "almost openly operated."[56] By 1898, at the very least, there were 161 in California who were in virtually every Japanese settlement. San Francisco had 38; Fresno, 30; Sacramento, 15; Vacaville, 7; Watsonville, 3; Hanford, 7; Bakersfield, 7; Los Angeles, 8; Stockton, 10; Santa Barbara, 6; Chico, 5; San Jose, 2; Marysville, 3; and other locales, 20.[57] Prostitutes turned up in other states as well. In May 1890 the Vancouver consul reported 50 in Seattle.[58] The San Francisco consulate recorded 71 known prostitutes in that city by 1891. Spokane had had 50 to 60 in 1889 and 17 in 1891. Portland had 19 in 1891.[59] The earliest known prostitutes in Montana were at Butte in 1884.[60] In 1897 the Tacoma consul reported 69 in Washington, 75 in Oregon, 23 in Idaho, 16 in Montana, and 12 in Utah.[61]

None of these consular figures can be interpreted literally and accepted as completely reliable. Because of geographical distances, local consulates could not check every female within their jurisdiction to ascertain whether or not they were prostitutes. Moreover, the prostitutes moved constantly from one locale to another, making the figures subject to sudden change. Yet the statistics are evidence that the prostitutes began to appear in the late 1880s and increased in the 1890s. They were dispersed widely on the Pacific Coast and in the western states and, likely as not, were more numerous than the statistics indicate.

From the 1870s China and Southeast Asia were the major overseas destination of Japanese prostitutes.[62] As an organized traffic, women were taken normally to the port of Nagasaki, and then smuggled out to Hong Kong and Shanghai, and later to Singapore, there to be sold and forced into prostitution. Many of them originated from Amakusa, a group of islands off the western coast of Kumamoto, where impoverished rural households, unable to survive economically, sold their daughters. Other young women were abducted or lured under false pretenses. Some of these women may have been sent to

the United States by the Chinese, in particular those who had been
sold to Hong Kong merchants before the late 1880s. How else can
one explain the presence in 1884 of Japanese prostitutes in Butte, Montana, a booming mining town with Chinese laborers? The women in
Butte, and perhaps others, having been sold to Chinese merchants in
Hong Kong, were probably rerouted to America to work as prostitutes in Chinese labor camps.

The majority of prostitutes in America were brought over by Japanese men. As agents of procurers or as procurers themselves, they
obtained women in Japan and transported them across the Pacific. As
soon as they landed in a port, they sold the women or engaged them
in prostitution. In many cases the procurers were former seamen who
had jumped ship and settled down in a port city. An early history of
the Japanese in the Pacific Northwest states that many prostitutes
"stowed away on sailing vessels . . . and became the prey of wicked
seamen who, in collusion with others who had already landed in
America, abetted their illegal passage."[63] Recalling his experience
shortly after the turn of the century, an Issei remembers an old seaman
who told of an unscrupulous agent in Nagasaki. This seaman said that
the agent

> told young girls from the countryside "if they went abroad, white
> families would employ them at high wages." Once he had groups of
> three to five girls, he sent them to Hong Kong or Singapore and most
> of them further on to the Pacific Coast. . . .
>
> Ship officers took a set commission from boatswains for each girl
> and delivered the girls to the procuring bosses. . . .
>
> Except for passenger-freighters, merchant ships were sailing vessels
> at the time and comprised from seventy to eighty percent of all cargo-
> bearing ships. Every sawmill company in the Pacific Northwest owned
> from ten to as many as fifty sailing vessels to transport lumber to var-
> ious ports of the world. Most of the cooks on these ships were Japanese;
> four or five were aboard each vessel. When the ships sailed for South-
> east Asia, they always stopped at Nagasaki and took on Japanese
> women.[64]

Some accounts indicate that the women were placed into boxes and
unloaded as cargo to avoid detection by immigration officials. Aware
of conditions on the West Coast, seamen played a prominent role in
the arrival of the prostitutes.

Other men travelled back and forth from Japan to the United
States, bringing women with them each time. According to the San
Francisco consul, for example, Watanabe Masanobu, an operator of

a Salt Lake City brothel, left San Francisco in November 1891 to procure additional women in Japan.[65] Similarly, Arai Seikichi, who ran a San Francisco brothel, sailed for Japan in February 1892 with the same objective in mind.[66] Hagiwara Makoto was another man who returned to Japan to procure women. In August 1891 he came back to San Francisco, where he had two brothels, with a woman he claimed was his cousin. He would have had three more women with him had he not been stopped by Japanese officials in Yokohama.[67]

The most notorious procurer was Hasegawa Genji of San Francisco. Instead of going to Japan, he had women shipped regularly to him. In May 1890 he was sufficiently well-off to hire counsel when two women for whom he had sent were denied landing permission and detained by immigration officials. With writs of *habeas corpus*, he got them released and put them to work in his brothels.[68] The following year, four other women were denied landing and detained. Hasegawa again sought their release through writs of *habeas corpus*, contesting the administrative decision of the immigration officials all the way to the United States Supreme Court.[69]

A few accounts of how individual prostitutes actually came are available. One is that of a woman who came from Amakusa itself, and who related her personal account to an Issei writer.

I'm a daughter of a farming household in Amakusa. Around 1889–90 a smooth-talking man appeared on my island. This man came to sell sea products processed at Nagasaki, and in the town he often told interesting tales. His stories were about foreign lands. Salmon was plentiful near Vladivostok; as children played in boats, the salmon jumped into them. Children used pearls and corals as toys on the beaches of Southeast Asia. Gold nuggets were waiting to be picked up on the riverbanks of America.

I got close to him at my grandmother's house. He tried to persuade me to go on a trip to Nagasaki. The distance between my home and Nagasaki was no more than the space between the nose and eyes. Since it took less than an hour by small boat to go there, I got on a boat with him one moonlit night. He took me to a seamen's inn in Nagasaki and fed me a nice meal.

On the next day I went with him to look at a foreign ship. It was a large steamship called the *Oceanic* bound for America. Boarding such a huge ship for the first time, I walked the decks enjoying the new experience. Then the man introduced me to a seaman on the ship. The seaman was about thirty-seven or thirty-eight years old, probably from Kyūshū, and very good-humored. He jokingly said, "Why don't you go to America on the ship?" When I replied, "I'd like to go and see

America, but since I don't know anyone there, I can't," he answered, "Nonsense, many Japanese are in America, and they're all rich. If you stick it out for two or three years, you can become rich to the tune of several thousand yen." When I said, "But my mother will worry about me," he answered, "If you write letters afterwards, she need not worry."

Just as I was half thinking about wanting to go and half worrying, the passengers quickened their pace as a noise like the clanging of a bell sounded. The ship had hoisted anchor and had left port. The man with whom I had come was nowhere to be seen. "Since the ship is on its way," the seaman said, "I'll take you to America. Don't worry at all."

The ship bobbed up and down on the Pacific Ocean. The waves gradually grew higher. The seaman put me in a room to sleep. "I'll bring you meals so don't leave it," he said. "If by chance you're discovered, you'll be thrown into the sea."

"If discovered, you'll be thrown into the sea"—that was frightening. True enough, thinking back on it now, I was a female stowaway, which was not a trifling matter.

The ship reached San Francisco after twenty days at sea. One evening the seaman dressed me in western clothes and took me off the ship. Pulled by his hand in the pitch darkness of the night, I just trailed behind him.

I arrived at an unknown house and was introduced to other women. I'll end my story here, for I'll tread upon people's reputations if I go into greater detail.[70]

The Nagasaki merchant and the seaman were in cahoots in the case of this woman. The merchant enticed her to go to Nagasaki and board the ship, and the seaman had her at his mercy once it sailed. Shanghaied in this manner, the woman arrived in San Francisco where she was delivered by the seaman to a procurer.

Another example recounts the story of an Oteru-san who was deceived under different circumstances.

Oteru-san was a person from Ejiri in Shizuoka Prefecture. A wealthy returnee from America was doing business in Ejiri at the time. Young people always clustered about him because he had lots of money and told unusual stories. When they did, he said, "If one went to America, even children could earn four to five dollars per day, and with a little more work one could make up to ten to fifteen dollars in a day." He also told them about the wonders of city life.

For young people already given to idle dreams, they naturally wanted to go to America where things were so beautiful and earn such money. Upon asking him how to get there, he said that he could help them since he had acquaintances on ships and any number of friends in America. Then he started to play his hidden cards. This well-to-do man had actually made his money in prostitution in America. On the surface he was engaged in a legitimate business, but in reality he was the boss of a kidnapping ring. Sometimes Oteru-san visited him with two or three other girls. In the end they were taken in by his words. One village festival night, they sneaked out of their homes and went to Yokohama with his assistance. From there they sailed for Seattle.

As soon as they landed in Seattle, their room was watched closely so that they could not meet other people. They thought it odd, but believed this was an American custom and didn't pay much attention. They came to Oakland from Seattle and were sequestered somewhere. The man who was attached to them locked the door whenever he went out. They felt suspicious, but they couldn't do anything. Then two women came one day. Consoled in many ways, the girls were told that they would be going to San Francisco to work with other girls. They went somewhat elated only to discover the house there was also strange with many women. They sensed it was not a respectable house. That evening the middle-aged woman who had come to get them informed Oteru-san, "You must work as a prostitute." "I was shocked," she remembered, "and said I couldn't do it. Please forgive me, but let me do some other work." The more she pleaded, they castigated her and ordered her to stop trembling. Her life of shame commenced from that point. As she recalled the past while crying, she said, "I made an error which determined my whole life."[71]

In contrast to the first woman, Oteru-san's arrival was connected with a man who had been in America. Operating as the boss of an abduction ring, this man coaxed young girls to leave their villages. With the aid of seamen, he sent her and others to the United States where, against their will, they were to be handed over to a procurer. In both cases verbal subterfuge rather than physical force was employed to induce them to leave Japan, and seamen were the crucial intermediaries.

A third and last example is that of Yamada Waka, a noted writer in Japan before World War II. A native of Kurigahama, a small fishing village near Yokohama, she too was induced to come to America by a man who had been here. Believing his exaggerated tales of riches in this country, she accompanied him to Seattle in 1902. Upon landing, he compelled her to become a prostitute in a Seattle brothel under the nickname, Oyae of Arabia. A sexist nickname, Yamada's rather ample buttocks and dark complexion apparently reminded Japanese men of an Arabian horse. In 1903, befriended by the Seattle correspondent of the *Shin Sekai,* she fled with him to San Francisco, only to be forced into prostitution again in a Chinatown brothel. Fortunately for her, she managed to escape and gained refuge in the Chinese Mission Home, a Presbyterian rescue mission in Chinatown, and through eventual self-education became a writer-critic upon her return to Japan. Although Yamada Waka arrived after the turn of the century, her initial fate illustrates the case of women brought by men who personally returned to Japan to secure them.[72]

Other prostitutes probably left Japan under different circumstances. In the three examples, the women were innocent country women who were ignorant of American conditions. Believing the tales men told them, they were lured to America and ended up as prostitutes after they landed. The exact geographical origins and the economic backgrounds of all the prostitutes are unknown. Thus, one can only speculate that there were other women, unlike the three, who were sold into prostitution before they left Japan, as were the young daughters of impoverished rural families in Amakusa who went to China and Southeast Asia.

Lacking personal memoirs, it is impossible to depict the life of the prostitutes fully. Fragmentary bits and pieces written by outsiders, however, offer a partial glimpse. No matter where the prostitutes were, pimp-gamblers who preyed upon them were invariably present. In 1891 approximately 250 to 260 Japanese resided in Seattle, but only 10 persons were employed legitimately. Apart from the 71 known prostitutes, the remaining people, in the judgment of a consular staff, were either vagrant types or pimp-gamblers who parasitically lived off the earnings of the prostitutes.[73] The same held true for other towns in the Pacific Northwest; 30 pimps in Spokane and 40 to 50 in Portland were attached to the prostitutes there in 1891. Colloquially referred to as *amegoro,* meaning American thugs, the pimps held the women as chattels in some cases. A representative of the Ministers' Association of Seattle wrote to the San Francisco consul in January 1892 and informed him of the "condition of the Japanese fallen women" in his city:

> We are informed that of the seventy to eighty [prostitutes] quite a number are . . . in virtual slavery, brought over . . . under false pretenses and kept . . . by bosses who hold them in bondage. . . . We are informed that certain individuals visit Japan, induce these unfortunates to come here, pay their passage under a contract that such amount shall be paid back out of the earning of the women, that these men then compel them to enter a life of shame, keep them under a system of

terrorism, take all their earning and keep them month after month in this condition of bondage; and that these women being ignorant of the value of our money thus pay many times the amount of their passage money though desiring to get out of the life of shame.[74]

Okina Kyūin, a noted early Issei writer, described the *amegoro* in the following way:

Amegoro were behind the women, men who had been in abject poverty in Japan or who had come to America with ambitions, but abhorred honest work and had gone the wayward path. To carouse and gamble, they duped women and forced them into prostitution. The worse ones fraudulently married several women and sold them off to the Chinese.[75]

The *amegoro* were not averse to violence. Holding women in bondage by coercion, they instilled fear even in the Japanese who were in legitimate occupations. Fearful of physical retaliation, the handful of ''respectable'' people in Seattle in 1891 refused to take action against the *amegoro* when asked to do so by a consular staff member. The San Francisco *Daily Report* in 1892 disclosed the presence of about 125 in San Francisco, with Hasegawa Genji as one of the leaders. As in Seattle, they too intimidated other Japanese in the city by threats of violence.[76] Such persons were capable of unforgivable deeds. Two of them kidnapped the thirteen-year-old daughter of a fellow immigrant in Portland in 1891, took the child to Salem, and forced her into prostitution.[77] In 1900 another individual sold his four-month-pregnant paramour to a Chinatown brothel in San Jose.[78]

Depending upon the clientele, the prostitutes were divided into three categories. The *hakujin-tori* catered exclusively to white men, the *Shinajin-tori* had Chinese customers, and the *Nihonjin-tori* dealt with Japanese. This division of prostitutes no doubt mirrored not only white American prejudices but Japanese prejudices as well. White men did not frequent brothels patronized by Asian men, nor did Japanese men associate with Japanese prostitutes who cavorted with Chinese men. In Seattle the houses of prostitution, known by names like Tokyo House, were located on or around King Street in the heart of the Japanese settlement, while those in San Francisco were all situated in or near Chinatown off Dupont Street (present-day Grant Avenue) and, ironically, on St. Mary's Street. Not all prostitutes worked in brothels. Innumerable small bar-restaurants, which hired *shakufu* or barmaids, proliferated in the inchoate immigrant communities in the 1890s. Not every *shakufu* was a prostitute, but some were, and they worked in these bar-restaurants rather than in brothels.

Many derogatory Japanese terms were applied to the prostitutes. A descriptive noun often employed by Japanese government officials was *senpu*, which means base women. Infused with negative meaning, it reflected the moral and bureaucratic biases of the officials who viewed the women as "undesirables," as blots upon Japan's national image. A prostitute who catered to white men was a *hakujinchō*, a white man's bird, birds being a common metaphor symbolizing prostitutes. A prostitute who slept with anyone was called a *mokugyo-kō*. A *mokugyo-kō* is a portable wooden drum commonly found in Buddhist temples. Oval in shape with two carved fishes at each end, it has a slit at the top which, to lascivious males, resembles the female organ. A fastidious prostitute was tagged a *nembutsu-kō*, *nembutsu* being to Buddhists what "Hail Mary" is to Catholics, a ritual invocation to the Amida Buddha. Compared to the *mokugyo-kō*, the *nembutsu-kō* was better, at least from a sarcastic male point of view. Another term, *iden*, designated a prostitute who moved from one house to another. This word originated from *iten*, which means to change one's domicile. The character *ten* of *iten* was replaced by *den*, meaning the buttock, so that the original meaning was altered to mean to move one's buttock, or, more coarsely, to move one's ass!

The prostitutes drew the attention of the American press very quickly. The Seattle *Post-Intelligencer* carried articles in February and April 1891 reporting on the arrest of Japanese prostitutes, and sarcastically noted, in the latter month, that "the Japs all gave half English, half Japanese names, such as 'Jap Mary' and 'Jap Lizzie' etc.," at the time they were booked.[79] In San Francisco, the *Bulletin* in January 1890 printed a story about them. Under the caption "Japanese women—Their Importation for Immoral Purposes," the story quoted a police official as saying that "the majority . . . are in houses of ill-fame, having been imported for that purpose," and that "their colony is growing" with "every steamer from Japan bringing reinforcements."[80] During the remainder of 1890 the San Francisco press published a few more items on Japanese women suspected of prostitution, but it was not until the following year that they became notably newsworthy.

In 1891 and 1892 the *Bulletin, Daily Report, Call,* and *Examiner* all printed sensational stories. In February 1891 the *Examiner* reported the arrest of two young Japanese prostitutes in a police raid which, it claimed, caused "consternation and alarm in the Japanese quarter."[81] A few months later, in May, the *Bulletin* took up where it had left off in 1890. Reviewing the past arrival of Japanese women, it said:

The first of them to arrive were imported for immoral purposes, and since that time scarely a steamer arrived . . . that did not carry one or two recruits for the army of abandoned women in this city. This colony increased slowly but surely until . . . one whole block was occupied exclusively by them. . . . [82]

Shortly afterward, using its favorite headline, "The Slave Trade," the *Daily Report* compared the Japanese to the Chinese:

The Chinese are not the only people in San Francisco engaged in the slave trade. For some years the Japanese have also been busily engaged in the traffic. . . . Nearly all the Japanese women who come to San Francisco are . . . destined for houses of ill-fame.[83]

The press coverage in the spring of 1892 had the same content and tenor. The *Examiner* stated emphatically that "Japanese women are imported for vicious purposes."[84] Continuing its self-proclaimed crusade against Japanese prostitution, the *Bulletin* declared that

the women here are of the lowest class, and, like the Chinese women, are imported only to lead a life of shame. Of course this is not true of all of them, but it is of far the greater number. Like the Chinese women, they are held in bondage and are obliged to turn over their wages of sin to their masters and importers.[85]

The *Call* parroted the *Bulletin:*

Six years ago there was hardly a Japanese woman to be found in this city. Now they are to be seen in great numbers.

They have taken exclusive possession of St. Mary's Street, where they hold forth without restraint by the police and hail every passerby with the familiar cry of the siren.

Perhaps Japan has sent us her very worst, but the samples seen here have given our people anything but a good opinion of Japanese morals.[86]

And the *Daily Report* warned of the danger ahead: "The importation of Japanese women for immoral purposes promises to become as notorious as the Chinese slave trade."[87] Likening Japanese prostitution to that of the Chinese, this adverse publicity was a part of the first agitation raised simultaneously against Japanese laborers by the San Francisco press.

Japanese government officials were appalled at the arrival and presence of the prostitutes. The San Francisco and Vancouver consuls forwarded frequent dispatches on them to the Foreign Ministry in which they consistently advised Tokyo to take steps to stop their departure from Japan. Highly sensitive to the American image of Japan and the

Japanese people, the negative press coverage heightened the consuls' sense of consternation. In February 1891 certain eastern newspapers carried an article on an alleged incident involving the "auction" of Japanese girls in San Francisco which alarmed Tateno Gōzō, the Japanese envoy in Washington, D.C., prompting him to order Chinda Sutemi, the San Francisco consul, to conduct an immediate inquiry. Chinda discovered that the story was fabricated, but stated in a March dispatch that "the rumor could not have spread if the vice of Japanese prostitutes had not already become a public scandal." Continuing, he predicted that:

> If matters are left as they are today, illicit Japanese houses inevitably will be established soon all over the country as in Hong Kong, Shanghai, and Singapore. . . . At present the Japanese are prone to incur the enmity of Americans like the Chinese. If we allow the prostitutes to carry on unhindered, what will be unavoidable is that prostitution will become a basic pretext in the hands of Japanese exclusionists.[88]

Chinda here expressed one of the great apprehensions shared by Japanese government officials. The prostitutes were not mere stains on Japan's national honor, although that was admittedly scandalous enough. Fully aware of what had happened to the Chinese, Chinda feared their presence would become, as he called it, a "pretext" for a campaign—similar to the Chinese exclusion movement—to exclude the Japanese. The San Francisco press would confirm his fear less than two months later when newspapers explicitly linked Japanese prostitution to that of the Chinese. To forestall the possibility, Chinda therefore concluded that "the most urgent task is to close up the avenues by which new prostitutes arrive in the city."[89]

The measures adopted by the Japanese government to curb the departure of prostitutes from Japan coincided with new immigration legislation in the United States. Congress amended previous enactments regulating immigration on March 3, 1891, creating the office of Superintendent of Immigration within the Treasury Department to oversee the operation of immigration stations. Along with earlier enactments, the new legislation prohibited the entry of certain classes of aliens, among them prostitutes. In the spring of 1891, two German tramp steamers sailed into San Francisco Bay carrying 120 Japanese laborers, including a number of women. In response to the consular dispatches on the prostitutes and the new legislation, the vice foreign minister had instructed Chinda to assign a consular staffer to the immigration station as an interpreter.[90] The idea was to cooperate with immigration officials to spot potential or actual prostitutes and prevent their debarkation whenever ships arrived with Japanese passengers. With Chinda's intervention and assistance, the majority of laborers aboard the two ships were allowed to land, but nine women were deported. Suspecting that they were prostitutes, Chinda did not intervene on their behalf. Thereafter Tokyo instructed all local passport-issuing offices in Japan to screen all applicants carefully to make certain they did not fall into the classes of aliens excluded by the new legislation. Though this measure did not completely halt the flow of prostitutes to America, it did reduce the number of new arrivals.

Student leaders in San Francisco were equally dismayed at the prostitutes. As early as 1889, the secretary of the Gospel Society appealed to the Japanese government to stop the passage of indigent persons.[91] In May 1891 other student leaders petitioned the Foreign Ministry to specifically curtail the departure of prostitutes from Japan. The petition in part read:

> Lately in the cities of California, Washington, and Oregon in America, Japanese women who ply the infamous trade, namely, prostitution, are increasing in number by the months. Among the cities, San Francisco is the most notorious with many women forming a block in a row of adjacent houses. Engaged in their illicit business, they sense no shame at all at the scandalous sight they present. Because they do not, a public outcry has been aroused among the American people, so that recent female arrivals are continually denied landing permission. . . . These women are a blot on our national image and national morality. . . . The reasons for the ban on Chinese immigration and the call for the expulsion of the Chinese were many and varied, but *the main one was that Chinese women were prostitutes.* . . . It is evident that, if this notorious vice spreads, America will adopt measures against us in the same manner as she did formerly against the Chinese (emphasis added).[92]

The petition reiterated Chinda's opinion. Asserting that the prostitutes dishonored Japan as a nation, it attributed the principal reason for Chinese exclusion to Chinese prostitutes. By analogy, if Japanese prostitutes increased in number, Japanese exclusion was a distinct possibility. Neither Japanese government officials nor student leaders alluded sympathetically to the plight of the prostitutes. They simply condemned them out of hand. Deeming the "face" of the Japanese nation and of the "respectable" Japanese residents of paramount importance, they feared that Japan and they would be judged by Americans in the same light as they themselves judged the prostitutes.

Government Contract Laborers to Hawaii

From 1885 to 1894 close to 30,000 laborers emigrated to the Hawaiian Islands under government auspices as contract laborers.[93] Based upon an 1884 preliminary agreement and an 1886 Immigration Convention between the Japanese government and the Hawaiian monarchy, the laborers signed contracts to work on Hawaiian sugar plantations for a three-year period. Like the student-laborers, these laborers were *dekaseginin*. Their goal was to earn as much money as possible with which to start life anew in their native village. Initially, the Hawaiian government assumed the cost of the steerage passage to Honolulu. Male laborers received nine dollars per month, plus a six dollar food allowance; female laborers earned six dollars, plus a four dollar food allowance. A work month was twenty-six days; ten hours of labor in the field and twelve in the sugar factory constituted a work day. Sugar planters deposited 25 percent (later reduced to 15 percent) of all wages with the Japanese consulate in Honolulu. The Japanese government insisted on this payment procedure to guarantee that no laborer would squander his or her earnings and that everyone would have the fare for the return passage. This movement of laborers to Hawaii was the beginning of mass labor emigration from Japan and the prologue to the arrival of laborers on the continental United States.

The laborers who went to Hawaii were organized into twenty-six separate contingents, and came from a limited geographical area. In southwestern Honshū, Hiroshima Prefecture ranked first with 11,122 laborers, or 38.2 percent of the total.[94] Lying adjacent to Hiroshima, Yamaguchi Prefecture ranked a close second with 10,424, or 35.8 percent. In Kyūshū, Kumamoto and Fukuoka Prefectures ranked third and fourth respectively. The former contributed 4,247 laborers, or 14.6 percent, while the latter added 2,180, or 7.5 percent. The four Prefectures combined to account for an astounding 96.1 percent of all the laborers. Certain districts within these four prefectures, moreover, contributed laborers disproportionately. Four districts in Hiroshima Prefecture, plus the city of Hiroshima, accounted for 9,183 laborers, or 81.6 percent of the Hiroshima total. All four were coastal districts facing the Inland Sea—Saeki, Takamiya, Numata, and Aki (present-day Asa combines Takamiya and Numata). Three districts in Yamaguchi Prefecture accounted for 9,203 laborers, or 88.3 percent of the Yamaguchi total. The three were Kumage and Kuga, two coastal districts lying west of Hiroshima Prefecture, and Ōshima, an island in the Inland Sea situated opposite Kuga and Kumage.

The method of recruitment determined this restricted geographical origin. Three principal figures were involved: Inoue Kaoru, Robert W. Irwin, and Masuda Takashi. Inoue was the foreign minister who negotiated the preliminary agreement and the Immigration Convention on behalf of the Japanese government. Irwin was in charge of recruiting and shipping laborers to Honolulu as special agent of the Immigration Bureau of Hawaii and as Hawaiian consul in Yokohama. Masuda was head of the Mitsui Trading Company. All three men knew each other very well, having been close business associates dating back to 1872. Inoue was Irwin's highest-placed contact in the Meiji government. The closeness of the two men is evidenced by the fact that Inoue had arranged Irwin's marriage to a Japanese woman. Although there is no conclusive evidence, it seems that Inoue urged Irwin to recruit laborers in Yamaguchi, his home prefecture. To undertake the actual job of recruiting, Irwin solicited the help of the Mitsui Trading Company. President Masuda recommended that recruitment take place specifically in Hiroshima and Yamaguchi Prefectures. Recruiting notices first appeared in a Mitsui-related newspaper, and the company dispatched agents to Hiroshima, Yamaguchi, Fukuoka, and Kumamoto for recruiting purposes. Irwin notified the governor of Tokyo of his intention to recruit laborers, and the governor passed on this information to all prefectural governors. Governor Hara Yasutarō of Yamaguchi Prefecture contacted the Mitsui Trading Company and offered to supply laborers from his prefecture. His local government even sent a native of Ōshima to the island to explain the details of recruitment and conditions in Hawaii. The first contingent of January 1885 consisted of 945 laborers. Selected from an estimated 28,000 applicants from across the nation, 420 of those chosen were from Yamaguchi and 222 from Hiroshima. Of the laborers from Yamaguchi, 305 were from Ōshima. The combined influence of Inoue, Irwin, and Masuda caused the initial selection to be heavily in favor of these two prefectures.[95]

Reports filed by the consul general in Honolulu reinforced the initial selection pattern. In 1886 Andō Tarō assumed the post of consul general. According to the terms of the 1886 Immigration Convention, the consul had the right to inspect all plantations which employed Japanese laborers to ascertain that the convention was being faithfully executed. As soon as he arrived in Honolulu, Ando conducted inspection tours and submitted reports to the foreign ministry. He reported that the planters were most pleased with the laborers from Hiroshima and Yamaguchi Prefectures—they were industrious, thrifty, and fastidious about the cleanliness of their living quarters and clothing. Although not as satisfactory as the laborers from Hiroshima and Yamaguchi, the laborers from Kumamoto and Fukuoka Prefectures were adequate, particularly if they were from agricultural villages. The least desirable laborers were those who had originated from areas near an urban center. Andō singled out the laborers from Chiba, Tokyo, Kanagawa, and Shiga as being "lazy and self-indulgent" and prone to "gambling." In the light of this evaluation, he recommended that future recruitment be restricted to "remote agricultural villages."[96] As a result the third contingent in 1886 consisted of 877 laborers who came exclusively from Hiroshima, Yamaguchi, and Kumamoto. The recruitment of all subsequent contingents took place almost entirely in these three prefectures plus Fukuoka.

The rural depression of the 1880s formed the economic background to this labor emigration to Hawaii. In 1873 the Meiji govenment had instituted a land tax system to generate a set income for itself. Based upon a fixed assessment of the value of land, it levied a 3 percent land tax on all landholdings, reduced to $2\frac{1}{2}$ percent in 1877. This land tax was not pegged to any fluctuation in the price of agricultural commodities, nor did it bear any relationship to crop failures or successes. And, unlike in the past, it had to be paid in cash rather than in kind. In the late 1870s, due to enormous military expenditures, the Meiji government's outlays far exceeded its income. To make up the deficit, the government issued 42 million yen of nonconvertible paper currency in 1878–79, and the result was runaway inflation. The major index of agricultural commodities, the price of rice, reflected the inflationary spiral. In 1877–78 the price of rice was 5.55 yen per *koku* (4.96 bushels); by 1879–1880 it rose to 8.01; and by 1881–82 it soared to 11.20. This inflation sharply reduced the government's revenues. Inasmuch as the land tax remained fixed as agricultural prices rose, the government's real income from the land tax declined proportionately. And since the land tax was the main source of income, the loss of revenue was all the more acute.

In 1881 the Meiji government set out to halt the inflation by driving down agricultural prices. It adopted drastic deflationary measures, among them the withdrawal of the previously issued nonconvertible paper currency from the economy. The government achieved its goal in a matter of several years. In 1882–83 the price of rice dropped to 8.93 yen per *koku;* in 1883–84 it dipped to 6.26; and by 1884–85 it plummeted to 5.14 yen, less than it had been in 1877–78. The steep downward turn in the price of agricultural commodities dealt a devastating blow to the rural economy. All farmers had their earnings cut drastically, and many small landowning farmers, obliged to continue to pay the fixed land tax, were forced into debt and eventually reduced to tenants. The first half of the 1880s witnessed violent peasant uprisings. Featuring demands for moratoria on the repayment of debts, and armed attacks on local usurers and large landowners, these uprisings attested to the widespread impoverishment of the peasantry caused by the Meiji government's deflationary policy.

A majority of the contract laborers who went to Hawaii came from landless or small landowning farming households which suffered the most from the rural depression. Recent research findings on three villages in Hiroshima Prefecture bear this out. Between 1885 and 1899, the village of Kuchita in Takamiya District sent out 288 emigrants—203 Hawaii, 73 to the United States, and 12 elsewhere. Of this total, 256 were males, and 206 were from agricultural households. Of all the households which contributed emigrants, the overwhelming number were either landless or small landholding households—87 had no land, 47 had three *tan* (1 *tan* = .245 acre) or less, and 25 had seven *tan* but less than 1.5 *chō* (1 *chō* = 2.45 acres). These households represented 81.9 percent of all the contributing households.[97] Between 1885 and 1894, the village of Hesaka in Aki District contributed 151 contract laborers. In 1890 this village, out of a total of 312 households, had 285 households engaged in farming. Of the 285 farming households, 49 were full tenants, 156 were part-owner/part-tenants, and 85 were full owners. With no single large landholding, 283 households cultivated eight *tan* or less of land each.[98] The third village is Jigozen, located in Saeki District. Between 1885 and 1899, this village sent out 793 emigrants—624 to Hawaii, 151 to the United States, and 18 elsewhere. During the Immigration Convention period, it contributed 297 contract laborers, ranking second behind the island of Nihojima in Aki District. Of the total of 793 emigrants, 564 were male, of whom 290 were from agricultural households and 238 were heads of household. No emigrant head of household owned more than one *chō* of land; the majority were either landless or tenants who farmed one to three *tan* of land.[99]

Rural households engaged in small-scale farming always depended upon supplementary sources of income. One source was the spinning of cotton yarn and the weaving of cotton cloth as a household industry. From Tokugawa times cotton was being grown in Hiroshima Prefecture, mainly around the city of Hiroshima and in the coastal districts. As the single most important cash crop, it represented 11.1 percent of the value of all agricultural commodities produced by the prefecture in 1877. That year there were only three modern spinning mills in all of Japan. By 1886 there were twenty-three, and one of them was completed outside the city of Hiroshima in 1882. Located in the village of Kami-Seno, it was operated by the Hiroshima Cotton Spinning Company. In 1883 this company opened a second mill in Saeki District.[100] Unable to compete with the modern mills, rural households were deprived of the supplemental income thay had earned by spinning and weaving.

Other unique factors explain the high number of contract laborers from Hiroshima and Yamaguchi Prefectures. The home of an old fishing community, the island of Nihojima contributed 999 laborers, the largest number of any single village or area. In 1884 the beginning of work on the Ujina Harbor construction project had a telling impact on the fishing village of Ōkō on this island. The people of Ōkō raised oysters and harvested the seaweed in the surrounding waters. The harbor project threatened to deny them their traditional water rights, thereby undermining the basis of their livelihood. Aware of the dire economic consequences, the people opposed the construction project, but their protests went unheeded. Once construction started in September 1884, a month before Robert W. Irwin began to recruit laborers, they had no choice but to seek work outside of Nihojima.[101] Economic pressures also affected Hesaka, primarily a rice-producing village. In 1889 heavy summer rains and pests adversely affected its rice crop so that it produced 695 *koku* less than in 1888. This drop in harvest corresponded with a sudden increase in emigration from Hesaka between 1889 and 1891.[102]

Of all the districts of Hiroshima and Yamaguchi Prefectures, Ōshima stands out as the one which sent out the highest number of laborers: 3,876. Many factors combined to induce the people of Ōshima to emigrate. During the late Tokugawa period, the island experienced a sharp rise in population. Two of the four towns in Ōshima illustrate this increase. Tōwa had a population of 3,050 in 1750, which multiplied five-fold to 16,616 by 1842.[103] Kuka had a population of 2,152 in 1737, which rose to 6,995 by 1842 and 8,365 by 1881.[104] The introduction of the sweet potato to Ōshima in the early eighteenth century was behind this rapid growth. Its cultivation provided the growing population with an inexpensive staple food. The population growth in turn forced people to seek work outside the island. Fishermen, seamen, stonemasons, carpenters, and others regularly left Ōshima to work temporarily in Hiroshima, Yamaguchi, northern Kyūshū, and Shikoku. Thus the practice of *dekasegi* was firmly established among the people well before 1885. As was the case with Hiroshima Prefecture, the Meiji government's deflationary policy wrought havoc on the island's rural economy, and the two modern mills of the Hiroshima Cotton Spinning Company also wiped out the spinning and weaving cottage industry in Ōshima.

Natural calamities added to the misery of the people of this region. In 1883 a major drought occurred, and in 1884 a storm caused widespread flooding.[105] Both destroyed crops in Ōshima and in the adjacent districts. In the summer of 1885, a Yamaguchi newspaper carried a story by a reporter who witnessed the terrible conditions in Kuga, Kumage, and Ōshima. The reporter wrote in part:

> The depression has gotten worse in every village, town, and district. But what strikes me most is the hardships paupers are having in surviving. The worse-off people are the fishermen and farmers in and around the port of Yanai, Kuga District, in Morotsu and Kaminoseki, Kumage District, and Kuka and Agenoshō, Ōshima District. Their regular fare consists of rice husk or buckwheat chaff ground into powder and the dregs of bean curd mixed with leaves and grass.[106]

In the village of Yashiro in Ōshima District, in 1886, another rainstorm caused a mountainside to collapse, and also caused severe flooding which destroyed 62 homes, killed 110 people, and left acres of land submerged under water.[107] Occurring right before and after 1885, these natural disasters gave the people of Ōshima and its adjacent districts an added reason to sign up for work in Hawaii.

The relative "success" of the first laborers inspired others to follow them. As a member of the first contingent, Iwase Kansuke of Kuka departed Yokohama aboard the *City of Tokyo* in January 1885. Ten months later he remitted 129 yen to his parents. This sum was remitted through the local government office, so that the townspeople quickly learned that it was Iwase who had sent it from Hawaii:[108] One hundred twenty-nine yen was an astronomical sum of money; Kuka stonemasons earned only 10 yen in the entire spring of 1885. Altogether 35 people from Kuka were members of the first contingent. Eighteen returned with a combined total of 2,365 yen. What 15 returnees did with their money is known. Three persons purchased a house or constructed a new home; 8 bought land; 2 saved their money; and 2 repaid outstanding debts.[109] One can imagine how greatly Iwase and these first returnees impressed the local populace. The improved life of the returnees was evident to everyone. They were living proof of the economic benefits one could gain by working abroad. Relatives, friends, and neighbors no doubt were excited by what they saw and heard; many became convinced that they, too, should go to Hawaii. By December 1891, Hiroshima laborers had remitted a total of $732,000 from Hawaii. Of this amount, $220,500 went into savings, $172,000 went towards the purchase of real property and household goods, $272,000 was earmarked for repayment of debts, and $67,500 went for miscellaneous expenses.[110]

Exclusive of money carried back in person to Japan, the contract laborers remitted a total of 2.6 million from Hawaii during the 10-year period from 1885 to 1894.[111] When the money carried back to Japan is added, the aggregate figure easily exceeded $3 million. A comparison of wages in Hawaii and in Japan will suggest the relative value of this sum of money. In 1885 a male contract laborer's earning of $15 per month in Hawaii was equal to 17.65 yen. In Hiroshima Prefecture, in 1885, woodcutters earned an average of 4.16 yen per month; stonemasons, lumbermen, and sake brewery workers, 3.64; and carpenters 3.36. Male agricultural field hands earned an annual income of only 9.98 yen.[112] Taking the example of Jigozen, in 1885 an ordinary carpenter earned 4.16 yen per month, while a day laborer earned 2.60.[113] The Hawaiian wages of 17.65 yen was more than four times that of a Jigozen carpenter and six times that of a Jigozen day laborer. In 1891 Hiroshima laborers remitted 270,732 yen. As another measure of the value of the remittances, this sum was equal to 54.3 percent of the 1891 budget of the Hiroshima Prefectural government.[114]

This Japanese government-sponsored labor emigration to Hawaii had far-reaching consequences. Contrary to what government officials expected, only 13,861 laborers, or less than half, returned to Japan— 2,034 died in Hawaii, while another 877 moved to the United States or elsewhere. The rest remained on the islands.[115] This first movement of contract laborers to Hawaii had the effect of stimulating further emigration, and the effect went beyond the limited geographical areas from which the laborers originated and spilled over into adjacent villages, districts, and even prefectures. By demonstrating the efficacy of overseas dekasegi, it encouraged many more people to seek work abroad. In short, the Hawaiian experience set the stage for the second phase of labor emigration from Japan.

Rise of Emigration Companies

The second stage began as the government-sponsored emigration to Hawaii was coming to a close, and was characterized by the rise of emigration companies which promoted labor emigration. Emigration companies were private business enterprises which recruited and shipped laborers abroad for profit. Established in December 1891, the first company was called the Nihon Yoshisa Emigration Company, a partnership of Yoshikawa Yasujirō, vice-president of the Nihon Yūsen Kaisha, a steamship company, and Sakuma Teiichi, a prominent Tokyo businessman. From 1892 this company shipped contract laborers to New Caledonia, Australia, Guadeloupe, and the Fiji Islands.[116] Other emigration companies such as the Meiji Emigration Company and Yokohama Emigration Company appeared later. Once the Japanese government pulled out of the labor emigration business in 1894, other companies were formed in rapid succession. No regulations or codes governed their operation at first. Many companies engaged in irregular practices, often of a fraudulent nature. They misled emigrants about wages and job conditions abroad. They exacted sundry fees under numerous guises. And they sometimes did not honor the obligations they had to the emigrants they had sent abroad. In 1893 the Meiji Emigration Company shipped 88 laborers to Canada. Upon their arrival in Victoria, British Columbia, these laborers learned that their wages and terms of employment were considerably different from what they had been led to believe. In 1894 the Yokohama Emigration Company shipped 84 laborers, likewise to Canada. These laborers reported that the company had issued bad foreign currency to them and that its agent in Canada refused to fulfill their employment agreement.[117]

To control the activities of emigration companies, the Japanese government in April 1894 promulgated a set of regulations known as the Regulations to Protect Emigrants.[118] This designation was somewhat misleading because the regulations were created to control emigration companies rather than to protect emigrants. An emigrant was defined as "any person who goes abroad to engage in labor." Labor was limited to agriculture, fishery, mining, construction, transportation, manufacturing, and domestic service. An emigration broker or agent was defined as "any person who engages in the business of recruiting and assisting emigrants to go abroad." All agents had to post bonds of 10,000 yen and obtain business licenses from the Ministry of Home

Affairs. No foreigner could be an agent. In applying for passports for emigrants, all agents had to present written agreements into which they had entered with their emigrants. The agreement had to specify the time the emigrants were to be abroad, the assistance rendered by the agents, the exact fee charged for the assistance, and the manner in which the agents would help the emigrants to return to Japan in case of illness or distress. No agent could send emigrants to any country or territory where he did not have a representative or with which the Japanese government did not have a treaty. All agents had to inform the government of their capital assets and business operations and the number and types of emigrants they were shipping abroad. The Ministry of Home Affairs was authorized to impose fines and revoke licenses if and when agents were found in violation of the regulations. Any emigrant who did not go through an agent had to have two sureties or guarantors who assumed responsibility for helping the emigrant to return to Japan in the event of illness or distress. Just as it was going out of the emigration business, the Japanese government drew up the Regulations to Protect Emigrants. With minor revisions, the regulations were enacted into law in April 1896.

Emigration companies flourished from that year on. In 1898 there were nine companies which shipped 12,393 laborers abroad. Of the 31,354 emigrants who left Japan in 1899, 21,515 were shipped by twelve companies.[119] Most of these emigrants were contract laborers furnished to Hawaiian sugar plantations under private agreements between the companies and planters. By 1906 there were thirty emigration companies and individual brokers.[120] Nine had their main offices in Hiroshima Prefecture, fifteen had agents who operated branch offices in Hiroshima. Emigration companies reached their peak between 1902 and 1907 when they sent a total of 98,429 emigrants abroad.[121] Besides the Hawaiian Islands, emigration companies shipped laborers primarily to New Caledonia, Australia, Guadeloupe, the Fiji Islands, Peru, Mexico, and later to Brazil. The five biggest companies were the Morioka Emigration Company, Hiroshima Kaigai Tokō Company, Nihon Emigration Company, Tokyo Emigration Company, and Kumamoto Emigration Company.

Some recent studies throw light on how the emigration companies operated. These studies suggest that the companies reinforced the original pattern of labor emigration by recruiting in established emigrant prefectures. With its main office located in Tokyo, the Nihon Yoshisa Emigration Company had a branch office in Hiroshima Prefecture. Its Hiroshima agent was Doi Tsumoru, a well-known local politician who was a native resident of Kamo District.[122] Between 1881 and 1887 Doi had been a member of the prefectural assembly, and in the early 1890s he was head of Gōta village in Kamo District. From 1892 the Nihon Yoshisa Emigration Company and its successor supplied most of the contract laborers who worked in the sugarcane fields of Queensland, Australia. The overwhelming majority of these laborers were from Hiroshima Prefecture. The company succeeded in recruiting laborers from Gōta and its environs and from the coastal villages of Aki, Saeki, Takamiya, and Numata, the four districts which had contributed the high percentage of contract laborers to Hawaii. As the Hiroshima agent of the emigration company, Doi recruited and selected the laborers himself, handled remittances from Queensland, and acted as an intermediary between the company and the families of the laborers. He commanded enough local respect and authority to carry out these tasks. In obtaining passports for the emigrants he recruited, his personal contacts in local government offices were important, for all passport applications had to be approved by heads of villages and districts, as well as by the prefectural governor, in a cumbersome process. As Gōta village head and onetime prefectural assemblyman, Doi had access to government officials at the village, district, and prefectural levels to expedite approval.

The Hiroshima Kaigai Tokō Company had widespread connections.[123] Founded in Hiroshima City in May 1893, this company received its license in October 1894 and began actual operation the following year. It had branch offices not only in Hiroshima villages, but in seven other prefectures as well. It had close ties to the Suo Emigration Company, a Yamaguchi-based firm with its main office in Kuga District, and the Kōsei Emigration Company, a Wakayama-based outfit. Three groups were involved in the Hiroshima Kaigai Tokō Company. Constituting the first group were four local prefectural assemblymen who founded the company: Mugida Tsukasaburō of Ashida District, Yamanaka Masao of Hiroshima City, and Segoshi Jūtarō and Doi Masao of Saeki District. The second group consisted of persons affiliated with the local Chūjō Bank which provided the capital to launch the company in business.

The third group was composed of members of the Patriotic League in San Francisco. In 1892, with Sugawara Tsutau as President, the members of the League established a commercial firm called the Nichibei Yōtatsusha in conjunction with the beginning of Japanese railroad labor contracting.[124] The first contractor was Tanaka Tadashichi. As a subcontractor of a Chinese subcontractor, Tanaka first supplied la-

borers in October 1891 to the Oregon Short Line, a subsidiary of
the Union Pacific running from Granger, Wyoming, to Huntington,
Oregon. Headquartered in Rock Springs, Wyoming, the Chinese subcontractor was supplying Chinese laborers to the Union Pacific under
William H. Remington, a white American. Tanaka was a former
seaman who had jumped ship in 1885. In Seattle he teamed up with
one of the Japanese prostitutes and took her to Ogden, Utah, where
he put her to work. In 1891 the Chinese subcontractor took a fancy
to the woman while visiting Ogden, and persuaded Tanaka to let him
take her back to Rock Springs as his mistress. Then Tanaka had the
woman prevail upon the Chinese to permit him to become his subcontractor.[125] Illiterate but shrewd, he set up his office in Nampa, Idaho,
and staffed it with student-laborers drawn from San Francisco. In 1892
Tanaka broke away from the Chinese subcontractor and supplied laborers directly under Remington. By September 1892 he had 500
workers employed on the Oregon Short Line, 150 of whom were
from Hiroshima Prefecture.[126] The Nichibei Yōtatsusha had access to
Tanaka and his laborers through Katsunuma Tomizō, a member of
the Patriotic League who was on the staff of Tanaka's Idaho office.[127]
Through this connection, the firm offered special mail handling, remittance, translation, and letter-writing services to the laborers.

In July 1893 the Hiroshima Kaigai Tokō Company and the Nichibei Yōtatsusha signed a formal agreement.[128] The emigration company
agreed to recruit and ship laborers to the San Francisco firm. For its
part the San Francisco company agreed to do three things. For emigrants who wished to visit certain places, the company would make
necessary travel arrangements. For those who wanted job referrals,
the company would offer employment information. And for those
who desired to work under its wings, the company would supervise
them on a job. In the event of groups of 100 or more persons, the
company would make special arrangements with the emigration company as to their disposition. Under the agreement, the Nichibei Yōtatsusha became the exclusive agent of the Hiroshima Kaigai Tokō Company in the United States, Canada, and Mexico.

The relationship between the Patriotic League and the Hiroshima
emigration company continued in Japan. In addition to Sugawara Tsutau, there were three other key figures in the Nichibei Yōtatsusha:
Hinata Terutake, Watanabe Kanjūrō, and Matsuoka Tatsusaburō. All
three were members of the League; Matsuoka worked in Tanaka's
office with Katsunuma. Along with Sugawara, these three men be-

came executives of the Hiroshima company upon their return to Japan—Sugawara in 1894, Hinata and Watanabe in 1895, and Matsuoka in 1897.[129] In 1895 Sugawara, Hinata, and others conducted an on-the-spot survey of conditions in Hawaii prior to setting up an office in Honolulu. Sugawara and Hinata eventually became successful politicians. Both were elected to the Diet as members of the Seiyūkai political party, Sugawara in 1898 and Hinata in 1902. Between 1895 and 1908 emigration companies based in Hiroshima Prefecture shipped a total of 41,297 laborers. The Hiroshima Kaigai Tokō Company accounted for 21,230 of this total, the vast majority of whom were sent to Hawaii.[130] The company's success was due in no small measure to its local and national political contacts which facilitated the recruitment and shipment of laborers. Conversely, it is said the the profits of the company, funneled into the coffers of the Seiyūkai, helped to finance the political careers of Sugawara and Hinata.[131]

Finally, there is the example of the Kyūshū Emigration Company.[132] Headquartered in Kumamoto City, this company operated between 1897 and 1908. By recruiting specifically in Kumamoto, Yamaguchi, and Hiroshima, it also reinforced the established pattern of geographical origins of Japanese emigrants. Up until the turn of the century, the company shipped emigrants from these three prefectures, mainly to Canada. Like the Nihon Yoshisa Emigration Company and the Hiroshima Kaigai Tokō Company, the Kyūshū Emigration Company had close ties to local politicians and to the Kokkentō, a local political party, in which every company official was enrolled. This party was headed by Tsuda Seiichi. Tsuda had studied in the United States and had recruited laborers in Kumamoto himself. In 1892 he was an agent of the Nihon Yoshisa Emigration Company, and in 1893 he recruited Kumamoto laborers who were shipped off to Queensland, Australia by the Tokyo-based company. To facilitate its financial transactions, the Kyūshū Emigration Company also had close connections with local banks through interlocking personnel. Many company officials served simultaneously as bank officers.

Laborers and the Continental United States

Labor immigration to the United States occurred in two distinct phases. From 1891 to 1900, the first phase, 27,440 Japanese, most of whom were laborers, were admitted.[133] From 1901 to 1907, the second phase, 42,457 more persons were admitted, augmented by upwards of 38,000 laborers who entered the United States via the Hawaiian Islands.[134] Agitation on the West Coast against the influx of Japanese laborers erupted fully in the spring of 1900. Fearful of diplomatic consequences, the Japanese government prohibited the passage of laborers to the continental United States and Canada in August, 1900, marking off the first phase of labor emigration from the second.[135] Two years later, in June 1902, it relaxed the restriction and permitted onetime laborers, who had returned to Japan, to go back to the United States. When such returnees applied for repassage, the government issued passports to them, and to the wives, children, and parents of residents in the United States as well.[136]

Of the 36,995 passports issued to persons destined for the continental United States from 1901 to 1907, only 5,316 were issued to laborers, presumably to former resident laborers who returned to the United States.[137] The balance were issued to persons classified as nonlaborers. Separate from the laborers who returned to the United States, the number of new laborers who came directly from Japan is impossible to determine. By obtaining student, commercial, and other passports under false pretext, a certain number no doubt managed to emigrate in spite of the government's restrictive policy. Still the restriction had the effect, however imperfect, of impeding and reducing direct labor emigration, so that indirect emigration via Hawaii became the main avenue by which laborers set foot on the Pacific Coast. Between 1894 and 1907 upwards of 127,000 Japanese arrived in the Hawaiian Islands, the bulk of whom were laborers shipped by emigration companies.[138] Because laborers were able to secure passports for Hawaii in the second phase, many of them used the islands as a stepping-stone to the United States.

The second phase ended abruptly in 1907. In California the clamor against Japanese immigration intensified in 1905, and the San Francisco school imbroglio of October 1906, in which the school board resolved to segregate Japanese pupils on the public schools, precipitated an international crisis. As a part of the solution, President Theodore Roosevelt issued an executive order on March 14, 1907, prohibiting those aliens whose passports had been issued for destinations other than the United States, from entering the country via insular possessions, the Canal Zone, or other nations. Congress had authorized him to take this action by amending immigration statutes in February. This meant that any Japanese who possessed a passport issued for the Hawaiian Islands no longer could enter the continental United States.[139]

As far as the United States was concerned, emigration companies could not operate freely because they were unable to ship contract laborers. In 1885 contract labor had been outlawed. Strictly defined, a contract laborer was any person who signed a contract to work at a job before he or she emigrated and whose passage was prepaid by someone else. Loosely interpreted, it could also mean any person whose passage was assisted and who was promised a job by relatives or friends already in the United States. The 1891 amendments to immigration statutes strengthened the ban on contract labor. Besides contract laborers, prostitutes, idiots, paupers, criminals, bearers of contagious diseases, and the insane were also excluded. As Japanese laborers landed from 1891 on, immigration officials considered many arrivals as belonging to the excluded classes. Classified as contract laborers, prostitutes, or paupers apt to become public charges, they were denied landing permission. An alien at the time had to have at least thirty dollars to satisfy immigration officials that he or she would not become a public charge.

Just as the arrival of prostitutes had alarmed Japanese government officials, so, too, did the landing of indigent laborers. As consul in San Francisco from 1890 to 1894, Chinda Sutemi filed numerous reports in which he voiced his consternation. Some laborers had barely scraped up the steerage passage fare and had little or no money. Many were dressed shabbily, and a few did not even possess passports. With the Chinese exclusion movement still fresh in his memory, Chinda was wary that such laborers would give rise to an anti-Japanese movement, already prefigured, in his opinion, by the San Francisco press coverage of the laborers. Based upon Chinda's reports, D. W. Stevens, American adviser to the Japanese Legation in Washington, D.C., expressed his own apprehension:

> Formerly the majority of the Japanese who came to San Francisco were of the student class. They arrived singly, or in small companies; and while they had often left Japan without definite plans and without proper provision for their support while abroad, they did not arouse criticism or hostility from the American press or people. Within the last year or so, however, a different class of Japanese have begun to come to the United States in comparatively large numbers. They are generally people belonging to the laboring classes, who have been induced to leave Japan by the hope of improving their condition. And, what is especially significant, instead of coming from the open ports or their immediate neighborhood, many of them come from remote parts of the interior.

This shift in the composition of Japanese arrivals, Stevens believed, would transform American public opinion towards Japanese.

> The feeling in the United States toward Japanese is very friendly. It is not too much to say, however, that there will, in all probability, be a change in this regard if indigent Japanese continue to arrive in this country. Already there are indications of such a change in California. Hitherto there has been a widely marked difference in the attitude of the people and press of the State toward the Chinese and their sentiments toward Japanese. But recently . . . it was possible to detect in the comments of the San Francisco press that same hostility so often displayed toward the Chinese.

And he concluded:

> There are unquestionably in Japan at present a number of persons engaged in promoting emigration to the United States simply to obtain the passage money of the immigrant. . . . The Imperial Government . . . should take immediate action in regard to this matter. . . . If there is any means of punishing the persons who for their own selfish ends lure Japanese away under false promises, the punishment should be prompt and severe. If there is a way to prevent indiscriminate emigration, it should at once be utilized. Neither the welfare of Japanese subjects, nor the credit of Japan, will be promoted by the continuance of the present condition of affairs.[140]

Warning of the negative consequences of unrestricted labor emigration, Chinda himself advised the Foreign Ministry to see that local authorities in Japan exercised strict control over the departure of laborers. Accordingly, the Foreign Ministry instructed all local authorities to screen all passport applications to make sure that applicants were neither contract laborers nor belonged to the other excluded classes of aliens.[141]

Limited to sending only so-called free emigrants to the United States, emigration companies played a minor role in promoting direct labor immigration to this country. Free emigrants were not contract laborers, strictly defined, because they did not sign employment agreements before leaving Japan. On the other hand, they did not cross the Pacific entirely on their own resources—they had the help of someone. Even before the appearance of emigration companies, innkeepers and others at the open treaty ports assisted individual emigrants to make the passage. Either the innkeepers had employment contacts in the United States, or the emigrants themselves had such contacts. The latter was clearly the case with many of the laborers who were denied landing permission in 1891. A native of Saeki District in Hiroshima Prefecture, Kojima Umekichi, for example, had received a letter from a friend in Napa County, California, informing him that a job could be obtained easily. Kubomoto Shintarō and Okada Kōshirō, both also from Saeki District, had been promised jobs by a man who operated a vineyard in Santa Rosa. Katō Unokichi, a native of Kanagawa Prefecture, had been offered help in getting a job by a friend who ran a lodginghouse in Seattle.[142] Even though emigration companies operated on a larger scale than innkeepers, they still were limited in the number and types of emigrants they could ship to the United States.

This limitation was tightened in 1898. One of the recurrent problems free emigrants faced was the agreements they signed with emigration agents in compliance with the 1896 Law to Protect Emigrants. Immigration officials often misconstrued such agreements as employment contracts and on that basis denied free emigrants landing permission by considering them to be contract laborers. To solve this problem, the Foreign Ministry decided in February 1898 that emigration companies did not have to enter into agreements with emigrants who were destined for the United States.[143] The ministry took a more radical step a month later. It prohibited companies from shipping any emigrant to the United States.[144] Although it lifted this ban in June, it adhered rigidly to its policy of not allowing any company to ship emigrants belonging to the excluded classes, as defined by American immigration statutes. To get around the restriction on immigration to the United States, emigration companies started to ship emigrants by way of Canada. This prompted the Foreign Ministry to adopt still another measure. In August 1898 it instituted a quota system for Canada limiting each emigration company to no more than 30 emigrants per month.[145]

Of the 27,440 Japanese admitted into the United States from 1891 to 1900, the annual average between 1891 and 1897 was less than 1,400. Since many students and other nonemigrants were included in this annual average, the number of laborers was much less. According to Japanese government statistics, only 165 free emigrants left Japan for the United States under the auspices of emigration companies between 1894 and 1898, which clearly indicates how the companies were hampered in shipping laborers to the United States. On the other hand, 4,048 free emigrants left Japan for Canada under the auspices of emigration companies between 1894 and 1900.[146] In fiscal 1897–98 the total admission figure was 2,230; in fiscal 1898–99 it increased to

2,844; and in fiscal 1899–1900 it leaped to 12,635. The sudden and dramatic rise at the turn of the century is attributable, not to emigration companies, but to Japanese railroad labor contractors on the Pacific Coast. To see how these contractors stimulated labor emigration from Japan, the labor-contracting system which emerged in the 1890s must first be examined.

CHAPTER

III

Labor-Contracting System

Labor Contractors

Labor contracting flourished from 1891 to 1907, coinciding with labor immigration to the United States. Newly arriving laborers, unable to speak English and unfamiliar with American labor practices, relied upon their fellow countrymen who were labor contractors for initial employment. The exceptions were those who obtained jobs through employment agencies or personal contacts. Labor contractors funneled laborers principally into the agricultural, railroad, mining, lumber, and fishing industries. The contractors' intermediary role between these industries and the laborers was premised on a demand for Japanese labor and a continual inflow of new laborers. Both conditions prevailed from 1891 to 1907, during which period the labor-contracting system extended from the Pacific Coast into the adjacent western states and Alaska.

Railroad labor contracting was on the biggest scale. It began with Tanaka Tadashichi on the Oregon Short Line. In 1894 he was ousted from this line. His expulsion was precipitated by his inability to account for money which he was supposed to have remitted to Japan for his workers. Members of the Patriotic League tried to succeed Tanaka, but they too were forced out, because they were implicated with him.[1] Tanaka was succeeded by Narita Yasuteru who in turn was followed by Kumamoto Hifumi. The latter, with his office located in

Pocatello, Idaho, furnished section hands under William H. Remington between 1895 and 1897.

After the modest inception on the Oregon Short Line, three major
contractors appeared in the Pacific Northwest. In late 1897 Remington secured contracting rights with the Northern Pacific and transferred his office from Salt Lake City to Tacoma, Washington.[2] Kumamoto, leaving another man in charge of his Pocatello office, joined
Remington in Tacoma where they founded the Tacoma Construction
and Maintenance Company in April 1898.[3] With Kumamoto as the
key Japanese, this company supplied section hands to the Northern
Pacific from 1898 to 1903 and 1905. In the second year of its operation, the company had 800 men employed on this railway.[4] As employees of Remington and Kumamoto, successive individuals managed
the Pocatello office, which continued to supply labor to the Oregon
Short Line. By 1901 Remington and Kumamoto had as many as 2,000
section hands.

Also established in 1898, the Oriental Trading Company of Seattle
was the second major contractor in Washington. This firm began
as a two-man partnership between Takahashi Tetsuo and Yamaoka
Ototaka, but became a three-man partnership with the addition of
Tsukuno Matajirō in 1899.[5] Two years later the three men incorporated, with each holding equal shares. Yamaoka was president, Takahashi vice-president, and Tsukuno treasurer. Unlike Kumamoto, who
was an agent of Remington, the Oriental Trading Company contracted directly with railroad companies, starting with the Seattle and
International Railway in early 1898. In December 1898 it entered into
a contract with the Great Northern and became the regular contractor
for this line from 1899. In 1904 it replaced the Tacoma Construction
and Maintenance Company as the contractor for the Northern Pacific
for a year, and from 1906 it permanently supplanted its rival and supplied laborers to the Northern Pacific as well as to the Great Northern.
At the zenith of the company's prosperity, it furnished no less than
2,500 to 3,000 laborers.[6]

Ban Shinzaburō, owner of the S. Ban Company of Portland, Oregon, was the third contractor in the Pacific Northwest. Ban first supplied section hands to the Southern Pacific line running from Portland
to the California stateline in 1892. Afterwards he contracted with
other lines, among them the Oregon Railway and Navigation Company, the Astoria and Columbia River Railway, and the Chicago,
Burlington and Quincy. As his contracting business prospered, Ban
diversified and divided his company into three departments. A con-

struction department handled all contracting of railroad and municipal works. A business department managed three retail stores located in Portland, Oregon, Denver, Colorado, and Sheridan, Wyoming. A lumber department operated a sawmill in Quincy, Oregon, which produced telephone poles with timber from forest land owned by Ban. In addition to all of these activities, Ban ran a dairy farm, producing butter and milk under a "Rising Sun" label, and a sugar beet farm on which he employed section hands in the off-season. At the height of his prosperity after the turn of the century, Ban probably had as many as 3,000 workers under his company.[7]

Four major contractors appeared in California, somewhat later than in the Pacific Northwest. The first instance of railroad labor contracting was in May 1892, when Hasegawa Genji, the San Francisco brothel operator, supplied 70 to 80 workers to the Southern Pacific.[8] For reasons unknown, his contracting business never expanded. Extensive railroad labor contracting awaited Kuranaga Terusaburō and Wakimoto Tsutomu who contracted with the Santa Fe Railway in 1899.[9] In 1900 Kuranaga established himself as an independent contractor after he gained exclusive rights to supply Japanese labor to the Southern Pacific.[10] Nishimura Ryūun then joined Wakimoto in supplying workers to the Santa Fe, with Nishimura located in Los Angeles and Wakimoto in San Francisco. In 1903 the two men quit the Santa Fe and moved to Cheyenne, Wyoming, in order to supply labor to the Union Pacific divisions in Wyoming, Colorado, and Nebraska. In 1906 Mitsuze Kōsaku contracted with the Western Pacific and furnished laborers from San Francisco.

The Japanese American Industrial Corporation of San Francisco was by far the biggest contractor in California. Founded in 1902 by Abiko Kyūtarō and others, this company supplied labor to the sugar beet, mining, and railroad industries. In 1903 it contracted with the Utah Sugar Company to furnish laborers to thin, hoe, and harvest sugar beets in Utah, and later in Idaho. The first contingent of laborers was dispatched to Garland where the Utah Sugar Company built a sugar refining factory. From 1903 the Japanese American Industrial Corporation also supplied labor to the Union Pacific Coal Company in southern Wyoming in cooperation with Nishiyama Gen. Nishiyama, an independent contractor based in Salt Lake City, had been furnishing laborers to this and other mining companies since 1898. In 1904 he joined the staff of the Japanese American Industrial Corporation. As to railroad contracting, the company began to supply section hands from 1904 to the Southern Pacific line east of Sparks, Nevada, and to the Union Pacific line west of Green River, Wyoming. It also supplied labor to the Western Pacific and the Nevada Northern. Railroad contracting complemented sugar beet contracting, for the former enabled the company to ship laborers to Utah on the Southern Pacific at no cost. The company had a branch office in Ogden and agents in Sugar City, Blackfoot, and Idaho Falls, all in Idaho, and in Sparks, Nevada. At the peak of its prosperity in 1906, the company had upwards of 3,000 laborers under its wings.[11]

Two major contractors operated in the Rocky Mountain region. The first was the E. D. Hashimoto Company owned and operated by Hashimoto Daigorō of Salt Lake City. Hashimoto entered the contracting business as an employee of the Oriental Trading Company. In May 1900 he secured an independent contract with the Denver and Rio Grande Railway and established himself in Salt Lake City. Subsequently, he supplied labor to the San Pedro, Los Angeles and Salt Lake City Railway. He contracted with mining companies from 1901 when he sent a few laborers to an American-operated coal mine in Mexico. Afterwards, he supplied men to mines in Wyoming and Utah, the largest number going to the Utah Fuel Company.[12] The second contractor was the Oriental Contracting Company of Denver, owned and operated by Takazuka Kichizō and Kiyama Teizō. Takazuka and Kiyama had worked at Kumamoto Hifumi's Pocatello office. In 1906 they replaced the E. D. Hashimoto Company as the contractor for the Denver and Rio Grande Railway. They also contracted with the Colorado and Southern Railway and with a few mines in southern Wyoming.[13] Although there were others, the companies and individuals mentioned here were the principal railroad contractors.

Most of these contractors shared a common background. They started out as student-laborers. Preceding the arrival of *dekasegi* laborers, they had worked part-time, attended schools, and learned English. A knowledge of American labor practices and some fluency in English were the minimum qualifications needed to become a contractor. No matter who he was, a contractor had to have this knowledge and fluency in order to negotiate with employers and to comprehend legal contracts. Abiko Kyūtarō is an outstanding example. A native of Niigata Prefecture, he landed in San Francisco in 1885. Of his own motive for leaving Japan, he said:

> The students who left for America from around 1882 did so because they heard that the growing economy there made it possible to work and study at the same time. Hearing this news, young men whose

ambitions were stifled in Japan crossed over to America. I was one of them.[14]

Abiko resided at the Gospel Society and studied English as he worked at menial jobs. He attended Lincoln Grammar School and graduated from Boys High School in 1891. In 1892 he enrolled at the University of California, but for unknown reasons he never graduated. In the 1890s he tried his hand at many businesses—he operated a restaurant and a laundry at one time; and he was a partner in a credit association. In 1899 he launched the *Nichibei Shimbun* which occupied his entire life. His fluency in English, combined with his knowledge of American labor and business practices, enabled him to enter the labor contracting business.[15] To manage the Japanese American Industrial Corporation, Abiko recruited former students into his firm. Senoo Hachirō, a 1901 Stanford University graduate, was a shareholder and staff member. A student-journalist, Washizu Bunzō was also a shareholder and staff member. A graduate of Waseda University, Kuroishi Seisaku was an employee. As a matter of fact, every staff member and shareholder in the company had some kind of student background.[16] Wakimoto Tsutomu, Hashimoto Daigorō, Nishiyama Gen, Kumamoto Hifumi, Mitsuze Kōsaku, and Takahashi Tetsuo all rose from the ranks of student-laborers.

Ban Shinzaburō and Yamaoka Ototaka were conspicuous exceptions. Ban had been in the service of the Foreign Ministry. In 1888 he was a secretary assigned to the Honolulu consulate. Three years later he was reassigned to Tokyo. In July 1891 the San Francisco consulate filed a disturbing report on Japanese prostitutes and pimp-gamblers in the Pacific Northwest. Foreign Minister Enomoto Takeaki dispatched Ban to investigate the matter further. During the course of his investigation, Ban toured British Columbia and the states of Washington, Oregon, Idaho, and Utah. Consequently, he was well informed of conditions not only in Hawaii, but in the western United States and Canada as well. Upon his return to Tokyo, he resigned from the Foreign Ministry. In March 1892 he came back to the United States and established himself as a contractor in Portland.[17]

Of all the contractors, Yamaoka had the most colorful background. A native of Shizuoka Prefecture, he was an activist in the People's Rights Movement. In 1886, in what is known as the Shizuoka Incident, he and others plotted to assassinate Meiji government leaders. Discovered before they were able to execute their plan, Yamaoka and his co-conspirators were arrested, tried, and found guilty. In 1887

Yamaoka was sentenced to a fourteen-year term and committed to a Hokkaidō prison. After serving ten years of his sentence, he was granted clemency in 1897. Yamaoka left Japan at once and settled down in Seattle. Few prisoners ever survived the hardships of prison life in Hokkaidō, especially the bitter, cold winters. The fact that Yamaoka survived speaks of the toughness and resiliency of his body and spirit.[18]

The remaining contractors had varied backgrounds. As already noted, Hasegawa Genji operated brothels in San Francisco. His profits probably enabled him to accumulate capital to enter the railroad labor contracting business. According to the standard explanation, Consul Chinda Sutemi persuaded Hasegawa to abandon prostitution in favor of legitimate business.[19] Tsukuno Matajirō landed in 1887 and ran a restaurant in Seattle. He provided much of the initial capital of the Oriental Trading Company out of the earnings from his restaurant. The backgrounds of Kuranaga Terusaburō, Nishimura Ryūun, Takazuka Kichizō, and Kiyama Teizō are unknown.

Methods of Recruitment

During the two phases of labor immigration to the United States, the railroad labor contractors engaged in different recruiting practices. The San Francisco-based contractors did not have any direct hand in inducing laborers to leave Japan. Rather, they relied on Japanese inns and boardinghouses that catered to new arrivals, and proliferated in the city in the late 1890s. In 1900 there were at least twenty-six such inns and boardinghouses, and the proprietors of these establishments supplied laborers for a set commission of three dollars per man. One of the largest proprietors was Tamura Tokunosuke, a native of Hiroshima Prefecture, who owned and operated three boardinghouses and the Tamura Hotel. He supplied labor to Ban Shinzaburō and other contractors. Kuranaga Terusaburō had agreements with eight boardinghouses and three employment agencies. As soon as he contracted with the Southern Pacific, he ran a daily three-quarter page ad in the *Shin Sekai* to recruit section hands. That the contractors in San Francisco did not send agents to Japan for recruiting purposes is not surprising, for railroad labor contracting in California did not thrive until the turn of the century. By that time the Japanese government had prohibited the direct passage of laborers to the continental United States and Canada.

In contrast, the contractors in the Pacific Northwest, having appeared earlier, promoted direct labor emigration. To explain the arrival of poor laborers, the Tacoma consul filed the following report in the spring of 1898:

> According to what I have uncovered, the cause of the continuous arrival of indigent laborers recently is the railroad labor contractors . . . who are abetting them . . . . For a small sum, they get some of their workers to send letters to friends at home telling them of the benefits of railroad construction work, thereby persuading many unknowing Japanese to come to this region. Some of these unknowing ones cannot even afford lodging when they reach an open port, and the contractors or their agents advance them money for clothing and travel expenses. In some cases, the contractors or their agents also temporarily loan the thirty dollars people must have at the time they enter the country.[20]

Although the consul did not mention specific names, he doubtless had in mind Kumamoto Hifumi and Ban Shinzaburō. They advanced passage fares and sometimes the thirty dollars steerage passengers needed to avoid being deported as paupers apt to become public charges. The consul also noted that the contractors promised a dollar commission to agents in open ports in Japan for every man they shipped.[21]

Yamaoka Ototaka returned to Japan in January 1899 and established a branch office of the Oriental Trading Company in Yokohama. The main function of this office was to advertise the employment his company offered in the Pacific Northwest. In December 1899 the Oriental Trading Company signed a major contract with the Great Northern. In anticipation of a high labor demand, it arranged to have 2,500 laborers shipped by the Morioka Emigration Company. The emigration company applied for passports for this number of men in March 1900, but the Foreign Ministry, fearful of exacerbating the growing clamor against Japanese labor which had already surfaced on the Pacific Coast, refused to issue them.[22] In April the Foreign Ministry made it even more difficult for laborers to obtain passports for the United States. It instituted a quota system, as it had for Canada in 1898. Each prefecture and municipality was alloted only 20 to 35 emigrants per month from February to September, and half this amount from October to January.[23] In May this quota was lowered to 4 to 10 emigrants per month.[24]

Faced with the government's restrictive policy, Yamaoka Ototaka resorted to illegal means. Through personal contacts with government bureaucrats in Shizuoka Prefecture, he had forged passports issued to laborers. In Shizuoka, his older brother, Yamaoka Kōzō, was secretary of the Seiyūkai branch with close connections to prefectural and village officials. To recruit laborers, Yamaoka Ototaka set up additional branches of the Oriental Trading Company in Kobe, Wakayama, Hiroshima, Kumamoto, and a few other places. Once he recruited laborers from outside Shizuoka, he had them change their domicile on paper to predetermined villages in Shizuoka. Family registries were falsified in these villages to reflect the change of domicile, and passport applications were processed with the approval of the village heads. The Shizuoka Prefectural government then issued the forged passports. Yamaoka Kōzō and his accomplices were ultimately indicted and charged with falsifying and forging public documents. According to the trial record, passports were issued in this manner from February to April 1900 at the rate of up to 200 a day.[25] The Oriental Trading Company claimed that it got 3,000 to 4,000 laborers into this country by this illegal method. The total number may be exaggerated, but the company unquestionably facilitated the departure of a sizable number of laborers. In sum, the recruiting activities of the labor contractors in the Pacific Northwest caused the dramatic increase in the number of new arrivals at the turn of the century and the high percentage of admission through the Pacific Northwest.

As soon as the Foreign Ministry prohibited all labor immigration to the continental United States and Canada in August 1900, all labor contractors experienced an acute labor shortage. As a result, on November 25, 1901, the contractors petitioned the Foreign Ministry. They complained of being unable to fulfill high labor demands, blamed the shortage of labor on the government's restrictive policy, and appealed to the ministry to allow the passage of laborers.[26] Kuranaga Terusaburō claimed that he had 1,500 workers, but that he easily could employ 3,000. Ban Shinzaburō said that he had 2,000 railroad workers, but required a minimum of 1,100 new laborers every year. Yamaoka Ototaka insisted that the Oriental Trading Company needed an annual average of 5,000 railroad workers. In appealing to the Foreign Ministry to lift its restriction, the contractors argued in terms of the economic development of immigrant society.

Since the Japanese government adhered firmly to its policy, the contractors turned to the Hawaiian Islands as an alternative source of labor. Statistics vary as to the number of laborers who migrated from the islands to the continental United States between 1901 and 1907. No figures are available for 1901. American statistics indicate that about 38,000 laborers migrated from 1902 to 1907. Japanese sources record that 31,720 left the islands for the mainland from 1902 to 1906.[27] If the 1907 figure, which unfortunately is unavailable, were added, this total would be higher. The annual breakdown of the 31,720 is as follows: 1,165 in 1902; 2,589 in 1903; 6,096 in 1904; 9,650 in 1905; and 12,220 in 1906. As can be seen, the number of laborers who left the Hawaiian Islands was small in 1902, increased steadily thereafter, and swelled to over 12,000 by 1906.

Mainland labor contractors and their agents induced this exodus. In 1902, San Francisco boardinghouse proprietors organized themselves into the Japanese Boardinghouse Keepers Association and entered into an agreement with the Pacific Mail Steamship Company.[28] The agreement covered a reduced rate for groups of laborers shipped by the association from Honolulu to San Francisco. If a group consisted of no less than 40 but no more than 75 persons, the steerage fare was $27 per person. If a group consisted of more than 75, the fare was $25 per person. The standard steerage fare was $35. Free passage was granted to one agent of the association for every group of 75 or less, and to two agents for every group of more than 75. The boardinghouse proprietors, intent on earning commissions from labor contractors, made this agreement with the steamship company so they could recruit laborers in Hawaii.

For the laborers on the islands, the main attraction of the West Coast was the wages. Compared to wages on sugar plantations, they stood to earn at least twice as much if they came to the mainland. The Japanese comprised a plantation work force of 30,640 laborers in 1902. The highest paid male plantation laborer earned $16.00 a month; a day laborer in Honolulu made 65¢ a day.[29] In stark contrast, in 1902, a Japanese railroad section hand on the mainland earned up to $1.25 per day. Taking advantage of this wage disparity, the Japanese Boardinghouse Keepers Association dispatched agents to Honolulu who advertised the higher West Coast wages in the local Japanese-language press. Notwithstanding the fact that the laborers had to pay a fee to the agents for arranging passage, the prospect of higher wages and the reduced passage fare were sufficient to induce them to leave Hawaii. Once the agents recruited enough laborers to form groups, they led them to San Francisco, travelling at no cost to themselves.

Not all labor contractors were satisfied with the arrangements they had with the boardinghouse proprietors. Given the limited number of laborers, the competition among the contractors was stiff. From 1904, therefore, most contractors started to send their own agents to Honolulu. The Japanese American Industrial corporation dispatched Kuroishi Seisaku to recruit laborers. To attract laborers to his company, he placed huge advertisements in the local Japanese newspapers. In 1906 Kuroishi advertised that men with his company could save no less than $250 a year from daily wages of $1.50 for agricultural workers and of $1.35 to $1.65 for railroad workers.[30] Wakimoto Tsutomu and Nishimura Ryūun sent their own agent to Honolulu to conduct similar recruiting campaigns. Their agent advertised wages of $1.35 to $1.60 for railroad workers on the Union Pacific.[31]

Since shipping lines did not have as many regular runs between Honolulu and Seattle or Portland as they did between Honolulu and San Francisco, contractors in San Francisco enjoyed a distinct advantage over those in the Pacific Northwest. Precisely because of this factor, Ban Shinzaburō of Portland is reported to have paid the highest commission for every laborer shipped to him.[32] The Tacoma Construction and Maintenance Company and the Oriental Trading Company adopted a bolder tactic. They made arrangements with shipping lines to transport laborers straight from Honolulu to the Pacific Northwest. In the summer of 1905 the Tacoma firm obtained 400 laborers in one shipment in this manner.[33] In the same year the Oriental Trading Company chartered the *Olympia*, a vessel of the Northwestern Steamship Company, and sent it to Hawaii to pick up laborers. Before the ship docked in Honolulu, the company advertised that it would pay daily wages of $1.30 from April to October and $1.10 for other months, and that it would furnish a set of work clothes, necessities, and food provisions, including rice, bean paste, and soy sauce. Charging $28.00 per laborer for the steerage fare and the booking fee, the company recruited 600 laborers in April and transported them to Seattle.[34]

The Oriental Trading Company expected an acute labor shortage in 1906. At the beginning of the year, Takahashi Tetsuo informed the General Superintendent of the Great Northern, George T. Slade, that his company intended to recharter the *Olympia* and send it to Honolulu three times in the spring.[35] His plan called for the ship to pick up 600 laborers on each trip. But contrary to Takahashi's plan, the *Olympia* sailed to Honolulu only twice. As had been done in the preceding year, the agent of the Oriental Trading Company advertised widely in the local Honolulu Japanese press. Due to competition from other contractors and the obstructive tactics of the Hawaiian sugar planters, however, the company recruited less than a third of the projected 1,800 laborers. In March the *Olympia* transported 350 laborers to Seattle, and in April fewer than 250 additional men.[36]

Japanese government officials tried to halt the exodus from Hawaii. As early as May 1902, the Honolulu and San Francisco consuls asked the Foreign Ministry for instructions. Consul Ueno Kisaburō of San Francisco was very wary of anti-Japanese sentiments in California and urged that the laborers in Hawaii not be permitted to migrate to San Francisco. He warned of the likelihood that local politicians and labor groups would make them a political issue in the 1902 election.[37] Under instructions from Tokyo, Ueno attempted to block the shipment of laborers. He persuaded the Pacific Mail Steamship Company to break its agreement with the Japanese Boardinghouse Keepers Association. Two other shipping lines which had agreements with the boarding-house keepers were also persuaded to refrain from selling tickets to Japanese laborers bound for San Francisco.[38] Meanwhile, Consul Saitō Miki of Honolulu contacted the Honolulu agents of the steamship companies and requested that they sell tickets only to persons who possessed special certificates issued by his consulate.[39] The passports of laborers in Hawaii had been issued only for the islands. Only if laborers received authorization from the Honolulu consulate in the form of special certificates were their passports valid for the continental United States. These efforts by the San Francisco and Honolulu consuls failed. The boardinghouse keepers and their agents in Honolulu threatened legal action against the shipping companies; with no legal grounds for refusing to sell tickets, the companies were forced to back down.[40]

In 1903 Saitō sought to influence the laborers himself. He released a consular notice in March, declaring that no one could migrate to the continental United States without his permission.[41] The notice read like an edict ordering everyone to remain on the islands. Accusing recruiting agents of purveying false information, it warned laborers not to give credence to their "honeyed words." Wages were not higher on the West Coast. Copies of this notice were posted at all plantations that employed Japanese laborers. In November, Saitō conveyed his message in person.[42] He toured the plantations and spoke directly to the laborers. Disputing all claims of higher wages on the West Coast, he insisted that wages and working conditions were better in Hawaii. His flexing of consular authority proved fruitless. For, contrary to his assertion, recruiting agents were not exaggerating nor lying. West Coast laborers in fact earned twice as much as their Hawaiian counterparts. No one, not even Consul Saitō, could convince the laborers to believe otherwise. Of the laborers who left Hawaii, many were new to the islands. By 1904 many new arrivals did not even bother to go to their assigned plantations. They just waited for the next ship bound for the mainland. Never intending to work in Hawaii, such laborers used the islands as a stepping-stone to the West Coast. In September 1904 Saitō estimated that half of the new arrivals had departed for the continental United States.[43]

Fearing the loss of the Japanese labor force, the Hawaiian sugar planters had also tried to intervene. In May 1902 two planter representatives had called on Consul Saitō and solicited his help in preventing laborers from leaving. In 1904 the planters wrote to the Japanese ambassador and asked for his assistance. When the number of departing laborers reached alarming proportions, the Hawaiian Sugar Planters Association raised the wages of field hands from $16 to $18 per month effective May 1, 1905. "It is hoped that the increase of wages . . . will have the affect of satisfying them with their work and surroundings so that they will remain in the islands," said President F. K. Swanzy.[44] To make it expensive to recruit laborers, the planters had the Territorial Legislature enact Act 57 of 1905 requiring all recruiting agents to be licensed at an exorbitant fee of $500.[45] Neither the licensing requirement nor the wage hike had the desired effect, however. Mainland recruiters willingly paid the licensing fee and continued to recruit laborers who left the islands in ever increasing numbers. Thus the planters too were powerless to halt the exodus.

This situation posed a dilemma to the Japanese government. On the one hand, it wanted to stop the migration to the mainland, and yet found itself unable to do so. On the other hand, it did not relish the thought of facing unilateral action by the American government. When Chinese laborers had been banned from American shores in 1882, the Ch'ing government had lost considerable face. If the United States prohibited only Japanese from immigrating, the Japanese people would be cast in an unfavorable light, and hence Japan would also suffer a loss of face. The full-scale eruption of the Japanese exclusion movement made the dilemma all the more acute. In February 1905 the San Francisco *Chronicle* launched its front-page editorial crusade against the influx of Japanese labor. Organized labor followed suit in May by establishing the Japanese and Korean Exclusion League (later called the Asiatic Exclusion League) and intensified the agitation for the exclusion of Japanese labor. Many anti-Japanese outbursts occurred after the disastrous earthquake of April 1906, but the major event took place in October when the San Francisco school board resolved to segregate Japanese pupils in the public schools.[46] Consequently, the

Foreign Ministry reached an impasse: it had to choose either to ban immigration to Hawaii on its own or consent to some kind of American measure curtailing migration from the islands.

Termination of Labor Migration from Hawaii

The migration was terminated by Theodore Roosevelt's executive order of March 14, 1907. Congress had authorized the president on February 18 to issue this order by amending immigration statutes. The amendment, drafted by Secretary of State Elihu Root, empowered the president to prohibit any alien from entering the United States via its insular possessions, the Canal Zone, or another foreign country if his or her passport had been issued for another destination. No mention of the Japanese was made either in the amendment or in the executive order itself, which allowed the Japanese government to save face. Since the Japanese were not singled out by name, the Japanese ambassador gave his tacit consent to the issuance of the order. Inasmuch as Japanese laborers in Hawaii had passports only for the islands, their migration to the continental United States thus came to an abrupt end.

The executive order stopped immigration to the United States via Mexico as well. The August 1900 Japanese government ban on labor emigration was applicable only to the United States and Canada. In addition to Hawaii, laborers were still able to obtain passports to Mexico. Between 1901 and 1907, the Kumamoto, Tōyō, and Tairiku Emigration Companies shipped a total of 8,706 contract laborers to Mexico.[47] These laborers were hired out to work as coal miners in Coahuila, copper miners in Baja California, railroad workers in Jalisco, and sugarcane field hands in Vera Cruz. Hashimoto Daigorō of Salt Lake City was the agent of the Kumamoto Emigration Company. In early 1901 he supplied 20 Japanese laborers to the Esperanzas mine in Muzquiz, Coahuila. Towards the end of the year, he sent an additional contingent of eighty-one men to this mine.

The state of Coahuila lies just south of Texas. Most Japanese coal miners at Esperanzas and other laborers in other locales abandoned their jobs. Working conditions were much worse and wages much less than expected. Strikes occurred often, and Japanese laborers beseeched the Japanese ambassador in Mexico City to rescue them from virtual slavery. Of the 8,706 contract laborers, more than 5,000 fled, among them some men who probably had no real intent of working in Mexico. The majority of the escapees found their way to the United States. A good deal of the Okinawan population of Southern California can be traced back to Mexico. Some 223 Okinawans in 1904 and 250 in 1907 were among the contract laborers shipped to the Esperanzas mine. Due to working conditions described as "a living hell," the vast majority abandoned the mine and entered the United States via El Paso, Texas.[48] Since Roosevelt's executive order prohibited the admission of any alien whose passport had been issued for another foreign country, and Japanese laborers in Mexico had passports issued for Mexico, Japanese immigration to the United States via Mexico also came to an abrupt end.[49]

Labor contractors vigorously protested the executive order. On February 15, three days before Congress passed the amendment, Abiko Kyūtarō had wired the foreign minister voicing his alarm. "We Japanese here are gravely concerned with the amendment," his telegram read, "for it will greatly impede our economic progress."[50] To sway public opinion in Japan, Abiko sent similar telegrams to various organizations, newspapers, political parties, and the Tokyo Chamber of Commerce, hoping to spur the Foreign Ministry to oppose the pending amendment. Eventually, mass protest meetings were held under the leadership of the labor contractors. On February 20, two days after the passage of the amendment, the Japanese of Los Angeles assembled for a protest meeting. Their telegram to the Foreign Ministry declared that, if the Japanese government acquiesced to the amendment, it meant the "self-destruction" of immigrant society, implying that the curtailment of migration from Hawaii would destroy its economic foundation.[51] The Japanese residents of Portland held a similar meeting on February 23. Out of the proceedings, a petition was drafted and submitted to the Foreign Ministry. Ban Shinzaburō headed the committee under whose name the petition was submitted. The petition enumerated the negative economic effects of the Congressional amendment, and appealed to the Foreign Ministry to permit direct labor immigration to the continental United States.[52]

Similar mass assemblies were held in San Francisco and Seattle. The San Francisco community dispatched Noda Otosaburō to Washington, D.C. in April. A staff member of the Japanese American Industrial Corporation, Noda was sent to confer with the Japanese ambassador to ascertain what his views were with respect to future labor immigration.[53] The Seattle community also sent a representative to consult with the ambassador. That person was none other than Takahashi Tetsuo. Besides going to Washington, D.C., Takahashi submitted a petition to the Foreign Ministry in the name of the Seattle community. While refuting all the allegations raised against Japanese labor, he appealed to the Japanese government to change its restrictive immigration policy. Like the petition of the Portland community, the Seattle petition asked the government to allow direct labor immigration.[54] To arouse public opinion in Japan, Yamaoka Ototaka returned to Japan in May. He conferred with many prominent persons and organizations for two months in an effort to apply pressure on the Foreign Ministry.[55]

Three basic reasons were behind the protests against the executive order. First, the protestors faulted the Foreign Ministry for what they considered its "spineless" acquiescence to the American measure. Indeed, the Japanese government had actually gone along with the order because it halted the migration from Hawaii in a face-saving manner. Secondly, they interpreted the order as an infringement of rights guaranteed by the 1894 U.S.-Japan Treaty of Commerce and Navigation. According to this interpretation, the freedom to travel from an American territorial possession to the continental limits of the United States was protected by the treaty. The protestors therefore faulted the Foreign Ministry doubly for failing to compel the United States to live up to its treaty obligations. Finally, and most significantly, the labor contractors who led the protest acted out of their economic self-interest. They knew their contracting business was doomed without an inflow of new laborers. The executive order meant that they would have only the existing labor pool on which to draw, and that pool would inevitably dwindle as time passed.

The Gentlemen's Agreement was the culminating event. To guarantee the effectiveness of the executive order, the American government needed the assurance of the Japanese government that it would adhere to its policy of not issuing passports to laborers for the continental United States. To obtain this assurance, the American ambassador to Japan initiated diplomatic negotiations with the Japanese foreign minister. The negotiations consisted of an exchange of notes between the two principals in the winter of 1907–8. The collective notes are known as the Gentlemen's Agreement. By the terms of the agreement, which came into force in the summer of 1908, the Japanese government pledged to issue passports to limited categories of people—merchants, students, diplomats, and tourists; bona fide Japanese residents in the United States who returned to visit Japan and wished to go back to the United States; parents, wives, and children of

such residents; and so-called "settled agriculturists" who were special
farmers bound mainly for Texas. The American government agreed
to permit the entry of all Japanese falling into these categories, but
reserved the right to deny admission to any laborer whose passport
was issued for any destination other than the United States. While
reaffirming the Japanese government's established emigration policy,
the Gentlemen's Agreement insured the effectiveness of the executive
order, and the two combined to terminate all labor immigration to
the continental United States, thereby causing the decline of the labor
contracting business and its gradual demise.

Contractor-Laborer Nexus

The majority of Japanese laborers in the United States worked under
the labor-contracting system. The laborers were distributed unevenly
on the western labor market. In 1909 some 10,000 were employed as
section hands by railroad companies throughout the western states.
This total was less than the peak of 13,000 to 14,000 in 1906. Twenty-
two hundred men worked in sawmills in Oregon and Washington.
Another 3,600 were employed by salmon canneries located in Alaska,
Oregon, and Washington; only a few hundred were engaged in the
fishing industry in 1909. Some 2,000 men were miners in Wyoming,
Utah, and Colorado; 200 were employed by a Colorado iron and steel
plant in Pueblo. Agriculture was by far the biggest employer. During
the height of the harvest season, upwards of 38,000 were employed
as field hands, of whom 30,000 were in California. All of these laborers were recruited and supplied by labor contractors. Approximately
22,000 to 26,000 persons were employed in the urban service trades
or engaged in small business.[56]

The relationship of the labor contractors to the laborers was very
exploitative. The railroad labor contractors operated on the biggest
scale profiting heavily at the expense of the laborers. In supplying
laborers to railway companies, the contractors earned income, but not
as paid employees of the companies. Their income came from fees
assessed on the wages of laborers. As a condition for employment, the
principal fee was a daily commission withheld from wages. First levied
by William H. Remington and Tanaka Tadashichi, every contractor
exacted this commission. In 1892 the laborers on the Oregon Short
Line earned $1.25 per day under Tanaka. His office charged a daily
commission of ten cents.[57] In 1899 Kumamoto Hifumi took ten cents

a day from his laborers who earned $1.10 per day on the Northern Pacific. Ban Shinzaburō's workers on the Oregon Railway and Navigation Company earned $1.10 per day in 1899, and Ban's commission was five cents. In the same year the Oriental Trading Company's commission was ten cents per day for its laborers whose daily wage on the Great Northern was also $1.10.[58] In 1900 Kuranaga Terusaburō's laborers on the Southern Pacific earned $1.00 per day, and he levied a commission of $1.00 per month.

This daily commission provided lucrative incomes for the contractors. Assuming a contractor exacted ten cents per day from a thousand laborers, his monthly income would have been $2,600 based on a twenty-six-day work month. Since every major railroad contractor had well over a thousand laborers, their monthly income from the daily commission was even greater than this assumed total. It is for this reason that Japanese immigrant sources refer to the contractors as "kings" who were the "objects of envy" of common laborers. Kumamoto is said to have earned up to $2,500 per month working under Remington.[59] How the two men divided the commission is unclear. In view of the fact that Remington posted the necessary bonds to secure contracting rights, he probably took the lion's share of the commission, perhaps all of it. In either case, Kumamoto—and other contractors as well—had additional sources of revenue, which easily explains the high income attributed to him.

There were many supplementary sources of income. On top of the daily commission, most contractors charged a so-called "translation-office fee" on a monthly basis. In 1899 Kumamoto and Ban both withheld a dollar per month from their workers' wages in the name of this fee. Profits from retail trade were another source. All contractors sold foodstuff and other goods to their laborers. They usually had agreements with railway companies to have goods shipped to their laborers free of charge or at a reduced tariff.[60] Still yet another source of revenue was the service fee charged for monetary remittances to Japan. Laborers regularly remitted money to Japan in keeping with their *dekasegi* mission. Upon request by laborers, the contractors withheld specified sums from wages and had the money remitted for them. This service began with Tanaka Tadashichi in 1892. Most contractors rendered the service through the Yokohama Specie Bank which had branches on the Pacific Coast. A medical fee was a final source of income. This one started with Tanaka too. Because of frequent cases of illness, Tanaka constructed a clinic in Nampa, Idaho, in 1892. To finance its construction and upkeep, he charged each of his workers an initial five dollars and withheld an added monthly medical fee of fifty cents.[61] Following Tanaka's example, most contractors established clinics and charged a monthly medical fee of fifty cents. All of these additional sources of revenue supplemented the income of the contractors. Together with the daily commission, they made labor contracting a highly profitable business.

The contractors were middlemen between American employers and Japanese laborers. For employers, they performed invaluable service. They recruited and supplied laborers, and they supervised them on the job through assigned overseers who knew English. In fulfilling this role, the contractors enabled employers to hire Japanese labor at a cheap rate without lifting a hand. The sole obligation the railroad companies assumed was to furnish housing, which in remote areas meant boxcars or makeshift sheds. The contractors' relationship to their laborers hinged on the latter's need for employment. The contractors had jobs to offer. Once laborers consented to work, they signed agreements authorizing the contractors to deduct the daily commission and other fees from their wages. In exchange for the authorization, the contractors sent them out to work under assigned interpreters and designated gang leaders and, in the event of sickness or injury, offered a kind of medical service. At additional cost they supplied goods and provisions and provided remittance service. Handling all affairs relating to the railroad companies, the contractors were buffers between the railroad companies and the laborers.

Consequently, the contractor-laborer nexus was crucial in any labor dispute. Whether grievances were over wages, working conditions, or other matters, disputes invariably involved the contractors, not the employers. In the spring of 1893 a conflict broke out between Tanaka Tadashichi and his laborers on the Oregon Short Line. The chief cause was Tanaka's inability to account for $15,000. This sum had been withheld from his laborers' wages for the purpose of remittance. Remington, under whose auspices Tanaka supplied laborers, fired him because Tanaka could not make up this large sum of money. On another occasion, in 1896, 200 laborers on the same line went on strike to demand higher wages. Interestingly enough, their demand was addressed, not to the Oregon Short Line railroad officials, but to Remington and Kumamoto. To satisfy the strikers, the two men negotiated a ten-cent daily wage hike with the railroad, and then summarily dismissed the strike leaders. These two examples illustrate the primacy of the contractor-laborer relationship in any labor dispute.[62]

The various fees exacted from the laborers were a natural source of conflict. A 1906 employment guide, published for prospective laborers, warned of their onerous nature. Pejoratively referring to the railroad labor contractors as "corrupt bosses," the guide asserted that they "deduct unreasonable prices for goods and provisions from wages" and that they "withhold commissions, sundry charges, and office and medical fees under numerous guises in collusion with agents and boardinghouses." From a worker's point of view, these levies were "tantamount to compensations paid to thieves."[63] The author of this guide based his judgment on his work experience. In 1902 a revealing dispute arose in connection with the daily commission. In defiance of Remington and Kumamoto, the head of the Pocatello contracting office and his laborers jointly asked the Oregon Short Line for a direct relationship. The principal bone of contention was the 10-cent daily commission which the laborers had been paying to the two contractors in Tacoma. In April 1905 the railway company replaced Remington with another white American who did not charge a daily commission.[64]

Despite the exploitative contractor-laborer relationship, open clashes were remarkably infrequent. To explain this apparent anomaly, the dependence of laborers upon the contractors cannot be overstressed. Unable to speak English and ignorant of American conditions, laborers found employment through the contractors who sent them out to the hinterland, to distant areas as far east as Montana, often in a matter of a day or two after arriving on the Pacific Coast. As soon as the laborers from Honolulu landed in San Francisco, the Japanese American Industrial Corporation had them transported to Nevada, Utah, and Wyoming on Southern Pacific boxcars. Given lunch boxes of rice balls with pickled plums, the laborers were instructed to come out only if they heard some one call out in Japanese either at Sparks, Nevada, or Ogden, Utah. With no knowledge of American geography, most laborers did not even know where they had been sent, let alone how to return to the Pacific Coast. If they quit prematurely, they would have to pay their own fare back. If they protested against the contractors, they were subject to dismissal. And if they were fired, they would have to fend for themselves. For those who neither knew English nor had employment options, it was understandable that they sought to avoid such a hapless fate. The particular circumstances of new laborers inhibited the overt expression of grievances.

With a year or so of work experience, seasoned laborers tended to leave their jobs. That such laborers left in a hurry as soon as they had options is apparent from the high turnover rate in the labor force of the Oriental Trading Company. When the Tacoma Construction and Maintenance Company and the Oriental Trading Company were in competition, they repeatedly stole laborers from each other, indicating that laborers quickly deserted one company for another when they had a choice.[65] But the two companies did not just compete with each other. They vied with other contractors for laborers. In 1906 Ban Shinzaburō had a contract with the Chicago, Burlington and Quincy. Offering twenty- to thirty-cent higher daily wages, Ban's agents advertised along the Northern Pacific line and lured away laborers supplied by the Oriental Trading Company. The numbers were sufficient to alarm the president of the Northern Pacific, prompting him to post a letter of protest to the vice-president of the Burlington.[66] Competition came from contractors in other industries as well. In April 1906 Takahashi Tetsuo reported losing half of his men on the Cascade Division of both the Northern Pacific and Great Northern to contractors from surrounding sawmills.[67] Later that year he lost 200 more men on the Montana Division to sugar beet contractors who paid higher wages.[68]

The railroad companies used bonuses and wage hikes as incentives to keep their laborers on their jobs. The Oriental Trading Company's 1906 contracts with the Northern Pacific and Great Northern stipulated that the summer daily wage rate for section hands would be $1.20, plus a ten-cent retroactive daily bonus for working through the season. The railroad companies added the bonus in anticipation of a high labor demand. In the spring, because some laborers began to abandon the lines, Takahashi urged the railroads to increase the wage rate. Citing the higher rates of competing railroads and other industries, he warned that he would not be able to hold his men at the existing rate.[69] Accepting his evaluation of the situation, both railroad companies raised the wage rate by ten cents, but neither this increase nor the bonus worked to hold all laborers on the lines. In the bonus period ending September 30, for instance, only 54 percent of the men on the Seattle Division of the Northern Pacific received bonuses.[70] In other words, only this percentage of the laborers on the division worked through the summer bonus period, indicating that the high turnover in the Oriental Trading Company's labor force continued in spite of the bonus and wage increase. In short, seasoned laborers escaped the exploitative contractor-laborer relationship by leaving the service of the company for other jobs.

Other factors also contributed to the lack of open clashes on the railroads. As section hands in the maintenance of way, the laborers were scattered over hundreds of miles in separate section gangs, making organized opposition to the contractors difficult. No source provides insights into the nature of the laborers' relationship to their gang leaders, nor of the gang leaders to the contractors. Yet even if the laborers had organized themselves successfully, unionization was impossible. The Brotherhood of Maintenance of Way Employees barred nonwhites from its membership. Finally, there was the *dekasegi* orientation of the laborers. This orientation inclined them to perceive working conditions as temporary, and therefore made them less motivated to seek change. Taken together, all of the foregoing reasons account for the absence of public labor disputes between the contractors and the laborers.

On the other hand the relationship between Japanese miners and their foremen appears to have been conflict-ridden. Under the auspices of Nishiyama Gen, Japanese laborers first entered the southern Wyoming coalfield in 1898. This coalfield, centered at Rock Springs, had a very heterogeneous labor force. Based upon a 1908 survey of seven mines, the United States Immigration Commission compiled information on 1,751 miners.[71] It found that 1,505, or 85.9 percent, were foreign-born, of thirty-two different national origins. Only 246 men were native-born. Indicating the arrival of new European immigrants, 39.9 percent of the foreign-born were of southern- and eastern-European origin. The 337 Japanese miners were the single largest group among the foreign nationalities—they made up 19.3 percent of the total. The Commission estimated that 512 Japanese miners in total were employed in all the southern Wyoming mines. As the labor contractor for the Union Pacific Coal Company, the Japanese American Industrial Corporation had problems controlling its miners. The corporation assigned agents to Rock Springs to act as foremen. In 1907 one such agent reported that Japanese miners literally ran successive foremen out of Rock Springs:

As a [Union Pacific Coal] company foreman, Nishiyama Gen recruited laborers and did office work. Several years ago he turned over all business affairs to the Japanese American Industrial Corporation. He continued to supervise Japanese work units, but did nothing for the laborers of other nationalities. Then, he resigned as foreman and handed over the job to the Industrial Corporation. The Industrial Corporation dispatched several employees one after another to take his place. The corporation thought that the only problem would be the Japanese miners' relationship to others, as it had been under Nishiyama. Unexpectedly, new internal conflicts broke out under the newly assigned foremen, which nullified Nishiyama's accomplishments achieved over the years. Things got so bad that external matters were all but ignored. No matter where they are, miners by nature are always tough to handle. Acting in unison at this mine, the Japanese miners attacked each new foreman. In effect, the supervised drove out their supervisors, and the Industrial Corporation had a huge headache.[72]

The contractor-laborer relationship in Alaska salmon canneries was unique in several respects.[73] Japanese laborers were employed by Alaska canneries from 1899, at first under Chinese labor contractors. The Alaska canning season normally extended from April to September, a long six-month period, during which the laborers had to pass tedious days with few amenities, either at sea en route to and from Alaska or at work in isolated canneries. One of the attractions of Alaska cannery work was the relative high wage. Japanese laborers earned a seasonal wage of $90 in 1900. This increased to $130 in 1901, and to $150 in 1903. By the 1905 season it reached $200. All laborers were given free transportation, room, and board, making the seasonal wage even more attractive because, in theory, it meant that the laborers, with no expenses to shoulder, could pocket their entire wages. Initially, the laborers were recruited by Japanese agents who worked for Chinese contractors. The first independent Japanese labor contractor appeared in 1901. He was followed by others who gradually displaced their Chinese counterparts. Each laborer who signed up for Alaska received an advance on his wages. In 1905 the advance amounted to $40. Before shipping out from San Francisco or Seattle, many laborers freely spent this advance on women and drink in anticipation of being away for a long time.

The long Alaska season enabled contractors to profit handsomely. They laid in stock goods and provisions on board ships and engaged in retail trade. The sale of food provisions was always brisk since the regular fare was never too palatable, especially aboard ship. No cash ever exchanged hands. The contractors issued coupons as a substitute for money. In exchange for signed coupons, they sold items at exorbitant prices which they deducted from the laborers' wages. The contractors or their foremen also promoted gambling among the laborers. Alaskan gambling was done on credit, and all loans were duly recorded and likewise deducted from wages. Much to their utter chargin, some laborers learned that they had no wages coming to them at the end of the season. Their contractors had gotten them to squander it all on costly goods and provisions and/or accumulated gambling debts. A few ended up actually owing money to the contractors.

The United States Immigration Commission reported on "the exploitation carried on by Japanese 'bosses' controlling Alaskan cannery laborers" in the following way:

> They secure the men through subagents . . . who receive a commission of five dollars per man, which is deducted from the wages of the men engaged. An advance is usually made by the packers to the "boss" in the spring . . . on the basis of the labor to be furnished. . . . They are advanced enough money to equip themselves for the trip, and a stock of goods is secured for boarding the men. In addition to these expenditures an extensive stock of eatables is bought, which is destined to be sold at high prices to the men en route. This is made possible by the fact that the food regularly furnished is poor and frequently insufficient in quantity. . . . The men buy these extra eatables and gamble at tables conducted by subbosses, on credit, their expenditures and losses being deducted from their total earnings for the season. The income of the "boss" is thus obtained from two sources—the sale of goods to the men at monopoly price and the profits realized from gambling. This income is comparatively large for the ability represented; frequently, if not generally, amounting to from two thousand to five thousand dollars for the year. It is entirely the result of the exploitation of the wages of Japanese laborers. . . . [74]

An Issei Alaskan cannery worker described his own experience. Although his description is of a later period (probably of the World War I era), it still captures vividly the general practice of avaricious contractors and foremen exploiting their laborers, so much so that some men had nothing to show for their labor at the close of a canning season.

> From what I observed, the first two or three months were taken up with *hana fuda* gambling. As the end of the season approached, the gambling became bigger and bigger. People played poker, and the losers lost more and more. Some lost their entire wages by the season's end or as early as a month before it closed. Those who did begged their contractors to give them the advance for the next contract season. They were thought of as "fools."
>
> There were always five or six "fools" in every camp. Foremen were elated when the number of "fools" increased, if even by one. One foreman bluntly blurted out: "This year I'm gonna return to Japan and get hitched and come back with my wife. I'm gonna go overboard and make more "fools."
>
> And just as this foreman said, thirteen men became "fools." Every man earned three hundred dollars. Thirteen men meant $3,900. That

was big money in those days. Cash was never used in Alaskan gambling. All betting was done on credit with foremen. . . .

I always said that no one could win in Alaskan gambling. A person like me who never gambled incurred the ire of foremen. Cannery boys were in a fix when they ran into wicked contractors.

The "fools" who returned to Seattle stayed in cheap hotels for twenty-five cents a night and begged for food at Chinese gambling houses. While enduring hunger, they waited for the next season. When they called at the contractors' office, they discovered they had outstanding loans of $150 to $200.

If they protested, "We didn't borrow that much," the matter was closed when they were told, "The ledger shows we loaned you X amount of dollars." . . . Contractors received five to six hundred dollars per boy from the companies they contracted with. Since they paid boys only three hundred to three hundred fifty dollars from this total, they earned sizeable sums of money. Contractors also received a hundred dollars per man as food allowance from the companies. They purchased rice, bean paste, soy sauce . . . , but this did not come to a hundred dollars. The balance went into their pockets.[75]

Agricultural labor contractors, notably in California, operated on a much smaller scale than their railroad counterparts, but were far more numerous. Beginning with Chinese immigrant labor in the 1870s, a contracting system had been established in Californian agriculture by which an alien labor force was organized.[76] As labor intensive crops, the cultivation of fruit and vegetables demanded a large pool of unskilled labor during the brief harvest season. This harvest labor force was supplied by Chinese labor contractors and composed of Chinese immigrant laborers at the outset. The Japanese entered California agriculture in 1888 when a few student-laborers worked as field hands in Winters near Vacaville. During the 1890s Japanese labor contractors began to supply Japanese labor to replace the Chinese labor force which was aging and declining. The number of Japanese laborers increased steadily after the turn of the century, so that by 1908 the Japanese became the dominant labor force.

Until the turn of the century, Japanese labor contractors engaged in laissez-faire competition. Without regard to other contractors, each contractor independently negotiated contract prices with growers and set wage rates for laborers. Frequently, they encroached on each other's territory by undercutting their competitors, and even by stealing each other's laborers. As intermediaries between the growers and laborers, all contractors performed the service of recruiting field hands and supervising them in the field. Just as the railroad labor contractors were not paid by the railroad companies for the services they rendered, the agricultural labor contractors were not paid by the growers either. They, too, earned income by levying a daily commission on their laborers' wages. In bunking and feeding their laborers, large contractors also earned income from the sale of goods and provisions. The growers had no direct dealings with the laborers at all; they did not even disburse wages. After the harvest was completed, the growers paid the contract price to the contractors directly. The contractors were responsible for paying their laborers out of the contract price in a disbursement procedure which differentiated labor contracting in agriculture from that in the railroad and mining industries.

Rampant competition had many negative consequences. To begin with, it placed the growers in an advantageous position. They were able to play off one contractor against another to drive down contract prices. Lower contract prices inevitably meant lower wages for laborers and usually lower incomes for the contractors themselves. A recurrent source of conflict in agriculture, absent in the railroad and mining industries and made possible by the method of disbursing wages, was the unscrupulous practice of agricultural labor contractors absconding without paying off their laborers. Known as *mochinige* in Japanese, this practice was common during the laissez-faire years. Unrestrained competition made it virtually impossible to prevent individual contractors from running away with the entire contract price. Contractors were usually paid by check. Seasoned laborers who had been victimized once never allowed contractors to go into town alone to cash checks. Hard experience taught them that it was wise to have some workers accompany the contractors into town. Such workers guaranteed that the contractors would return to labor camps to pay off their laborers. Early guides warned incoming immigrants of this dastardly act of *mochinige*.[77] For the contractors who engaged in it, it was their way of realizing the dream of *ikkaku senkin*, of striking it rich overnight, but at the expense of their own laborers.

Concrete cases can be cited, but not before the 1906 San Francisco earthquake. Immigrant newspapers carried stories of *mochinige*. Unfortunately, however, the newspapers of the pre-earthquake period, except for scattered issues, have not been preserved. Examples drawn from the post-earthquake period will have to serve as illustrations of the early incidents. In July 1906 Abe Kumakichi of Glendale, a strawberry labor contractor, abandoned his laborers and fled with $1,500.[78] Two months later, Fujiwara Kumatarō absconded with $2,000, deserting 60 men who had harvested hops in Sonoma County. A reward of $50 was posted for information leading to Fujiwara's whereabouts.[79] A year later, two other contractors known only as Komoto and Tachimi fled Hanford without paying 50 laborers who had harvested grapes in the surrounding vineyards. As soon as the laborers learned of their disappearance, they frantically searched in all directions but to no avail. The two culprits escaped with $1,500.[80] Alarmed at the frequency of *mochinige* incidents, the *Shin Sekai* suggested in September 1906 that laborers should obtain photographs of all labor contractors and forward them to the newspaper office in the event of *mochinige*. To publicly censure contractors who engaged in this act, this newspaper promised to print their photographs.[81]

Agricultural labor contractors formed local groups to try to control the ''corrupt'' element among them. In 1900, for example, sugar beet contractors in the Sacramento area banded together to cooperate with each other. For the 1900 harvest season, they all agreed to pay wages of $1.25 per day for ten hours of labor and to contract with growers at a rate of $1.60 per ton with a minimum guarantee of ten tons per acre.[82] They also agreed to boycott any grower who refused to contract at this rate and to censure any contractor who failed to abide by the wage and contract price agreement. In this way the contractors hoped to eliminate harmful competition and regulate the contract price to their own collective advantage. Similarly, in 1908, 53 contractors in the Fresno area joined together to form the Central California Contractors Association. These contractors agreed to a uniform rate of $1.65 per ton with which to contract with local grape growers for the coming harvest season.[83] To deter and punish renegade contractors, both of these contractors' groups and others resorted to public censure by employing several methods. First, they publicized the ''immoral'' activities of ''corrupt bosses'' in the immigrant press. Newspapers regularly printed scandalous stories of such contractors, listing their hometown addresses in Japan and often carrying their photographs, especially in *mochinige* cases. Secondly, they appealed to the local Japanese consulate and other immigrant organizations to blacklist the contractors. Thirdly, they wrote to the village or town in Japan from which the contractors originated and notified local government offices of the contractors' misdeeds in the United States. These methods of public disclosure inhibited potential renegades and socially ostracized those who were already guilty of grave misconduct.

Workers' Daily Life

Before the turn of the century, the conditions of agricultural labor camps were primitive. Labor contractors led their labor gangs from one camp to another, often plodding long distances between farms and orchards. Men usually carried blankets with them as their bedding. *Buranke-katsugi*, literally meaning a person who shoulders a blanket, was the Japanese term for a migratory agricultural laborer. Fresno camps were the worst. Referring to the early 1890s, one description reads as follows:

> During those days around Fresno, laborers did not even carry blankets. They slept in the fields with what they had on. They drank river water brought in by irrigation ditches. When they felt hungry, they devoured fresh grapes. If they ate supper, it consisted of flour dumplings in a soup seasoned with salt. Vegetables were unheard of. Slaving away from 4:00 a.m. to 9:00 p.m., this unhealthy life was intolerable.[84]

In 1900 a *Shin Sekai* reporter toured the Fresno area. He described the labor camps in this language:

> The camps are worse than dog and pig pens. They are totally unfit for human beings to sleep in. Rain and moisture seep down from the roofs. Winds blow nightly through all four walls. It's like seeing beggars in Japan living beneath bridges. No one, not even dirt-poor peasants, wants to live in such unpleasant and filthy surroundings. These camps are the reason why so many robust workers become ill and die.[85]

A 1903 guide depicted the camps in these words:

> Twenty to thirty Japanese sleep alongside each other in fieldsheds on the edge of fruit orchards. These sheds are called camps. There are well built camps as well as makeshift ones. Most of the latter have no beds. Men sleep with bedding on straws spread over dirt floors.[86]

Combined with the primitive conditions of labor camps, the hard labor caused many agricultural laborers to fall ill and die. In 1908 the Japanese Association of Fresno compiled death statistics for the years 1898 to 1907. It found that 182 laborers died in Fresno County during this decade.[87] The causes were not enumerated. The Sacramento Betsuin Book of the Deceased is more revealing in this respect. Established in 1900, this Buddhist church maintained detailed records during its first three years. Ninety-nine persons are recorded to have passed away between 1900 and 1902 in the Sacramento area.[88] The overwhelming majority were young men in their twenties and thirties who died either in county hospitals or at one of two Japanese clinics in the city. "Sickness" is listed as the general cause of deaths, with heat stroke, beriberi, and tuberculosis as the most frequently cited specific illnesses. Among those who died in the Sacramento area, many were laborers who originated from Aichi Prefecture, concentrated in the delta region. Of the people from this prefecture, 58 persons (including six women, but excluding children) died between 1894 and 1914.[89]

According to Japanese consular statistics, a total of 3,836 Japanese died in California between 1906 and 1913.[90] The annual breakdown by number and causes is shown in the table on page 85.

This chart leaves much to be desired. Some of the causes of death listed are not specific, especially those in the "other" categories. It is not clear what is meant by "early infancy." Does it mean the first days or months or years of infancy? And the lack of deaths due to venereal diseases is hard to believe. Be that as it may, the chart still shows an unquestionable high death rate among Japanese immigrants. In 1910 California's Japanese population was 41,356. This means that that the total number of deaths between 1906 and 1913 was equal to 9.2 percent of the 1910 Japanese population. If the deaths caused by the common childhood diseases (smallpox, measles, scarlet fever, whooping cough, and diphtheria), the puerperal state, and early infancy are subtracted from the total of 3,836, the balance is 3,410. During the period in question, the Japanese population was composed primarily of male laborers in their twenties and thirties, so that it can be inferred that this balance represents, with minor adjustments, the deaths of adult males. As to the causes of deaths, 138 are attributed to suicides and 476 to "other external causes" which presumably include accidents and homicides. The balance of 2,796 represents deaths caused by illnesses, with tuberculosis, pneumonia, typhoid, and intestinal disorders ranking the highest. A second inference which can be drawn is that these deaths by illnesses were mainly of laborers who toiled under poor, unsanitary, and often dangerous working conditions, particularly in California agriculture.

Japanese laborers had few wholesome recreational outlets. Gambling was a major source of recreation, since it offered a hope, however illusory, of striking it rich instantly. In 1914, Kawakami Kiyoshi, a leading Issei publicist who wrote in English, retold in his book, *Asia at the Door*, a story relating to the 1911 Chinese Revolution. A friend had informed Kawakami that it was not really Chinese immigrants in America who had supported Sun Yat-sen when he led the revolution. On the contrary, it was Japanese laborers. Kawakami's friend did not mean to say that the Japanese had financed the revolution directly. He meant that the source of the remittances sent by the Chinese to support Sun Yat-sen was the Japanese laborers who squandered their earnings in Chinese gambling houses. "In California alone," according to this story, "these gambling dens used to levy from the Japanese a toll of several million dollars every year."[91] In retelling this story, Kawa-

NUMBER OF DEATHS BY CAUSES IN CALIFORNIA'S JAPANESE POPULATION, 1906–1913

Cause	1906	1907	1908	1909	1910	1911	1912	1913	Total
Typhoid	44	58	49	37	18	20	25	25	276
Malaria	4	2	0	7	1	2	3	4	23
Smallpox	0	0	0	0	0	0	0	0	0
Measles	0	0	0	0	1	0	1	5	7
Scarlet Fever	1	0	0	2	9	0	0	0	12
Whooping Cough	0	0	0	0	0	0	6	4	10
Diphtheria	1	5	1	4	2	1	0	4	18
Influenza	4	0	0	0	1	0	2	0	7
Other General Epidemic Diseases	4	17	7	8	2	3	2	2	45
Tuberculosis, Lungs	58	53	57	70	64	77	50	69	498
Tuberculosis, Other	30	20	17	32	27	29	32	29	216
Cancer	7	12	8	6	11	5	11	3	63
Venereal Diseases	0	0	0	0	0	0	0	0	0
Other General Diseases	9	8	7	5	19	14	10	17	89
Meningitis	16	39	30	19	24	20	16	18	182
Diseases of Nervous System	6	12	7	19	4	12	11	15	86
Pneumonia	23	41	25	30	32	27	62	67	307
Other Diseases of Respiratory System	6	14	16	20	12	11	15	11	105
Diseases of Circulatory System	18	24	23	11	16	21	26	17	156
Diarrhea and Enteritis—under 2 years	14	25	31	28	40	33	51	76	298
Diarrhea and Enteritis—over 2 years	6	6	3	4	4	3	8	7	41
Other Diseases of Digestive System	28	33	35	22	27	30	29	37	241
Nephritis and Other Non-Venereal	7	20	8	14	12	5	13	18	97
The Puerperal State	8	5	4	9	9	12	12	19	78
Early Infancy	8	25	28	27	43	41	43	63	278
Suicide	10	9	24	16	15	24	20	20	138
Other External Causes	61	81	47	42	45	70	57	73	476
Other Causes	11	8	5	18	6	12	19	10	89
TOTAL	384	517	432	450	444	472	524	613	3,836

kami was appealing to American authorities for help in stamping out
the Chinese gambling establishments.

The story was not a hyperbole. Dating back to the nineties, Japanese laborers regularly patronized Chinese gambling houses. In most
rural communities, Japanese immigrants lived alongside Chinese immigrants in segregated quarters. The Chinese operated the houses in
these quarters. In Fresno, for example, the gambling joints were clustered in an area known as China Alley, around which the Japanese
resided. In 1908, according to a Japanese Congregational minister,
there were 19 houses in operation which took in approximately
$200,000 from Japanese laborers during the 1907 harvest season.[92] One
of the biggest houses, operated by a Lee Troy, provided free wine,
beer, and tea and had a moving picture display which was changed
every week to attract customers. In the Sacramento delta region, Japanese and Chinese immigrants lived together in Isleton, Walnut Grove,
and Courtland, towns in which Chinese gambling houses thrived.

In 1908 Hanihara Masanao, Second Secretary of the Japanese Embassy, traveled throughout the western United States and the Pacific
Coast and observed Japanese immigrant life at first hand. He witnessed
the Japanese living next to the Chinese in almost every settlement he
visited. In Walnut Grove, he was appalled to see "the Japanese and
Chinese living together in filthy, winding alleys criss-crossing each
other." All of the Chinese quarters were "gambling dens" in which,
in his opinion, "the Chinese fattened themselves by squeezing dumb
Japanese laborers."[93] Hanihara's observation reflected the anti-Chinese
bias of Japanese government officials. Going back to the late nineteenth century, Japanese officials always blamed the Chinese immigrants for arousing the hostility of Americans. The Chinese were regarded as "coolie" laborers who worked for cheap wages and
undermined the position of white workmen. Indifferent to American
morals and customs, they openly engaged in such vices as gambling
and prostitution. Japanese officials feared that Americans would identify the Japanese with the Chinese. From Hanihara's bureaucratic
point of view, Japanese immigrants who lived alongside the Chinese
and patronized Chinese gambling houses were making this identification a real possibility.

Warning of the pitfalls of Chinese gambling, a 1902 labor hand-
book, published in San Francisco for incoming Japanese immigrants,
contained these words of admonition:

> As a laborer in the countryside, you will toil from dawn to dusk with
> only shots of whiskey and cigarettes to enjoy. Beware of gambling!
> Why did you leave your home and cross the wide Pacific to endure

hardships in this foreign land? It was of course to enrich your family and benefit the homeland. Then, why try to forget your long days of toil by gambling? You will lose your hard earnings in a single night. If it were your countrymen who take your earnings, it would not be so bad, but, alas, they will all be Chinese. Gambling corrupts the spirit, harms the body, and causes wives, children, and relatives at home to suffer unnecessarily. Be sure to avoid it![94]

In 1908 the *Shin Sekai* decried the prevalence of gambling and carousing among Japanese laborers. In an editorial entitled "Debauchery and Gambling," it rhetorically asked its readers, "What did you come to America for?"[95] The *Nichibei Shimbun* blamed the popularity of gambling on the *dekasegi* orientation of the laborers. Gambling offered the laborers the pipe dream of striking it rich overnight and returning to Japan as wealthy persons.[96] A writer in the *Beikoku Bukkyō*, monthly organ of the Buddhist Mission of America, echoed the views of the *Nichibei Shimbun*. He also blamed the *ikkaku senkin* mentality, adding that a lack of alternative recreational outlets was also an important factor.[97]

Japanese laborers were addicted to two Chinese gambling games in particular.[98] The first was a lottery called *baahk gap piu* in Cantonese, which means a white pigeon card. In China doves were used to announce the results of lotteries in rural areas. Thus the lottery card came to be known as a white pigeon card. A variant of this lottery is known as keno today and is played widely at Las Vegas casinos. The keno lottery card has eighty numbers. A player buys a card and selects certain numbers. The pay-off is calculated by the number of numbers the player hits in the lottery. The more numbers he hits, the bigger the return. Conversely, if the player hits fewer than the minimum, he or she receives no pay-off at all. The Chinese lottery card was different. Instead of eighty numbers, it had eighty Chinese characters taken from an old school primer on Chinese characters. These characters gave the original Chinese lottery a dimension lacking in contemporary keno. Since each character had a separate meaning, a player could select characters to compose a poem or a sentence. Approximating the Chinese pronunciation, the Japanese called this lottery *bakapyō* or *bakappei*. The Japanese *baka* means a fool; *pyō* and *pei*, following the Chinese *piu*, mean a card. Hence the Japanese pronunciation had the double meaning of a white pigeon card and a fool's card. To make the latter meaning explicit, the Japanese always wrote for *baka*, not white pigeon, but the characters "horse" and "deer," which means a fool when combined into a compound.

The second game was *fantan*. The Japanese called this game *shiigo* or *shiikoi* derived from the Japanese pronunciation of another Cantonese word, *sei gok*, which means four corners. *Fantan* was played with old Chinese coins or any small objects. The coins were placed on a table and covered with a brass cup. The game opened with the removal of the cup. The exposed coins then were removed four at a time by a tapered rod. The object of *fantan* was to wager on how many coins would be left at the end, determined when there were four coins or less remaining on the table. *Sei gok* or four corners were the possibilities represented by "four gates" marked on the table. A heavenly gate represented one coin, an upper gate two, a lower gate three, and an earthly gate four. Stakes were placed on one or any two gates, and only bettors on the winning gate or corner received payoffs from the house. All others lost.

Simplicity was the hallmark of *fantan*. Because it required little equipment, it could be played anywhere. The only items needed were old coins, a brass cup, a tapered rod, and a table. Yet even these items were not essential. Old coins could be replaced by small stones or beans, and any rice bowl and chopstick could serve as a brass cup and tapered rod. In lieu of matted tables with betting gates or corners marked, any large sheet of paper penciled with the betting spots could be used on floors. Moreover, *fantan* could be played by anyone. The betting and pay-off procedures were the quintessence of simplicity. As long as he or she could count to four, any moron could understand how to play the game. And for those prone to taking big risks, it had the ever-tempting and simple double-or-nothing wager. The potential for legerdemain lay in this very simplicity. A house croupier handled the rod and removed the coins from the table. All bets were placed openly. This enabled the croupier to see which corners were bet more heavily than others. Aware of the betting on the table, an experienced croupier was in a position to control the outcome of the game if he removed more than four coins at any time. By a sleight of hand, he could regulate the number of remaining coins to decide the outcome in favor of the house. If the heavenly gate representing one coin was bet most heavily, the croupier saw to it that two or more coins were left on the table at the end. That the hand is faster than the eye is a truism. No wonder Japanese laborers lost at *fantan*!

Other recreational outlets, if they can be called that, were poolhalls and bar-restaurants catering to migratory laborers. These small businesses sprang up wherever Japanese laborers appeared, but especially in urban areas where the laborers waited out the off-season. Poolhalls were often combined with barbershops and bathhouses. In 1912 San Francisco had 41 Japanese-operated poolhalls. In the same year Sacramento had 21 poolhalls and 25 bar-restaurants; Stockton 6 poolhalls and 11 bar-restaurants; Fresno 19 poolhalls and 11 bar-restaurants; and Los Angeles 35 poolhalls and 30 bar-restaurants.[99] Some poolhalls had high-sounding names such as the Imperial Poolhall, National Poolhall, and Miyako Poolhall. Many were named after specific geographical areas in Japan—the Kinokuniya Poolhall after Wakayama Prefecture, the Higoya Poolhall after Kumamoto Prefecture, and the Nankaiya Poolhall after Kagoshima Prefecture. A few were named after specific villages, as was the case with the Tawara Poolhall of Los Angeles named after a fishing village in Wakayama Prefecture.

Poolhalls and bar-restaurants served as important social havens from the hardships and tedium of labor. In addition to providing the game of pool, poolhalls served as a general meeting place for workers to renew old friendships, to exchange work information, and to simply while away leisure time. Many catered to fellow countrymen from the same prefecture or village. Bar-restaurants were a place where workers ate sorely missed Japanese food and, following a time-honored Japanese custom, imbibed alcoholic beverages, usually cheap wine and whiskey, frequently to the point of a drunken stupor. Laborers were drawn to bar-restaurants for another reason. With *shakufu* or barmaids, the bar-restaurants had the attraction of offering female companionship. Without wives or sweethearts, the laborers craved such companionship and, however fleeting it may have been, sought it in the bar-restaurants. On Sundays railroad section hands used handcars to go into towns. Since Japanese-operated bar-restaurants did not exist in remote areas, railroad laborers in isolated places had to be content with drinking by themselves. In 1906 a gallon of wine, enough for a cheap high for several men, cost twenty-five cents.

With few women in early immigrant society, prostitutes were the sexual outlet for Japanese laborers. Hardly any description of the houses of prostitution or of the prostitutes in them are available. Of the few, there is this depiction of Japanese prostitutes on Brooklyn Place in San Francisco Chinatown:

> The girls were exhibited in a kind of cage. Each was dressed in a gaudy red garment. Each had painted cheeks, and a peculiar wreath-like ornament upon the head, which instead of being a crown of a pure and noble womanhood was the emblem of shame.[100]

In 1908 the Japanese prostitutes in Fresno's China Alley were described as follows:

There are close to fifty to sixty Japanese prostitutes in this place. . . .
They construct crude hovels of two nine-by-nine foot rooms in several
filthy three to four feet wide alleys wedged in a slum area and accessible
by side and rear entrances. When evening sets in, they show off their
''wares'' by leaving the doors open and wearing grotesque bright Japanese and Chinese garments with cribs by their sides.[101]

Venereal disease must have been a common ailment among Japanese
laborers. This can be inferred from advertisements which appeared
in the immigrant press praising the efficacy of medicines for curing
gonorrhea. The *Shin Sekai* carried continuous advertisements for ''Ri-
tanol for Gonorrhea,'' claiming it could heal this disease in forty-
eight hours. According to the ads, only one bottle, costing $2.50, was
necessary.[102]

IV

Labor Organizing and Organized American Labor

Earliest Japanese Immigrant Labor Bodies

Just as Japanese laborers were entering the western labor market in the 1890s, the AFL emerged as the dominant force in the American labor movement. In the late nineteenth and early twentieth century, the presence of Asian immigrant labor posed a fundamental issue to the labor movement. Should the movement, in the name of class solidarity, recruit and enlist Asian laborers into its ranks, or should it exclude them, in the opposite cause of racial separatism? Save in rare instances, organized labor's answer to this question was to pursue a one-sided policy of racial exclusion. The AFL was primarily a federation of craft unions composed overwhelmingly of skilled white workmen, the aristocracy of American labor. Unskilled labor had no place in the federation. Skilled minority workers were either relegated to segregated locals or excluded from union membership altogether. As far as Asian immigrant labor was concerned, the AFL adhered to an exclusionary policy. Regardless of skill, it denied membership to all Asian laborers. The AFL was also at the forefront of anti-Asian exclusionary movements designed to bar Asian labor from American shores. Beginning with Chinese immigration, it successively opposed Japanese, Korean, East Indian, and Filipino immigration to the United States.

Although outside the structure of the American labor movement, Japanese immigrant laborers were not indifferent to modern labor problems. Belying the belief held in most labor quarters that Japanese immigrants were wholly ignorant of modern labor practices, many student-laborers became knowledgeable about trade unionism. Indeed, the very beginning of the modern Japanese labor movement can be traced to a group formed by a handful of student-laborers in San Francisco. Established in 1891, this group was called the *Shokkō Giyūkai* (The Friends of Labor) whose founding members were Takano Fusatarō, Jō Tsunetarō, Sawada Hannosuke, and a few others. For many years this group was thought of as only a study group which examined solutions to labor problems in the West with the goal of applying those solutions to labor problems in Japan in some distant future. Recent research reveals that the members of the *Shokkō Giyūkai* actually anticipated organizing workers in Japan, so that it was an incipient labor organizing body rather than a mere study group.[1]

Takano Fusatarō was the key figure.[2] A native of Nagasaki, Takano was born in 1868. In 1878 his family moved to Tokyo where his father engaged in the hostelry and marine transport business. The father died in 1880. After completing elementary school in Tokyo, Takano lived with an uncle in Yokohama. In 1886 this uncle passed away, which prompted Takano to cross the Pacific. Once he landed in San Francisco, he worked as a school-boy and studied English. In the fall of 1887 he returned to Japan temporarily, and in 1888 he opened a small general store in San Francisco. This store never got off the ground and failed. From 1889 Takano became an itinerant laborer who worked at various jobs and pursued an independent course of study. While employed at a sawmill in Mendocino County in 1889, his interest in trade unionism was stimulated by his reading of *The Labor Movement: The Problem of To-day.* Edited and in part written by George E. McNeil in 1887, this book presented a history of the American labor movement with an emphasis on the Knights of Labor. In 1890 Takano wrote an essay, which appeared in a Tokyo daily, attributing the strength of the American working class to its ability to organize itself. In 1891 he wrote another essay, which appeared in the same Tokyo daily, expounding on the need to organize labor in Japan. In 1891 Takano started to translate *Wealth and Progress,* an 1887 treatise on wages by George Gunton. Gunton was active in the American labor movement and had been associated closely with Ira Steward, the Boston machinist who was a leader of the eight-hour day movement. Takano completed his translation in 1892. In light of the foregoing, Takano's membership in the *Shokkō Giyūkai* strongly suggests that this first labor body embraced the practical goal of organizing workers in Japan.

Takano's correspondence with AFL President Samuel Gompers strengthens this interpretation. Takano corresponded with him from 1894 to 1898.[3] In his first letter of March 6, 1894, he explained his interest in the American labor movement:

> Having been attracted by the well doings of American Workingmen since my arrival in this country a few years ago, my thought has been turned upon Japanese laborers whose condition viewed from social and material standpoint is most pitiful and has caused me to determine to try to better their condition upon my return home. In order to do so, I intend to study as much as I can of the American labor movement while I live in this country.

Linking the goal of educating workers with that of organizing them, Takano continued:

> As you are aware, there is no labor organization in Japan at present and the cause of this non-existence, I believe, is the prevailing ignorance among the working people. This being the case, to educate the working people is the most important step to be taken in amelioration of their condition. I further believe that this educational work must be carried by organized efforts, that is to say, we must organize the working people in order to educate them.

Skilled American workmen in AFL-affiliated unions were organized along exclusive craft lines. In contrast to this organizing principle, the Knights of Labor organized workers on an industrial basis. The first method of organization excluded all workers outside of any given craft; the second included all workers in any given industry regardless of craft or skill. Takano favored the Knights of Labor method of organizing:

> I am inclined to consider that it is preferable to adopt the form of K. of L. as a temporary method in organizing the Japanese workmen, bringing whatever number of them there is who is willing to join under one organization and start the educational work at once.

To contemplate organizing workers in Japan was one thing; to organize Japanese workers in America was another. Jō Tsunetarō, another founding member of the *Shokkō Giyūkai,* reflected the dilemma faced by Japanese laborers in this country. Jō arrived in 1888 as a representative of the Tokyo Shoemakers' League, a guild organized in 1886 for self-protection against rapacious investors. In 1887 the *Kokumin no Tomo,* a popular journal for youth published in Tokyo, carried an article on Chinese immigrant shoemakers in San Francisco. Jō was dispatched by the League to investigate the possibilities of Japanese shoemakers obtaining employment in the city. Concluding that the prospects were good, Jō reported back favorably to Tokyo. He made the acquaintance of Takano Fusatarō while working as a dishwasher in a San Francisco hotel. In 1889 Sekine Tadayoshi, a fellow member of the League, joined Jō, and the two men opened a small shoe shop on Mission Street. Shortly after, they contracted with an American shoe manufacturer. Sekine then returned to Japan and escorted back 15 shoemakers who commenced to manufacture shoes under a trade-mark borne by other shoes produced by white shoemakers in other shops under contract with the same manufacturer. In February 1890 matters came to a head as the Boot and Shoemakers' White Labor League learned of the secret contract into which the manufacturer had entered with the Japanese. The union pressured the manufacturer to remove the trade-mark from the Japanese-produced shoes and to break his contract with them. In the end, Jō and Sekine had to close their shop under heavy union pressure.[4]

In 1892 Jō and his fellow shoemakers organized the *Nihonjin Kutsukō Dōmeikai* (Japanese Shoemakers' League). Unlike the *Shokkō Giyūkai,* which anticipated organizing workers in Japan, this League represented a defensive reaction to organized white labor in San Francisco. It was a response to the plight in which the shoemakers found themselves. Jō and his associates had experienced at first hand the hostility of white union shoemakers and had lost their jobs on their account. More likely than not, Jō was aware that the Boot and Shoemakers' White Labor League had endeavored to drive out the Chinese from the shoemaking industry. As a defensive strategy, therefore, the Japanese elected to specialize in shoe repairing in order to avoid competing with white shoemakers. Accordingly, they reopened their shop in May 1890 as a repair shop, and thereafter every new shop they opened specialized in shoe repair.

Thus the character of the Japanese Shoemakers' League was considerably different from that of the *Shokkō Giyūkai,* even though Jō was a founding member of both organizations. The League was not a labor union. Above all else, its purpose was to protect the Japanese in shoe repairing. The League started with 20 members; this number increased to 167 by 1904 and reached the peak of 327 by 1909. To eliminate harmful competition, the League controlled membership, regulated the opening of new shops, and set repair prices. Five existing members had to endorse candidates for membership. Membership dues amounted to 50¢ per month for master journeymen and 35¢ per month for journeymen and apprentices. All members had to contribute an additional 50¢ per month up to a maximum of $50 towards a common business fund. As a part of cooperative buying, a portion of this fund was allocated to keeping a stock of goods in a supply house operated by the League. If a journeyman wished to open his own shop within six months after admission into membership, he had to pass a technical test. Only apprentices who had served a master journeyman for one year and had passed a technical test could open their own shops. If they had served for two years, the test was waved. All new shops had to be opened at a distance of more than 1,190 feet from any existing Japanese shop. Any member who opened a shop where no Japanese-operated shop existed was entitled to a loan of up to $50 from the business fund. No member could charge less than the minimum repair prices set by by-laws.[5] In sum, the Japanese Shoemakers' League was a kind of guild which sought to protect the Japanese in the shoe repairing niche into which they retreated in the face of white union hostility.

The *Shokkō Giyūkai* was reconstituted in Japan as the *Rōdō Kumiai Kiseikai* (Society for the Promotion of Trade-Unions) in July 1897. Among its founding members were Takano Fusatarō, Jō Tsunetarō, and Sawada Hannosuke, who had all returned to Japan. The members of this society successfully organized the first industrial union, the *Tekkō Kumiai* (Iron Workers' Union), in December 1897, and simultaneously launched the *Rōdō Sekai* (Labor World), the first labor journal, under the editorship of Katayama Sen. These events marked the real starting point of the modern labor movement in Japan, a movement through which Takano, Jō, and others realized the *Shokkō Giyūkai's* original goal of organizing Japanese workers. Such was not to be the case in this country. Symbolizing the dilemma of Japanese immigrant laborers, the Japanese shoemakers retreated to shoe repairing as non-union workers when they were ousted from the shoemaking industry by the Boot and Shoemakers' White Labor League.

The 1903 Oxnard Strike

In 1903 Japanese and Mexican sugar beet workers in Oxnard, California, went out on an historic strike.[6] More than any other event, this strike forcefully raised the fundamental issue of whether organized labor would admit Asian laborers into its ranks, or, as the Boot and Shoemakers' White Labor League did, stick to a policy of racial exclusion. Situated in Ventura County, Oxnard was named after the promoters of the local sugar beet industry. In 1897 three brothers—Henry, James, and Robert Oxnard—began the construction of a sugar beet processing factory on the townsite. These three men had established the American Beet Sugar Company, which operated the factory when it was completed in 1898. In 1899 Henry and James Oxnard also founded the Bank of Oxnard which offered loans to growers who cultivated sugar beets under contract with the American Beet Sugar Company. Oxnard's sugar beet industry expanded rapidly—in 1900 the factory processed 63,000 tons of sugar beet; in 1901 160,000 tons; and in 1903 almost 200,000 tons. The factory employed 700 white workers in 1903.

Japanese and Mexican laborers were employed as field hands by the local growers. Formed in 1902, the Western Agricultural Contracting Company (WACC) was the major labor contractor. Its Japanese department, responsible for recruiting Japanese labor, was headed by Inose Inosuke. Inose was a native of Ibaragi Prefecture who, like so many other labor contractors, had risen from the ranks of the student-laborers. He had worked at one time as a cook in the sugar beet factory. In 1903 he operated a retail store and was a stockholder in the American Beet Sugar Company.[7] Of the first contingent of laborers recruited by the WACC in 1902, 443 were Japanese and 175 were Mexican. Highly successful in recruiting laborers, the WACC's labor force harvested almost 75 percent of the 1902 sugar beet crop in the Oxnard area. Laborers recruited by small independent contractors harvested the balance.

The virtual monopoly of the WACC was an important factor behind the 1903 Oxnard strike. Small independent contractors, numbering in the neighborhood of 12, were in danger of being eliminated altogether or reduced to subcontracting under the WACC. At the beginning of 1903, Inose recruited 120 Japanese from San Francisco and assigned them to work under a subcontractor. The newly recruited laborers, many of whom were student-laborers, protested this assignment to a subcontractor as a violation of the promises which had been made to them. After an initial protest meeting among the Japanese, a series of meetings took place between Japanese and Mexican workers, and, on February 11, 500 Japanese and 200 Mexicans joined hands and formed the Japanese-Mexican Labor Association (JMLA), with Baba Kozaburō as president. Baba was an independent contractor who opposed the growing monopoly of the WACC. The workers raised three issues in forming this union. First, they accused the WACC of paying less than it promised. Secondly, they attacked the subcontracting system because they had to pay a daily commission twice, once to the WACC and again to the subcontractors. Thirdly, they criticized the WACC policy of compelling all workers to buy at designated stores as a condition of employment. Such stores, they charged, sold goods at inflated prices and paid kickbacks to the WACC. Once the union members voted to strike to break the monopoly of the WACC, the union achieved remarkable success in a brief period. By the first week of March, it had 1,200 members or 90 percent of the entire labor force out on strike.

The WACC countered by creating another labor organization. Called the Independent Agricultural Labor Union, it was launched on March 21 with Inose as a member of the Board of Directors. Its avowed purposes were to preserve harmonious labor relations and to defend its members from any person or body preventing them from working. Then, on March 23, a violent shooting incident erupted in which a striking Mexican worker was killed; two other Mexicans and two Japanese were wounded. A few days later, negotiations began between the local growers, the WACC, and the JMLA. The union demanded the right to contract directly with all growers. The WACC offered to permit the union to contract for 2,000 of the 7,000 total acres it had under contract, provided that the WACC workers be non-union and that all strikers return to work. The union in turn proposed that the apportionment of acreage should be based upon the number of men the JMLA and the WACC each had. Union membership had reached 1,300. The WACC, the union claimed, had only 60 men.

A final settlement was reached on March 30. The WACC agreed to cancel all existing contracts with one exception. That exception was its contract with the Patterson Ranch covering 1,800 acres owned by the American Beet Sugar Company. The union conceded this acreage to the WACC. Local growers accepted a negotiated contract

price of $5.00 to $6.00 per acre for thinning and hoeing. Through
this final settlement, the JMLA succeeded in breaking the monopoly
of the WACC, which itself was a significant victory. It is not clear,
however, if the union actually contracted for the acreage relinquished
by the WACC. If the union did contract in fact, it functioned as a
true labor union and made all labor contractors superfluous. On the
other hand, if it did not, the small independent contractors must have
contracted with the growers separately in accordance with the negotiated settlement. If this occurred, the pre-WACC contracting system
was reestablished with laborers still working under labor contractors.
Victory in this case meant the demise of subcontracting, but not of
the labor-contracting system as a whole.

Whatever the outcome was, this Oxnard strike had far-reaching
implications. The American labor movement had failed to organize
agricultural workers. The strike raised the question of whether or not
the movement in California would organize such workers and admit
them into union membership. Since the striking Oxnard sugar beet
workers were Japanese and Mexican, the strike raised another basic
question of whether or not organized labor would admit agricultural
workers who happened to be members of racial minorities. In southern California local labor councils looked favorably upon the JMLA.
Fred C. Wheeler and John Murray, Jr., two local leaders, supported
the strikers. Both were socialists affiliated with the Los Angeles
County Council of Labor, and under their influence the Council addressed these two fundamental questions in a resolution after the
March 23 shooting incident:

> Whereas, For the first time in the history of organized labor on the
> Pacific Coast an opportunity has come to organize agricultural laborers;
> and
>   Whereas, About one thousand such laborers of Mexican and Japa-
> nese nationality have been organized at Oxnard, California, and have,
> for two months, bravely maintained a strike against starvation wages
> and iniquitous conditions; and
>   Whereas, They have proved their courage and manhood by passing
> calmly through the trial of seeing many of their numbers shot down
> by the opposition and have emerged from this ordeal with unbroken
> ranks; and
>   Whereas, The complete organization of agricultural laborers is nec-
> essary for the protection of all working men; now, therefore, be it
>   Resolved, By the Los Angeles County Council of Labor that we
> declare our belief that the most effective method of protecting the

American workingman and his standard of living is by the universal organization of the wage-workers regardless of race or national distinction.

Resolved, That while we are utterly opposed to the unrestricted immigration of the various Oriental races, we heartily favor the thorough organization of those now here, and believe that the fact that men are able to do our work when we strike is sufficient reason why they should be organized, regardless of race or color.[8]

Encouraged by this resolution, J.M. Lizarras, the Mexican secretary of the JMLA, applied for an AFL charter under the name of the Sugar Beet and Farm Laborers' Union of Oxnard. Upon receiving the application, Samuel Gompers expressed his willingness to issue a charter but with a crucial condition. Gompers stipulated that "your union will under no circumstance accept membership of any Chinese or Japanese."[9] In other words, Gompers was prepared to grant a charter to Lizarras on the condition that his union bar Asian laborers from membership. Much to the credit of Lizarras, he refused to accept any charter under such a racist term. "We would be false [to the Japanese] and to ourselves and to the cause of Unionism," he answered, "if we . . . accepted privileges for ourselves which are not accorded to them." And Lizarras concluded: "We therefore respectfully petition the A.F. of L. to grant us a charter under which we can unite all the Sugar Beet & Field Laborers of Oxnard, without regard to their color or race. We will refuse any other kind of charter. . . ."[10]

The significance of the Oxnard strike cannot be overstressed. Gompers' condition that the newly formed union must bar Japanese and Chinese laborers was consistent with AFL's opposition to all Asian immigration. The AFL had opposed Chinese immigration in openly racist terms. In 1893 its national convention asserted that the Chinese "are a degraded people, and bring with them nothing but filth, vice and disease. . . ."[11] Gompers himself said, in 1901, that:

Every incoming coolie means the displacement of an American, and the lowering of the American standard of living.

So much more vice and immorality injected into our social life in its place.

We can not afford to trifle with a race of people so utterly unassimilative, so ruinous to our general prosperity, and so blighting to our every prospect.[12]

In 1901 Gompers co-authored *Some Reasons for Chinese Exclusion: Meat vs. Rice, American Manhood Against Asiatic Coolieism, Which Shall Survive?*, an inflammatory tract written as a part of the AFL's successful drive to have the 1892 Chinese Exclusion Act, known also as the Geary Act, extended beyond 1902.

In opposing Japanese (and Korean) immigration, the AFL linked it to the preceding Chinese immigration. In 1904 the AFL national convention adopted its first anti-Japanese resolution. The resolution called for the 1902 Chinese Exclusion Act to be amended to include the Japanese and Koreans because it "had been succeeded by an evil similar in general character, but much more threatening in its possibilities, to-wit: the immigration to the United States and its insular territory of large and increasing numbers of Japanese and Korean laborers."[13] The *American Federationist,* official organ of the AFL, articulated the racial reasons against Japanese laborers. Regardless of origins, all white men were capable of uplifting themselves by joining the American labor movement. Ignorant workmen, even those newcomers of southern and eastern European background, could be taught the fundamentals of unionism. "If some of them are slow to learn," this was no cause for alarm since "in the end they will stand shoulder to shoulder with those faithful workers who never tire of teaching them that unity is strength." Japanese were of a different species. They were incapable of being unionized, a presumed fact which differentiated them from their white brethren:

> Their God is not his God. Their hopes, their ambitions, their love of this country are nothing to him. It is a question of making some money which he can not get in his own country. That is all. Otherwise he must always remain the stranger. He will come, stay, and leave us as a stranger. Herein lies the greatest danger. I say that our interest can never become his. He can not be *unionized.* He cannot be *Americanized* (italics included).

Here Americanization was equated with unionizing. Since the Japanese could not be Americanized, they could not be unionized. So the inexorable conclusion was: "This, then, is the all-important reason why Japanese as well as Chinese labor should be excluded from competing with American labor."[14]

In his own person, Takano Fusatarō gave the lie to the judgment that the Japanese as a race could not be unionized. Samuel Gompers himself knew this fact through correspondence with Takano during the 1890s. Indeed, Takano kept him informed of the promising beginnings of the Japanese labor movement. Gompers recalled his encounter with Takano in the following way:

In the 'nineties I met Fusataro Takano. . . . He became very much interested in the labor movement and came down to my office to ask me for information on our trade union movement which would be helpful to Japanese workers. . . . When he was ready to return to Japan, I helped him to establish relationship with various labor papers that would enable him to sell an occasional letter containing Japanese labor news. During a number of years I kept in touch with Takano and supplied him with information of developments in the American labor movement. He spread among his fellow-workers information of trade unionism and helped to kindle a spirit that afterwards found expression when there was opportunity for Japanese workers to organize.[15]

Other AFL leaders and rank-and-file members knew of Takano through articles he contributed to American labor journals from 1894 to 1899. Undoubtedly through Gompers' intercession, these articles appeared in the *American Federationist* and *Coast Seamen's Journal,* organ of the International Seamen's Union of the Pacific, an AFL-affiliated union headquartered in San Francisco. In publishing the articles, the *American Federationist* identified Takano as a special correspondent and on one occasion as "our organizer in Japan."

Takano's articles covered the condition of labor in Japan and the rise of the Japanese labor movement. In 1894 Takano wrote of the need to launch a modern labor movement. "Agitation among the thinkers of the country," he said, was "the first step to be taken in Japan, to be followed [by] an organization" to educate "the working people . . . , to protect the interest of the working people, and lastly . . . to *organize the working people*" (italics included).[16] In 1896 Takano described the working conditions in modern Japanese cotton mills as a "mockery of our national integrity and a blot upon our civilization" which demanded an "immediate solution."[17] In 1897 he reported on the formation of the *Rōdō Kumiai Kiseikai.* Noting that four of its founders had been original members of the *Shokkō Giyūkai* in San Francisco, Takano assured Gompers that the four, including himself, were all "staunch advocates of trade unionism."[18] In 1898 he announced the establishment of the *Tekkō Kumiai* which he predicted would have "a bright future."[19] In numerous other articles, Takano discussed strikes, wages, female labor, factory legislation, and farmers in Japan.[20]

The purpose of Takano's writings was to inform organized American labor of the state of Japanese labor. If AFL officials and union members read Takano in earnest, they would have learned that the Japanese were interested in modern labor problems and had actually started their own labor movement. Yet Takano in no way altered Gompers' or the AFL's anti-Japanese policy. In 1905 Gompers, probably addressing an all-white audience, is reported to have said that "the caucasians are not going to let their standard of living be destroyed by negroes, Chinamen, Japs, or any others."[21] Devoid of any pretension to racial tolerance, this statement expressed the crude racism behind Gompers' earlier refusal to allow the admission of Japanese or Chinese laborers into the Sugar Beet and Farm Laborers' Union of Oxnard. In line with the final outcome of the Oxnard strike, the AFL never deviated from this policy of racial exclusion until the 1930s, keeping Japanese and other Asian workers outside the structure of the American labor movement.

Socialists and Anarchists

Japanese immigrant socialists and anarchists who appeared shortly after the turn of the century were keenly interested in modern labor problems. In Japan, the socialist movement started with the formation of the *Shakaishugi Kenkyūkai* (Socialist Study Society) in 1898.[22] As the name implies, this was a study group whose aim was "to examine the principles of socialism and determine whether or not they are applicable to Japan." Most of the original twelve members were Christians; three were Christians who had studied in America. Four members eventually played some kind of role in the activities of immigrant socialists and anarchists. These four were: Katayama Sen, Abe Isoo, Kaneko Kiichi, and Kōtoku Shūsui. In 1901 this study group formed the *Shakai Minshūtō* (Social Democratic Party), the first socialist political party. As soon as the proclamation and platform were released, however, the Meiji government declared the party illegal. Ordered to disband, the party was reconstituted as an educational body, headed by Abe Isoo, which sponsored public lectures on socialism and labor problems. It dared not step into the political arena since the Public Peace Preservation Act of 1900 prohibited labor agitation with the aim of organizing labor unions to fight for better wages and improved working conditions.

During the Russo-Japanese War of 1904–05, Christians and socialists protested the war, and the Meiji government clamped down on the anti-war dissenters.[23] Kōtoku Shūsui was the most outspoken socialist. In late 1903 he formed the *Heiminsha* (Commoners Society) with Sakai Toshihiko when war with Czarist Russia appeared imminent. This society published a journal in which Kōtoku started his anti-war campaign before the opening of official hostilities. Once the war broke out, his voice became more strident and his anti-war campaign took on the color of a crusade. In November 1904 Kōtoku was charged with violating the National Press Law, tried and pronounced guilty, and sentenced to five months' imprisonment.

After the war and the inauguration of the Saionji Cabinet in January 1906, the government adopted a conciliatory policy. Under this circumstance, socialists organized the *Nihon Shakaitō* (Japan Socialist Party) in February. Mindful of what had happened to the first socialist party, the founders incorporated the key phrase "we advocate socialism within the limits of the law" into the party constitution. Inasmuch as this party emphasized the use of parliamentary means to advance the welfare of the working class, the government momentarily tolerated its existence. But within a year the efficacy of parliamentary tactics came under fire. The leading critic was Kōtoku who advocated what he called "direct-action" at the first annual party convention. By direct-action Kōtoku meant the use of massive general strikes which he interpreted as the only means by which the working class could obtain power. An intense debate over this issue occurred between moderate Christian socialists and radical anarcho-syndicalists. As a result, the two sides worked out a compromise, yet elected to delete the phrase "within the limits of the law" from the party constitution, which promptly impelled the government to step in and order the dissolution of the party. Thus the Japan Socialist Party suffered the same fate as its predecessor. Subsequently, the socialist movement split into independent factions.

The High Treason Affair of 1910 marked the end of the early socialist movement. This affair involved the wholesale arrest of socialists and anarchists with the disclosure of a "plot" to assassinate the Emperor.[24] In a trial wrapped in secrecy, 26 defendants were found guilty despite the lack of conclusive evidence. The court ordered 12 of the defendants executed, 12 imprisoned for life, and 2 committed to definite terms in the military. Kōtoku was among the 12 defendants sentenced to death and actually executed in January 1911. The Meiji government contrived this affair in order to suppress the socialist movement. Historians call 1911 the beginning of a "cold, wintry period" for socialists. Driven underground or into exile abroad, they did not resurface until after World War I.

Student-laborers were predominant among Japanese immigrant socialists. By the beginning of 1904, there were two groups akin to discussion societies, one in San Francisco and another in Oakland, which came under the influence of Japanese socialists who visited the United States. The first to arrive was Katayama Sen. Katayama's initial visit to this country lasted twelve years. While working at menial jobs, he attended many different schools. He obtained B.A. and M.A. degrees at Grinnell College, Iowa, and a B.D. degree at Yale University. In 1896 he returned to his homeland and founded Kingsley Hall, a settlement house located in Tokyo at which he gave orientation sessions to youth wishing to go abroad. Based upon his own American experience, he wrote his first guide to America in 1901. Entitled *Gakusei Tobei Annai* (Student Guide to America), this guide was an instant success, selling two thousand copies within a week.[25]

In 1902 Katayama formed the *Tobei Kyōkai,* an organization which encouraged youth to emigrate to the United States. Katayama always linked this organization to the Japanese labor and socialist movements, of which he was a founder and leading figure. As editor of the *Rōdō Sekai,* he used the journal as the news outlet of the *Tobei Kyōkai* and made subscribers automatic members. When the *Rōdō Sekai* was renamed the *Shakaishugi* (Socialism) in March 1903, Katayama continued to employ the newly titled journal as the *Tobei Kyōkai*'s news outlet. In this way he influenced many youth to emigrate as he promoted the labor and socialist movement. In 1904 he returned to the United States to attend the National Convention of the American Socialist Party in Chicago and then to proceed to Amsterdam for the Sixth Congress of the Second International. In San Francisco he spoke on socialism before Japanese immigrant groups and organized the *Sōkō Nihonjin Shakaitō* (San Francisco Japanese Socialist Party).[26] One of the founders was Iwasa Sakutarō who had come to the United States with the assistance of the *Tobei Kyōkai.* According to Iwasa, who then managed the Gospel Society, this party dissolved as suddenly as it was formed. He was supposed to draft up a party constitution and by-laws, but never got around to this task. "Our minds had not progressed to the idea of starting a movement," he later recalled, and so 38 original members drifted away.[27] Yet they did undertake one activity: an anti-war meeting. Influenced by Kōtoku Shūsui's anti-war campaign, they held the meeting at the San Francisco Methodist Episcopal Church, joined by the Oakland group led by Uyeyama Jitarō and Takeuchi Tetsugorō, amid accusations of being Japanese traitors. Following the heels of Katayama, Abe Isoo visited San Francisco in 1905. Abe, too, addressed different immigrant groups, but his moderate brand of Christian socialism did not appeal to the young immigrant socialists. The decisive influence had to await the arrival of Kōtoku.

Upon his release from Sugamo Prison, Kōtoku decided to visit the United States to recover his health and observe the socialist movement here. To Albert Johnson, a veteran anarchist in California with whom he had corresponded before his imprisonment, he wrote that he had entered Sugamo "as a Marxian Socialist and returned as a radical Anarchist" and that he wished to criticize Japan from "where the pernicious hand of 'His Majesty' cannot reach."[28] He had in mind the possibility of making San Francisco a "logistical base of operation" for Japanese socialists, much as Switzerland had become for Russian revolutionaries.[29] He landed in San Francisco in December 1905. Much to his delight, he was whisked off to the San Francisco branch of the *Heiminsha* established by Oka Shigeki and others.

Thus Kōtoku's six-month sojourn began. During this short period, he engaged in many activities. He contributed articles on socialism to the *Nichibei Shimbun*. He attended the weekly Sunday night meetings of the San Francisco *Heiminsha* branch and joined the American Socialist Party. He conducted study sessions on socialism at the Gospel Society; after the Great Earthquake of April 1906, he moved to Oakland where he conducted similar sessions. He met a wide variety of people, including members of the newly organized Industrial Workers of the World (IWW). Established in 1905, with the Western Federation of Miners as its mainstay, the IWW stood for industrial unionism. Contrasted with the AFL, the IWW admitted workers on an industrial basis, regardless of skill, race, sex, or national origins. As a precursor of the Congress of Industrial Organizations (CIO), it militantly championed the cause of industrial unionism in opposition to the narrow craft unionism and racial exclusion practiced by the AFL. Kōtoku lamented that "the majority of Japanese workers, not only are ignorant of socialism, but also do not know of the existence of the IWW." Yet he was not pessimistic. "Among the Japanese in Oakland, there are new knowledgeable students and socialist thought is very prevalent," he observed. "If the comrades in San Francisco and in Oakland join hands and work together," he believed, "their influence will be considerable."[30]

The chief product of Kōtoku's sojourn was the *Shakai Kakumeitō* (Social/Revolutionary Party). Established in June 1906 in Berkeley, it brought the socialists of San Francisco and Oakland together for political action. While the party had about 40 members, the active core probably did not exceed 15. Reflecting the strong influence of Kō-toku, the party platform read:

1) We shall abolish the current system of industrial and economic competition, making all land and capital the common property of the people, thereby rooting out the cause of poverty;

2) We shall reform the traditional and superstitious class system and guarantee equal rights to all;

3) We shall eliminate national and racial prejudices and strive for true brotherhood and international peace;

4) To achieve the aforesaid goals, we recognize the necessity of uniting with the comrades of the world to carry out a great social revolution.[31]

The Social Revolutionary Party appeared in public almost immediately after its establishment. On the evening of June 10, on the corner of 8th and Franklin Streets in Oakland, it attempted to hold a street rally. Several hundred persons had congregated at this site in the heart of the Japanese and Chinese settlement. Party members made a grand entrance with red flags inscribed in black with the Chinese characters *"Shakai Kakumeitō."* No permit had been secured. The police prohibited the rally and arrested two party members.[32] Subsequent to this inauspicious debut, the party supported the International Seamen's Union of the Pacific which went on strike for higher wages in mid-June. Shipping companies sought Japanese workers as scabs through Japanese employment agencies. In the name of the international unity and brotherhood of workers, the party issued two leaflets exhorting Japanese not to become scabs, and party members descended upon the docks to dissuade those who had gone to sign up.[33]

The party's support of the Seamen's Union was ironic. As an AFL-affiliate, the union was at the forefront of the anti-Japanese exclusion movement. Union President Andrew Furuseth had definite racial biases and unwaveringly endorsed Japanese exclusion.[34] Samuel Gompers himself had dismissed Katayama Sen as a "presumptuous Jap" with a "leprous mouth whose utterances show this mongrel's perverseness, ignorance and maliciousness. . . . "[35] American socialists also favored exclusion, making the Social Revolutionary Party's action doubly ironic. While proclaiming the international solidarity of workers, American socialists rallied behind organized labor's opposition to all Asian labor immigration. In 1906 the California Socialist Party adopted a resolution favoring restriction.[36] The National Executive Committee of the American Socialist Party adopted a similar resolution in 1907.[37] Some socialists marshalled economic reasons to mask their position on the question. Others justified exclusion by theoretical subterfuge:

> . . . The rational Japanese socialist . . . will certainly see that if the capitalists in Japan can ship their surplus millions to America, the Japanese labor movement, if it depends, as those who favor unlimited immigration into this country assert, on the "philosophy of misery" will be injured by this deportation of the very element that tends to make the misery in Japan sufficiently keen to breed revolution.[38]

Disguising the racial motive, this line of reasoning concluded with the assertion that "the working class of each nation owes its first duty to itself." The working class of America was by definition the *white* working class! Other socialists were open racists. Ernest Untermann, for example, bluntly said: "I am determined that my race shall be supreme in this country and in the world."[39]

The racial factor behind the rising clamor for Japanese exclusion did not escape the attention of Japanese socialists. In 1905 Abe Isoo observed that "it is rooted in race prejudice."[40] In 1907 the Japan Socialist Party sent an open letter to American socialists on the exclusion question. Signed by Kōtoku Shūsui, Sakai Toshihiko, and Nishikawa Kōjirō, it read:

> Comrades: We believe that the expulsion question of the Japanese laborers in California is much due to racial prejudice. The Japanese Socialist Party, therefore, hopes that the American Socialist Party will endeavor to bring the question to a satisfactory issue in accordance with the spirit of international unity among workingmen. We also ask the American Socialist Party to acquaint us with its opinion as to this question.[41]

The American Socialist Party never answered this open letter. Kaneko Kiichi, through whom the letter was distributed, pinpointed the issue when he asked "whether or not American socialists are going to be true to the exhortation of Marx—'Workingmen of all countries, Unite'—or whether they are to encourage contention and division on the ground of race prejudice."[42] Although he was listed as an original member of the Social Revolutionary Party, Kaneko was not in California. He was active as a socialist in Chicago, and later in Kansas. In his judgment, American socialists had revealed themselves to be uniformly bigoted:

> I was really disappointed to have found that the Socialists in this country are not altogether good fighters. . . . Not only have they been silent in this matter but they have vainly tried to narrow their socialism by

joining with the cheap political grafters and so-called labor leaders in
the disapprobation of Japanese immigration. So far as I know, not a
single Socialist paper in this country spoke out plainly on this Japanese
question without showing race prejudice.[43]

In short, the Social Revolutionary Party emerged in the midst of the
exclusion movement, and Japanese socialists were aware that American
socialists, too, were very much a part of it.

Two subsequent events brought the Social Revolutionary Party
into sensational light. The party's official journal was called the *Kakumei* (Revolution). Published out of a lodginghouse operated by Uyeyama Jitarō in Berkeley, the first issue appeared on December 10, 1906.
Somehow a copy found its way into the hands of the secretary of the
San Francisco School Board who passed it on to the newspapers. An
uproar ensued caused by an English passage which read: "Our policy
is toward the overthrow of Mikado, King, President as representing
the Capitalist Class as soon as possible, and we do not hesitate as to
means."[44] The San Francisco *Chronicle* headlined its story "Secret Service Men on the Trail of Japanese Publishers—Japs Favor Killing of
President Roosevelt." The San Francisco *Examiner* echoed the *Chronicle:* "Japanese Anarchists Publish Paper Urging President's Death."
The San Francisco *Call* had an almost identical tone: "Japanese Socialists Threaten Roosevelt—Violent Pronouncement Is Issued." And the
Berkeley *Daily Gazette* voiced its own alarm: "Hotbed of Japanese
Anarchists Located Here—the Yellow Peril." In each instance the cen-
tral focus was placed on the implied threat to assassinate President
Theodore Roosevelt.[45]

The authorities began an investigation and the question of responsibility became crucial. The Japanese consul explored with immigration
officials the possibility of having the responsible persons deported. Ultimately, the matter came before a Special Board of Inquiry of the San
Francisco Immigration Commission, and Takeuchi Tetsugorō, who
assumed responsibility for publishing the *Kakumei,* was ordered to appear before it. A native of Iwate Prefecture, Takeuchi had arrived in
1903 as a draft evader. He appeared with Austin Lewis, a lawyer and
one-time socialist candidate for the governorship of California. To
exonerate himself, Takeuchi pleaded his knowledge of English was so
deficient that he made the error of titling his journal "Revolution"
instead of "Evolution." According to the existing statutes relating to
anarchists, Takeuchi could not be deported. The government either
had to prove that he had been an anarchist at the time of his entry,

or that he had been in the country less than three full years and had committed an overt act of anarchism. Takeuchi had only expressed anarchistic thoughts.

The *Kakumei*'s content was anarchistic, especially the Japanese section which exuded youthful exuberance. In the first issue, an article covered the historical development of socialism. Deeming parliamentary tactics *passé*, it ended with the exhortation: "People, wake up! And arise! Arise and seize your freedom! Seize your happiness! Destroy evil governments, the enemies of freedom, with bombs!" Another article expounded on the revolutionary usage of the bomb:

> The only revolutionary means is the bomb. The bomb is also the means to harvest the revolution. The bomb is also the means to destroy the bourgeoisie. Today, with the merging of capital and the rapid growth of the poor, the different policies of reform and parliamentarianism are equivalent to a child squirting a water pistol into a conflagration.[46]

An anti-Emperor system current also ran through the pages of the *Kakumei*. Labelling the Meiji shibboleth *"chūkun aikoku"* (loyalty to Emperor and love of Nation) as a "slave morality," the journal expressed contempt for the institution as a tool of the ruling class, a denial of scientific knowledge, and a vestige of superstitious belief. The third issue reprinted Kōtoku Shūsui's speech on "direct-action" which he delivered at the first annual convention of the Japan Socialist Party.

The next incident spelled the end of the Social Revolutionary Party. On the morning of November 3, 1907, a few party members tacked on the entrance of the Japanese consulate in San Francisco an "Open Letter to Mutsuhito Emperor of Japan" and distributed copies throughout the Japanese community. The letter declared that the Emperor and the writers had evolved from "monkeys" and therefore were "equals"; that the Emperor is responsible for the poverty and suffering of the poor; that he is "vanity" personified if he believes the "fabrications" scholars relate about his divine origins. And it concluded:

> When spring arrives, flowers bloom; when summer comes, fruit ripen; this is the power of nature. When revolutions arise, it is not because someone brings them about; they arise naturally. And terrorism comes at the end of the process.
>
> Don't mistake this for an empty armchair theory. Terrorism is now succeeding in both Russia and France. Our terrorism will appear after careful study of the successes and failures of terrorism in these advanced

nations. Mutsuhito, pitiful Mutsuhito, your life will not be long. A bomb planted beside you will soon explode. Farewell![47]

This open letter was signed "Anarchist-Assassin." The local Japanese community rose up in arms, for November 3 was *Tenchōsetsu,* a Japanese national holiday commemorating the Meiji Emperor's birthday, which most Japanese immigrants honored with nationalistic reverence. The Japanese consul again tried to have the responsible party members deported. Because a few members had drafted the open letter without consulting everyone, a split occurred within the party. So what began as a small youthful group of Issei socialists and anarchists organized for political action came to a sudden ending, with members either returning to Japan or dispersing to other locales.

Fresno Labor League

Another more meaningful organization succeeded the Social Revolutionary Party. This was the *Furesuno Rōdō Dōmeikai* (Fresno Labor League) established in August 1908. In 1908 upwards of 5,000 Japanese laborers converged on the Fresno area to pick grapes. The appearance of a former member of the Social Revolutionary Party led to the formation of the Labor League. The central figure was none other than Takeuchi Tetsugorō. After the split in the party, he first went to Vacaville where he worked as an agricultural laborer. From there he moved to Fresno and organized Japanese field hands into the Labor League which became an incipient labor union with a sizable membership of about 2,000 workers.[48] From its inception the League grappled with the concrete problems of Japanese harvest hands. Neither anarchistic in tone nor in fact, the League goals were:

1) to prevent the lowering of wages and to secure the highest possible;
2) to attack vigorously the unfair competition of corrupt labor contractors; and
3) to unify members to take concerted action to elevate the status of workers and to gain the confidence of grape-growers.[49]

As the 1908 picking season opened, several renegade Japanese labor contractors appeared. The Central California Contractors Association, composed of 53 Japanese labor contractors, set $1.65 per ton as the rate for harvesting grapes. All contractors had agreed upon this set rate. The Association foresaw some difficulties with one of the biggest vineyards, the 900-acre Tarpey Ranch, because of troubles during the previous season. In early August, contrary to the set rate and to the dismay of the Association, three contractors from Kings County contracted with this vineyard for $1.25 per ton. The Association appealed to Japanese laborers to boycott these "corrupt" contractors. Issuing a circular couched in nationalistic language, it claimed that it was the duty of Japanese laborers to remit money to enrich Japan, while the contractors in question were only interested in lining their own pockets at their workers' expense. The *Shin Sekai* lined up behind the Association. It accused the three contractors of lending substance to the charge that Japanese laborers worked for cheap wages. Japanese laborers, in its view, should be demanding the same wages as white workers.[50]

The three goals of the Labor League were formulated within the context of this controversy. The $1.25 per ton rate inevitably meant lower wages for any laborer who was hired by the three contractors. The Labor League actively opposed the contractors, dispatching members to Fowler and other places to obstruct their attempts to recruit laborers. The League members were so effective that no Japanese would work for the three contractors, forcing them to hire Mexican, Indian, and Korean laborers to fulfill their contract with the Tarpey Ranch. The Labor League also opposed the Contractors Association, and Takeuchi himself endeavored to secure a contract with the Tarpey Ranch on behalf of the League. To this extent, despite Takeuchi's failure, the Labor League can be interpreted as an effort to organize Japanese laborers free from labor contractors into a genuine agricultural labor union.

The League published a weekly from November 1908 to September 1909. Called the *Rōdō* (Labor), its editorial staff was composed of Takeuchi and Matsushita Zenpei in Fresno and three former members of the Social Revolutionary Party who had remained in the San Francisco area. From the few extant issues of the *Rōdō*, it is possible to get an idea of its content. Articles attacking the Emperor system, the capitalist class, and militarism were prominent, along with a constant appeal to workers to unite:

According to recent statistics, out of 1,000 persons 343 ruling class members live to the age of 60 year olds, but only 256 members of the working class. Why is this so? We workers die early from physical ailments caused by excessive labor, by working in dangerous factories or in mines with inadequate facilities. Or by working long hours with an injury, by unsanitary living conditions injurious to health, and by mental disorders caused by living in perpetual poverty.

But no matter how dangerous the work is, no matter how long the working hours are, we workers have no right to air our grievances. For if we express our likes and dislikes, we will never be able to secure work and will starve pitifully to death.

If one thinks in these terms, what difference is there between workers today and the slaves of old? . . .

Today the workers of the world are awakening to how wretched their conditions are. The workers in Japan are awakening. This is natural. Thus we workers also must unite.[51]

Other articles advocated the public ownership of land and the means of production. Labor unions

cannot take effective measures to cope with the evils which arise from the private property system and laissez-faire economic competition, nor with unemployment and dips in wages which accompany economic depressions. . . .

Thus if we workers are to seek our own welfare, we must not stop at denouncing exploiting employers, greedy merchants, and corrupt bosses. We must go one more step forward and destroy the private property system which always spawns unemployment and poverty. We workers must make all land and the means of production public property for society as a whole and eradicate laissez-faire competition.[52]

In 1909 the Labor League undertook two major activities. First, it convened a labor convention which coincided with the start of the grape-picking season. Representatives from Sacramento, Los Angeles, San Francisco, and Fresno addressed an audience of 300 workers. Declaring that the welfare of workers could be only advanced by "worker unity," the Labor League resolved:

1) to affiliate with labor groups in other locales and to establish Labor League branches elsewhere to further the labor movement;

2) to publish an English monthly to educate and inform ignorant anti-Japanese elements; and

3) to affiliate with labor groups in other locales to ban Chinese gambling.[53]

Secondly, the League held a joint rally in Japantown with the Fresno branch of the IWW. The Fresno branch head as well as Italian and Mexican IWW speakers addressed the rally. Echoing the IWW, Takeuchi himself talked on the international brotherhood of workers and the necessity of workers to unite irrespective of color or nationality.

Despite the resolutions passed at the labor convention, the League failed to expand its activities. It neither established branches in other localities nor published an English monthly. Indeed, it ceased publication of the *Rōdō* on September 14, 1909. One explanation for this setback is the lack of funds; litigation costs to defend Takeuchi in a court case drained the League's limited financial resources. Japanese immigrant newspapers were not sympathetic to the League. The *Sōkō Shimbun* (*San Francisco News*) in particular carried caustic articles by Ōtsuka Zenjirō, a conservative who assailed the League as an anarchist organization. Infuriated by these articles, Takeuchi had gone to San Francisco in November 1908 ostensibly to challenge Ōtsuka to a public debate. Instead, a knife fight occurred between the two men, resulting in costly legal expenses to defend Takeuchi in court.

Yet the cessation of the *Rōdō*, coupled with the League's failure to expand its activities, was a symptom of a larger problem. The League undoubtedly experienced the inherent problem of organizing a migratory labor force. The fact that most Japanese laborers remained in the Fresno area for only the harvest season—a short two and a half months—made it difficult, if not impossible, to maintain an ongoing, cohesive organization. The composition of the labor force also changed with each new season. In addition, the League faced a hostile Japanese immigrant press and local Japanese community opposition. Local groups obstructed the League by branding it an anarchist organization. And when news of the High Treason Affair in Japan reached Fresno in 1910, it made it impossible for anyone identified with Kōtoku Shūsui, as Takeuchi and other immigrant socialists were, to operate in any Japanese community. Signalling the end of the League, Takeuchi left the Fresno area sometime in 1910. Hence the League lasted only two years, but its short duration in no way detracts from the fact that it was a significant early attempt to organize Japanese field hands into an agricultural labor union.

Japanese Coal Miners and the United Mine Workers of America at Rock Springs, Wyoming

There was one notable exception to organized labor's exclusion of Japanese labor. That was the case of the United Mine Workers of America (UMWA) whose locals in southern Wyoming admitted Japanese (and a few Chinese) coal miners in 1907. Concentrated in the southern part of the state with Rock Springs as the center, the Wyoming coal industry dates from the appearance of the Union Pacific Railroad, which was constructed across southern Wyoming in the 1860s. The railroad first exploited the rich bituminous fields there to fuel its locomotives, opening mines at Carbon and Rock Springs in 1868 and at Almy in the following year.[54] In 1869 Wyoming's total coal output did not exceed 50,000 tons, but the nascent industry rapidly expanded as the Union Pacific and independent coal companies later opened additional mines, principally in the two southwestern counties of Sweetwater and Uinta. By 1907 Wyoming ranked twelfth in the nation among coal-producing states and second only to Colorado in the Rocky Mountain region. Representing 1.3 percent of national coal production, the state produced 6.2 million tons in that year. Of this aggregate figure, the southern field, mined by seven separate coal companies, accounted for 4.5 million tons, with Sweetwater and Uinta Counties alone producing 3.9 million tons.[55] Operating through its subsidiary, the Union Pacific Coal Company, the Union Pacific Railroad was the major coal producer with extensive mineral rights. The Union Pacific Coal Company's 1907 output of 2.9 million tons, mined at Rock Springs in Sweetwater County, at Cumberland in Uinta County, and at Hanna in Carbon County, constituted 64.4 percent of the southern field's total production. The unrivalled giant of the seven coal operators, the company employed 2,899 out of the 4,935 men who worked the southern mines in 1907.[56]

   In the late nineteenth century, the labor movement in Wyoming followed the national pattern in many ways.[57] In the early 1880s local assemblies of the Knights of Labor were formed by coal miners and railroad workers at Almy, Rock Springs, and Carbon. Almy with 700 men was the biggest mining camp in the territory, and the local assembly there had considerable influence in community affairs. Yet no assembly had wage-scale or working agreements with the Union Pacific. As the Knights of Labor declined in the next decade, newly organized locals of the American Railway Union (ARU) replaced the assemblies. Active ARU unions existed all along the Union Pacific line at Cheyenne, Laramie, Rawlins, Green River, and Evanston at the time of the Great Pullman Strike of 1894. These locals participated in that strike. Ending in disastrous defeat for Eugene V. Debs and the ARU, the strike marked their demise. The UMWA was founded in 1890, but never penetrated into Wyoming in the 1890s. Limiting its activities to east of the Mississippi, the union struggled to establish itself in the older coalfields of Pennsylvania, Ohio, Indiana, Illinois, Alabama, and a few other states. Thus Wyoming's coal miners were unorganized until after the turn of the century.

Occasional letters from Rock Springs published in the *United Mine Workers' Journal* allude to the obstacles which hindered the formation of local unions. In 1903 one miner penned a series of illuminating letters. Claiming that he had been "agitating among the men," he found that "the majority of the English-speaking people are in favor of being organized." "Of course there are forty-four different nationalities here," he continued in referring to the heterogeneity of the labor force, "but the only ones I think that will be troublesome are the Chinese, but they are not strong enough to cause much trouble." If the UMWA deemed it worthwhile to dispatch organizers, he recommended persons who "can converse in different languages—Finnish, Japanese and Italian, included."[58] He also described the Union Pacific's employment policy. "A man comes here to the U.P. mine," he wrote, "and asks for a job. The boss will ask him what nationality he is." According to the correspondent, the boss did "this in order to hold a balance between the nationalities so they can't get together and agree on anything." In the end, once the boss "finds out what nation he belongs to, and if there is not too many of that nationality here he will get a job, otherwise not."[59]

Efforts to organize meant summary dismissal. The same miner said that his boss "intended to fire every man that looked like a United Mine Worker."[60] He reported that he in fact had been discharged three times because of his organizing activities. He was released first by the Central Coal and Coke Company, the major coal operator at Rock Springs next to the Union Pacific. He then secured work with the Union Pacific Coal Company, only to be fired again. Finally, he became a section hand with the Union Pacific Railroad, but once again met the identical fate. Blacklisted by all three companies, he lost all means of livelihood, since there were no other sources of employment at Rock Springs. To him the mining town, understandably, was a "tough place" that "will take time and money to organize . . . because when a man gets fired . . . there is nothing that he can get to do. . . . "[61] Another miner wrote of similar experiences. He and a handful of men actually formed a UMWA local. To guard against company spies, they met "two miles in the country on Sunday morning before breakfast."[62] In spite of this precaution, his employer learned of his secret activities and promptly dismissed him.

These letters attest to the severe handicaps under which labor organizers worked at Rock Springs and suggest fundamental reasons why the miners remained unorganized. Staunchly anti-union, the Union Pacific Coal Company and the Central Coal and Coke Company fired anyone suspected of union sympathies, preventing the UMWA from making inroads into the mining camps of Rock Springs. Through the divide-and-rule practice of hiring many foreign nationalities, they kept labor in a state of disunity. In connection with the Union Pacific's employment policy, the Wyoming *Tribune* observed that the company's "employment of miners of various nationalities has been adopted with success, it being found almost impossible to hold these various races together."[63] In short, Rock Springs, the center of the southern Wyoming coal industry, was a bastion of anti-unionism.

UMWA locals were founded at Rock Springs in 1907. The circumstances of their origin are crucial to an understanding of why the UMWA admitted Japanese and Chinese miners. In the late spring of that year, UMWA organizers from northern Wyoming appeared at Rock Springs and launched a unionization drive. UMWA locals had been organized in northern Wyoming at Dietz in Sheridan County in 1903. Together with the UMWA locals of Montana, the northern locals constituted District 22. Originally, the UMWA national executive board had assigned southern Wyoming to District 15, whose principal jurisdiction was Colorado, but the board reassigned it to District 22 in October 1903. Having been invited to organize the southern coalfield by some of the miners of Rock Springs, Thomas Gibson, District 22 president, and other district officials arrived at the mining town on May 19, 1907. Michael F. Purcell, a member of the international executive board, appeared on the following day.

The organizing drive proved successful. Within a brief time, the miners of Rock Springs rallied behind the call to establish UMWA locals. The organizers planned a mass assembly of miners on the evening of May 21, which fell on Tuesday. Aware of this scheduled meeting, the Union Pacific Coal Company and the Central Coal and Coke Company posted notices throughout the mining camps during that day, warning their miners that if they joined the UMWA they would be terminated. The coal operators threatened to lock out anyone who enrolled in the union. The evening assembly, held at the local opera house, attracted a throng of miners. Thomas Gibson and Michael F. Purcell appealed to them to join the UMWA. Besides the outside organizers, local Italian, Finnish, Austrian, Swedish, and Slavic miners spoke in their native tongues and voiced support for the establishment of local unions. At the close of the meeting, approximately 400 miners stepped forward and signed up with the union organizers.[64]

The next day the coal operators carried out their threat. They locked out the miners who had signed up, but the reprisal did not discourage other miners. On the contrary, it had the reverse effect of galvanizing the miners to unite against the operators. As word of the unionization drive and of the operators' lockout spread, other miners joined the UMWA who in turn were locked out. By May 23, Thursday, the operators were forced to close down most mines for lack of nonunion miners, and the Central Coal and Coke Company, as an added reprisal, began to order its miners to vacate company housing. Two days later the shutdown was complete; Rock Springs did not have a single mine in operation by Saturday. Every nationality was represented among the pro-union miners, except the Japanese and Chinese who continued to report to work. In the ensuing week, on May 28, the Union Pacific Coal Company rounded up the Japanese and Chinese, who had been employed in various mines, and had them, along with a few white miners, escorted by sheriff's deputies to one mine. This concentration of the nonunion labor force, consisting predominantly of Japanese miners, enabled the company to resume operation of one mine. During the second week of the lockout, however, save for this solitary mine, the shutdown continued.

Confronted by the solidarity of the miners, the operators attempted to drive a wedge between them. Both the Union Pacific Coal Company and the Central Coal and Coke Company on June 1 offered a flat 10 percent wage increase, applicable across the board, to any miner who elected to resume work.[65] While the operators still refused adamantly to recognize the UMWA, they guaranteed that no miner would be penalized for pro-union sentiments. This offer was calculated to split the ranks of the pro-union miners, but the ruse did not work. The locked-out miners maintained their unity of purpose and declined to report back to the mines. The wage hike enticingly dangled before the miners failed to induce them to break ranks, forcing the operators to realize their inability to stop the formation of UMWA locals.

A logical tactic for the operators would have been to replace the pro-union labor force with other miners. The operators did not have such an option as far as more Japanese miners were concerned. Two months before the labor dispute at Rock Springs broke out, Theodore Roosevelt had stopped the Japanese labor exodus from the Hawaiian Islands by his executive order of March 14, 1907. The sudden decline that this brought about in Japanese labor contracting precluded the operators from obtaining additional Japanese miners. The *Mineral In-*

dustry, an annual devoted to the mining enterprise, went so far as to assert that "the utter impossibility of securing any kind of efficient labor prevented the [Union Pacific] company from opposing the union organizers."[66] With no alternative supply of labor, the operators were unable to bring in a substitute labor force.

The Union Pacific Coal Company therefore announced an emergency conference of all coal operators in the southern field and union officials of District 22 to avoid a continuation of the lockout. Convened on June 8 in Omaha, Nebraska, at the home office of the Union Pacific Railroad, the conference produced a temporary settlement. All southern coal operators agreed to grant recognition to UMWA locals, to permit union organizers to enter unorganized camps, and to raise wages by 10 percent. Thomas Gibson and Michael F. Purcell, the union representatives who participated in the conference, agreed to order all miners back to work under these terms. No specific contract was worked out by the two sides. Instead they deferred negotiation of this matter until July 15, at which time they agreed to meet again in Denver, Colorado. Having gained recognition, a 10 percent wage boost, and the right to organize the entire southern field, the miners of Rock Springs accepted the temporary settlement and returned to work on June 10. In less than three weeks, the UMWA had scored a major victory.

John Mitchell, president of the UMWA, played a role in setting up the Omaha conference. In the midst of the shutdown, the Union Pacific appointed John J. Hart as new manager of its coal operations in southern Wyoming. Upon assuming his post on June 1, Hart arranged the Omaha conference with Mitchell. Mitchell himself was no fiery labor radical. Disavowing belief in irreconcilable class conflicts, he espoused a philosophy of cooperation between labor and capital.[67] In accord with his philosophy, he maintained cordial relations with a number of coal operators and managers. Mitchell personally knew Hart who sought out his help to settle the dispute at Rock Springs. Just prior to the Omaha conference, Mitchell wrote to an union associate that "prospects are very favorable for a satisfactory settlement of our difficulties at Rock Springs and vicinity." His judgment rested on the fact that "John Hart took charge of the management of the U.P. Company last Saturday and immediately communicated with me asking that some one be authorized to negotiate a settlement," which Mitchell did by designating Thomas Gibson and Michael F. Purcell.[68] Two days after the conference, he wrote about Hart to Harry N. Taylor, his closest confidante among coal operators:

I presume you have learned that John Hart has been given management of the Union Pacific Coal Company's operations in southern Wyoming. Rock Springs has been the citadel of nonunionism for many years. Just before John took over we had succeeded in organizing Rock Springs and the company had closed down the mines, but I am pleased to say that immediately upon taking charge, John communicated with me, a conference was arranged and a settlement effected. I am of the opinion that John has an important place and I hope he gets along all right.[69]

How Mitchell's friendship with Hart influenced the outcome of the Omaha conference is unclear. What is indisputable is that the conference was arranged by Hart with Mitchell.[70]

Japanese miners were admitted into the newly recognized UMWA locals after the Omaha conference. The miners of Rock Springs on June 9 held a mass rally to welcome Gibson and Purcell back from Omaha and to celebrate their victory. At this jubilant celebration, Purcell is reported to have said that "nothing should be held against the men who had not as yet joined the union" and that "they should be received with open arms."[71] To complete the task of unionizing, organizers quickly entered the mining camps outside of Rock Springs at Cumberland, Superior, Kemmerer, Frontier, Oakley, Hanna, and other places where Japanese miners were also employed. In mid-June the Wyoming *Tribune* published rumors that the UMWA would demand the discharge of all Japanese nonunion miners, but on July 9 quoted Thomas Gibson as saying "that arrangements are now being made to organize the Japanese miners in the west."[72]

On behalf of the Japanese miners, three Japanese labor contractors took the initiative and negotiated with a union committee for admission into the union.[73] Unfortunately, what transpired between the Japanese and union representatives is impossible to ascertain, for there are no detailed accounts of the negotiations. That the union formally considered the admission of Asian miners is verifiable, nevertheless. The UMWA international executive board on June 28 entertained a motion in regard to this question. Specifically entitled "The Japanese in Southern Wyoming," the motion read "that wherever Japanese or Chinese are employed in or about the mines, our organizers be instructed to admit them into our organization."[74] Seconded by Michael F. Purcell, the motion was passed by the members of the board, including John Mitchell, without any recorded discussion or dissent. Whatever happened in the local negotiations, the UMWA international executive board on June 28 officially sanctioned the admission of Japanese and Chinese miners in southern Wyoming.

In preparation for the Denver joint conference, District 22 union officials convened a district convention of Wyoming locals in Denver on July 10. The convention featured the election of a scale committee and the formulation of demands that were to be presented to the coal operators. Since it had been decided at Omaha that any negotiated contract should cover the entire state of Wyoming, delegates of northern UMWA locals attended the convention. As official delegates from Rock Springs and Frontier, the three Japanese labor contractors— Kondō Chikai, Suzuki Rokuhiko, and Ueda Heitarō—took part in the proceedings. The Colorado and Wyoming press ascribed great significance to the appearance of the Japanese delegates. The Rocky Mountain *News* declared: "For the first time in the history of the United States, Japanese . . . are present as recognized delegates at a convention of union men. The other delegates are exceedingly friendly toward them, and the least intimation of a slight towards the Japs is received belligerently."[75] The Denver *Post* stressed how the Japanese conducted themselves. "The Japanese . . . are the most interested of the delegates in what is going on. They are regular in their attendance and do not hesitate to take part in the discussions." White delegates, the *Post* reported, were trying "to find out just what sort of union material the little brown are making in the miners' organization."[76] Underscoring the importance the Denver press attached to the presence of the Japanese, both newspapers published large photographs of them. The Wyoming *Tribune* viewed the sight of the Japanese "sitting among the delegates of white persuasion" as a "singular spectacle."[77] With the 1885 massacre of Chinese miners at Rock Springs in mind, the Cheyenne *Daily Leader* described the event as a "most remarkable paradox" and interpreted it as evidence of the "reincarnation of the union spirit among the miners."[78] The *United Mine Workers' Journal* was less effusive. In a terse editorial, it stated that "one of the most agreeable features of the convention of District 22 is the presence of . . . Japanese delegates thereto."[79]

The Denver joint conference opened on July 15 as scheduled. John Mitchell himself participated in it. Although arriving in the mile-high city to recuperate from illness, he still managed to join the contract talks. During the conference, the three Japanese delegates conferred with him, and shortly after their meeting handed him a written proposal. According to the three men, because of "different language, custom and manners," there had been "misunderstandings" between Japanese laborers and the union, including "a Sheridan local agreement" which had "discriminated" against the Japanese.[80] To avert future misunderstandings, they proposed that Mitchell accept one of two schemes. The first called for the election of a Japanese officer in each district, subdistrict, and local where Japanese miners were employed. Such officers would govern the Japanese miners in accordance with UMWA regulations. The second entailed the establishment of an "Oriental or Japanese Department" in each district, subdistrict, and local where Japanese miners were employed which, presumably with hired staff, would perform the same role as elected Japanese officers.

In drafting this proposal, the Japanese delegates assuredly had in mind organized labor's hostility towards Japanese labor in Wyoming and elsewhere. A few Japanese section hands worked for the Chicago, Burlington and Quincy in and around Sheridan in 1907, but there were no Japanese miners employed in the surrounding coal mines. The so-called Sheridan local agreement, signed between the Northern Wyoming Coal Operators' Association and the northern UMWA locals, contained a clause which had excluded Japanese miners from northern Wyoming.[81] Opposition to Japanese miners also existed in northern Colorado where they were excluded in like manner. In 1904 the northern UMWA locals first sent a delegate to the UMWA national convention. A delegate from Dietz, Wyoming, submitted a "Japanese resolution" in that year, the first of its kind ever considered by the national body. Advocating the exlusion of Japanese labor, the resolution read:

> We . . . view with alarm the pouring of cheap Japanese labor into our western States. We believe that Americans today, as in 1776, stand for independence and the noblest manhood; the Japanese laborer, as we find him in our mines and other industries, stands for neither. The Jap, like the Chinaman, works for whatever the company is pleased to pay him, and returns a portion of his earnings regularly to a Japanese agent, who is called "boss," doubtless to evade technically the law prohibiting contract labor.
>
> He holds firm allegiance to his native country, and scorns the idea of American citizenship.
>
> Morally and industrially he is a curse to the American nation, and should be excluded from our shores.
>
> Therefore, we pray Congress to enact a law excluding the Japanese as well as the Chinese.[82]

Combined with the Sheridan local agreement, this 1904 anti-Japanese resolution, proposed by the Wyoming delegation, reflected the penetration of the Japanese exclusion movement into the Rocky Mountain region. Actually adopted by the UMWA national convention, it was referred to national officials for appropriate action.

Conforming to the established policy of the AFL, the UMWA national leadership opposed all Asian immigration. As UMWA president from 1898 to 1908, John Mitchell consistently backed organized labor's demand for the exclusion of all Asian immigrants. In 1901 he favored the reenactment of the Geary Act to extend Chinese exclusion beyond 1902. "It is especially important to mine workers that this law be re-enacted," he reasoned, "as we should unquestionably be the first to feel the baleful effects of Asiatic competition. . . . "[83] Here Mitchell touched upon the basic rationale for his opposition to Asian immigration. To him Asian laborers had a lower standard of living than native or immigrant white workers. Consequently, white workers suffered degradation as they were thrown into competition with them. In order to preserve the higher standard of living of American labor, it therefore was imperative to terminate all immigration from Asia. Moreover, Asian laborers were unassimilable. Mitchell never deviated from this position. In March 1904 he stated it succinctly: "I am opposed to the admission of the Chinese and Japanese because these two races always work for low wages and can not be assimilated."[84]

The *United Mine Workers' Journal* was equally, if not more, anti-Japanese. Echoing Mitchell's position, the journal in 1901 editorially favored amending the Geary Act "to exclude all Asiatics, the Japanese as well as the Chinese."[85] As organized labor in San Francisco intensified its agitation against Japanese immigration and attracted national attention to this issue, the journal carried many anti-Japanese articles, many of which were reprinted from publications of the Asiatic Exclusion League and the Sailors' Union of the Pacific. During the 1906 San Francisco school crisis, the journal even endorsed the city school board resolution segregating Japanese pupils in the public schools. Going well beyond the argument of adverse labor competition, it justified the board's action because of "the utter abuse of morals or anything pertaining to morality among the Japanese." In its judgment, "the people of California are clearly within their own rights and should stand firm against the encroachments of this immoral race."[86]

The proposal submitted to John Mitchell by the three Japanese delegates at the Denver joint conference is clear evidence that they were aware of the UMWA's hostility to Japanese labor. As far as they were concerned, the admission of the Japanese miners into the UMWA did not guarantee equal treatment. Thus they tendered the proposal to Mitchell in order to insure fair treatment within the union. The Japanese delegates undoubtedly also had a personal motive. For once the Japanese miners were admitted into the union, all Japanese labor contractors became superfluous. The contractors no longer were in a position to control them. So the delegates thought of themselves as potential elected officers or hired staff members in the two alternative schemes. Both motives, one altruistic and the other personal, lay behind their proposal.

Mitchell refused to accede to the proposal. He rejected the plan of a special department. If such a department were to be established for the Japanese and Chinese, it meant that similar departments would have to be set up for other nationalities. Arguing that it would be divisive, he declined to endorse the plan. He likewise saw no merit in the idea of specially elected Japanese union officers. In his opinion, regardless of race, color, or nationality, all union officials should be elected on the basis of their qualifications. Nevertheless, "as a matter of expediency and for the better understanding of all," Mitchell conceded that "it is necessary in some communities to make selection of local officers and interpretors [sic] from among those speaking different language[s]." And "in the case of the Japanese," he concluded, "it would be advisable, indeed necessary, to have one Japanese interpretor [sic] in each local union of which Japanese are members."[87] In sum, except for acknowledging the need for interpreters, Mitchell turned down the proposal of the Japanese delegates.

As a result of the Denver joint conference, the Wyoming coal operators and the UMWA signed the first statewide agreement in the history of the Wyoming coal industry.[88] By the terms of the agreement, all operators recognized the eight-hour day and the check-off system. They also agreed to an average wage increase of 20 percent and to improved working conditions, including specific provisions governing safety, health, and checkweighmen. The United Mine Workers' Journal extolled John Mitchell's role in the negotiation of the contract, calling it the "latest exhibition of his wisdom and ability" and "a dual victory" for both the miners and the operators.[89] Effective September 1, 1907, the agreement settled the labor dispute in the southern Wyoming coalfield. In the sequence of events which led up to this final settlement, the UMWA had admitted Japanese miners.

In contrast to the UMWA's general opposition to Asian labor, the union's acceptance of Japanese miners at Rock Springs appears incongruous. The explanation of this apparent paradox lies in the reasons the UMWA admitted them. Certain inferences can be drawn from the known facts. The local negotiations between the Japanese

labor contractors and union representatives took place after the Omaha
conference but before the international executive board's decision to
admit Asian miners, that is, between June 9 and June 27. From the
contractors' point of view, it was in their self-interest to have sought
the admission of the Japanese miners into the union once the operators
recognized the UMWA at the Omaha conference. The union had
won, and the contractors were fearful that the union would insist
upon the dismissal of the Japanese miners. In such an event, they
would have lost their income as contractors. It makes sense for them
to have negotiated with the union to salvage what they could. Similarly, it stands to reason that the Japanese miners wanted to be admitted into the union because they faced the prospect of losing their jobs.

The self-interest of the Japanese side coincided with that of the
union as well as of the operators. On the one hand, being the single
largest group of miners, the Japanese (with the few Chinese) would
have posed a potential threat to the fledgling local unions if they had
not accepted them. For as long as the Japanese miners were employed
as nonunion miners, and at a cheaper wage rate, the operators could
have manipulated this nonunion labor force to their own advantage.
Asian miners always had been paid less than white miners; in the first
five months of 1907 the Union Pacific Coal Company's basic daily
wage differed by $1.10—Asians started at $1.65, whites at $2.75.[90]
From this perspective, it was also decidedly in the self-interest of the
union to have admitted the Japanese miners, notwithstanding the ani-
mosity it harbored towards them. On the other hand, the operators
had recognized the union for lack of an alternative supply of labor and
could not afford to dismiss the Japanese miners. Expecting a shortage
of labor in the fall months when coal demand always rose, they needed
the sizable Japanese labor force. That the Union Pacific Coal Company
was in fact experiencing an acute labor shortage was confirmed in
August 1907 by a report in the *Cheyenne Daily Leader*.

In theory, the union should have demanded the elimination of the
wage disparity between white and Asian miners to deprive the operators of the economic benefits derived from it. Yet when the first union
contract came into effect, the differential was reduced, not abolished
altogether. The Union Pacific Coal Company's basic daily wage disparity was cut from $1.10 to 30¢ and remained at this level through
two successive contract periods through 1910.[91] In the bargaining between the union and the operators, the operators, in all likelihood,
agreed to the reduction in the wage differential but not to its entire
elimination in order to preserve some economic benefits, to which

position the union must have acquiesced as a compromise. One Japanese source intimates that in return for the union's admission of Japanese miners, the operators promised not to bring in any new Japanese miners.[92] Although uncorroborated by other sources, such a deal seems highly plausible, as it would have assured the union that the Japanese labor force would not be enlarged, making the union more amenable to accept the existing Japanese miners, while permitting the operators to retain the very labor force they needed. And the compromise in the wage differential as well as John Mitchell's labor philosophy of cooperation and friendship with John J. Hart would have been consonant with the deal. Since the operators did not have the option of enlarging the Japanese labor force, their promise not to bring in any new Japanese miners was not a real concession. Rather their concessions consisted in the recognition of the union and the narrowing of the wage differential between the white and Asian miners.

In all probability, therefore, the local unions admitted the Japanese miners because of unique local exigencies in negotiations with the Japanese labor contractors and the coal operators, and in advance of the UMWA international executive board's decision. This inference is reinforced by the presence of Michael F. Purcell at the June 28 session of the board. Purcell undoubtedly participated in the local negotiations, and, likely as not, he explained the Rock Springs situation to the board members and persuaded them to sanction the local unions' action. Interpreted in this manner, the UMWA's acceptance of Japanese miners was not a real paradox. Local conditions dictated the policy of admission in spite of Mitchell's and the union's antipathy to Japanese labor. This interpretation dispels the paradox and strengthens the plausibility of the inference that the local unions accepted the Japanese miners before the international executive board decided to do so. The interests of the Japanese miners, the local unions, and the coal operators all happened to have converged in the unique labor situation that prevailed in southern Wyoming in 1907. For pragmatic reasons rooted in that situation, the newly organized local unions admitted the Japanese miners. Thus this notable exception to organized labor's exclusion of Japanese labor was not the result of labor solidarity.

The Ludlow Massacre and Japanese Miners

Kept outside the structure of the American labor movement, some Japanese immigrant workers acted as strikebreakers, sometimes with disastrous consequences. In 1914 a tragic affair occurred near Ludlow,

Colorado, the site of the infamous Ludlow Massacre. Situated north
of Trinidad, Ludlow lies in the heart of the southern coalfield in the
State of Colorado. The coal miners of this region went on strike in
September 1913. This strike turned into a protracted, bitter struggle
which erupted into open industrial warfare between the strikers and
coal operators. Absentee owners controlled the coal mines of southern
Colorado, and ruthless, anti-union managers operated the mines under
feudal conditions. The principal absentee owner was John D. Rocke-
feller, Jr. who had a controlling interest in the two biggest coal companies, the Colorado Fuel and Iron Company and the Victor-
American Fuel Company. Japanese immigrant miners were caught in
the middle of the striking miners and coal operators. Tragically, four
Japanese strikebreakers were killed by the union side.

The Colorado coal mining labor force was dominated originally by
English-speaking miners. This changed as a result of a previous strike
which occurred in 1903–4. During and after this strike, the coal operators recruited many Mexican, Italian, Slavic, and Greek immigrant
laborers into the southern field as nonunion miners.[93] Japanese immigrant workers were also brought in, but not in large numbers. Okajima Kinji was the main Japanese labor contractor. In 1903 he was
managing the S. Ban Company's labor office in Sheridan, Wyoming.
Taking advantage of the labor vacuum created by the strike, Okajima
supplied Japanese laborers to the southern coalfield as strikebreakers.[94]
In 1908 the United States Immigration Commission surveyed the
composition of the mining labor force in the southern field. It found
that foreign-born miners predominated with eastern- and southern-
European immigrants in the majority. On the other hand, it only
found 66 Japanese miners, but noted that many Japanese had left the
mines to work in other industries or in agriculture.[95]

In 1913 the coal operators were determined to crush the strikers
from the outset. They refused to recognize the UMWA as the bargaining agent of the miners, and quickly employed strikebreakers under the protection of heavily armed company guards. The striking
miners were not only up against the hostile coal operators, but also
the political establishment of the State of Colorado. Governor Elias
Ammons backed the operators and mobilized the state militia against
the strikers. On April 20, 1914, the shameful Ludlow Massacre occurred when the state militia, composed in part of company guards,
fired machine guns and rifles into a tent colony which had been erected
by the striking miners. Evicted from company housing, the tent colony served as the temporary living quarters of the miners and their

families. The militia killed 21 persons, among them 11 children and 2 women. In swift retaliation, enraged striking miners laid siege to numerous mining camps, setting ablaze company buildings, destroying mules, and killing or expelling strikebreakers and company guards. To quell this open warfare and restore civil order, federal troops had to be called in. Altogether, the strike claimed the lives of 66 people.[96]

Japanese immigrants in Colorado did not stand aloof from the 1913–14 strike. The Japanese-language newspaper, *Kororado Shimbun*, published in Denver, covered the strike closely and reported on the situation of Japanese miners. Indeed, on September 23, 1913, the first day of the strike, it featured an editorial which advised Japanese miners to side with the union miners. It recalled that the Japanese had first entered the southern coalfield as strikebreakers. Foreseeing a violent confrontation between union and nonunion miners, the *Kororado Shimbun* believed that it was not in the interest of Japanese miners to scab. Citing the example of Japanese union miners in southern Wyoming, it encouraged the miners in southern Colorado to seek admission into the UMWA. It also warned Japanese labor contractors of the folly of supplying strikebreakers and urged the Japanese Association of Colorado to adopt a pro-union policy.[97] According to one of the Japanese labor contractors, Okimoto Seiichi, the Japanese contractors withheld Japanese laborers from the mines at the beginning of the strike because they felt the UMWA held the upperhand. Once they thought the situation had shifted in favor of the coal operators, however, they began to supply strikebreakers.[98] At the time of the Ludlow Massacre, there were approximately 100 Japanese miners working in the southern field. The *Kororado Shimbun* reported 40 at Oakview, 11 at Green Canyon, 24 at Forbes, and a few more at other mines.[99]

The tragic killing of the four Japanese strikebreakers took place at the Forbes mine eight days after the Ludlow Massacre. Before the massacre, the tent colony at this camp had been razed twice by state militiamen and company guards and a striking miner had been killed. The mining camp at Forbes was at the bottom of a canyon surrounded by steep hills. On the morning of April 29, approximately 300 armed strikers, many of them Greek immigrants, took up positions on the canyon heights overlooking the mining camp. These men were bent on seeking revenge for what had happened earlier at Forbes, and also, of course, for the Ludlow Massacre. The Greek miners were also out to avenge the death of their leader, Louis Tikas, who had been slain outside of Ludlow. The strikers swarmed down upon the camp and set twelve buildings afire. Thirty-seven mules perished in a burning barn. Nine men were killed; the four Japanese strikebreakers—Itō Kotarō, Niwa Masukichi, Hino Tetsuji, and Murakami Jōbei—died in a burning shack. Another Japanese was injured and had to be hospitalized.[100] Testimony presented before the United States Commission on Industrial Relations, which investigated the Ludlow Massacre, uniformly described these Japanese victims as "Japs."

Those Japanese miners who survived the reprisal attacks immediately withdrew from the mines. The *Kororado Shimbun* favored a "wait-and-see policy."[101] It made no sense for the Japanese, in its opinion, to continue as strikebreakers and incur the wrath of union miners. Significantly, the Japanese union miners at Kemmerer in southern Wyoming appealed to the Japanese in southern Colorado not to scab. After the killings at Forbes, they forwarded copies of a written appeal to the Japanese Association of Colorado and asked the association to distribute them.[102] Under federal mediation, a final settlement was reached between the striking miners and coal operators at the end of 1914. In January 1915 Kawabata Minoru, a labor contractor at the Delagua mine of the Colorado Fuel and Iron Company, assessed the lesson of the 1903–4 and 1913–14 strikes. According to Kawabata, these strikes had "proven that the union could not win," and so he believed that the Japanese "should side with the coal operators."[103] Throughout the 1913–14 strike, the Japanese Association of Colorado had never adopted a pro-union position. Kawabata was an active member of the association, as were other Japanese labor contractors. One Japanese miner took issue with Kawabata and the Japanese Association of Colorado. "Labor unions are essential," he said, "in order for workers to protect their own interest." The labor contractors who belonged to the association were only looking after "their own self-interest."[104] This union issue in Colorado was never resolved because most Japanese miners preferred to stay away from the southern coalfield after 1914 as a result of the tragic deaths at the Forbes mine.

Suzuki Bunji and the American Federation of Labor

The exclusion of Japanese immigrant workers from the ranks of organized labor appeared to change during World War I. In the middle of the war, the AFL, seemingly contradicting its long-standing anti-Asian policy, suddenly welcomed a Japanese representative of labor from Japan. Handpicked by the Japanese government, the representative was Suzuki Bunji. As a "fraternal delegate" from Japan, Suzuki attended the annual conventions of the California State Federation of Labor and the AFL in 1915 and 1916. His appearance at these conventions marked the first time an Asian delegate ever participated in the proceedings of the AFL at either the state or national level. Suzuki was dispatched by the Foreign Ministry to conduct diplomacy in a private capacity. He established contacts with AFL leaders in an attempt to moderate their hostility towards Japanese immigration and Japanese immigrant workers. For their part, AFL leaders received Suzuki with considerable cordiality, so much so that a few labor historians have interpreted the AFL's reception of Suzuki in a very positive light.[105] From the point of view of Japanese immigrant laborers, however, such an interpretation has no validity, since Suzuki's private diplomacy did not effect any change in the AFL policy of racial exclusion.

It is not altogether clear who conceived the original idea of having a Japanese labor delegate visit the United States. Dr. Sidney L. Gulick, a clergyman associated with the Federal Council of the Churches of Christ, arranged Suzuki's 1915 visit with Paul Scharrenberg, secretary of the California State Federation of Labor. Gulick went to Japan at the beginning of 1915 as a member of a "Christian Embassy" dispatched by the Federal Council to present its viewpoint on the Japanese immigration question. Constituting almost a counter-movement by himself, Gulick was the most active opponent of the exclusion movement. He had been a missionary to Japan, was a member of the Commission on Relations with Japan of the Federal Council, and author of many anti-exclusion tracts and the influential book, *The American Japanese Problem*, published in 1914.[106]

Before sailing for Japan, Gulick conferred with California trade-union leaders in San Francisco. At that time, according to his account, "Mr. Scharrenberg . . . made the suggestion that one important method for promoting mutual understanding and friendship between Japan and America was to arrange for the exchange of Fraternal Delegates by the respective working classes of the two countries."[107] Because of this suggestion, Gulick began to search for an appropriate labor candidate upon his arrival in Japan. He informed Vice Foreign Minister Matsui Keishirō that "the suggestion by Mr. Paul Scharrenberg" should be interpreted as "an olive branch" held out by the "bitterest opponent of the Japanese," meaning the California State Federation.[108] On the other hand, Frederick W. Ely, labor editor of the San Francisco *Bulletin,* assigned the original idea to Gulick. Ely wrote that Gulick, in discussions with California labor leaders, had proposed having a Japanese representative of labor come to the United States "as a means of bringing about a better understanding among the wage earners of Japan and the United States."[109] Other writers have also credited Gulick with the idea.[110]

Regardless of who first proposed it, Gulick actively searched for a labor delegate during his stay in Japan. The Foreign Ministry presented an initial obstacle. When Gulick first sought the assistance of the Ministry, Vice Foreign Minister Matsui advised him that "a representative should be chosen from among the Japanese residents . . . in the United States." His reasoning was simple: "There exist at present in Japan no labor unions from whose members a delegate suitable for the purpose can be selected."[111] Matsui concurred with Consul Numano Yasutarō of San Francisco who earlier had reported that it would be difficult to find a representative of labor because labor unions were outlawed in Japan. Moreover, since "subversive persons" had been active in the labor movement, Numano believed it unlikely a candidate acceptable to the Foreign Ministry would be found.[112] Almost immediately after Matsui rebuffed Gulick, Foreign Minister Katō Takaaki ordered Numano to select someone within his consular jurisdiction.[113] The attitude of the Foreign Ministry reflected the Japanese government's general policy towards labor, especially after the High Treason Affair. The Ministry associated anyone engaged in labor organizing with subversive socialists and anarchists.

Despite the initial uncooperativeness of the Foreign Ministry, Suzuki Bunji was designated as the labor representative, with even the eventual blessing of the Foreign Ministry. In 1915 Suzuki was president of the *Yūaikai*, a conservative labor body headquartered in Tokyo. He had founded it in August 1912 in the aftermath of the High Treason Affair. Neither a trade union nor a socialist organization, the *Yūaikai* was a mutual-aid society oriented towards social reformism with a membership of slightly over 7,000 in 1915. Philosophically, it stood for the elevation of the moral character of workers and the promotion of harmony between labor and capital.[114] Suzuki, aware of the legal ban on trade-unions, organized this labor group in such a way that police authorities tolerated its existence. Suzuki did not have a working class background. A graduate of Tokyo Imperial University, he was an intellectual social reformer rather than a worker. A practicing Christian, he once had been the personal secretary of Reverend Clay MacCauley, pastor of the Tokyo Unitarian Church. Through his association with missionaries, he had learned to speak English, which enhanced his candidacy as the labor delegate for whom Gulick was searching.[115]

Shibusawa Eiichi played a major role in the selection of Suzuki. Shibusawa was an active proponent of what he called "people-to-people diplomacy" to promote and preserve harmonious United States–Japan relations.[116] For him, such diplomacy entailed direct, private contacts between the people of the two countries over and beyond formal diplomatic intercourse. Shibusawa had cultivated ties with American business circles, but not with the American working class. Gulick first met Shibusawa in January 1915 and ask him for help in finding a suitable representative of labor. Gulick was introduced to Suzuki in early February by Abe Isoo, a prominent Christian and professor at Waseda University. Abe had known Gulick since the latter's early days as a missionary in Japan, and he recommended Suzuki to him as an appropriate labor candidate.[117] Suzuki's candidacy was endorsed by Soeda Jūichi, president of the Industrial Bank of Japan, who served as an advisor to the *Yūaikai*. Soeda, in turn, recommended Suzuki to Shibusawa. At Gulick's request the Foreign Ministry interviewed Suzuki and his *Yūaikai* associate, Yoshimatsu Sadaya.[118] At that point Foreign Minister Katō, foreshadowing a reversal of policy, cabled Consul Numano instructing him to suspend his search for a labor representative in California.[119]

The decision to send Suzuki was reached in the spring. Gulick returned to San Francisco towards the end of March. To catch up on the latest local developments, the consulted with Consul Numano, Ushijima Kinji, president of the Japanese Association of America, and Dr. Harvey H. Guy, professor at the Pacific School of Religion and advisor to the Japanese Consulate of San Francisco. Everyone urged Gulick to notify Scharrenberg about Suzuki and Yoshimatsu. Gulick paid a call on him in April. When informed of the two possible delegates, Scharrenberg said that he would extend a cordial welcome to them as "fraternal delegates" from Japan at the forthcoming convention of the State Federation.[120] Convinced that there was no danger of the two men being manipulated for anti-Japanese purposes, Gulick was confident their coming would produce positive results. Changing his own opinion, Consul Numano came to share Gulick's optimistic outlook. Scharrenberg's response offered "a good chance" for "an appropriate labor delegate from Japan . . . to contact and mingle with labor leaders here."[121] It was a golden opportunity to forge a link with organized labor in the United States. Thus Numano recommended that the Foreign Ministry approve Suzuki and Yoshimatsu, his companion-to-be, as representatives of Japanese labor.

The Foreign Ministry granted formal approval in May. Gulick notified Suzuki that Scharrenberg "assures me that you and Mr. Yoshimatsu will be acceptable" and advised him to mail copies of his *Yūaikai* credentials to Scharrenberg and to Frank Morrison, secretary of the AFL. Simultaneously, he reminded Suzuki of the purpose of his mission. "You understand," Gulick cautioned, "that the purpose . . . is not to try and open the way for additional coming of Japanese labor to this country," but to bring "the fraternal greetings" of the *Yūaikai* and to study "the conditions of labor and the methods of labor organization" in the United States.[122] In other words, Gulick warned Suzuki that he should skirt the immigration issue during his contacts with American labor leaders. Gulick also informed Shibusawa of Scharrenberg's favorable response. To prepare for any unforeseen events, he asked Shibusawa for special authority. He requested that he—along with Numano, Guy, and Ushijima—be authorized to "immediately step in and stop the proceedings" if anything "untowards happens" and "return" Suzuki "promptly back to Japan."[123]

Shibusawa interviewed Suzuki three times in order to make his own assessment of Suzuki's qualifications. Upon being duly impressed, Shibusawa endorsed Suzuki and used his influence to persuade Foreign Ministry officials to consider him seriously as a representative of Japanese labor.[124] Consul Numano's report on Gulick's fruitful meeting with Scharrenberg proved to be decisive. Based upon it, final negotiations occurred between Shibusawa, who assumed private responsibility for Suzuki, and the Foreign Ministry. Vice Foreign Minister Matsui notified Shibusawa of the Ministry's approval on May 1.[125] A week later, concurring in effect with Gulick, Foreign Minister Katō directed Shibusawa to have Suzuki and Yoshimatsu sent back immediately to Japan "in the event anything unfavorable arises."[126] Notwithstanding the Japanese government's anti-labor policy, the Foreign Ministry approved Suzuki as a representative of labor for diplomatic reasons. Having screened him carefully, the Ministry considered him a moderate who could be relied upon to establish "safe" ties with American labor leaders, thereby possibly contributing to the broad diplomatic goal of countering the anti-Japanese exclusion movement.

Suzuki departed for the United States in June. He had his own motives for embarking on his mission. The Foreign Ministry's designation of him as a representative of Japanese labor meant that he was recognized, at least implicitly, as a legitimate labor leader. This in itself enhanced his personal stature as well as the standing of the *Yūai-kai* as a labor body. Secondly, his trip afforded him an opportunity to observe the American labor movement at first hand. Thirdly, he stood to win enormous prestige in Japan if he carried out his mission success-fully. Suzuki landed in San Francisco in early July well in advance of the State Federation and AFL conventions scheduled for October and November. In the intervening time, he acquainted himself with Cali-fornia labor leaders like Paul Scharrenberg, William T. Bonsor, secre-tary of the Anti-Jap Laundry League, and Patrick H. McCarthy of the San Francisco Building Trades Council. He spoke before labor groups, among them the Executive Council of the State Federation and the San Francisco Labor Council. And he inspected Japanese settlements and addressed immigrant groups.[127]

The State Federation convention was held at Santa Rosa. Delegates representing unions of San Francisco laundry workers objected to the seating of Suzuki and Yoshimatsu on the opening day. They charged that the *Yūaikai* was not a bonafide trade-union, that the two men did not represent the working class of Japan, and that they were agents of the Japanese government. William T. Bonsor made these allega-tions prior to the convention in the *Labor Clarion,* official organ of the San Francisco Labor Council and the State Federation.[128] Since no proof was presented, however, the committee on credentials seated the two men as fraternal delegates without voting rights. At the same time, the committee reaffirmed the State Federation's stand on Asian immigration, declaring that the seating of the two Japanese "in no way affects our attitude or modifies our demand for the exclusion of all Asiatic laborers from our shores."[129] Suzuki addressed the conven-tion on the second day. He spoke in general of the Japanese labor movement and in particular of the *Yūaikai* as an infant labor body.[130] Heeding Gulick's warning about the purpose of his mission, he side-stepped the immigration issue completely. Suzuki's speech had been prepared by Kawakami Kiyoshi. In 1915 Kawakami was the head of the Pacific Press Bureau which the Foreign Ministry had founded in 1914 in order to distribute news favorable to Japan to American news-papers.

It appears that the delegates to the State Federation convention wel-comed Suzuki and his associate. Neither Suzuki nor Yoshimatsu re-corded being treated rudely or insultingly. Indeed, Suzuki felt warmly received because the delegates applauded his speech and approached him in a friendly manner. He even participated in nightly social events. Only one thing upset Suzuki. "We felt badly," he said, when "the convention adopted an anti-Asiatic resolution,'' even though it was passed as ''an annual ritual'' to which few paid serious attention.[131] The resolution expressed opposition ''to the patronizing or employing of Asiatics in any manner'' and favored the ''extension of the Chinese Exclusion Law so as to bar all Asiatics.''[132] With a touch of forced bravado, Suzuki declared that he had yielded nothing to Charles Child, head of the Anti-Jap Laundry League who had contested his seating and sponsored the resolution. Suzuki told him, as he ''shook'' his ''fist in Child's face,'' that he had no objection to Japanese exclusion for ''economic reason,'' but that he could not condone it if it were based upon ''race prejudice.''[133] Suzuki granted validity to the economic reason American trade unionists advanced to justify Japanese exclusion. The Anti-Jap Laundry League, Suzuki believed, went beyond the economic rationale and raised objectionable racial reasons for exclusion. Apart from Child and his group, however, Suzuki was elated by the overall reception he received at the State Federation convention.[134]

The AFL convened its national convention in San Francisco. As a fraternal delegate, Suzuki delivered an address before this assembly, too. ''We look upon you as our big brother whose guidance and cooperation will give great impetus to the growth of the labor movement in Japan,'' he said in terms flattering to the delegates, emphasizing the advanced state of the AFL compared to the backwardness of labor in Japan.[135] And he consciously eschewed the exclusion issue. During the convention, Ushijima Kinji feted President Samuel Gompers at a private banquet held at the Palace Hotel. In attendance were Suzuki, Yoshimatsu, Paul Scharrenberg, Sidney L. Gulick, Harvey H. Guy, and Consul Numano. Along with Gompers, Shibusawa Eiichi, who had also come to the United States, was present as an honored guest, too. Later Shibusawa entertained California labor leaders at a second banquet. These social gatherings were held to establish personal relations with state and national officials of the AFL.[136] At the close of the national convention, Consul Numano filed a report to Tokyo lauding Suzuki. In his judgment, Suzuki had ''given a positive impression to all delegates'' with the ''enthusiastic support of Paul Scharrenberg and Frederick W. Ely.'' All in all, he had ''fulfilled his mission'' by establishing friendly contacts with American labor leaders.''[137]

Before returning to Japan, Suzuki undertook an unanticipated task with respect to Japanese immigrant workers. He helped to organize an immigrant labor group, named the Japanese Labor League of America, as a by-product of his exposure to organized American labor. At Suzuki's behest, and with the approval of Consul Numano, this body merged two existing labor associations, one of day laborers in San Francisco, and one of laundry workers in Oakland. Its main aims were "to improve the economic and social status" of Japanese immigrant labor and "to cooperate with white labor groups to attain the high ideal of Japanese-American accord."[138] As already noted, Suzuki acknowledged the validity of the economic reason advanced by American trade unionists against Japanese immigrant labor. Although he never specified the precise means he would employ, he launched the Japanese Labor League with the goal of elevating the condition of Japanese labor so as to nullify that reason. Thus this new organization started with essentially a conservative aim, narrowly restricting its purpose to seeking organized labor's acceptance of Japanese immigrant workers.

Katayama Sen's brief association with the Labor League illustrates this conservatism. Katayama had returned to the United States in 1914 because his life in Japan as a socialist had become intolerable after the High Treason Affair.[139] In 1915 he was living in exile in San Francisco where he eked out a living as a domestic worker. He attended meetings preceding the launching of the Labor League in which he was suggested as a possible manager of a labor club being planned as an adjunct to the new body. Katayama was on the Japanese government's official list of subversives. Consul Numano looked askance at his presence and did not relish the thought of his becoming such a manager. From Numano's perspective, his participation would have discredited the League, for it would have been identified inevitably with Katayama and, by extension, with socialism.

To avert this undesirable outcome, Consul Numano ordered Katayama to sever his connection with the League and to refrain from taking any part in its activities.[140] Save for a very few, Japanese immigrants shunned Katayama as a dangerous man. Although he had never been an anarchist, he was linked indirectly with Kōtoku Shūsui, and so the dark shadows cast by the High Treason Affair stalked him even in San Francisco. Without the support of his fellow domestic workers, Katayama acquiesced in the Consul's order.[141] His acquiescence, however, did not signify endorsement of the League. When it was inaugurated publicly in December, he had Oka Shigeki, a fellow immigrant socialist, distribute leaflets at the San Francisco Buddhist Hall where the ceremonies were held. The leaflets implied that the League had been formed by outsiders who wished to manipulate it for the sake of diplomatic goodwill, not by Japanese immigrant workers themselves for their own welfare.[142] In any event, Numano's ousting of Katayama was in keeping with the League's conservative goal.

As a major proponent of Japanese exclusion, Senator James D. Phelan of California became alarmed over the welcome accorded to Suzuki and Yoshimatsu. In a letter to Scharrenberg, he warned that the State Federation's reception of the two men had "a bad moral effect," giving the "false impression . . . that the workers of California are indifferent" to Japanese exclusion. "Anything which weakens the hands of your representative in Washington," he continued, "weakens the cause in which we are all concerned—the prevention of the displacement of the white population of California by the Japanese." The seating of the Japanese labor delegates had made it appear that "our . . . working men . . . have been won over to the 'Brotherhood of Man' sentimentality, skillfully preached by Japanese proponents. . . . ''[143] Phelan appealed to Scharrenberg to erase this erroneous impression.

Scharrenberg replied that the position of the State Federation remained unchanged:

> We have not modified our views upon the Japanese menace. We fully realize the danger of the so-called "Gentlemen's Agreement" and we are anxious to have enacted an exclusion law which will effectively and permanently bar these little brown men from our shores.
>
> Our objection to the Japanese . . . is not . . . based upon trivial or sentimental reasons. We object to them for economic reasons, we know Californians cannot compete with them and maintain an American standard of living.

Scharrenberg also explained the motives behind the reception given to Suzuki and Yoshimatsu. "Our kind treatment of the two delegates from Japan" was to foster "a better understanding between the wage workers of Japan and . . . America" and to show "that we have no grievances against the Japanese as long as they remain in Japan.''[144] This exchange of letters occurred in October. To clear up the misconceptions about the State Federation's position on Japanese immigration, Scharrenberg later issued a press release to which he attached the correspondence. The release reiterated that the "kindness and courtesy toward our visitors should not be construed to mean a weakening in labor's demand for the exclusion of all Asiatic workers from our shores.''[145]

Scharrenberg summarized the result of Suzuki's visit in the following way:

Mr. Suzuki . . . has . . . learned from first hand observation that the organized workers of America who demand the exclusion of all Asiatics from these shores are not nearly as bad nor as unreasonable as they have been pictured by the jingo press of both countries. Mr. Suzuki will be able to tell his constituents of the friendly and cordial reception he received in quarters alleged to be the hotbeds of anti-Japanese agitation. He will be able to explain that the organized workers of America place their main reliance on self-help, and that they are anxious to aid and encourage the workers in Japan to do likewise.[146]

In other words, organized labor had been able to educate Suzuki about its stand on Japanese immigration. Here Scharrenberg alluded to what was probably the real motive behind the welcoming of Suzuki. Portrayed in some quarters as unreasonable for its anti-Japanese position, organized labor's reception of Suzuki had been to demonstrate to the Japanese in Japan and the American public how eminently "reasonable" it was.

There was probably another related motive. In 1915 Scharrenberg lobbied for an amendment to the 1913 California Alien Land Law, an amendment which would have eliminated the right to lease agricultural land altogether.[147] When he conferred with Sidney L. Gulick at the beginning of the year, he was planning to have such an amendment introduced into the state legislature. He knew then that any anti-Japanese bill, including his own, would meet stiff opposition. Japan's entry into World War I on the side of the allies and the scheduled opening of the Panama-Pacific International Exposition made anti-Japanese measures inopportune. Anticipating harsh criticism, Scharrenberg hoped to mollify his critics by treating Suzuki with utmost courtesy while upholding organized labor's anti-Japanese policy. All of this suggests that Gulick, in all likelihood, was correct in assigning the original idea of inviting a Japanese labor delegate to Scharrenberg.

Suzuki's relative success in 1915 enabled him to return to the United States the next year. In the summer of 1916 Frederick W. Ely advised Shibusawa Eiichi to send Suzuki again to attend the 1916 conventions of the State Federation and the AFL. Of all the reporters of the commercial press of San Francisco, Ely was the most sympathetic to the Japanese side. In 1915 he gave Suzuki very favorable coverage in his labor column in the *Bulletin*. He believed that Suzuki had influenced trade unionists in a constructive way, and he pledged to Shibusawa that "I shall do all in my power to help him . . . profit from the visit." Ely also proposed that the *Yūaikai* invite Samuel

Gompers and Scharrenberg to visit Japan. Predicting that they would accept an invitation, he wrote "that much lasting good would result and that a long step would be taken to insure permanent peace between the people of the two nations."[148] Meanwhile, Foreign Minister Ishii Kikujirō inquired of Hanihara Masanao, the new consul in San Francisco, if it would be advisable to have Suzuki attend the 1916 conventions.[149] Hanihara recommended that the Foreign Ministry grant him permission, and the Ministry approved Suzuki's second trip without hesitation.[150]

As he had done the preceding year, Suzuki first attended the State Federation convention, this time held at Eureka in October. He was seated as a fraternal delegate over objections raised again by members of the Anti-Jap Laundry League. Suzuki spoke to the convention about the progress made in the Japanese labor movement since his first visit, and then extended an invitation to the convention to send a fraternal delegate to Japan in 1917. "I sincerely hope that you will send your delegate," he said, "with a view to instructing and guiding your younger brothers in Japan."[151] The delegates accepted the invitation by resolution. When the State Federation first welcomed Suzuki in 1915, Scharrenberg had had to reassure Senator James D. Phelan and others of his body's unchanged policy towards Japanese immigration. Just as the reception of Suzuki then had not involved any shift in policy, so, too, the acceptance of this invitation did not mean any lessening of opposition to Japanese immigration. The delegates again resolved to continue "our unswerving stand upon exclusion until such time as immigration will not prove a menace to our own unions, our working people, and our standard of living."[152]

In addition to extending the invitation, Suzuki brought up the subject of Japanese immigrant workers for the first time. He told the delegates that "Japanese wage earners living in America have come to understand your ideals and aspirations" and that "they have been rapidly assimilated into your system."[153] Suzuki referred to their conduct in a recent strike to substantiate this claim. San Francisco culinary workers had gone out on strike in August, and not only had Japanese workers joined them in sympathy, but Japanese employment agencies had refused to furnish scab workers.[154] Suzuki stressed that, "though the Japanese were not union men, they respected the wishes of the union men and walked out with them."[155] In recounting this fresh example of labor solidarity, Suzuki undoubtedly was raising the question of whether or not the State Federation was willing to organize Japanese immigrant workers and enlist them into its ranks. What he had assidously avoided in 1915, he now consciously broached, albeit in an indirect way.

When the Anti-Jap Laundry League introduced an anti-Asian resolution, a debate over the question of organizing Asian immigrant workers arose. The resolution was like others the convention had adopted for six successive years. It opposed "the patronizing or employing of Asiatics in any manner" and advocated amending "the Chinese Exclusion Law so as to cover and bar all Asiatics."[156] Hugo Ernst, head of the San Francisco Waiters' Union and a socialist delegate, spoke out forcefully against the resolution. "I see no good reason for going on year after year passing this resolution," he said. To Ernst, the central issue was the unwillingness of the State Federation to organize Japanese immigrant workers. "If the Japanese are properly organized," he argued, "they will be removed as a source of unfair competition in the labor market." And inasmuch as the economic argument against them was fundamental, he viewed unionization as "the only logical solution" and hoped that "the time will come when the uselessness of passing resolutions will be recognized."[157] Harry Mohr, head of the Street Car Men's Union of Oakland, echoed Ernst's opinion: "We should organize the Asiatics who are already in this country and put them on an equal basis with the white men."[158] Other delegates, among them James Maloney of the Los Angeles Web Pressmen's Union, voiced similar sentiments. These opponents of the Anti-Jap Laundry League favored a resolution sponsored by Mohr which called upon the Executive Council of the State Federation "to take immediate steps having for its object the organizing of all Asiatics in the State of California."[159]

A compromise settled the difference between the two resolutions. On the one hand, the convention adopted the first without amendment and referred the second to the Executive Council. On the other hand, it passed a third resolution which instructed the Council "to gather data relative to the feasibility of organizing labor unions of the citizens of the United States of Asiatic origins."[160] Since the overwhelming majority of Asian workers were immigrants who were ineligible to citizenship, this third resolution had no meaning. Being a small minority, the opponents of the Anti-Jap Laundry League could neither prevent adoption of the first resolution nor force passage of their own counter resolution. The most they were able to accomplish was to ask for a meaningless study of the feasibility of organizing American-born Asian workers. In this indecisive way, the debate on admitting Asian workers closed.

Suzuki listened intently to the debate. To him, the adoption of the Anti-Jap Laundry League sponsored resolution was "unfortunate," but it did not make him pessimistic. For he believed that the majority of delegates voted for the resolution "to protect themselves for economic reasons."[161] Convinced of the validity of the old economic argument, Suzuki interpreted the voting in terms of economic motives. In addition, he felt it made sense for the convention to have deferred the question of organizing Asian workers for a year until the Executive Council had time to investigate the matter. Since the delegates had opposed Japanese immigrant workers for so long, they could not be expected to do an abrupt about-face without appearing to be devoid of principles. What gave Suzuki room for optimism was that the debate on organizing Asian workers had been "unprecedented."[162] In the not distant future, he foresaw the possibility of the State Federation reversing its policy and actually admitting Asian immigrant workers.

To prepare for that day, Suzuki founded the Japanese Federation of Labor. Larger than its 1915 predecessor, this new organization ostensibly unified existing fraternal bodies of tailors, domestics, day laborers, barbers, laundry workers, and cobblers in San Francisco, Oakland, and Berkeley. Its broad purposes were "to protect the rights and privileges of Japanese workers . . . and to improve their welfare" by cooperation and possible affiliation with "white labor groups."[163] The founding of the Japanese Federation, Suzuki thought, would make the State Federation amenable to admitting Japanese immigrant workers since its existence proved that they were organized and only awaiting recognition by American trade unionists.

Frederick W. Ely supported Suzuki's strategy. In a sympathetic account of Suzuki's new "Central Labor Council," he reported that it included "nine Japanese labor unions, with a combined membership of close to 2,000. . . . " Its aims were:

> to eliminate the "unfair" competition of Japanese wage earners by seeking to establish the same wages, hours of labor and conditions that are maintained by the organized white wage-earners, and to raise the standard of living among the Japanese wage-earners in this country. When this is accomplished . . . , not only in California, but in Washington and Oregon, it can no longer be charged . . . that the Japanese . . . are a menace to the white wage-earners because they work longer hours and for less money than do their white brothers.

According to Ely, Suzuki hoped that "within another year the American Federation of labor will authorize the affiliation of the Japanese labor unions," but until then "separate organizations [would] be maintained, with the same wages and conditions as have been established by the A.F. of L."[164] There is not a shred of evidence that the Japanese Federation ever operated to maintain such wages and conditions. Contrary to Ely's reportage, the new organization was a paper federation of fraternal bodies, publicized as a "Central Labor Council," to seek the admission of Japanese immigrant workers into the State Federation.

Suzuki acted with the consent of the Japanese consul who supervised the formation of the Japanese Federation. A consular staff member was present at all preparatory meetings. Consul Hanihara Masanao was concerned with the participation of a specific person, just as Consul Numano Yasutarō had been concerned with Katayama Sen in 1915. This time the person in question was Ogawa Kinji who operated a watch repair shop in Berkeley. Suzuki had appointed him to the Board of Directors of the Japanese Federation. Ogawa's name appeared on the Japanese government's list of subversives, too. He had been a member of the Social Revolutionary Party and had been involved in the 1907 lèse-majesté incident. Hanihara pressed Suzuki for an explanation of why he had appointed Ogawa to the Board in view of his anarchist background. Suzuki replied that, fearing Ogawa might stir up trouble if left out, he considered it wiser to put up with him on the Board. Hanihara dutifully recorded the foregoing account in his report to Tokyo, concluding that Ogawa "has not acted radically as he did in the past."[165] Apparently persuaded by Suzuki's explanation, Hanihara did not insist on Ogawa's removal from the Board.

After founding the new body, Suzuki proceeded to Baltimore where he attended the AFL national convention in November. While still in San Francisco, he posted a personal letter to Samuel Gompers inviting him to Japan. Upon his arrival in Baltimore, he presented the *Yūaikai*'s formal invitation which predicted that Gompers' appearance in Japan would "prove a great encouragement to the working people of Japan" and would "aid in the promotion of peace between the two countries."[166] In his address to the convention, Suzuki adroitly mentioned Japanese immigrant workers. He said that he had organized the Japanese Federation in San Francisco, which he, too, called a "Central Labor Council." Seattle already had "a strong Japanese union." And he claimed that in other Pacific Coast cities Japanese workers "have been asking me to come and help organize their local unions and labor councils." All this burst of activity was "a harbinger of the spring," indicating that Japanese immigrant workers soon would be organized fully.[167] In so describing how Japanese workers were organizing themselves, Suzuki again obliquely posed the question of whether or not the AFL was prepared to admit them into its ranks. For if the Japanese were organized, how could the AFL continue to adhere to its policy of barring them from union membership? Ely had predicted that the AFL national convention would consider this question, but no debate of any kind arose at the convention. In contrast to what occurred at the State Federation convention, the delegates did not consider the question at all.

Japanese Ambassador Satō Aimaro, at Suzuki's suggestion, invited the entire California delegation to a private banquet during the national convention. He hosted such figures as Paul Scharrenberg, Frederick W. Ely, Daniel P. Haggerty, former president of the State Federation, John A. O'Connell, secretary of the San Francisco Labor Council, and others. The Japanese and American sides both delivered speeches, with the latter repeating the economic rationale for upholding Japanese exclusion. Ambassador Satō "felt a great sense of satisfaction" with the social event since "no one uttered a single offensive word about Japan."[168] Suzuki detected a softening in O'Connell's attitude towards Japanese.[169] But whatever the results of the banquet were, it was a part of the ongoing effort to induce the AFL to alter its long-standing policy of racial exclusion. Towards the close of the national convention, the delegates adopted a resolution accepting the invitation to send a fraternal delegate to Japan in 1917.

Suzuki's private diplomacy had no effect on organized labor's anti-Japanese policy. Nothing came of the two 1916 resolutions on organizing Asian workers, which the State Federation convention had referred to its Executive Council. Scharrenberg reported the Council's decision to the 1917 convention. "Your Executive Council," he said, "is not prepared to recommend the use of the Federation's funds for organizing work among Asiatic workers in California."[170] Scharrenberg gave no reason for this decision. He did not even present findings of the feasibility study of organizing American-born Asian workers, which the Council had been asked to conduct. Suzuki's activities had aroused a hope, however faint, that the State Federation would organize and admit Asian immigrant workers. That hope was dashed by the Executive Council's decision. Neither the State Federation nor the AFL dispatched a fraternal delegate to Japan. Scharrenberg and Gompers were scheduled to visit Japan and attend ceremonies scheduled to commemorate the fifth anniversary of the *Yūaikai,* but cancelled their trips because of United States entry into World War I. In 1919 Suzuki returned to the United States to attend the first international labor conference. He addressed the AFL national convention again, but nothing eventful resulted from this third visit.

Scharrenberg is a key person to understanding the State Federation's policy of racial exclusion. He was groomed for his job as editor of the *Coast Seamen's Journal* by Walter Macarthur who, along with Andrew Furuseth, had led the International Seamen's Union of the Pacific in opposing Chinese immigration in the nineteenth century.[171] He inherited the anti-Asian ideology of his mentor as an article of faith and saw himself in the role of perpetuating organized labor's opposition to Asian immigration. As a longtime secretary-treasurer of the State Federation, he was a consistent advocate of Japanese exclusion and the AFL's chief spokesperson on this issue. He led the State Federation into the Japanese Exclusion League and the California Joint Immigration Committee, in which he worked closely and tirelessly with the arch exclusionist, V.S. McClatchy.[172]

Scharrenberg always disclaimed racial prejudice, but his frequent reference to the white race belies his denial. He was convinced that organized labor, beginning with its agitation against Chinese workers, had saved California from being inundated by Asians.

> If it had not been for the early labor agitators, I think this Pacific Coast would have filled up with Chinese. They came drifting in . . . at a tremendous rate, and once they were here, why, they just displaced the white workers. It was the hell-raising of Dennis Kearney and those early sandlotters that was responsible for the Chinese Exclusion Act. . . . It was the hell-raising of the agitators that maintained California for us and our kind of people.[173]

By "our kind of people," Scharrenberg of course unmistakably meant white people. Hawaii was the example of what would have happened to California if organized labor had not opposed Japanese immigration. So numerous and entrenched were the Japanese in the territory, the islands no longer could be preserved, to cite his favorite phrase, "as a heritage to the white race." In 1922 Scharrenberg wrote:

> Hawaii is the most complete and convincing object lesson to the mainland as to what would have happened in California if the workers of the state, and the people generally, had not been so determined to hold the state as a heritage to the white race.[174]

Later warning of the perils of Filipino and Mexican immigration, he repeated that it had "been the historic mission of the California labor movement to take the lead in every movement to preserve our State as a heritage to the white race."[175] Scharrenberg recognized no legitimate Asian presence in California. Neither makers nor bearers nor recipients of the state's "white" heritage, the Asians were intruders.

Except for Japanese immigrant workers, all parties involved in Suzuki Bunji's private diplomacy reaped some benefits. As a result of his contacts with AFL leaders, Suzuki gained considerable prestige in Japan which he used to build the *Yūaikai* into a full-fledged labor federation during the post–World War I years. The brief optimism generated by his mission was of passing benefit to the Foreign Ministry and Shibusawa Eiichi. Organized American labor also benefitted, for its reception of Suzuki enabled it to assume a facade of being "reasonable" about its opposition to Japanese immigration and Japanse immigrant workers. Scharrenberg was able to "educate" Suzuki about the rationale behind the State Federation's stand on Japanese exclusion, to the extent, indeed, that Suzuki accepted the validity of the economic argument. Samuel Gompers threw the full weight of the AFL behind President Woodrow Wilson's foreign policy during World War I. To marshal support for it, Gompers solicited the backing of European trade unionists in the name of international labor solidarity. The AFL was able to pay additional lip service to that solidarity by welcoming Suzuki as a publicized "fraternal delegate" from Japan.

As a Japanese publicist, Kawakami Kiyoshi believed that Suzuki's private diplomacy had been effective. In his opinion, Suzuki influenced organized labor to change its attitude towards Japanese immigrant workers. As evidence of this change, Kawakami referred to "a very clever and exceedingly pertinent observation" made by Walter Macarthur. At one of the banquets hosted by the Japanese side, Macarthur said that "the more I see you, the less you look like a Jap!" Kawakami interpreted this statement to mean that, "if Japanese and Americans only get together, the barrier between the two must gradually vanish."[176] Ostensibly, Macarthur had changed his negative opinions of the Japanese by coming into contact with them. Indeed, according to Kawakami, California labor leaders in general had shown "a disposition to deal more squarely with the Japanese" by welcoming Suzuki and debating the desirability of organizing Japanese immigrant workers.[177] In general, Kawakami drew a very rosy picture of Suzuki's private diplomacy.

Katayama Sen reached an opposite conclusion. Katayama had no

illusions about the AFL policy of racial exclusion. In 1917 he summarized his own views in the *Heimin,* a monthly he published out of
New York City. In his opinion, there had never been any competition
between organized white workers and Japanese immigrant workers.
The only reason for the "anti-Japanese movement" was "racial prejudice" which had been "purposely incited against the Japanese." San
Francisco labor leaders had manipulated the Japanese labor issue "in
order to get the labor vote." "Labor leaders like Shorenberg (sic) and
others framed up the anti-Japanese movement," according to Katayama, by "putting up every imaginable scheme and false pretext
shamelessly." When this method proved to be no longer effective,
the leaders "changed their tactics and began to speak of the Japs
favorably. . . . " Katayama saw the AFL's courting of Suzuki Bunji
as further evidence that "the anti-Japanese movement was merely a
worked-up scheme by the trades union leaders to get labor's votes."[178]
During the World War I period, AFL leaders ceased to utter anti-
Japanese statements because they realized that such statements no
longer guaranteed labor votes. Instead, they welcomed the likes of
Suzuki and dined with Japanese diplomats as another method of ad-
vancing the cause of Japanese exclusion.

V

Permanent Settlement

Abiko Kyūtarō: His Ideal and Influence

The transition from sojourning to permanent settlement was a gradual process. Of all immigrant leaders, Abiko Kyūtarō played a key role in this process. As the longtime publisher of the *Nichibei Shimbun* and as a highly respected, if not *the* most respected, immigrant leader, he, more than anyone else, influenced many Issei to sink their roots in American soil. Abiko was a visionary who foresaw a permanent future for Japanese immigrants in this country. He believed that the *dekasegi* ideal was an obstacle to the realization of that future, and that it lay at the root of the many unsavory features of Japanese immigrant life. During the anti-Japanese exclusion movement, he exhorted his countrymen to abandon the *dekasegi* ideal. As his solution to the exclusion question, he formulated an alternative ideal of permanent settlement and persuaded many immigrants to adopt it, thereby laying the real foundations of Japanese immigrant society.

Abiko believed that the exclusion question could be solved amicably. He never interpreted the question purely in terms of economic competition, political demogoguery, or simple racism, although he acknowledged that all of these factors were involved in one way or another.[1] Some degree of economic competition existed between Japanese immigrants and Americans, to be sure, but that was not sufficient to explain the anti-Japanese hostility. Most Japanese were not in direct competition with white workers, occupying as they did different sectors of the labor market. Assuming however that Chinese immigrants had been in such direct competition, Abiko reasoned that Americans wrongly identified the Japanese with the Chinese, thus conjuring up the specter of economic competition. He felt that, while political demogogues were numerous enough, they were offset by other people who were sympathetic to the Japanese. The racial animus towards the Japanese, unlike that towards the blacks, included a white fear that Japanese had superior traits which made them formidable opponents against whom Americans could not compete.

Fundamentally, Abiko viewed the exclusion movement as a problem of ignorance. Americans were ignorant of Japan and Japanese immigrants, and their ignorance was at the bottom of all the misunderstandings which fueled the movement. Abiko was that rare student-laborer who mastered English. Not only did he learn to read and write, he also learned the art of speaking, to such an extent that he was capable of delivering public speeches in his adopted tongue. His fluency enabled him to socialize freely with Americans, an ability which enhanced his stature as an immigrant leader. Abiko had an abiding faith that communication and education could dispel misunderstandings and clear the way for a solution to the exclusion question. In keeping with that faith, he maintained cordial relations with many Americans, including the likes of V.S. McClatchy, the archexclusionist.

Abiko felt strongly that Japanese laborers, for their part, had to cast off the *dekasegi* ideal with which they landed.[2] The ideal was selfish at bottom. Under its sway, Japanese immigrants were only interested in earning money as quickly as possible and returning to Japan. In their minds, in Abiko's judgment, this orientation justified doing anything to expedite the goal of returning, as rationalized by the Japanese proverb *"tabi no haji wa kakisute"*—there is no shame away from home. It was behind the failure to honor contracts and to respect cherished American customs. Fostering an indifference to the immigrant land, it precluded any notion of making a contribution to American society. Abiko also attributed the shortcomings within immigrant society itself to the sojourning mentality. It was behind the frequent early cases of agricultural labor contractors absconding without paying their laborers. It accounted for the unsanitary labor camps with makeshift bunkhouses, and the widespread prevalence of gambling as an illusory way of striking it rich. And it promoted short-term "speculative" ventures for quick profit rather than sound, long-term, economic undertakings. Abiko was convinced that, as long as the *dekasegi* ideal persisted, immigrant society could never be established on a solid foundation. It would continue to be composed primarily of itinerant male laborers whose life had no roots in American society.

Abiko realized that, to facilitate the transition to permanent settlement, Japanese laborers had to develop an economic and social stake in American society.[3] Abiko believed that the laborers were ideally suited to take up farming. Seeing agriculture as the economic foundation of permanent residency, he encouraged laborers to settle on land and become agricultural producers. This not only would give them an economic stake in this country, but would also place them in a position to make real contributions to American society. Simultaneously, Abiko urged all men who became farmers and shopkeepers to summon wives from Japan. Settled family life, he reasoned, would socially reinforce the economic basis of permanent settlement by motivating the immigrants to improve their living environment and by eliminating gambling, carousing, and prostitution from immigrant society. The elevation of the quality of immigrant life and the elimination of its undesirable features, in turn, would deprive the exclusionists of any real substance in their anti-Japanese rhetoric.

Abiko disseminated his ideal of permanent settlement through his newspaper, which by 1910 had become the leading immigrant daily with subscribers throughout California and in the Pacific Northwest and Rocky Mountain region. The *Nichibei Shimbun* adopted the slogan *dochaku eijū*, meaning settlement on land and permanent residency, and consistently advised Japanese laborers to take up farming. Short-term farming for quick profit would not do, however, Farming had to be on a secure, long-term basis in keeping with the ideal of permanent settlement. To keep track of the growth of Japanese immigrant agriculture, the newspaper published the *Nichibei Nenkan* (Japanese American Yearbook) between 1905 and 1918. The yearbook carried the names of all farmers by prefectural origins, state, and locale, their form of land tenure and acreage holdings, and their crop specialities. For the benefit of farmers, the yearbook also contained samples of share and cash-lease agreements and offered detailed economic analyses of costs in operating farms and in purchasing land.

In 1909 the first conference of Japanese farmers in California was held at Stockton.[4] The farmers exchanged opinions as to how to advance Japanese agriculture. As a result of this first conference, the farmers resolved to support a monthly publication. Called the *Hokubei*

Nōhō (North American Agricultural Journal), it first appeared in 1910 and was published by Noda Otosaburō and edited by Chiba Toyoji. Both men were associated closely with Abiko. Noda was an old business colleague as a stockholder and staff member of the Japanese American Industrial Corporation. Chiba was in the employ of the *Nichibei Shimbun*, compiling the *Nichibei Nenkan*. Not surprisingly, the *Hokubei Nōhō* echoed Abiko's ideal by urging Japanese laborers "to discard the *dekasegi* mentality and to become American entrepreneurs."[5]

Abiko was fond of referring to the Japanese immigrant experience in Utah and Idaho as an example of how the exclusion question might be settled in California. No anti-Japanese exclusion question of the order found in California existed in those two states. The Japanese were employed initially by the Utah Sugar Company as field hands to thin, hoe, and harvest sugar beets. Others were hired as railroad section hands, or as miners. Some of these laborers later became farmers who grew sugar beets under contract to the Utah Sugar Company. Both as laborers and farmers, the Japanese not only contributed to the prosperity of the Utah Sugar Company, but they also actually created jobs for local white workers who were employed in the company's sugar refining factories. Abiko attributed the lack of anti-Japanese agitation in Utah and Idaho to these economic contributions made by the Japanese and suggested that the pattern could be repeated in California.[6]

The Japanese settlements of Livingston and Cortez were concrete manifestations of his ideal in California. Abiko was not just an idealist. He practiced what he believed. In 1906 the Japanese American Industrial Corporation prospered greatly as the Japanese labor exodus from Hawaii peaked. All Japanese labor contractors operated for personal profit. Abiko was different in terms of what he did with his earnings. Instead of pocketing his profits, he reinvested in land to promote the common good. In 1906 Abiko and his associates established the American Land and Produce Company, an agricultural land company. With the self-declared goal of "laying the basis of settlement on land and permanent residency," this company purchased 3,200 acres of undeveloped land in Livingston. It then subdivided this large tract into 40-acre parcels and resold the parcels to those who wished to settle down on the land as farmers. A handful of pioneer settlers moved onto the land in 1907 to form what came to be known as the Yamato Colony. To avoid competing with established local businesses, no Japanese opened a shop in the town. The Japanese patronized white shopkeepers in the belief that this would facilitate their acceptance by the townspeople. Unlike the situation in other locales, all the Japanese in Livingston became landowning farmers. In Abiko's view, because they contributed to the local economy both as consumers and producers, they constituted a desirable element in the local population and provided a model solution to the exclusion question.[7] The Japanese settlement of Cortez started later, but it too was in accord with Abiko's ideal. In 1919 he organized another land company in cooperation with a white American. Purchasing 2,000 acres of land in Cortez, he again subdivided the land into small plots and resold them to those immigrants who wished to settle on it.[8]

Settlement on Agricultural Land

Statistics of farm holdings reflect the growth of Japanese agriculture in California. According to U.S. Census data, there were only 37 Japanese farms in 1900 with a combined acreage of 4,674 acres.[9] The earliest Japanese figures indicate that, in 1902, 350 Japanese farmed 17,250 acres in Northern California.[10] By 1910, and again based on U.S. Census data, the total acreage increased sharply to 99,254 acres on 1,816 farms.[11] The Nichibei Shimbun compiled much higher statistics. Broken down into four categories, the figures between 1905 and 1913 are as follows:[12]

JAPANESE AGRICULTURAL LANDHOLDINGS, 1905–1913

Year	Owned	Cash-Lease	Share-Lease	Contract	Total
1905	2,442	35,258	19,573	4,775	61,858
1906	8,671	41,855	24,826	22,100	97,452
1907	13,815	56,889	48,228	13,359	131,292
1908	15,114	55,971	57,578	26,138	155,581
1909	16,449	80,232	57,001	42,276	195,958
1910	16,980	89,464	50,399	37,898	194,742
1911	17,765	110,442	62,070	49,443	239,720
1912	26,571	124,656	56,053	38,473	245,753
1913	26,707	155,488	50,495	48,997	281,687

As can be seen, the 1910 aggregate figure of 194,742 acres is considerably higher than the corresponding U.S. Census total. The discrepancy is partly explainable by the Nichibei Shimbun's inclusion of acreage under contract. The newspaper compiled its statistics from local Japanese reports which included the names of individual owners, lessees, and contractors, and the acreage each farmed. Thus the Nichibei Shimbun statistics undoubtedly are more accurate than that of the U.S.

Census, giving a truer picture of the dramatic rise and growth of Japanese immigrant agriculture. By 1913 the 281,687 acres were being farmed by 6,177 farmers.

Japanese laborers who became farmers passed through four overlapping stages of farming.[13] Dating back to 1894 or thereabouts, they began as contract farmers. In this mode of farming, Japanese cultivated land under contract for a set wage. They did not manage farms nor did they sharecrop in any way. Providing their labor to landowners, contract farmers were wage-earners of a kind. This method of farming was common in the cultivation of sugar beets, beans, potatoes, and hops, crops which necessitated large-scale operation with many laborers. To meet the high demand for labor, contract farmers often acted as labor contractors. They supplied Japanese laborers and supervised them in the fields, making such contract farmers more than just the hired hands of landowners. For Japanese laborers, contract farming was attractive because it required no capital and offered a way out of the ranks of labor.

The second stage was share-tenancy. Shares of landowners and sharecroppers depended on what the landowners provided. If landowners only furnished land, the share was fifty-fifty; but if they also supplied horses, implements, and other essentials, their share was greater. Conversely, if sharecroppers had their own horses, implements, and other necessities, their share was greater. In 1909 the minimum cost of horses and implements needed to cultivate 100 acres was $1,377.[14] Contrasted with contract farming, share-tenancy could require a sizable amount of capital. Sharecroppers had an incentive to be productive, since the size of their set share was relative to their productivity. If they worked hard and produced more, their set share increased proportionately. Along with this advantage of share-tenancy went the risks of crop failure. Crop failure meant little or no returns. Still, share-tenancy was better than contract farming because it could be more profitable.

Cash-leasing was the third stage. Cash leases varied from one to ten years; most extended from three to five years. The method of rental payment normally was divided into two installments. The first was due when leases were signed, and the second became due after harvest. Next to the purchasing of land, this mode of farming required the most capital. In 1909 the annual rental outlay for 40 acres of land suitable for the cultivation of table grapes was $1,000.[15] Compared to contract farming and share-tenancy, cash-leasing was more desirable because it enabled Japanese to become independent farmers who enjoyed the entire fruit of their labor.

The outright purchase of land was the last stage. In 1909 the *Nichibei Shimbun* presented an economic analysis of purchasing and farming a 40-acre grape vineyard. This analysis assumed the land was undeveloped. The price of 40 acres was $2,400, paid off in installments of $400 a year over a six-year period. No profits accrued until the fourth year of farming. Excluding the cost of labor and assuming the possession of horses and implements, the projected outlay of the first three years was $2,049.[16] This sum included the annual installment and interest for the land, the annual payment and interest for water rights, and the cost of water and of grape seedlings. Japanese immigrants who had sufficient capital purchased land, but such persons were a small minority among all Japanese farmers.

A combination of factors facilitated the process by which laborers settled down on land.[17] From the landowners' perspective, Japanese were desirable farmers. In the first decade of the twentieth century, Japanese laborers occupied a dominant position in California agriculture, and landowners had the perennial problem of competing for a limited supply of labor. Inasmuch as Japanese farmers always employed fellow immigrant laborers and acted as labor bosses over them, many landowners solved this problem by allowing Japanese to till their land. As the number of Japanese farmers grew, the competition for Japanese labor intensified, and other landowners who had been reluctant to lease land to Japanese followed suit in order to assure themselves of an adequate supply of labor. Japanese laborers themselves had a strong desire to leave the ranks of labor. Farming to them meant regular employment and a settled way of life. In addition, it meant the possibility of family life. According to Japanese government regulations, farmers were eligible to summon wives from Japan. The strong desire of the Japanese to farm was exhibited in their willingness to pay higher rents in cases of cash-leasing. Once on the land, they improved it and did not demand the living quarters usually provided to white tenants. These added considerations further induced landowners to lease land to Japanese.

Japanese farmers began with little or no capital. They accumulated and acquired it by various means.[18] As contract farmers and sharecroppers, they accumulated savings which they used to move on to cash-leasing or landownership. But savings were not the only source of capital. In the production of fruit and vegetables, shippers known as commission merchants advanced money and supplies. To obtain transportation and wholesale monopolies over crops, commission merchants advanced cash in exchange for liens on crops, and in some instances subleased land, which they had leased themselves, to Japanese farmers. Sugar beet companies also subleased land and supplied a portion of the capital necessary to grow sugar beets. Another important factor was the pooling of resources by two or more persons to form partnerships, a widespread practice among Japanese farmers.

The 1913 California Alien Land Law

Just as Japanese immigrants were settling on land, California enacted the 1913 Alien Land Law. The law itself avoided direct reference to the Japanese, employing instead the phrase "aliens ineligible to citizenship," but it was definitely legislated with them in mind. It prohibited individual Japanese, and companies the majority of whose members or stockholders were Japanese, from purchasing agricultural land, and restricted the leasing of such land to three years. It also banned Japanese from bequeathing or selling to a fellow immigrant any agricultural land they already owned. The Nichibei Shimbun expressed the anger felt by the Japanese. It editorialized that the law manifested the "height of discriminatory treatment" to which Japanese immigrants were subject. Ostensibly a people of a first-rate power, Japanese were being "accorded worse treatment than people of third-rate southern and eastern European nations living in the United States."[19] At the same time, the Nichibei Shimbun warned Japanese immigrants "not to waver" in their determination to settle down permanently. The law had enough loopholes in it, so that it was not a barrier to settling on land.

Japanese farmers quickly took steps to protect existing landholdings. The most pressing problem was the ban on the transfer or sale of agricultural land from one Japanese to another. Once a Japanese farmer passed away, he was unable to bequeath his farm to his kin as long as they were aliens ineligible to citizenship. Four actual cases arose. One was that of Yokoi Hideyoshi, a resident of Florin. He died on September 6, 1913, leaving a 36-acre farm and a will which stipulated that his land should be divided equally between his wife and parents.[20] Japanese landowners who planned to return to Japan faced the problem of being unable to sell their holdings to another alien Japanese. Yet the law did not prohibit the transfer or sale of stocks in landholding companies. Governor Hiram W. Johnson signed the law on May 19, and it became effective on August 10. As early as June, the Nichibei Shimbun strongly urged Japanese farmers to form land companies to solve this problem. According to a comprehensive report of the San Francisco Japanese consul, Japanese owned a total of 29,735 acres in California as of the end of 1913.[21] There were 141 land companies at the end of 1913, of which 100 held agricultural land totalling 10,249 acres. Out of those 100 companies, at least 65 were organized in 1913, the overwhelming number in July and early August right before the effective date of the law.

Japanese farmers also had the problem of meeting payments on land purchased before the 1913 law. The case of the Yamato Colony is an excellent example. In February 1914 Abiko Kyūtarō submitted an application for a $56,000 loan to the San Francisco branch of the Yokohama Specie Bank.[22] As an important reason for his loan request, Abiko cited the paramount urgency of retaining existing landholdings in view of the prohibition against the purchase of additional land. Of the original 3,200 acres purchased by the American Land and Produce Company, 1,500 acres had been paid off, while 1,000 acres had been lost in 1910 with the liquidation of the Japanese American Bank, a Japanese immigrant bank which had held the mortgage. The loan application was for the balance of 720 acres and the $56,000 was earmarked for making outstanding payments and developing this remaining acreage.

Japanese immigrants always lacked access to adequate banking facilities. Before 1911 there were nine Japanese immigrant banks of various sizes.[23] By 1910 all but two went out of existence; the two biggest, the Golden Gate Bank and the Japanese American Bank, were liquidated in 1910.[24] The two surviving banks were the Nippon Bank of Sacramento and the Industrial Bank of Fresno. Most Japanese farmers managed without the aid of Japanese immigrant banks. The outstanding exceptions were the Yamato Colony farmers whose land was purchased with the backing of the Japanese American Bank. As editor of the *Hokubei Nōhō,* Chiba Toyoji lamented the lack of financial assistance available to Japanese farmers. Many sociologists have stressed the importance of the *tanomoshi-kō,* or Japanese-style rotating credit union, in the economic life of the Japanese immigrant.[25] Contrary to their evaluation, Chiba discounted the *tanomoshi-kō* because it could not generate large enough capital for agricultural development and could be fouled up by one or two irresponsible persons.[26] Similarly, the *Nichibei Shimbun* bemoaned the lack of an adequate rural bank and the insufficiency of the *tanomoshi-kō.* To solve this problem, some people entertained the idea of having the Japanese government establish a rural bank, but nothing ever came of it. In order to preserve existing landholdings in the light of the 1913 law, this problem took on added urgency in 1914. In Abiko's opinion, the two surviving immigrant banks of Sacramento and Fresno did not have the resources to loan large sums of money. Uncertainties had been generated regarding the position of Japanese farmers, and however well disposed a few American banks may have been, the risks foreclosed possibilities of loans from them.

The only institution to which Japanese farmers could turn was the Yokohama Specie Bank with its branches in San Francisco and Los Angeles. With the disappearance of immigrant banks, the branches of this bank had a virtual monopoly over immigrant savings from 1911. The Yokohama Specie Bank operated as an exchange bank and did not loan money to Japanese immigrants. So an anomalous situation existed in which the bank absorbed immigrant savings, but offered very little in return. The branches provided the service of remitting money to Japan, yet that was a far cry from granting loans to help the immigrants develop economically. As of the end of September 1913, the Yokohama Specie Bank held $11 million in immigrant savings in the two branches and in the home bank in Japan itself.[27] In 1913 the Japanese grape growers of Bowles requested a loan of $30,000 from the bank. The branch heads of San Francisco and Los Angeles were not authorized to grant loans. They only extended short-term loans to Mitsui Bussan and certain other trading firms with the approval of the home bank. Hence the San Francisco branch rejected the Bowles grape growers' request. Despite the endorsement of the local Japanese consul, Abiko's loan application met the same fate. The Yokohama Specie Bank took the position that it was not a commercial bank in the business of lending money.[28] This early experience with the lack of access to adequate financial institutions was to recur in an acute form in later years, but it did not halt the expansion of Japanese immigrant agriculture at this juncture.

Indeed, notwithstanding the 1913 Alien Land Law and the lack of bank loans, Japanese agriculture grew between 1914 and 1920. Japanese statistics indicate the following increase in acreage:[29]

JAPANESE AGRICULTURAL LANDHOLDINGS, 1914, 1918, 1920

Year	Owned	Cash-Lease	Share-Lease	Contract	Total
1914	31,828	155,206	72,040	41,300	300,474
1918	30,306	336,721		23,608	390,635
1920	74,769	192,150	121,000	70,137	458,056

Until the economic boom ushered in by World War I, the growth was characterized exclusively by increases in the acreage of leased land.

From a combined cash and share acreage of 227,246 in 1914, this acreage rose to 336,721 by 1918, while the owned acreage decreased slightly in the corresponding span of time. But in 1919 and 1920 the acreage of owned land rose sharply. World War I caused a great expansion in American agriculture. With a sudden demand for agricultural commodities accompanied by rising prices, American farmers enjoyed unprecedented prosperity during the war years. Sharing in the general prosperity, Japanese farmers increased their landholdings in these two years. Purchasing land in the name of their American-born children or land companies, they more than doubled the 1918 total of 30,306 acres to 74,769 by 1920.[30] The 1918 total acreage of 390,635 peaked to 458,056 acres by 1920, the highest total acreage Japanese farmers were ever to cultivate.

It would be erroneous to claim that the 1913 Alien Land Law had no negative consequences, however. Chiba Toyoji presented a perceptive critique in 1917.[31] In the few cases in which landowners died with deeds still in their names, their land sold at public auction for 30 to 40 percent less than the going market value. The three-year leasing limitation discouraged many farmers from cultivating fruit, grapes, and other crops which required a longer commitment of time, money, and labor. On the other hand, it rekindled the desire among some farmers to return to Japan, causing them to neglect their physical environment and to gamble on uncertain one-year crops. Finally and most importantly, the 1913 Alien Land Law forced all Japanese immigrants to live with the stigma of being aliens ineligible to citizenship and subject to discriminatory treatment.

In 1918 there were a total of 7,973 farmers, 4,560 of whom had wives, with 6,510 children, adding up to an aggregate of 19,043 persons.[32] These farmers and their dependents comprised 27.5 percent of the Japanese population of 68,982 in California. In 1918 there were still 15,794 agricultural laborers, 1,666 of whom had wives with 1,508 children. The total agricultural population therefore was 38,011, or 55.1 percent of the total Japanese population. These figures taken together indicate the degree to which many laborers had settled successfully on land and the primary importance which agriculture had assumed in the economic life of Japanese immigrants.

Japanese Associations

Social institutions reinforced the economic foundation of permanent settlement. Formed as the shift to permanent settlement was taking place, the key political organizations of the Japanese immigrants were the so-called Japanese associations. Wherever a significant number of Japanese settled, whether in California, Oregon, Washington, or elsewhere, they established local associations. All associations operated within the framework of a three-tiered hierarchy. Local Japanese consulates occupied the upper tier, while local associations represented the third tier. Situated on the middle level were so-called central bodies, which provided the link between the local consulates and local associations. In the Pacific Northwest, locals in Washington and Montana were affiliated with the Northwest American Japanese Association that was established in 1913 and based in Seattle under the Seattle consulate. Locals in Oregon, Idaho, and Wyoming were affiliated with the Japanese Association of Oregon, headquartered in Portland and formed in 1911 under the Portland consulate. The Japanese Association of America, the first of the central bodies, was organized in 1908 in San Francisco under the San Francisco consulate, and originally embraced all locals in California, Nevada, Utah, Colorado, and Arizona. In 1915, however, the Central Japanese Association of Southern California was founded in Los Angeles under the Los Angeles consulate to which locals in southern California, Arizona, and New Mexico affiliated. In 1923 Seattle had 15 affiliated locals, Oregon 10, San Francisco 40, and Los Angeles 21. From 1914 to 1929 these four central bodies (excluding Los Angeles in the first two years) combined with the Japanese Association of Canada to form the Pacific Coast Japanese Association Deliberative Council, which, though not a fourth tier, was an additional organ that addressed itself to problems common to the Japanese in the United States and Canada. This hierarchy was the product of a special relationship into which all associations entered with the Japanese government.

To understand the origins of the associations, it is important to examine their predecessors. The earliest precursor dates from the late nineteenth century. In 1891 Chinda Sutemi, the Japanese consul in San Francisco, organized the Greater Japanese Association. The body's purposes were ''to increase friendly intercourse among Japanese residents, to promote mutual aid in times of need, and to safeguard the Japanese national image.''[33] Reflecting the consul's prominence in the organization was the fact that Chinda was the president with his term of office coinciding with his tour of duty in San Francisco. Though this association tried to speak on behalf of all Japanese in and near the city, it failed. The heterogeneous composition of the Japanese population made it all but impossible to bring everyone under the fold of a single organization. As the earliest precursor of the Japanese associations, the significance of the Greater Japanese Association lies not so much in its failure as in its foreshadowing the influence local consuls would have in later organizations. However limited its membership and activities may have been, however, it did last through the 1890s. But since anti-Japanese incidents were still isolated events, Japanese immigrants, fragmented into diverse interest groups, felt no compelling need to band together into a large organization.

The turn of the century witnessed a sharp change with the beginning of the Japanese exclusion movement.[34] In March 1900 the San Francisco Board of Health announced that it had discovered a victim of the bubonic plague in Chinatown. Anti-Chinese elements raised the specter of an epidemic engulfing not only the city but the entire state. After ordering the quarantine of Chinatown, city officials on May 19 issued a compulsory inoculation order applicable to all Chinese and Japanese within the city limits. Less than two weeks prior to this order, the first public anti-Japanese meeting had been held on May 7 at which the question of the extension of the Chinese Exclusion Act had been linked to the new issue of curtailing Japanese immigration. In direct response to these events, key immigrant leaders convened an emergency meeting on May 22 that was attended by 31 persons. To stay the inoculation order, they decided to seek a court injunction, which they successfully obtained on May 28. Three days later, a larger meeting was held at which Japanese residents discussed establishing an organization to cope with future problems. As a result, the assembled residents organized the Japanese Deliberative Council of America, the purpose of which, as subsequently written into its charter, was "to expand the rights of Imperial subjects in America and to maintain the Japanese national image."[35] By dint of external pressure in the form of the beginning of the exclusion movement, Japanese immigrants came together for the first time.

Just as outside pressure compelled the immigrants to form the council in the first place, so, too, did ensuing external events cause them to expand it. During the first five years of its existence, the council was restricted to the city of San Francisco. The sole exceptions were the ties it had with similar bodies in Oakland and San Jose. The full-scale eruption of the exclusion movement in 1905 forced immigrant leaders to realize the need for a statewide organization. Shortly after the San Francisco *Chronicle* launched its anti-Japanese editorial crusade in late February, a spokesman of the council travelled throughout California and urged local Japanese communities to send representatives to San Francisco for a conference. In May representatives of local groups and members of the San Francisco council convened to discuss the formation of a statewide organization. Rather than immediately form such an organization, the delegates instead set up regional ad hoc committees to foster the establishment of local councils. At the second conference, held in Fresno the next year, the locals officially affiliated with the San Francisco council, which was designated the central body and renamed the United Japanese Deliberative Council of America. This network of councils consisted of 11 affiliated locals in 1906, and stayed mostly intact until 1908.[36] Yet mere affiliation did not automatically produce a cohesive statewide organization. The network had been created, ideally at least, to unify Japanese immigrants to fight the exclusion movement; but if local affiliates did not derive benefits from affiliation, they were free to sever their ties. The formation of the Japanese Association of America in 1908 fundamentally altered the nature of the affiliation between the central body and locals, and the change itself was related to another external event, the Gentlemen's Agreement of 1907–8.

Once the two governments concluded the agreement, the Japanese government faced the administrative problem of implementing it. Because Japanese immigrants were scattered throughout the western states, the government had the difficult task of determining who in fact was a bona fide resident. In the course of the negotiations, the American government had suggested that the Japanese government devise a system of compulsory registration of all Japanese in the United States and issue certificates of registration.[37] The possession of such a certificate, to be issued by local Japanese consulates beginning on January 1, 1908, was to be considered the only valid document allowing Japanese laborers to continue to reside in the United States. The Japanese government at first refused to consider any system of registration, arguing that it was virtually impossible for its consular staff to contact and register Japanese immigrants who were dispersed so widely. Moreover, and even more important, the government feared that, if it consented to the American suggestion, it would signify that Japanese who did not register, and hence did not possess certificates of registration, would forfeit their right to stay in this country. The American government broached this matter in late November 1907 and, in spite of Japanese refusals, continued to insist on some kind of system of registration. The Japanese government finally acceded to a modified system in February 1908.[38] As proposed by the Japanese side, the system of registration did not entail either legal coercion or the forfeiture of the right to remain in the United States. But it did have a measure of extralegal coercion as it was eventually implemented and actually practiced. Under the modified system, the Japanese government delegated certain bureaucratic functions to the Japanese associations. This delegation of functions became the basis of the special relationship between the government and the associations.

During and after the negotiation of the Gentlemen's Agreement, significant related events occurred. In December 1907 the Japanese Foreign Ministry transferred Koike Chōzō, the consul general of New York City, to San Francisco, and simultaneously elevated the status of the San Francisco consulate to a consulate general. These actions undoubtedly reflected the importance Tokyo attached to the city in view of the growing exclusion movement. Other reasons were involved, too. The majority of Japanese immigrants resided within the jurisdiction of the San Francisco office, and the consular staff there would have to implement any agreement which might finally be reached. The Foreign Ministry also wished to control the activities of Japanese immigrant socialists and anarchists, especially after the November 3, 1907, incident in which a few members of the Social Revolutionary Party had blasphemed the Meiji Emperor.[39] This called for an experienced diplomat like Koike. As soon as he assumed his new post, Koike advised immigrant leaders to disband the United Japanese Deliberative Council of America. From the start the organization had been plagued by financial problems and factional strife, and the Los Angeles council even disaffiliated itself from it in January 1908.[40] At the behest of the new consul, prominent leaders, rather than reform the existing body, organized the Japanese Association of America on February 4, 1908, as a new central body.

The relationship of the newly formed central body to the Japanese government was established in the course of the year. In April Consul Koike hinted that the Japanese Association of America might be granted authority to process applications for certificates issued by the consulate and might share the fees charged for them. The new central body then convened a conference of local bodies, regardless of whether they had been affiliated to the old council, to discuss this possibility in July. Local representatives were informed that, if the Foreign Ministry delegated such authority, it would be bestowed on the new central body and local associations affiliated to it. Unaffiliated locals would be excluded. The parley closed with the representatives voting in favor of the idea, and a formal petition was submitted to the consul, which the Foreign Ministry approved in December. Consul Koike had laid down the condition of affiliation as an incentive to locals to affiliate in order to create a wider, more cohesive network of associations. From the point of view of the locals, they clearly stood to gain if they affiliated. They not only would secure the delegated authority, but they would also benefit financially. That the condition proved to be an effective incentive can be seen in the dramatic rise of affiliated locals. The old council had but 8 affiliates when it was dissolved. The Japanese Association of America had 22 in 1908; by 1909 it had 30.[41] In sum, the Japanese government decided to use the tighter network of Japanese associations, which it had nurtured, to solve the administrative problem of implementing the Gentlemen's Agreement.

The system of delegated bureaucratic authority was known as the "endorsement right." Effective January 1, 1909, in accordance with the authorization granted by the Foreign Ministry, the San Francisco consul delegated this right to the Japanese Association of America, which in turn redelegated it. When the consulate first instituted the system, two hierarchical arrangements governed the relationship between the consulate and local associations. On the one hand, the Japanese Association of America redelegated the right to locals directly affiliated to it in a three-tiered hierarchy; on the other hand, it redelegated the right to regional central bodies, which again redelegated it to smaller locals affiliated to them in a four-tiered hierarchy. The latter arrangement was established in Sacramento and Los Angeles. At the beginning the Japanese Association of America functioned concurrently as the central body and as the local association of San Francisco, and administered the endorsement right in the city. In December 1913 the Japanese Association of San Francisco was formed, making it no longer necessary for the central body to perform two roles, so that it redelegated the right to the new San Francisco local. In theory the consul or the central body, or the regional centrals while they existed, had the power to withdraw the endorsement right from associations to which they had delegated it.

The consulate issued certificates in conjunction with the endorsement right. There were basically two types of certificates: one type related to the Gentlemen's Agreement, and the other was tied to Japanese laws. In the first category fell the certificates which permitted bearers to journey to Japan and return to America alone or accompanied by spouses, children, and/or parents; to take a trip to other countries and return to the United States; or to summon spouses, children, and/or parents without going to Japan. These certificates attested to the fact that the bearers were bona fide residents of the United States. Certificates for annual draft deferments were the main ones in the second category. Any Japanese male who had not fulfilled his Japanese military obligation and resided abroad could have his service deferred as long as he submitted a certificate to the government office in his home district indicating that he was living in a foreign country. Other certificates in this category were connected with family registries and concerned such matters as births and deaths, marriages and divorces, adoptions and inheritances. For all these certificates, Japanese immigrants had to apply at the association within whose jurisdiction they lived. Based on the delegated endorsement right, the associations performed the bureaucratic job of "endorsing" certificate applications to see that applicants in fact were bona fide residents within their jurisdiction, and that the socio-economic data in the applications were accurate. Once the applications were processed, the associations forwarded them to the consulate where they were approved or rejected. If they were approved, the consulate issued the appropriate certificates. As far as the United States was concerned, the primary administrative problem of the Gentlemen's Agreement was how to determine who was a bona fide resident in America. The Japanese government solved it by delegating the responsibility of making this determination to the local associations.

Local associations were entrusted with one other bureaucratic function. In May 1909 the Foreign Ministry announced that overseas Japanese had to register at the closest consular or embassy office in the foreign country in which they resided.[42] Effective October 1, 1909, according to a new regulation, all overseas Japanese had to register by March 31, 1910. The Foreign Ministry also delegated to the Japanese associations the responsibility for such registration, which in the United States actually took place from April 1 to September 30, 1910. To make certain that as many persons as possible registered, the San Francisco consul stipulated that no future certificates would be issued unless applicants had registered with an association. When the associations forwarded applications to the consulate, they were instructed to indicate on them whether applicants had registered or not. The Japanese government had assured the American government in the negotiation of the Gentlemen's Agreement that it would institute a modified system of registration. On February 23, 1908, Foreign Minister Hayashi Tadasu had informed American Ambassador Thomas J. O'Brien that, although the Japanese government could not legally force Japanese residents to register, it could "indirectly make registration highly desirable, if not indispensable in the majority of instances, by refusing to grant certificates to non-registered persons."[43] Hence the consul's new administrative condition was linked directly to this assurance conveyed by Foreign Minister Hayashi to Ambassador O'Brien. Eventually, the Seattle, Portland, and Los Angeles consulates delegated the same bureaucratic functions to the central body within their respective jurisdiction.

A measure of control was built into this system of delegated authority. All consuls occupied the top tier in the three-tiered hierarchy. Their authority naturally rested on the power with which their office was vested by the Foreign Ministry. As official government representatives, they had general influence over Japanese immigrants. Their added influence derived from their responsibility to see that the delegated authority was being efficiently and fairly exercised by the associations. To administer the endorsement right, they assigned the task of supervising local associations to the central bodies. When they issued administrative directives, they sent them to the central bodies which in turn directed local associations to carry them out. The three-tiered hierarchy served as a convenient administrative channel for the consuls.

The system of delegated authority enabled local associations to exercise control over Japanese immigrants. Local associations became semi-government offices for all intents and purposes, with their officers endowed with the status of quasi-government bureaucrats. If an immigrant wanted one or more of the certificates issued by the consulate, he had to apply at a local association. If the local association considered him guilty of acts detrimental to the welfare of the Japanese community, it could refuse to process his application. In fact, local associations declined to handle the applications of persons they considered incorrigible—hoodlums, prostitutes, prostitution ringleaders, chronic gamblers, corrupt labor contractors, political extremists, and the like. And the central bodies as well as the consulates invariably backed up their refusal to handle the applications of such persons. Once the network of associations was organized tightly, it made it very difficult for an immigrant who had his application refused by one association to have it accepted by another. Sensitive to American criticisms of Japanese immigrant behavior, local associations endeavored to coerce Japanese immigrants to behave in an ''acceptable'' manner or suffer the consequence of being deprived of the certificates issued by the consulates. Local associations also were privy to personal information which gave them extra leverage over the immigrants. When local residents registered, they were required to list their home addresses in Japan and to submit detailed socio-economic data and photographs of themselves. With this information, local associations were able to keep track of Japanese immigrants and inform each other of anyone who stepped out of line.

The Japanese Immigrant Family

The family was the key social institution. Between 1900 and 1920 many men summoned wives from Japan. In 1900 there were only 410 married women in immigrant society. This number increased to 5,581 by 1910 and leaped to 22,193 by 1920. These women enabled many immigrant men to enjoy a settled family life which socially reinforced the economic foundation of permanent settlement. Married women entered immigrant society in one of three ways. Some wives who had been left behind in Japan were summoned by their husbands. Other women married single men who returned to Japan to seek brides. These women came to the United States with their spouses. Two factors limited the number of bachelors who returned to Japan to seek brides. Few could afford the time and expense of such a trip, which included the heavy outlays for marriage required by Japanese social custom. Some returnees faced the possibility of being inducted into the military. All Japanese men living abroad enjoyed deferments, but lost their deferred status if they returned for more than thirty days. The time spent in finding an appropriate bride, in entering into a formal engagement, and in getting married often exceeded a month.

Thus many bachelors resorted to the so-called picture-bride practice, the third way by which women entered immigrant society. The picture-bride practice did not diverge sharply from traditional Japanese marriage custom. In Japan, marriage was never an individual matter, but always a family affair. Heads of household selected marriage partners for family members through intermediaries or go-betweens. An exchange of photographs sometimes occurred in the screening process, with family genealogy, wealth, education, and health figuring heavily in the selection criteria. Go-betweens arranged parleys between families at which proposed unions were discussed and negotiated. Although at such meetings prospective spouses normally met each other for the first time, it would be unusual for them to talk to each other. After all, the meetings were for the benefit of the heads of family, and not designed for future couples to become acquainted with each other. If the families mutually consented, engagement and marriage ensued.

In general, the picture-bride practice conformed to this marriage custom. Single immigrant men had brides picked for them by their parents or relatives. Along with photographs of themselves, the men forwarded information about their lives in America, which go-betweens used in negotiations with parents of eligible daughters. The practice deviated in only one important respect from conventional marriages: bridegrooms were physically absent at wedding ceremonies. Still, the practice satisfied all social and legal requirements governing marriage in Japan. Marriages were legal as long as husbands fulfilled a simple bureaucratic condition: they had to enter the names of their brides into their own family registries. By meeting this requirement, men became legally bethrothed no matter where they resided. That they had never laid eyes upon their brides nor had participated in wedding ceremonies was of no consequence. In accordance with this practice, the majority of wives who entered immigrant society between 1910 and 1920 came as picture-brides.

To control the entry of married women, Japanese consulates set rigid standards. The fundamental yardstick was economic. Only men who had proven means of supporting families were qualified to summon wives. All laborers were ineligible until 1915. Rare exceptions were made for those in urban occupations—for example, butlers, waiters, and cooks—if they commanded high wages and could provide proof of continuous employment and savings of at least $1,000. Businessmen and farmers were eligible, but they had to meet specific criteria. A businessman had to have an annual gross income of $1,200 or more, a farmer had to have an annual profit of $400 to $500, and both had to have savings of at least $1,000 as well.[44] In 1915 the Japanese government modified its requirements to make laborers eligible. Effective July 1, 1915, all male residents of the United States, including laborers, became eligible to summon wives, provided they had savings of $800. To reduce the possibility of fraud, Japanese consuls required that men who applied to bring over their wives had to submit bank deposit books as proof that this sum had been in their accounts for no less than five months preceding the date of applications.

Women had to satisfy specific government regulations too. If they were picture-brides, their names had to be entered into their husbands' family registries six months prior to their passport applications. This requirement, Japanese officials believed, impeded procurers from obtaining prostitutes disguised as picture-brides. After 1915 picture-brides also had to meet an age regulation. They could not be more than thirteen years younger than their spouses. This age limit was set on the premise that too wide a disparity was not conducive to harmonious marriages. If there were extenuating circumstances, however, the regulation was waived. All Japanese emigrants had to pass physical examinations at ports of embarkation. American immigration statutes prohibited the admission of bearers of contagious diseases. Immigration inspectors were especially alert for those afflicted with trachoma and hookworm, two fairly common diseases in Japan. Aware of American regulations, the Japanese government administered physical examinations to all departing women to make sure that they had neither.

No single motive explains why Japanese women came to the United States. In the case of married women who had been left behind in Japan, they responded to their spouses' summons to join them. Most picture-brides simply obeyed parents. Bethrothed by parental arrangement, they, too, came to join their spouses. To refuse would have been an act of filial disobedience, a grave moral offense. Economic motives no doubt were also involved. Some daughters became picture-brides to help their families through hard times or to put a younger sibling through school. By working in this country, they expected to be able to remit money to their families. For women who found themselves in social predicaments, marriage with men abroad offered an avenue of escape. For such women life in America held out hopes for a new beginning, a future in a country which evoked images of material comfort unimaginable at home. Some women came for even more fundamental economic reasons—they lacked sufficient food, clothing, and shelter.

Regardless of motives, all women were beset by common problems as soon as they landed. Their first encounter with America was the ordeal of passing through the labyrinth of the immigration station. Most women arrived as third-class steerage passengers for whom an immigration inspection was a grim experience. Inspectors examined them more scrupulously than first- or second-class passengers. Advance briefings about what to expect did not allay anxieties. Many questions worried the women no end. Were their papers in order? Each wife had to have a valid passport, a certified copy of her husband's family registry, and a health certificate. Would she pass the physical examination? That she had been found free of trachoma and hookworm in Japan was no guarantee she would. Would her husband be at the immigration station to welcome her? Some wives did not know. All husbands had to appear in person to receive wives. Picture-brides gazed upon their spouses for the first time in the station. Such anxieties were compounded by fear of the unknown and by lack of knowledge of English.

Wives were matched up with husbands at the immigration station. Immigration officials required husbands to present documents to avert mix-ups. First, they had to have certificates issued by the Japanese consulates which attested to their identity and occupation. Second, they had to have additional proof of employment. Farmers had to show land titles or lease agreements, businessmen had to show commercial licenses, and salaried workers had to produce letters signed by employers. Third, they had to have bank deposit books as evidence of their ability to support wives. If everything was in order, officials released wives into the custody of husbands. Prior to 1917, the American government did not recognize picture-bride marriages, so that picture-brides and their spouses had to be remarried in a ceremony in order to be considered legally married in the United States. Group ceremonies were conducted in the immigration station at the beginning; later they were held in hotel lobbies or churches by special arrangement with immigration authorities. In 1917 the State Department granted legal recognition to picture-bride marriages, allowing picture-brides and their spouses to dispense with this second wedding ceremony.

Many picture-brides were genuinely shocked to see their husbands. Sometimes the person was much older than he appeared in his photograph. As a rule husbands were older than wives by ten to fifteen years, and occasionally more. Men often forwarded photographs taken in their youth or touched up ones that concealed their real age. No wonder some picture-brides, upon sighting their spouses, lamented dejectedly that they had married "an old man." Husbands appeared unexpectedly different in other ways. Some men had photographs touched up, not just to look youthful, but to improve their overall appearance. They had traces of facial blemishes and baldness removed. Picture-brides understandably were taken aback because such men did not physically correspond with their photographs at all. Suave, handsome-looking gentlemen proved to be pockmarked country bumpkins. A few disillusioned picture-brides declined to join their husbands and asked to be sent back to Japan. Others who had married distant relatives or men they had known in their villages as young girls were disappointed, perhaps, but not crestfallen.

Almost all women landed wearing Japanese kimonos and sandals. As a part of their initiation into American society, it was common for husbands to take their wives to a clothing store to outfit them in a set of western clothes. Of all the strange items of apparel, corsets were the most uncomfortable. Newly outfitted women had trouble breathing while wearing something so constricting. Western-style shoes were no less uncomfortable. The enclosed, pointed toe of shoes, particularly of fashionable, high-lace boots, were not suited for Japanese women whose feet, shaped since childhood by open slippers and sandals, were wide and flat. Pointed shoes were painful to wear and impossible to walk in at first.

Other more serious problems lay in store. Besides sending touched-up photographs, Japanese immigrant men were sometimes disingenuous in other ways. To enable parents or relatives to find brides easily, they often exaggerated their own attractiveness as future husbands.[45] Keepers of small Japanese-style inns or boardinghouses referred to themselves as hotel operators. In Japan, the word "hotel" connoted something much larger than either, conjuring up images of modern, multistoried brick or concrete structures. Similarly, sharecroppers passed themselves off as landowning farmers, small shopkeepers as big merchants, hotel bellboys as elevator engineers, railroad section foremen as labor contractors. A female reader of the *Shin Sekai* once wrote that, if the newspaper ever printed the letters men forwarded to Japan in seeking picture-brides, the men would have to cringe in shame. She believed that these letters were devoid of sincerity.[46] A few men were culpable of more than hyperboles; they relayed utterly false information about themselves. A picture-bride in one case discovered that her husband was an itinerant gambler instead of being the landowning fruit grower he had claimed to be.[47] Picture-brides had no way of verifying information about their spouses. In general, they believed what they heard from go-betweens until they arrived in the United States and learned otherwise.

Women quickly came into contact with American realities through work. The majority went into rural areas. Scattered throughout the western United States, many entered labor camps operated by their husbands. Alternatively, women entered farmlands on which their husbands tilled the soil as share or cash tenants. This was especially common in California where Japanese immigrant agriculture flourished the most. In urban areas, women entered small businesses in which their husbands were engaged: laundries, bathhouses, bars, markets, restaurants, boardinghouses, and poolhalls. Or they became domestic servants, seamstresses, or cannery workers. But no matter where they ended up, a life of unending labor was their lot. Ideally, Japanese women were supposed to confine themselves to the home as "dutiful wives and intelligent mothers" (*ryōsai kenbo*). Very few immigrant women could afford to limit themselves to these two roles.

Economic realities forced the majority to assume a third role as workers whose labor was indispensable in the operation of labor camps, farms, and small businesses.

Living and working conditions generally were primitive. In rural areas women had to draw water for cooking, washing, and bathing from wells. Kindling wood was the source of heat. Frequently, women had to cook for large gangs of workers employed by their husbands. Makeshift wooden shacks on farms and small rented rooms in towns usually served as initial living quarters. Working from dawn to dusk left little time to socialize, even less to devote oneself to the leisure arts or to learn English. Women were compelled to work in order to survive, a reality which made them aware of the hyperboles and falsehoods their husbands had told before marriage.

This harsh reality was behind marital scandals known as *kakeochi* or desertion of husbands by wives. The immigrant press regularly printed *kakeochi* notices. A typical notice announced that a married woman and a "scoundrel," both named specifically, had "disappeared," meaning that they had absconded together. The notice included their physical description, place of origin in Japan, and even photographs. Husbands who had been deserted, or local immigrant organizations, placed these notices in the immigrant press and offered rewards for information leading to the discovery of the guilty parties. The *Shin Sekai* ran a typical notice in 1909 submitted by Kojima Aizō of Walnut Grove announcing that his wife, Tsuta, had fled with Miki Jōkichi.[48] A native of Wakayama Prefecture, Miki was described as 33 to 34 years old, 5 feet 2 inches, 115 pounds with dark complexion and a scar at the nape of his neck. A native of Yamaguchi Prefecture, Tsuta was described as 28 years old, 5 feet, 110 pounds, with fair complexion. The notice stated that the two had vanished together on December 12. Kojima offered a reward of $25 to any party furnishing information as to their whereabouts. The *Nichibei Shimbun* printed many similar notices. In 1912, for example, it ran one submitted by Ōshima Suematsu of Hanford who declared that his wife, Tora, had run off clandestinely with Ono Ken'ichi.[49] Ōshima also offered a reward of $25.

Desertion stories appeared in the immigrant press as often as *kakeochi* notices. As early as April 1908, the *Shin Sekai* reported the case of Odawara Toshiko, who ran away from Sacramento to Stockton with her paramour.[50] In 1914 the *Taihoku Nippō* of Seattle carried a story about Nishizaki Juta who was depicted as a moral derelict.[51] He had seduced the wife of Hashimoto Yoshirō of Tacoma, and harbored her secretly until the local Japanese association uncovered his hideaway and had them arrested. Legal charges were dropped once Nishizaki agreed to pay Hashimoto $600. *Kakeochi* stories typically preceded notices. The *Shin Sekai* ran a story on September 20, 1916, on Kimura Haru, wife of Kimura Masaki, who left Loomis with her 2½-year-old child. Having suffered a miscarriage, she went to Sacramento ostensibly to regain her health. There, by prearrangement, she met Shimizu Fudeki who had been employed by her husband on his fruit orchard. The two then disappeared. A notice of this desertion appeared on September 21. The *Nichibei Shimbun,* in another story, reported on February 14–15, 1916, that Yamaura Toshie, wife of Yamaura Chiyozō of Lodi, abandoned not only her husband but her child as well. A notice of her desertion appeared on February 18.

All stories contained variations of the desertion theme. The detail differed depending upon the story. A picture-bride deserts right after arriving; another deserts after living with her husband for a spell. An older married woman leaves her husband and children, while another takes her infant with her. A woman and her paramour plot to steal her husband's hidden money before absconding together. A woman is caught and sent back to Japan, while another is placed in a church-operated women's home. The men with whom women run off range from young laborers to roving city salesmen, to partners in their husbands' farms or businesses, and even to professional gamblers. Most stories are written in a tragic vein; a few have elements of the comic. All have didactic overtones. Embellishments and distortions undoubtedly crept into many of the reports. Newspapers, after all, published *kakeochi* stories to attract readers and thereby enlarge their circulation. Yet the stories were not imagined by reporters; they were based upon actual incidents.

The publication of *kakeochi* stories and notices by the immigrant press was also a means of social control. The publicity exposed to public shame those women who deserted their husbands. Branded as "adulteresses" or "immoral hussies," women who deserted were ostracized and inevitably forced to move to new locales. The *Nichibei Shimbun* printed two notices in July, 1913, one announcing that Ōmoto Mine had deserted her husband in Alameda, and another that Furube Shizue had left her husband in Oxnard. Both women fled eastward to Utah.[52] Remote places, however, were not always safe havens, as a Stockton man found out when he deserted his own wife and ran away with another man's. The two were apprehended in

Medford, Oregon, as they were heading for Seattle, by local Japanese residents who recognized them.[53]

Complementing the immigrant press were the Japanese associations which acted as the moral watchdogs of Japanese communities. Association leaders became alarmed in 1916 over the rate of desertion. As evidence of a rising rate, the *Nichibei Shimbun* reported that the local association of San Francisco had received an inordinate number of *kakeochi* notices from other associations.[54] In the spring, secretaries of local associations affiliated with the Japanese Association of America deliberated on the problem of desertion at their annual meeting. They described the state of marriages within the jurisdiction of their association, and to account for marital failures, enumerated such factors as the drinking and gambling habits of husbands, the disillusionment of picture-brides, and the gaps in age and education among spouses. To the horror of the assembled males, a few cases were cited in which picture-brides had had affairs with seamen or other men aboard ships en route to the United States. This prompted the Japanese Association of America to issue a guide to the United States for women and to have it distributed at ports of embarkation in Japan. First published in 1916, it was reissued in 1919.[55] The guide instructed women on how to conduct themselves aboard ship, how to manage a household, and how to behave in American society. It reminded them that they had the "responsibility" of never revealing "domestic scandals" to Americans, for such scandals were sources of "embarrassment" to all Japanese. In October 1916 the Japanese Association of America asked the Tōyō Kisen Kaisha, a Japanese steamship company, to assign matrons to ships to supervise young women en route to the United States, and also petitioned the Foreign Ministry to direct other Japanese shipping lines to do likewise.[56]

All Japanese associations treated absconding couples as outcasts. The Western Idaho Japanese Association is a case in point. In September 1923 this association received a letter from the North American Japanese Association of Seattle notifying it that Araeda Asako had absconded with Amano Sanji.[57] She had deserted her sick husband, Araeda Aiji, and her child. Photographs of her and her paramour were enclosed. The Seattle association asked the Idaho association to be alert to their possible appearance in its jurisdiction and to have no dealings with them until Asako returned to her husband and Amano made proper restitution. Three weeks later the Idaho association received another letter, this one from the Japanese Association of Watsonville,

California, with photographs attached.[58] The letter asserted that Kasa-
matsu Chika had deserted her husband and three children and had run
off with Kuramoto Hikosuke. Japanese associations communicated in
this manner with each other, and as a matter of common policy refused to have any dealings with absconding couples. The network of
associations made it well-nigh impossible for such couples to escape
detection, even when they left one state and settled down in a Japanese
community in another. If they wished to elude social ostracism altogether, they had no choice but to resettle in a place where there were
no Japanese.

Marital estrangement was at the bottom of desertions. No woman
took desertion lightly. Living in an alien land reinforced the traditional
subordinate role of Japanese women. With little or no knowledge of
the English language and of American society, wives had to depend
upon their husbands for almost everything. This dependency, coupled
with the threat of public exposure, inhibited desertion. As a general
rule, therefore, women who deserted had to be those who were very
desperate. Becoming a social outcast, to them, was better than enduring conjugal relations which had degenerated to an insufferable level.
Kawai Michiko, a prominent Christian educator in Japan, observed
the picture-bride practice at first hand in 1917. She felt that ''an out-
dated attitude'' exhibited by men in America was the main cause of
marital conflicts. Despite changes in ideas and practices in Japan, the
men clung to archaic notions, which they had learned from their fathers in the nineteenth century, about the absolute subordinate role of
wives.[59]

Notwithstanding all the hardships Japanese immigrant women had
to endure, the majority did not desert their husbands, and thus enabled
many men to enjoy a settled family life. The emergence of the Japanese
immigrant family was reflected in the dramatic increase in the number
of American-born, or Nisei, children between 1900 and 1920. At the
turn of the century, there were only 269 children; by 1910 the number
grew to 4,502, and by 1920 it multiplied more than sixfold to 29,672.
Most women gave birth to these children through midwifery. Nearly
every Japanese settlement had midwives. If a settlement did not have
one, women relied upon those who worked in neighboring communities. Many pregnant women in the Imperial Valley, for example,
entered Los Angeles maternity clinics that were staffed with midwives. In isolated rural areas, husbands served as midwives or women
gave birth unassisted, even cutting and tieing the umbilical cord themselves. Most women never had prenatal or postnatal care. They

worked until a few days before delivery and resumed work shortly after. The birth of Nisei children accelerated the transformation of Japanese immigrants from sojourners to permanent settlers as the Issei generation eventually identified its own future with that of its children in America. In sum, the entry of women into immigrant society was integral to the process by which Japanese immigrants sank roots in American soil.

Termination of Picture-Bride Practice

In 1919 the agitation against the picture-bride practice emerged in California. Senator James D. Phelan, anticipating his 1920 reelection campaign, started the agitation in March. Japanese women were easy targets. Phelan and others attacked the picture-bride practice as an uncivilized ''Asiatic'' custom, a throwback as it were to barbarism by which women were married off without regard to love or morality. They alleged that the practice violated the Gentlemen's Agreement which had been negotiated to curtail labor immigration from Japan. Deviously undermining the agreement, Japanese female laborers were entering the United States under the guise of being ''homemakers.'' To make matters worse, these women produced children, enabling Japanese immigrants to circumvent the 1913 California Alien Land Law. Exclusionists charged that the Japanese were buying agricultural land in the name of their offspring who were American citizens. Lastly, they saw the increasing number of Nisei children as dangerous increments to the Japanese population because the children, like their parents, could never be assimilated into American society. From the vantage point of the Japanese consul in San Francisco, this agitation peaked in September. Judging the situation to be truly grave, Consul Ota Tamekichi wired the Foreign Ministry on October 5 and recommended that it cease issuing passports to picture-brides. In his words, such a measure would have the effect of ''taking away the most effective source of agitation from the exclusionists.''[60]

While waiting for Tokyo to make up its mind, Consul Ota called a meeting of the executive board of the Japanese Association of America. He asked the board members to declare publicly that they were opposed to the picture-bride practice. Originating from immigrant leaders, such a stand, Ota felt, would mollify the exclusionists. The executive board agreed with him, and on October 31 issued a press release in English which declared that the practice ''should be abolished because it is not only in contravention of the accepted American conception of marriage, but is also out of harmony with the growing ideals of the Japanese themselves."[61] In this sequence of events, it was the consul who first recommended to Tokyo the termination of the picture-bride practice, and who then wrested the agreement from the executive board of the Japanese Association of America. No affiliated local association nor any other central body was consulted by the board in arriving at its decision to go along with Consul Ota.

As soon as the press release became public, a veritable storm of criticism came down upon the Japanese Association of America. The *Nichibei Shimbun* and its publisher, Abiko Kyūtarō, attacked the statement as well as the way in which it had been issued. While not blind to the shortcomings in the picture-bride practice, Abiko had always supported the practice as the most economical and practical way for single men to get married and to summon their brides. Editorially, the *Nichibei Shimbun* had criticized the Foreign Ministry's $800 requirement which, in its opinion, had effectively disqualified most single men. Moreover, the five-month deposit requirement had impeded the economic development of immigrant society. Capital was essential for development. The five-month deposit requirement meant that large sums of money languished in savings accounts at low interest rates, sharply reducing the amount of capital available to farmers and businessmen for investment purposes. Both requirements had retarded the realization of permanent settlement.[62] From Abiko's point of view, marriage was a fundamental human right which no one had a right to abridge. The content and tone of the *Nichibei Shimbun*'s coverage of the executive board's public statement were so caustic that Consul Ota reported that Abiko was "playing on the ignorance of the masses."[63] The *Taihoku Nippō* of Seattle and the *Rafu Shimpō* of Los Angeles sharply voiced their own opprobrium in major editorials.[64] The other three central bodies of Seattle, Portland, and Los Angeles quickly denounced the Japanese Association of America, arguing that it did not have the authority to release the statement without consulting them first. Affiliated locals felt that the executive board had acted beyond its prescribed authority and convened an extraordinary session of representatives.

The extraordinary session met from November 29 through December 1 in a tense atmosphere. Besides the representatives of local associations, interested spectators packed the meeting hall. On the first day, Consul Ota addressed the assembly and asked local associations to support the action of the central body. Although he had yet to be notified of Tokyo's final decision, he believed his government would concur with the executive board's press release. The spectators responded by roundly booing Ota, and he accused them of being "ruffians" sent by Abiko to disrupt the proceedings.[65] The three-day session was taken up with the board members defending their action in the face of hostile charges that they were hirelings of the consul. On the last day, every officer and staff member of the central body formally resigned. The session in no way, however, repaired the damage that had been done; it merely provided a forum for local associations to vent their anger. On December 6 the Foreign Ministry informed the Japanese ambassador to the United States of its decision to cease issuing passports to picture-brides effective March 1, 1920.[66]

Japanese immigrants did not acquiesce quietly in this decision. Many local associations, both in and outside of California, convened emergency meetings at which local residents adopted protest resolutions. Even so staunch a conservative as Ikeda Kandō of Oakland appeared at a San Francisco protest meeting to voice his own opposition. With the single exception of the *Shin Sekai,* all immigrant newspapers editorially condemned the decision of the Foreign Ministry. From the immigrant perspective, the Foreign Ministry had had the option of upholding the immigrants' right to marriage through the picture-bride practice. Instead Tokyo had chosen to abolish the practice unilaterally in order to placate anti-Japanese exclusionists. In 1920 there were still 24,000 single, adult males within immigrant society, the overwhelming majority of whom were laborers. These laborers were single, not because they preferred bachelorhood, but because they had not been able to meet the $800 requirement. Now they were doomed to perpetual bachelorhood. The only way for them to get married was to return to Japan, a journey few laborers, if any, could afford to make. Seen in this context, the termination of the picture-bride practice was an unforgivable instance of the Japanese government sacrificing the welfare of Japanese immigrants on the altar of what it perceived as diplomatic necessity.

Struggle Against Exclusion

Adaptation to American Society

During the transition from sojourning to permanent residency, Japanese immigrants adapted themselves to American society in many ways. In the first place, immigrant leaders undertook periodic moral reform campaigns in an attempt to eliminate the "unsavory" features of Japanese immigrant life. From 1908 these campaigns had the goal of eradicating gambling and prostitution. Local Japanese association leaders led the campaigns in most communities; religious leaders, Christian as well as Buddhist, sometimes spearheaded them in other locales. In 1899 the first Buddhist temple was established in San Francisco; later, others were founded in quick succession in other locales. Anti-gambling drives were held in virtually every Japanese settlement. To discourage the patronizing of Chinese gambling houses, community leaders issued notices warning of the deleterious moral effects of gambling. Such notices were posted in Japanese-operated restaurants, stores, hotels, poolhalls, bars, bathhouses, and boardinghouses, and even on street corner buildings around which Japanese workers congregated. The leaders also monitored the gambling houses in their effort to dissuade Japanese gamblers from entering them.

If simple persuasion failed to work, the leaders released the names of incorrigible gamblers to the immigrant press, and in some instances they forwarded the newspaper articles in which the names appeared to relatives in Japan. Both tactics were employed to shame the gamblers to such a degree that they would give up gambling. All local Japanese associations compiled and maintained a list of chronic gamblers and kept each other informed whenever such gamblers moved from one locale to another. As another deterrent, local Japanese associations refused to handle certificate applications of known habitual gamblers unless they reformed themselves. The only exceptions were the applications for certificates needed to obtain annual draft deferments. In rural farming communities, the anti-gambling campaigns always coincided with the beginning of the harvest season when large numbers of migratory workers appeared.[1]

In 1915 the anti-Chinese gambling campaign took on a decidedly nationalistic character. Shortly after declaring war against Germany, the Japanese government formulated its notorious Twenty-one Demands through which it sought to take over German territorial rights in China and presented the demands to the Chinese government in 1915. If China had acceded to the demands, she would have had to concede to Japan all the rights in Shantung Province she had been forced to surrender to Germany. To protest the policy of the Japanese government, the Chinese in the United States patriotically rallied behind their homeland and initiated a boycott of Japan-made goods being sold in this country. In direct reaction to this boycott, Japanese immigrant leaders renewed their anti-Chinese gambling campaign and couched it this time in nationalistic terms. The Chinese boycott presented a new opportunity for the Japanese to stop patronizing Chinese gambling houses. According to the new nationalistic interpretation, the Japanese losses in the houses were a source of "national humiliation." Any Japanese immigrant who frequented the houses was a "national disgrace" and a person who possessed, regrettably, only the "outer shell of the Japanese spirit" (Yamato damashii no nukegara). In other words, the Chinese boycott of Japanese goods gave every self-respecting Japanese immigrant a compelling reason to turn the tables and boycott Chinese gambling houses altogether.[2]

Soon after the United States declared war against Germany, Japanese immigrant leaders conducted the anti-gambling campaign with renewed determination. In general, immigrant leaders saw the United States entry into World War I as an opportune time to eradicate gambling, once and for all, from Japanese immigrant society. To accomplish this goal, they established special anti-gambling committees within every local Japanese association. In June 1918 the Japanese Association of America instructed all of its affiliated local associations to survey the actual state of gambling within their respective jurisdictions. The local associations were asked to investigate the number, names, and addresses of gamblers, their movements from one locale to another, their estimated total losses and the percentage of losses to Chinese gambling houses, and the specific losses of Japanese businessmen and farmers.[3] The survey by the associations revealed that Japanese immigrants were losing an estimated $3 million annually, the large bulk of this total to the Chinese.[4]

In July 1918 the Japanese Association of America issued a directive to the newly formed anti-gambling committees. This directive ordered them:

    1) To encourage Japanese immigrants to report the names and addresses of all gamblers;

    2) To order all hotels, boardinghouses, labor camps, and stores to expel all gamblers and to prohibit gambling altogether;

    3) To compile and distribute lists of gamblers, to report the names of incorrigible ones to their native places in Japan, to publish their names in the immigrant press, and to cooperate with local authorities to compel them to engage in legitimate labor;

    4) To photograph all arrested gamblers, to publish their photos in the immigrant press, and to furnish local police with evidence damaging to gambling house operators; and

    5) To establish alternative recreational facilities for Japanese laborers.[5]

In accordance with this kind of anti-gambling guideline, local anti-gambling committees strove to stamp out gambling in their local areas.

As a religious group, Japanese immigrant units of the Salvation Army conducted the most zealous anti-gambling crusade.[6] The Japanese Salvation Army was headquartered in San Francisco and had branches in various rural communities. Kobayashi Masasuke was the founder and leader. He landed in the United States as a student-laborer in 1902. He first attended Stanford University briefly, and then became an employee of the Japanese American Industrial Corporation. Later he entered a Salt Lake City college. From 1911 to 1918 he served as a secretary of the Japanese Interdenominational Board of Missions in San Francisco, an umbrella organization founded in 1911. This board initially had jurisdiction over all Japanese Christian churches in northern California, and later over all churches in southern California as well. In 1918 Kobayashi returned to Japan to attend the Salvation Army school in Tokyo and became a disciple of the Japanese leader,

Yamamuro Gunpei. He came back to the United States the following year and established Japanese units of the Salvation Army within Japanese immigrant society.

Kobayashi viewed the prevalence of gambling as a pernicious evil corrupting the moral fiber of Japanese immigrants. Under his leadership, the Japanese Salvation Army campaigned against Chinese gambling all through the post-World War I years, with an intense fervor often bordering on fanaticism. Many local anti-gambling committees worked hand-in-hand with the Salvation Army. Kobayashi did not hesitate to seek the help of local law-enforcement officers and municipal government officials to achieve his goal of wiping out Chinese gambling houses. In 1920 his moral crusade produced a martyr. Takeba Teikichi, a member of the Stockton Anti-Gambling Committee, was killed by gangsters who opposed the Salvation Army's anti-gambling crusade. Despite the efforts of the Salvation Army, however, neither Chinese nor Japanese gambling establishments were ever stamped out completely. That the Salvation Army had to conduct its crusade year after year testifies to the fact that it was never really very successful. Blithely ignoring the anti-gambling crusades, Japanese immigrants continued to gamble.

Moral reform campaigns also featured efforts to rid the Japanese immigrant communities of Japanese prostitutes and other so-called undesirable elements. Soliciting the cooperation of local police authorities, local Japanese associations had Japanese prostitutes, pimps, and brothel operators arrested periodically. In 1908 the Fresno Japanese Association established a Moral Reform Committee headed by Kitazawa Tetsuji, pastor of the Japanese Methodist Episcopal Church. In 1908, and again in 1909, Kitazawa filed complaints against the Japanese prostitutes who worked in the China Alley area and had them, along with their pimps, arrested by the local police. In Fresno, the chief brothel operator was Iwata Hidekuni, whom Kitazawa also had arrested. Iwata owned the building in which the prostitutes worked. After a prolonged legal battle, immigration authorities were able to deport him in 1914 as an undesirable alien.[7] Local immigrant leaders also filed charges against persons they considered "shiftless vagrants" and had them arrested, too. The Stockton Japanese Association had such persons picked up regularly by the local police, who turned around and expelled them from the city. To insure that they would not return, the association maintained a list of names and photographs and warned all those who had been banished that it would have them rearrested if they dared to come back to Stockton.[8]

Apart from purging Japanese immigrant society of "unsavory" elements, Japanese immigrant leaders wrestled with the question of how, and to what degree, Japanese immigrants should assimilate themselves into American society. A 1911 lèse-majesté incident raised this question in a special way. On November 3, 1911, the small Japanese immigrant community of Bakersfield, California, assembled to commemorate the Meiji Emperor's birthday. With representatives of various local organizations participating in the program, the commemoration was held at the Bakersfield Buddhist Hall. Takeda Shōjirō represented the Bakersfield Japanese Methodist Mission. Takeda reportedly paid no respect to the Emperor's portrait, an important ritual in the commemoration of the Emperor's birthday. Two days later at a meeting in the Methodist Mission, he was alleged to have said that such a ritual was a form of "idolatry" which Christians should not observe.[9] As a local *cause célèbre,* Takeda was accused of being a "traitor" for his behavior and utterances.

At the heart of this lèse-majesté affair was Reverend Kitazawa Tetsuji of Fresno. Because of adverse newspaper coverage of Takeda's remarks, as the minister responsible for supervising the Bakersfield Methodist Mission, Reverend Kitazawa went to Bakersfield. On November 17 he presented a talk in which he made the distinction between the act of showing respect and its meaning. Although the act appeared outwardly uniform for all people, the inner meaning differed. Kitazawa believed that three different meanings could be ascribed to the Emperor's portrait. Some people respected the Emperor in Japan through the portrait; other people respected the portrait as a portrait and nothing more; and still others respected the portrait as the embodiment of some transcendental value. Christians, Kitazawa said, looked upon the portrait as only a portrait and paid respect only in this sense. In addition, he defined the difference between "respect" and "worship." The former was a secular term used to denote human relationships based upon ceremonial propriety; the latter was a religious term used exclusively to designate man's relationship to God. Kitazawa said that, while Christians should "respect" the Emperor's portrait, they should never "worship" it. To show respect was "an individual choice," and any failure to show it "did not violate any law."[10] The *Shin Sekai* interpreted Kitazawa's talk as "pouring oil into a small fire" because he had "justified" Takeda's conduct.[11]

The furore quickly spread to Fresno. In addition to being the pastor of the Fresno Japanese Methodist Episcopal Church, in 1911 Reverend Kitazawa was also the president of the Japanese Association of Fresno.

Due to the discrepancy between the public explanation of his talk and the earlier newspaper coverage of it, a dissident group led by Taira Chizan, Yoshii Setsunan, and Itō Banshō met in Fresno and decided to send a delegation to Bakersfield to investigate exactly what had occurred in that city. In spite of the initial uproar, the board of the Fresno Japanese Association gave Kitazawa a vote of confidence, rejected his resignation, and declared the matter closed. On December 6 a public hearing was convened at which the Fresno delegation to Bakersfield presented its findings and accused Kitazawa of having uttered anti-Emperor statements. As a result, the people who attended this hearing adopted a resolution which denounced Kitazawa as a *fukeikan* or disrespectful turncoat and called upon the Japanese Association to take punitive measures.[12] Upon being presented with this resolution, the board refused to implement it and most members promptly resigned. As the last but most significant event of the year, on December 27, a special membership meeting of the association was convened. The members adopted a second resolution which also condemned Kitazawa as a *fukeikan,* relieved him of his post as president, and actually expelled him from the association.[13] Since the majority of officers had already resigned, the execution of this membership resolution had to await the election of new officers in January.

This action was the harbinger of a prolonged and bitter conflict which divided the Fresno Japanese community into two hostile camps. The regular annual membership meeting took place in January 1912, and the newly elected officers decided to execute the resolution. The first public notice of expulsion appeared on February 14. The Japanese Association of America responded by withdrawing the endorsement right from the Fresno Japanese Association on the grounds that "under present circumstances" it "could not advance the welfare of the Japanese" and broke off relations with it.[14] Meanwhile, the former members of the Fresno Japanese Association who disagreed with the action against Reverend Kitazawa organized another association. Launched in March, this second association was known as the Fresno County Japanese Association. Efforts by the older association to regain the endorsement right—through negotiation with San Francisco, by direct appeals to Consul General Nagai Matsuzō, and even through a mediator—all proved fruitless. Thus two associations came to exist, one old and one new, each claiming to represent the Japanese community of Fresno.

This unprecedented situation was not settled until 1914. Aggravating the situation, the Japanese Association of America recognized the new association in April 1912 and bestowed upon it the endorsement right. Throughout the rest of the year, there were many unsuccessful attempts at mediation. Exacerbating matters even more, in March 1913 a group of men from the old association, led by Taira Chizan again, invaded the office of the Fresno Japanese-language newspaper, assaulted its editor, and vandalized the office. The newspaper had carried a series of vituperative articles which called the old association "a total fraud."[15] Renewed efforts at mediation occurred again, but to no avail. The eventual reconciliation did not take place until January 1914, at which time by common consent both the old and new associations merged to form a new association.

Since 1891 Christians had aroused suspicions and enmity in Japan when the noted Christian, Uchimura Kanzō, had refused to pay his respect to the Emperor's portrait.[16] This most celebrated lèse-majesté affair led to an acrimonious debate between the critics of Christianity and its defenders during the 1890s. Led by Inoue Tetsujirō, the critics attacked Christian teachings as incompatible with the Meiji state. Because Christianity stressed the equality of all men, it made no basic distinction between different races and nations. To the critics, the Meiji Constitution was premised on the uniqueness of the Japanese people. Because Christianity taught universal love and charity, it transcended the limited ideals of the Meiji state. Because Christianity emphasized salvation in another world, it was antithetical to the secular orientation of the state. And lastly—and here the critics were the harshest—because Christianity did not teach filial piety, it did not inculcate loyalty to the Emperor. Indeed, Christians recognized a higher authority in God! These criticisms of Christianity were reinforced by the Christian participation in and leadership of the socialist movement at the turn of the century. During the Russo-Japanese War, Christians like Uchimura Kanzō and Kinoshita Naoe added their voices to the anti-war campaign begun by Kōtoku Shūsui, providing additional ammunition to the charge that they were disloyal subjects.[17] And the later public association of Christians with anarchists, especially after the disclosure of the High Treason Affair, made them even more suspect.

The Bakersfield lèse-majesté affair was a reflection of this anti-Christian bias. Reverend Kitazawa was labelled a "disloyal" Japanese with "subversive ideas" by the anti-Kitazawa forces who defined themselves as Japanese "patriots." In March 1912 the leaders of the old Fresno Japanese Association, in cooperation with Soejima Hachirō and others in the San Francisco area, convened a conference in Oakland of so-called "Imperial Subjects."[18] Soejima was a founder and onetime publisher of the *Shin Sekai* and a recognized conservative community leader. Naming the Bakersfield affair another "Uchimura Kanzō Lèse-Majesté Incident," the participants at the conference denounced the Japanese Association of America, the Fresno County Japanese Association, and even Consul General Nagai for their failure to take punitive measures against Reverend Kitazawa. Soejima declared that "Consul General Nagai" and the "Japanese Association of America . . . were protecting a 'fukeikan' and had subversive ideas."[19] Kitazawa Tetsuji was a "traitor," and anyone who protected him was also a "traitor." Consul General Nagai, the Japanese Association of America, and the Fresno County Japanese Association were traitors because they protected Kitazawa.[20]

Since the *Nichibei Shimbun* refused to condemn Reverend Kitazawa, it came under heavy fire. The anti-Kitazawa forces linked the newspaper to Kōtoku Shūsui and the Social Revolutionary Party, implying that the publisher, Abiko Kyūtarō, had socialistic leanings. They accused Abiko of having assisted the socialists by letting them reside in the Gospel Society, by allowing Kōtoku to conduct meetings there, and by permitting him to be a guest contributor to the *Nichibei Shimbun*. To insinuate that Abiko had more than sympathy with socialists, they noted that he had had Sagitani Seiichi on his staff, a person who was identified with the Social Revolutionary Party. Associating Abiko in this manner with Kōtoku, the anti-Kitazawa forces hoped to discredit the executive council of the Japanese Association of America as well because Abiko was a council member.

That the local Bakersfield incident mushroomed into this type of lèse-majesté affair is not surprising. Subsequent to the High Treason Affair, the Japanese immigrant community became ultra-sensitive to instances of "disrespect" towards the Meiji Emperor. His death in the summer of 1912 no doubt reinforced this sensitivity. Coming as it did less than ten months after the execution of Kōtoku and others, all socialists and anarchists were by definition "treasonous" persons, whether in Japan or America. In America, the words and deeds of the members of the Social Revolutionary Party and the Fresno Labor League, both of which could be traced to Kōtoku, were tangible evidence for this judgment. And their protest activities in response to the High Treason Affair left no room for any doubt. From November 1910 to February 1912, Issei socialists and anarchists issued open letters and held rallies in San Francisco and Oakland in cooperation with American socialists, including the noted writer, Jack London. On the

day after the execution of Kōtoku and others, nineteen persons held
an all-night vigil in San Francisco and declared that "the deranged
Japanese government, heedless of the worldwide protest movement,
had murdered the warriors of humanism and the forerunners of the
Japanese revolution."[21]

To be sure, all Christians were not considered *ipso facto* disloyal.
Yet with the historical bias against them, suspicions lurked. In San
Francisco back in 1902, well before the socialists and anarchists had
arrived on the scene, an instance of Christian "disrespect" had occurred within Japanese immigrant society. In that year Sakon Yoshi-
suke had written critically of the Meiji Emperor in the *Yorokobi no
Otozure,* the monthly organ of the San Francisco Japanese Methodist
Episcopal Church. His opinions raised considerable debate, and the
ensuing controversy forced Sakon to resign his job as editor of the
monthly and his position as an English instructor in the church.[22]
In the conservative patriots' mind, Reverend Kitazawa was another
"disloyal" Christian. And given the activities of the socialists and
anarchists in the intervening time, his conduct called for prompt, unequivocal condemnation in the name of the Meiji shibboleth *chūkun
aikoku,* literally meaning loyalty to the Emperor and love of nation.
The anti-Kitazawa forces used this slogan as their rallying call.

This Bakersfield incident indirectly raised the question of the adaptation of Japanese immigrants to American society. In order to rebut
the anti-Kitazawa forces and to serve Abiko's ideal of permanent settlement, the *Nichibei Shimbun* reinterpreted the meaning of *chūkun
aikoku* in 1913.[23] This shibboleth did not mean that Japanese immigrants ought to adhere to a form of narrow Japanese nationalism or
insular island mentality in the United States. On the contrary, it
meant that they should prove to the world that the Japanese as a
people were capable of adapting themselves to live and work outside
of Japan. If they settled on land and progressed economically, they
would demonstrate this capacity to Americans, and, by extension, to
the world. In addition, the shibboleth did not mean that Japanese
immigrants ought to cling to an archaic Japanese tradition. Rather, it
meant that they should exhibit certain enduring traits inherited from
the ancient Japanese past. One of these traits was the Japanese capacity
"to assimilate." If the immigrants adopted "American customs and
manners" and changed their "thoughts and sentiments" to conform
to those customs and manners, according to the *Nichibei Shimbun,* they
would be true to their own past.[24] If a Japanese immigrant truly believed in Japanese overseas development, it was unfitting for him to

cling to archaic ideas and customs or to yearn after a retired life of ease in Japan. In sum, the real meaning of *chūkun aikoku* was to sink roots in American soil and adapt oneself to American society.

The argument that Japanese immigrants should adapt themselves to American society had two basic components. Anti-Japanese exclusionists charged that Japanese immigrants could never be assimilated into American society. Since the Japanese were racially and culturally so far removed from Western civilization, the exclusionists maintained, they would always constitute an unassimilated, non-white, alien element in American society. In order to refute this allegation of unassimilability, Japanese immigrant leaders looked at the question of assimilation from two angles. A majority favored what was called *gaimenteki dōka*. This form of assimilation involved only outward appearances. According to its proponents, Japanese immigrants had to adapt their external appearance to conform to American life.

To begin with, all Japanese immigrants, regardless of sex, had to adopt American clothing. They had to refrain from wearing Japanese national garments in order to avoid being perceived as foreign interlopers. From a Japanese perspective, Americans perceived Chinese immigrants as unassimilable aliens, in part, because the Chinese had refused to adopt American clothing. Aware of this fact, as early as 1892 Tanaka Tadashichi had insisted that the Japanese railroad section hands working under his office wear American work clothes, and even eat American food, to differentiate themselves from Chinese laborers.[25] During hot summer days in Japan, it was common for Japanese workers to wear only a loincloth or a light Japanese-style bathrobe with wooden clogs. Wary of Japanese workers being seen as "backward Asiatics," Japanese immigrant leaders sternly admonished anyone who walked around in such scanty Japanese outfits, no matter how hot it was.

Gaimenteki dōka was not limited to clothing. It also involved adapting one's physical living environment to conform to American ways. Living quarters and furnishings had to meet specific American standards as much as possible. Conversely, things visibly and conspicuously Japanese, such as large signs written in Japanese, had to be eschewed as much as possible. Outward appearances were also important in terms of how Americans perceived Japanese immigrant couples. Accordingly, wives were advised to walk alongside their husbands, not behind them, so as to avoid reinforcing the negative stereotype of Japanese women as being enslaved by Japanese men. Japanese immigrants were encouraged to follow well-established American customs as well. Since the United States was a nation of Christians, Japanese immigrants had to observe the sabbath as a day of rest rather than working seven days a week. Instead of celebrating Japanese national holidays, they had to commemorate American ones like Independence Day and Thanksgiving Day. Japanese immigrants also had to participate in important local events in order to gain recognition as being an integral part of local American communities. All of this, too, fell within the scope of *gaimenteki dōka*.

In 1911 the Japanese Association of America launched what it called "a campaign of education." This campaign had a threefold purpose. First, it aimed to educate people in Japan about the real condition of Japanese immigrants in the United States. Based upon prejudice or misinformation, many people in Japan had a distorted understanding of the anti-Japanese exclusion movement and the reasons behind it. Some even blamed the immigrants for arousing the hostility of white Americans. Secondly, the campaign sought to educate Americans about Japan and the Japanese immigrants in the belief that ignorance was behind the effectiveness of anti-Japanese agitation. Thirdly, the campaign was designed to disseminate the idea of permanent settlement among the immigrants. To achieve these three purposes, the Japanese Association of America invited two very prominent persons from Japan. The first was Nitobe Inazō, a noted American-educated intellectual and educator; the second was Shimada Saburō, a member of the National Diet and a well-known Christian.

Both men arrived in September 1911 and went on lecture tours on behalf of the Japanese Association of America.[26] In speaking before Japanese immigrant audiences, Nitobe and Shimada invariably advised Japanese immigrants to settle down in the United States. Nitobe specifically exhorted them to learn English and adopt American concepts of morality. Rather than cling to Japanese ways, Japanese immigrants had to adapt themselves to American society in accordance with an old Japanese proverb—*gō ni haette wa gō ni shitagae,* or when in Rome do as the Romans do. This proverb also counseled adaptation as a temporary expedient. The Japanese Association of America had adopted a policy of popularizing the idea of permanent settlement and adaptation. Association leaders believed that, if the idea was advanced by such prominent persons as Nitobe and Shimada, Japanese immigrants would be inclined to listen and take the idea to heart. From 1913 many other prominent Japanese reiterated the idea of permanent settlement and adaptation.[27]

The proponents of *gaimenteki dōka* were fond of using an analogy drawn from the Japanese family system. To justify their position, they conceived of Japanese immigrants as being analogous to adopted persons in Japan. In Japan, an adopted person had to conform to the ways of his adopting family. Normally, his own family was poorer than the adopting family. Consequently, an adopted person's status, whether as a son or husband, was low, placing him in a very difficult and often almost impossible situation. But no matter how trying his situation, an adopted person was compelled to make himself acceptable to his new family. The situation of Japanese immigrants was akin to that of an adopted person. By emigrating from Japan, Japanese immigrants had left their own family, Japan, and had been adopted by the United States, which of course was incomparably wealthier than Japan. Even though they encountered immense hardships, Japanese immigrants were obliged, as with all adopted persons, to adapt themselves to their new adopted family, the United States. They had to cease being objects of exclusion and make themselves acceptable to this country. And if they did, they enabled their own family, Japan, to preserve its face in the international arena. This adoption analogy, readily understood by any Japanese immigrant, made adaptation a temporary but necessary expedient for survival in the United States.

A minority of Japanese immigrant leaders favored another form of assimilation known as *naimenteki dōka*. Those who adhered to this type of assimilation believed that *gaimenteki dōka* was insufficient. Since the first form of assimilation involved only external appearances, it did not go far enough. Real assimilation meant the adoption of American values. Some leaders attached primary importance to secular values, such as American democratic principles and practices; others stressed the primacy of American Christian religious values. In either case, the proponents of this second form of assimilation went much further than those of the first.

American Protestant ministers, many of whom had been missionaries in Asia, were prominent among the defenders of Chinese and Japanese immigrants. The Reverend Otis Gibson, under whom the first Japanese immigrants founded the Gospel Society, was one of the chief defenders of Chinese immigrants in the nineteenth century. Such men as Sidney L. Gulick, member of the Commission on Relations with Japan of the Federal Council of Churches of Christ, Herbert B. Johnson, superintendent of the Japanese Methodist Episcopal Mission, Ernest A. Sturge, superintendent of the Japanese Presbyterian Mission, and Harvey H. Guy, professor at the Pacific School of Religion, were prominent in opposing the anti-Japanese exclusion movement. These Christian ministers always equated assimilation with conversion to Christianity, singling out Asian converts as living refutations of the allegation that Asian immigrants were unassimilable.

In 1877 Otis Gibson published *The Chinese in America*, a defense of Chinese immigrants. Convinced of the superiority of the English language, the Christian religion, and the American Republic, Gibson was a smug nineteenth century white missionary. Of the English language, he wrote:

> The English language is eminently the language of intellectual power and activity—the language of Christian evangelization. The heathen who, living in England or America, learns to understand and to speak the English language can never be the same heathen that he was before. A door has been opened into the shady chambers of his mind and soul which, whether he wills or not, lets in a constant stream of intellectual light and spiritual life. Our whole language, to the pagan, is full of new thoughts. It is the language of progress, the language of inventions, of investigation, and of discovery. It is the language of civil liberty and equal rights. It is the language richly freighted with Christian faith and hope; a language full of Christian songs and prayers and experiences. A people who, to any considerable extent, learn to use the English language in this age of the world, no matter how stagnant the civilization to which they have belonged, will of necessity, by the power of the new ideas with which the language is filled, be aroused to intellectual activity, to a higher and better culture, and to a new spiritual life.[28]

To Gibson, Chinese immigrants were fortunate in being exposed to the United States, the sublime epitome of a Christian civilization:

> It has been reserved for this 19th century and this Republican Government of these United States of America to witness the first great experiment of aggregated paganism in actual contact with the best form of Christian civilization which the world has ever seen, on Christian soil, in the midst of a Christian people, with Christian institutions, and under the regulations of a powerful Christian government.[29]

The "aggregated paganism" coming into contact with the Christian civilization of America was of course the Chinese immigrants. The result was the inexorable uplifting of the Chinese:

> The tendency of the lower, according to its measure of power, is to corrupt, weaken, and poison the higher and better; while it is the tend-

ency of the higher and better, according to its measure of power, to arouse, vitalize, energize, purify, and uplift the lower and the decaying. And this process is taking place to-day in the contact of the Chinese with the Christian civilization of the United States.[30]

Without the smugness of Otis Gibson, Sidney L. Gulick also interpreted evangelization among Japanese immigrants as an important measure of their assimilation into American society. The Christian missions among the Japanese immigrants were "working powerfully for the assimilation of the Japanese."[31] In citing the work already accomplished by Japanese Christians among their fellow immigrants, Gulick concluded that "whoever will consider the efforts put forth by Japanese leaders and also by the rank and file to adapt themselves to the conditions of life here, to learn our ways, and conform to our standards will surely realize that much has already been done and that the prospects for the future are hopeful."[32] The initial success of the Christian missions was proof that Japanese immigrants could be assimilated. In Gulick's opinion, there was a fundamental difference in "the attitude and spirit of a Japanese who has become a Christian" from the attitude and spirit of a Japanese who had not. That difference lay in the fact that "a Christian Japanese is ready to go more than halfway in establishing right relations with American neighbors." "No more important step could possibly be taken by American Christians in the Americanization of Orientals living here permanently," he was convinced, "than in providing adequate support for aggressive Christian work among these peoples from the Far East."[33]

Unlike Japanese immigrant Buddhists, Japanese immigrant Christians had a crucial link to the larger society through men like Gulick and the missionary structure under which Japanese immigrant churches operated. In 1912 Miyazaki Kohachirō, a member of the Japanese Interdenominational Board of Missions, reviewed the board's evangelizing activities among Japanese immigrants. With regard to the question of assimilation, he reported that the board had "stressed . . . the necessity of assimilating into American society, the need to understand the spirit of Christ in order to assimilate, and that the only way of understanding the spirit of Christ was to believe in Him."[34] Here Miyazaki, too, explicitly equated assimilation with conversion. In his Christian version of *naimenteki dōka*, Japanese immigrants had to "believe in Christ" in order to assimilate into American society. By adopting such a position, Japanese Christian leaders affiliated with the Interdenominational Board of Missions cemented their relationship with the white clergymen who defended them in the public arena.

Japanese publicists always upheld the assimilability of Japanese immigrants. Kawakami Kiyoshi was the foremost publicist. Born in 1879, he was a native of Yamagata Prefecture. In his youth he had been a socialist who identified himself so much with Karl Marx that he assumed Karl as his own first name in English. Kawakami was acquainted with Katayama Sen, Abe Isoo, Kōtoku Shūsui, and other early Japanese socialists; indeed, he was among those who founded the short-lived Shakai Minshūtō (Social Democratic Party) in 1901. In August 1901 Kawakami came to the United States as a student and studied political science at the University of Iowa. After graduating with an M.A., he launched his career in this country as a bilingual journalist and writer.[35] From 1914 to 1920 he served as director of the Pacific Press Bureau, a Japanese government-established and controlled news agency. Turning away from his youthful fling with socialism, Kawakami acted as an unofficial publicist of the Japanese Foreign Ministry throughout much of his career.

Kawakami traced the assimilability of the Japanese to their historical experience. The Japanese were not originally a homogenous people, according to Kawakami. Different races with different cultures inhabited the Japanese archipelago at the dawn of Japanese history. Tolerant of each other, these races gradually mixed biologically to form the Japanese people. Subsequently, the Japanese people absorbed elements of Chinese civilization and adapted them to their own society. During the nineteenth century, the Japanese again exhibited the same habit of importing and incorporating foreign elements. They adopted aspects of Western civilization and creatively transformed feudal Japan into a modern industrial state. In sum, throughout their history the Japanese as a people had manifested an extraordinary capacity to assimilate foreign cultures under changing circumstances.[36]

The assimilability of the Japanese was further evident if one compared Japanese immigrants to Chinese immigrants. To substantiate this claim, Kawakami cited Sidney L. Gulick as an authoritative source. He quoted Gulick's opinion that "the Japanese go to the West in order to acquire all the West can give," while "the Chinaman goes steeled against its influences." The Chinese were impervious to change. A Japanese, on the other hand, was "susceptible to every change in his environment."[37] Kawakami added that Japanese immigrant communities were not plagued by so-called hatchet men whose deeds strike "terror in the hearts of all denizens . . . of Chinatown." In stark contrast to Japanese settlements, Chinatowns were "filthy quarters."[38] Gulick actually drew an even sharper distinction between the Chinese and Japanese. In an unquoted passage, he said:

Contrast a Chinaman and a Japanese after each has been in America a year. The one to all appearances is an American; his hat, his clothing, his manner, seem so like those of an American that were it not for his small size, Mongolian type of face, and defective English, he could easily be mistaken for one. How different is it with the Chinaman! He retains his curious cue (sic) with a tenacity that is as intense as it is characteristic. His hat is the conventional one adopted by all Chinese immigrants. His clothing likewise, though far from Chinese, is nevertheless entirely un-American. He makes no effort to conform to his surroundings. He seems to glory in his separateness.[39]

This kind of self-serving comparison with Chinese immigrants did not originate with Kawakami, or with Gulick. Beginning with the first student-laborers in the late nineteenth century, Japanese immigrants always differentiated themselves from Chinese immigrants. From the student-laborers' point of view, Americans had excluded the Chinese, understandably and justifiably, because the Chinese were lower class laborers who had not adapted themselves to American society. The student-laborers almost uniformly perceived Chinese immigrants in an unsympathetic, negative light and often repeated harsh American criticisms of the Chinese. In 1892, a student-laborer described the Chinatown of San Francisco as "a world of beasts in which, behind its outward facade, exists every imaginable depravity, crime, and vice known to the human world—assault, homicide, gambling, illicit business, prostitution, robbery, and drunken disorder."[40]

According to the *Aikoku,* the weekly organ of the Patriotic League, the Chinese in the United States represented the "lower class" of China. They were "conservative" and "obstinate" in their "opposition to American ways." In contrast, the Japanese in the United States represented the "upper class" of Japan. They were "progressive" and "resourceful" and "adapt themselves to American customs."[41] Here the *Aikoku* echoed Fukuzawa Yukichi's famous essay on "Abandoning Asia" with which most student-laborers were familiar. The essay appeared in the *Jiji Shimpō* in 1885.[42] In it, Fukuzawa had argued that Japan had to divorce herself from China and Korea. The two neighboring countries on the Asian continent were mired hopelessly in a conservative tradition and therefore doomed to perpetual backwardness. If Japan aspired to make progress, she had to forsake Asia and become a part of the Western world. Sharing Fukuzawa's point of view, the *Aikoku* looked upon Chinese immigrants as representatives of a stagnant and decaying Asia from which Japan had already parted company.

Americans of course generally did not distinguish the Japanese from the Chinese. They tended to identify the members of both immigrant groups as Asiatics, Orientals, or Mongolians. In fact, anti-Japanese exclusionists characterized the Japanese as being equally as undesirable as the Chinese had been. As early as 1892, the San Francisco *Bulletin* reported that, "like the Chinese," the Japanese "are here for the purpose of acquiring enough money to enable them to end their days in leisure in their native land, and they have no intention of settling down here and making this place their home." Moreover, "like the Chinese, . . . few of them in this country are married. The women here are of the lowest class, and, like the Chinese women, are imported only to lead a life of shame."[43] The Japanese always felt indignant and insulted whenever they were lumped together with the Chinese because their own self-image set them distinctly apart. In the same year a Japanese graduate of Berkeley High School wrote in the *Oakland Enquirer* that he wished "to inveigh with all my power" against American newspapers which "compared" the Japanese "to the truly ignorant class of Chinese laborers and condemned [the Japanese] as bearers of some mischievous Oriental evils." Japanese student-laborers were different and deserved to be recognized as "diligent and self-supporting young men" who were "in search of truth, knowledge, and light!"[44]

According to Kawakami, Japanese immigrants were assimilable by other standards as well. Compared to European immigrants, their literacy rate in their native language ranked higher. Their knowledge of the English language was equal to or exceeded that of their European counterparts. More than anything else, the example of their children conclusively proved the assimilability of the Japanese people. Born on American soil and influenced by the American environment, Nisei youngsters were thoroughly Americanized. Having "caught the Yankee spirit," Kawakami wrote, "these children . . . disdainfully call the newcomers from Japan 'Japs.'" When told that they themselves are also Japanese, "they proudly cock their heads and indignantly swear that they are not Japs but 'Mericans." Japanese immigrant parents were "proud" that their children were "Americans and want them to learn all that is good of American ideas and manners."[45] Kawakami described the children in this way to underscore the fact that they were American not only by nationality but also in spirit.

All in all, Kawakami projected an exaggerated picture of the Japanese immigrants' identification with and affection for the United States:

> Even in the present untoward circumstances, the Japanese in America have proved themselves surprisingly loyal to the country which harbours them. How fond they are of this great country! And how proud! Their enthusiasm is almost contagious. They are resolved that nobody shall speak in their presence disparagingly of the United States. Now and then there come to these shores Japanese who have spent a few years in Germany or France or England and who are naturally inclined to belittle America, its arts, its literature, its universities, its cities, and even its charming womankind. Such impudent critics had better beware, lest their compatriots in America admonish them rather unceremoniously. In spite of all the inconveniences and disagreeable experiences that annoy them, the Japanese in America, especially the educated class, appreciate that this is a country of freedom and opportunity. They breathe the atmosphere of freedom and they revel in it. Here is a country which is singularly free from official red-tape; where nobody is called upon to sacrifice the best years of his life for military duties; where officials are in the true sense of the term the servants of the people; where social caste has never been established; where all the blessings of modern civilization—schools, libraries, museums, and what not—are placed at the disposal of every one. After all, it is a pretty good country, this great Republic of brothers, and the Japanese are quick to appreciate it. When they are treated more kindly, and more squarely, and more in accord with the true spirit of the Republic, there is no doubt that they will become even more devoted to this country.[46]

As a Stanford University professor of Japanese studies, Ichihashi Yamato also upheld the assimilability of Japanese immigrants. A native of Aichi Prefecture, he had come to the United States in 1894 at the age of sixteen. He attended the public schools of San Francisco, and eventually graduated from Lowell High School in 1902. In 1903 he matriculated into Stanford from which he received two degrees in economics: an A.B. in 1907 and A.M. in 1908. From 1908 to 1910 Ichihashi served as an assistant in the Economics Department at Stanford and as a special agent of the United States Immigration Commission. In the latter capacity, he conducted field studies of Japanese immigrants under Harry A. Millis who directed the commission's investigation of Japanese immigrants living throughout the western United States. From 1910 Ichihashi attended Harvard University and obtained his Ph.D. in 1913. From 1913 to 1943 he taught Japanese studies at Stanford.[47]

Ichihashi was active in the campaign of education to enlighten the American public about Japan and Japanese immigration. In 1912 the Japanese Association of America commissioned Ichihashi to write a pamphlet which would present factual information on Japanese immigration. Entitled *Japanese Immigration: Its Status in California,* the pamphlet was issued in 1913 and again in 1915 in an expanded edition. According to Ichihashi, the Japanese people possessed "a natural faculty for assimilation" because they were "sensitive to their environment." Japanese immigrants were not the "scum" of Japan, so they could not be classified as "coolies." They were young men and women who brought as much capital to this country as European immigrants had and who were the most literate among all the foreign-born people residing in the United States. Regarding their adaptation to American life, Ichihashi maintained that "they are eager and make a strenuous effort to learn of American institutions, and to speak, read and write English, and in fact, 'have made unusually good progress' in this regard."[48]

Ichihashi's private views of his fellow immigrants were not quite so sanguine. In 1915 he candidly expressed his opinions to Consul General Numano Yasutarō of San Francisco. He placed no stock at all in the ability of Japanese immigrant leaders to contribute anything towards improving Japanese-American relations. The Japanese Association of America had "proved most inefficient." His harsh judgment was that "not a single contribution" had "ever been made by it." Ichihashi considered it "a pity" that someone like Ushijima Kinji, the Potato King, had been made its president. "If no better substitute could be found," Ichihashi said, "the presidency of the Association should be made inconspicuous." To control all the associations, he advised Consul Numano to "further bureaucratize" them:

They should be put under the absolute control of the Consulate . . . and should be guided to do what they should and to avoid what they should. . . . This is a confession of one who has prized democracy above all things, and has watched with a keen interest for the last twenty years its evolution among the Japanese here. They are by nature not democratic, and there are no stimuli to make them so. They are at least twenty years behind the intelligent Japanese at home and lord only knows how [many] years they are behind the intelligent Americans.

They have not been in touch with the progress here or at home. They must be ruled from above. . . . [49]

Publicly, Ichihashi upheld the assimilability of Japanese immigrants, but privately he believed otherwise. In his opinion, the immigrants, out of touch with progress, were hopelessly behind the times. Despite residing in the United States for years, they had not embraced democratic principles and practices, leading Ichihashi to his elitist conclusion that they needed to be "ruled from above."

Kanzaki Kiichi, perhaps, best exemplified the public posture of Japanese immigrant leaders on the question of assimilation. He was among the few Japanese graduates of the University of California. In 1920 he appeared before the House Committee on Immigration and Naturalization which held hearings on Japanese immigration. As the general secretary of the Japanese Association of America, Kanzaki testified that "assimilability" was a "part of the Japanese racial characteristics," as evidenced by "the rapid growth of modern Japan." He defined "assimilation" as an "adjustment to the new conditions" in the United States and an "adaptation" to her "social, political, industrial, and cultural institutions." By this definition, Japanese immigrants had assimilated into American society, for their "ideas and ideals, both social and political and cultural, have been greatly, if not completely changed, even to the point of 'conversion.'" Indeed, Kanzaki went so far as to assert that "a sense of brotherhood and social equality and a rising spirit of democracy and internationalism," though "foreign to the Japanese . . . , are fast winning the hearts" of Japanese immigrants.

As further evidence of their assimilability, Kanzaki recited how Japanese immigrants had participated in the national Americanization campaign since 1918. He reported that Japanese associations had encouraged Japanese immigrants to contribute funds for Liberty Bonds, the American Red Cross, and War Saving Stamps. The associations had also promoted the study of English among the immigrants and imparted a "knowledge of American life, its form and spirit," to them, "so that they may easily understand Americanism to the fullest extent. . . . "[50] In 1919 the Pacific Coast Japanese Association Deliberative Council had adopted a policy of promoting the study of English among the immigrants and of imparting a knowledge of American society to them.[51] The council had adopted this policy as another manifestation of *gaimenteki dōka* in response to the national Americanization campaign, and the four central bodies and their affiliated local

Japanese associations had implemented it to varying degrees. The Japanese Association of America hired an American-educated person and sent him on a lecture tour within its jurisdiction to educate Japanese immigrants about American society.

Finally, Kanzaki argued that the American-born children of the Japanese immigrants incontrovertibly proved the cultural assimilability of the Japanese people. Kanzaki reiterated Kawakami Kiyoshi's earlier public stance. By virtue of their American birth and upbringing, the children were "more American than Japanese in their ideas and ideals, their language and manners, their modes of thinking, and attitude toward life in general."[52] In another context, Kanzaki summarized the degree of assimilation of the Japanese immigrants. "The native born Japanese are one hundred per cent American," he wrote, "while foreign born Japanese are at least fifty per cent American in spite of the many obstacles put in their way."[53] What retarded the complete assimilation and Americanization of the latter were the "barriers" erected against Japanese immigrants. Kanzaki cited such barriers as racial prejudice, alien land laws, and residential segregation. The single most important barrier was the denial of naturalization rights, since it prevented Japanese immigrants from participating in the American political process. Kanzaki concluded that "it is . . . obvious that the Japanese can not be assimilated to the fullest extent" as long as these barriers persisted. In the final analysis, "the question of assimilation can never be solved permanently," he said, "unless equality of races and equality of opportunity are established, unless all the barriers [to] assimilation are melted away, and unless the time element is given its full power of transformation."[54]

Nisei Education and Dual Nationality

The adaptation of Japanese immigrants to American society was also reflected in their changing ideas regarding the future of their American-born children. In the late nineteenth and early twentieth century, Japanese immigrants recognized no Nisei problem. The prevailing *dekasegi* ideal precluded the recognition of any problems peculiar to Nisei children in the United States. To educate the first-born children, the immigrants established Japanese language schools very early, the first one in Seattle in 1902 followed by others in San Francisco, Sacramento, and other locales. Coinciding with the *dekasegi* ideal, the purpose of these first schools was to educate the children to enable them to enroll in the public schools of Japan. In 1932 an Issei educator succinctly described this initial orientation:

In the past the majority of Japanese in America and Canada were under the sway of the *dekasegi* spirit. We crossed the vast Pacific in order to earn money. The land here was only a temporary place to earn a living, a travel lodge as it were, with our real home being in Japan where the cherry blossoms bloom. Hence we thought we had to educate our children accordingly. Some of us sent our children back to Japan to be cared for and educated by grandparents, siblings, or other relatives at home. For those unable to send children back . . . , we felt compelled to offer a "Japanese" education to them here. To achieve this end, we founded special schools—Japanese schools and language institutes. During this period, these schools mainly had the purpose of preparing the children to return to Japan.[55]

In California, a recognition of a Nisei educational problem surfaced in 1908. The first editorial on Nisei education in the *Shin Sekai* appeared in May 1908.[56] While not dogmatically opposed to the establishment of "pure" Japanese schools, the editorial questioned the value of such schools in view of the likelihood that school-age Nisei youngsters would be sent to American public schools. The *Beikoku Bukkyō* carried an interesting article in September 1908.[57] The article was devoted to the ignorance of Japan exhibited by Nisei children. When asked about what they would like to become, some children replied that they aspired to become the Emperor of Japan. According to the article, this answer reflected the baneful influence of the American environment. Under the sway of the American folk belief that anyone could aspire to become the President of the United States, such children erroneously equated the Emperor with the President. This example was an omen of grave problems which loomed in the near future. In 1908 the Japanese Association of America conducted a survey to determine the exact number of Nisei children in the San Francisco area.[58] Upon discovering a sizable number of school-age children, immigrant leaders formed a special group to discuss the educational problems of the Nisei. Organized in early 1909, this group was called the *Mokuyobikai* or Thursday Club.

In the summer of 1909, the *Shin Sekai* raised a fundamental question regarding dual nationality.[59] Based upon the principle of *jus soli,* all Nisei children had American citizenship by virtue of being born on American soil. At the same time, they were Japanese subjects based upon the opposite principle of *jus sanguinis.* Since Japanese law determined nationality by paternal descent, all Nisei with Japanese fathers

automatically had Japanese citizenship. The *Shin Sekai* editorialized
that this dual nationality of the Nisei would become a thorny problem
in the future, especially in view of the military service obligation in
Japan. Rather than wait until the problem became a pressing reality,
the newspaper advised immigrant parents to decide whether or not
they were going to settle down in the United States. If they were
settling down permanently, they should raise their children as Americans and, accordingly, seek to solve the problem of dual nationality.
These first signs of a shifting attitude did not signify the erosion of
the *dekasegi* ideal. They were simply an early recognition that the
American-born generation had unique problems which warranted serious attention.

This realization soon manifested itself in a new educational plan.
After studying the educational problems of Nisei youngsters, the
Thursday Club drafted a plan for a new Japanese language school to
accommodate the growing number of Nisei children in San Francisco.
"The cardinal principle" of the plan was that the education of the
Nisei "must be principally the assimilation of American customs and
manners, supplemented by education in other essential ideas so that
they will not forget the motherland."[60] This plan called for a kindergarten and primary division. The former would accommodate pre-
school children to teach them English in order to prepare them for
American public schools. To insure that they would learn "proper"
English, the kindergarten division would employ white American
teachers. The primary division would offer supplementary education
in Japanese ethics, history, geography, and language to school-age
children who were already attending American public schools. In January 1910 the Thursday Club submitted this plan to the Japanese Association of America for its consideration.

In January 1910 the Japanese Association of America convened its
annual assembly with representatives of affiliated local associations.
The Thursday Club plan appeared on the agenda, and the assembly
adopted the plan without any modification.[61] To find a qualified principal for the future school, the assembly voted to seek the assistance
of Nitobe Inazō in Japan, and appointed a special education committee
empowered to implement the plan. In June, this newly appointed
committee, using the identical language of the Thursday Club, affirmed that the education of the Nisei "must be the assimilation of
American customs and manners." The Thursday Club plan embodied
a definite change in ideas. In place of the simple notion, derived from
the *dekasegi* ideal, that the Nisei should be educated to enable them to

enter the public schools of Japan, it recognized the primacy of an American public school education and the importance of assimilating into American society. The adoption of the plan by the Japanese Association of America and its affiliated local associations indicated that this change in ideas was not limited to the members of the Thursday Club, but was shared by other immigrant leaders as well.

Subsequently, a full-scale debate on the subject of Nisei education occurred within immigrant society. A speech by Consul Nagai Matsuzō of San Francisco sparked it. In July, Consul Nagai delivered an address at Alviso near San Jose. The occasion was the opening of a new Japanese language school. As a Japanese diplomat, Nagai was an advocate of permanent settlement. He believed that Japanese immigrants had to discard their *dekasegi* ideal. He also believed that Nisei children should be educated exclusively as Americans. Nagai frankly expressed his opinions at the opening of the Alviso school, going as far as to assert that Japanese language schools were not necessary at all.[62] Nagai's speech shocked his audience. After all, they had assembled to celebrate the opening of the new Alviso school. Shortly after, Takahashi Hōnen, principal of the new school, publicly assailed Nagai, and the ensuing publicity surrounding Nagai's speech produced a lively debate on the education of the Nisei.

As the debate was carried on, most participants did not see an irreconcilable conflict between a Japanese and an American education.[63] The debate focused on the relative value of each. Some stressed the central importance of an American education; others upheld the primacy of a Japanese education; still others assigned equal weight to both a Japanese and American education. Special terms were coined to distinguish these different positions. *Beishu Nichijū* designated the first position, while *Nisshu Beijū* represented the second. *Setchūron* described the third position, *setchū* being the Japanese word meaning compromise. Notwithstanding these designations, however, the debate was never very clear, for no one precisely defined the meaning of a Japanese and American education. Those who favored the primacy of a Japanese education insisted that it should be based upon the old Meiji shibboleth, *chūkun aikoku*. Yet no one bothered to elaborate on the exact content of such a Japanese education. Be that as it may, the fact that Japanese immigrants engaged in this debate indicated that they had begun to modify their views on the education of the Nisei as they themselves were casting off their *dekasegi* ideal.

Between 1911 and America's entry into World War I, the Japanese immigrants' perspective on the second-generation problem changed decisively. In 1911, in accordance with the Thursday Club plan, the Kimmon Gakuen or Golden Gate Institute was inaugurated in San Francisco. Headed by Kamada Masayoshi, who had been recommended by Nitobe Inazō, it was to become the largest school in northern California. The Thursday Club had been endorsed by the Japanese associations as a model for all schools in other locales, but no organization had been formed to unify the schools into a single system. The schools all functioned independently—they set their own goals, formed their own curriculum, and selected their own textbooks. One effect of the debate on Nisei education was to draw attention to the need to create a unified system under which all the schools could be operated. In 1910, and again in 1911, the *Shin Sekai* suggested repeatedly that a statewide conference of educators should be convened to consider this matter, but it was not until 1912 that a such conference was actually convened.[64]

Sponsored by the Japanese Association of America and held in San Francisco, the 1912 conference marked a watershed in the on-going debate on Nisei education. For the first time, immigrant educators from throughout the state of California assembled together. Thirty-four educators in all attended the conference, which focused on the goal of Japanese language schools. The educators adopted three broad resolutions. Pertaining to the fundamental purpose of the schools, the first two resolutions read:

> 1) The main objective will be to educate future permanent residents of the United States; and
>
> 2) Recognizing the necessity of an American education, Japanese schools will provide supplementary instruction in Japanese and education about Japan.[65]

The debate over the relative value of an American and Japanese education was settled. Declaring that the Nisei should be educated as permanent residents, the educators unequivocally accepted the primacy of an American public school education. In the words of Kamada Masayoshi, the educators' long-run goal was

> to produce individuals who will be able to stand up for the rights and privileges of the Japanese people among Americans. To achieve this end, we must enroll Nisei children in American public schools and have them educated in the same manner as white children. To teach them about Japan and the Japanese language, we must provide supplementary education in Japanese schools.[66]

By adopting the two resolutions, immigrant educators abandoned, once and for all, the old idea rooted in the *dekasegi* ideal that the Nisei should be educated to enter the schools in Japan.

The educators retained certain Japanese educational ideas. They made the distinction between intellectual (chi), moral (toku), and physical (tai) education. An American public school education, they believed, satisfied the requirements of an intellectual and physical education, but not those of a moral education. The educators insisted that the moral education of the Nisei had to be based on the Imperial Rescript on Education. Promulgated in 1890 by the Meiji Emperor, the Rescript was the moral underpinning of the entire Japanese educational system until the end of World War II. It read:

> Our Imperial ancestors have founded Our Empire on a basis broad and everlasting and have deeply and firmly implanted virtue; Our Subjects ever united in loyalty and filial piety have from generation to generation illustrated the beauty thereof. This is the glory of the fundamental character of Our Empire, and herein also lies the source of Our education.
>
> Ye, Our subjects, be filial to your parents, affectionate to your brothers and sisters, as husbands and wives be harmonious; as friends true; bear yourselves in modesty and moderation; extend your benevolence to all; pursue learning and cultivate arts, and thereby develop intellectual faculties and perfect moral powers; furthermore advance public good and promote common interests; always respect the Constitution and observe the laws; should emergency arise, offer yourselves courageously to the State; and thus guard and maintain the prosperity of Our Imperial Throne coeval with heaven and earth. So shall ye not only be Our good and faithful subjects, but render illustrious the best tradition of your forefathers.[67]

The Imperial Rescript on Education was part and parcel of the Emperor ideology promoted by the Meiji government. In 1889 the Meiji Constitution had been promulgated. The ruling oligarchy drew it up in such a way that the Japanese Emperor system was the bedrock upon which the Meiji state rested. The constitution incorporated the myth that the Imperial line had been "unbroken for ages eternal," embodied the principle that political sovereignty inhered in the Imperial institution, and declared the Emperor to be "sacred and inviolate." Written as the foundation of all moral education, the Rescript was designed to buttress the constitution. Apart from reaffirming old Confucian virtues, loyalty and obedience to the Emperor were extolled by the Rescript. Moral precepts were defined in public terms, allowing for no separation between the sphere of the state and that of a private citizen. According to the constitution, the Emperor was the head of the state. Loyalty and obedience to the Emperor, therefore, were synonymous with loyalty and obedience to the Meiji state.

As the Rescript was expounded upon in later years, a family analogy was applied to the relationship of the Emperor to his subjects. The Japanese nation was conceptualized as akin to a family-state. The Emperor was the head of this family-state with all the households of Japan being its members. So the people's relationship to the Emperor was analogous to ordinary family relationships governed by Confucian moral precepts. Just as household members had to be loyal and obedient to their householdheads, so, too, all households had to exhibit the same virtues in relation to the Emperor.[68]

All immigrant educators did not give unqualified support to the Rescript as the moral foundation of Nisei education. Some had misgivings and qualified their acceptance of the Rescript. Such educators were wary of promoting what they called "parochialism" among Nisei youngsters. The Rescript had been promulgated with the Japanese people in Japan in mind. If those aspects of the Rescript which were unique to Japan were emphasized unduly, they were afraid that they would create an insular mentality among Nisei children which would hinder the children's ability to adapt to American society. To avoid this pitfall, they interpreted the Rescript as broadly as possible and advised their associates to focus on its universal precepts such as the exhortation to "extend benevolence to all."[69]

At this first conference, the educators also set down the secondary aims of the Japanese language schools. With the growing number of Nisei children, the language barrier between parents and children had become a matter of grave concern. By teaching the Japanese language, the language schools were to alleviate family problems by reducing the existing communication gap. Another secondary purpose was the inculcation of pride in Nisei youngsters. The educators feared that the children would develop "an inferiority complex" unless they were exposed to Japanese culture. Hence the language schools also served to instill a positive Japanese identity in the children. But whatever the secondary aims were, this first conference produced a much clearer perspective on the education of the Nisei. The educators committed themselves firmly to educating Nisei children as permanent residents of the United States.

In subsequent annual conferences, the educators changed their perspective on Nisei education. The second conference, held in June 1913, witnessed the establishment of the Japanese Teachers Association of America, a body composed exclusively of educators and persons interested in education, whose purpose was "to study and solve all educational problems pertaining to Japanese children in America."[70] The Japanese Association of America had convened the first two conferences. To divorce education from politics and to unify the language schools in California, the educators organized this association as an independent body. The educators also debated two important questions. First, they took up the subject of curriculum. Despite the fact that they agreed on the fundamental goals of the language schools, no uniform curriculum had been developed. Each school created its own curriculum, teaching many different subjects and using many different textbooks. To establish a uniform curriculum, the educators decided to limit instruction to three basic subjects: language, history, and geography, augmented by group singing. No specific classes on *shūshin* or moral education were to be offered. Rather, moral education was to be taught through the three basic subjects. This in itself was a departure from the standard practice in Japan where moral education was always taught as a separate subject.

Secondly, the educators deliberated on the question of textbooks. Most schools used the textbook series compiled by the Ministry of Education in Japan. Was this series appropriate for the education of the Nisei? The educators answered that the series was inappropriate because it was geared specifically for Japanese children in Japan. The textbooks featured stories drawn from Japanese history, society, and culture. They also had didactic stories on the moral teachings of the Rescript on Education, most of which of course were alien to Nisei children. To be suitable for Nisei children, a textbook series had to be adapted to the American environment in which the children were being reared. This assessment reflected yet another change in the educators' perspective on Nisei education.

Events which preceded the second conference influenced the proceedings and the assembled educators. Right before the conference opened, the California State legislature had enacted the 1913 Alien Land Law. During the spring and early summer months of 1913, many prominent visitors from Japan arrived in California to observe the Japanese exclusion movement at first hand. Among them were two Japanese Diet members, Ebara Soroku and Hattori Ayao, who actually addressed the second conference and urged the educators to adapt their educational goals and practices to the United States.[71] At the same time, another eminent person, Shiga Shigetaka, published an article entitled "The Uselessness of a Japanese Education" in the immigrant press. In it Shiga claimed that a Japanese education, being insular and narrow, ill-prepared the Japanese people for overseas expansion.[72] Thus he advised Japanese immigrants to stress an American education for their children.

Subsequently, Japanese immigrant leaders turned to the problem of dual nationality. In 1914 this problem appeared on the agenda of the first meeting of the Pacific Coast Japanese Association Deliberative Council. The Northwest American Japanese Association of Seattle proposed that the council seek revisions in the Japanese Nationality Law to enable the Nisei to renounce their Japanese citizenship. The council adopted the proposal, and in 1915 the Northwest American Japanese Association submitted a formal petition to the Japanese government asking for an amendment to the Japanese Nationality Law.[73] Two longtime immigrant leaders, Arai Tatsuya of Seattle and Toyama Noriyuki of Los Angeles, lobbied in Tokyo on behalf of the council, working through Ebara Soroku and Shimada Saburō, two legislators familiar with the problem of dual nationality. As a result of the petition and lobbying, the Japanese Diet amended the Japanese Nationality Act in 1916.[74] This first amendment allowed the parents or guardians of Nisei who were 14 years old or younger to renounce their youngsters' Japanese citizenship on their behalf; it also allowed those Nisei who were 15 to 16 years old to renounce it themselves. Male Nisei who were 17 years old or more, however, were subject to a precondition. They could forswear their Japanese citizenship only if they had fulfilled their Japanese military obligation. Complementing the Japanese immigrant educators' commitment to educate the Nisei as American citizens, this first amendment partially solved the problem of dual nationality.

After World War I, anti-Japanese exclusionists began to voice increasing alarm at the growing number of Nisei children. They leveled many charges, most of them utterly groundless. According to the exclusionists, by granting Japanese citizenship to Nisei children, the Japanese government considered the children as loyal subjects of Japan. Japanese language schools were indoctrinating the children with Emperor worship or so-called Mikadoism. Unassimilable and alien like their parents, the children posed a threat to American society because they had American citizenship. Indeed, Japanese immigrants were evading the 1913 Alien Land Law by purchasing agricultural land in the name of their children. Thus, in 1919, the California Oriental

Exclusion League proposed a constitutional amendment to deny citizenship to those children whose parents were aliens ineligible to citizenship, even though the children were born on American soil.[75]

This renewed agitation had an impact on the Pacific Coast Japanese Association Deliberative Council. The council convened twice in 1920, once in February for an extraordinary session and again in June for a regular meeting. In 1918 it had formed an educational committee to study the question of unifying all language schools and of compiling an appropriate textbook series for Nisei children. Only five textbooks had been compiled by 1918 to replace the Japanese Ministry of Education series which had been deemed inappropriate back in 1913. During the 1920 sessions of the council, the council discussed, not the unification of the schools nor the question of textbooks, but the very *raison d'être* of the schools.[76] Abe Toyoji opened the discussion. As a representative of the Japanese Association of Oregon, he argued that the schools "contradicted" the policy of Americanization which had been adopted by all Japanese associations because the schools actually impeded the Americanization of the Nisei. He therefore proposed that the council adopt a public stand in favor of their elimination; barring that, he wanted the council to recommend that the schools be transformed into institutions to teach English to the parents of Nisei children.

The council delegates reacted differently to Abe's proposal. A few flatly opposed it. Some delegates suggested an amendment to the effect that the education offered by the Japanese language schools must not conflict with the policy of Americanization adopted by the associations. Others felt that the council had no authority to abolish the schools, however desirable the goal may be. Such persons recognized that most schools were not under the control of Japanese associations, making them unwilling to endorse any public declaration which advocated their abolishment. In 1921 the council reconsidered the same question with Abe reasserting his point of view.[77] No action resulted from these deliberations. Yet the fact that the council members entertained the idea of doing away with the schools indicated the extent to which the anti-Japanese agitation influenced the thinking of some Japanese association leaders.

The council did take action on other matters. Mindful of the campaign to deprive the Nisei of their American citizenship, it adopted the policy of promoting Nisei civic organizations. Such bodies were to teach the Nisei how to protect and exercise their American citizenship rights. Yet this was more easily said than done because the Nisei generation was still so young. In 1920 there were only a handful of adult Nisei. In 1922, a small group of Nisei formed the Seattle Progressive Citizens' League, and in 1923 an equally small group launched the American Loyalty League in California. Both these groups had the financial support of the Japanese associations and were organized at the behest of Japanese association leaders.[78] The council also reconsidered the problem of dual nationality. To expedite the process of renouncing Japanese citizenship, the Japanese Association of America published a pamphlet on behalf of the council in 1922. This pamphlet explained to the parents of Nisei youngsters the 1916 amendment to the Japanese Nationality Act and the renunciation procedures.[79] To disseminate this information as widely as possible, local Japanese associations distributed the pamphlet to all Japanese residents living within their jurisdictions.

Still the 1916 amendment was not altogether satisfactory. Males 17 years old or older had to fulfill their Japanese military obligation before they could renounce their Japanese citizenship. To eliminate this precondition, in 1922, the council again petitioned the Japanese government.[80] This second petition produced the 1924 amendment to the Japanese Nationality Act. Much more liberal than the first amendment, this one allowed retroactive renunciation of Japanese citizenship without any precondition. Moreover, it abolished automatic Japanese nationality based upon paternal descent. In order to obtain Japanese citizenship for their children, parents were now required to notify the closest Japanese government office within 14 days after birth that they desired Japanese citizenship for their offspring. Otherwise, the children would not possess it. Going much further than the 1916 amendment, the 1924 amendment removed the last legal obstacle to solving the problem of dual nationality.

External pressures also had a telling impact on Japanese immigrant educators. Japanese language schools proliferated over the years. In 1914 there were 31 schools in California; by 1923 this number increased to 55.[81] In 1915 the teachers of southern California organized the Southern California Educational Society. This group adhered to the same goals as the Japanese Teachers Association of America, its counterpart in northern California. In the words of its president, Shimano Kōhei, the educational work of the society was dedicated to "the Nisei who will live and work permanently here, not to those who will return to Japan."[82] In October 1920 the Japanese Teachers Association convened its annual conference as the California electorate was preparing to vote on the 1920 alien land initiative measure.

Japanese immigrant educators reacted to the renewed anti-Japanese agitation in several ways. Some schools used the Japanese term *shō-gakkō* or elementary school as a part of the official name of their schools. To avert the possibility that such schools might be misinterpreted as being modeled on Japanese elementary schools in Japan, the educators decided to designate all schools as *gakuen* or institutes. To reflect this change in name, they renamed the Japanese Teachers Association as the Association of Japanese Language Institutes. The same substitution of nomenclature occurred in southern California. The educators also redefined the goal of the institutes to read: "Based on the spirit of American public schools, the purpose . . . is to supplement good civic education."[83] By civic education they meant the instruction in American citizenship offered by the public schools. The educators incorporated this redefinition of purpose into a new constitution and forwarded an English translation to the State Superintendent of Public Instruction in the hope of mollifying the exclusionists.

In 1921 the California state legislature enacted a law regulating private foreign language schools. The law regulated the operation of schools, the certification of teachers, and the content of instructional materials. According to its provisions, no foreign language school could operate during public school hours, and periods of instruction could not exceed one hour per day, six hours per week, and thirty-eight weeks per year. To be certified to teach in a school, all teachers had to pass a state examination in English competency (reading, writing, and speaking) as well as in American history and institutions in English. All textbooks and curricula had to be approved by the Superintendent of Public Instruction. Finally, the Superintendent was authorized to inspect any school and to withdraw the certificates of teachers at any time. This law became effective on July 30 as Section 1534 of the California Political Code.

All Japanese language institutes became subject to this new enactment. The examinations in American history and institutions in English and in English competency were deferred until 1923. As a compromise, Japanese teachers were allowed to take the examination in American history and institutions in Japanese in 1921 and 1922. To prepare them for the 1921 examination, the Japanese Association of America and the Central Japanese Association of Southern California sponsored special Teachers' Training Institutes in San Francisco, Fresno, and Los Angeles. The program in San Francisco lasted for two weeks with 127 teachers enrolled in classes on American history and institutions.[84] Various white Americans presented the lectures in these

classes. Sam H. Cohn, Assistant State Superintendent of Public Instruction, personally appeared on the first day to explain what the
state would expect from the Japanese teachers in the upcoming examination.

Japanese teachers took the examination in the fall under Sam H.
Cohn's watchful eyes. In San Francisco, the examination consisted of
seven questions on history and seven on institutions. Five in each category had to be answered. The examinees pondered such historical
questions as:

> What two questions were definitely settled by the Civil War?
> What was Washington's policy in foreign affairs? How has it af-
> fected the foreign policy of America?
> What is meant by the Monroe Doctrine?
> Discuss the territorial expansion of the United States from the origi-
> nal 13 colonies, explaining how each acquisition was made.

Turning to the questions on institutions, the examinees encountered
such biased questions as:

> Compare the form of government of the United States with that of
> Japan in regard to similarities and differences. Point out the strength
> and weakness of each.
> Why is it essential that a teacher should be familiar with the institu-
> tions of the country in which he resides? Illustrate.
> Instructing Japanese children in their relation to American institu-
> tions, what points would you consider most needful of emphasis?

In 1922 the questions on institutions were more slanted:

> What restrictions are placed on immigration into the United
> States? Are these restrictions just? Why?
> Explain your view as to whether the State should or should not have
> control of "foreign language schools."
> Give the essential qualities of a "good" citizen. How may these be
> developed in young children?[85]

These questions were patently absurd. Were the examinees to reply
that the immigration restrictions against the Japanese were just? That
the government of Japan was a terrible tyranny and that of America
a wonderful democracy? Or that the state should require the examination they were compelled to take? Yet the examinees had no choice
but to answer the questions to please their examiners. In 1923 the
examinees took a similar examination in American history and institutions in English. As reference books for the Japanese teachers, the

Japanese Association of America purchased 200 copies of four American textbooks: Charles A. Beard and William C. Bagley, *The History of the American People;* Frank A. Magruder, *American Government;* Charles A. Beard and Mary R. Beard, *American Citizenship;* and *Civics for New Americans,* a manual on citizenship for new immigrants.

Assistant Superintendent of Public Instruction Cohn selected Kuno Yoshisaburō of the University of California to read the examination papers. Kuno was an assistant professor of Japanese in the Department of Oriental Languages. An Issei maverick, he was often at odds with Japanese immigrant leaders. He enraged them in October 1920 when he published a series of articles in the Oakland *Tribune.* Entitled "A Survey of the Japanese Situation," the series alleged that Japanese consuls controlled the Japanese associations and that Japanese immigrants had managed to evade the 1913 Alien Land Law.[86] From the immigrant leaders' perspective, Kuno played into the hands of the exclusionists by giving the California electorate reasons for voting for the 1920 alien land initiative measure. As to the Japanese language institutes, Kuno felt that Nisei children were being unduly forced to attend them. He disapproved of the institutes because, in his opinion, they were creating "hyphenated Americans" with "two loyalties."[87] Upon reading a batch of the 1921 examination papers, Kuno wrote to Cohn that he was "astonished" that "the majority of . . . teachers are unfamiliar with . . . American history and American institutions. . . . " He condescendingly judged "their average intellectual ability" to be "approximately that of an 8th grade pupil in the United States." In his entire teaching experience, he had "never before come across so many low-grade papers in a single lot."[88] Notwithstanding Kuno's harsh judgement, in 1921, out of 156 teachers who took the examinations administered in San Francisco and Fresno, 125 received licenses.[89]

To comply with the requirement relating to textbooks, the Japanese Association of America and the Central Japanese Association of Southern California cooperated to compile an acceptable new textbook series. Representatives of the two central associations formed a special education committee entrusted with the task of compiling it. Until the series was completed, state officials approved selected translations of the Japanese Ministry of Education series on an interim basis. The new alternative series, consisting of sixteen volumes, took two years to complete. The State Superintendent approved it officially in August 1923.[90] This series was uniquely American; it neither had lessons in Japanese history or geography, nor any reference to the Japanese Emperor. The compilers drew upon and translated from American textbooks. Stories about George Washington, Abraham Lincoln, Betsy Ross, and other American figures were so prominent that the series was overwhelmingly American in content.

Nevertheless, neither the 1921 legislation nor the Japanese immigrant compliance with it satisfied anti-Japanese exclusionists. In 1923 the California state legislature enacted a more stringent law. Authored by the rabid anti-Japanese State Senator J.M. Inman, this measure limited enrollment into foreign language schools to children who had completed the fourth grade. In addition, it included a provision outlawing all foreign language schools by July 1, 1930. The United States Supreme Court indirectly nullified this new California enactment in a timely ruling. Just as the governor was on the verge of signing the bill into law, the high tribunal ruled that a 1919 Nebraska statute was unconstitutional. The Nebraska statute banned the teaching of a foreign language to any child who had not completed the eighth grade. Rendered in June 1923, the court ruled in a case involving a person who had taught German to a ten year old in a parochial school.[91] Reasoning that the Nebraska statute exceeded the powers of the State, the court struck down the statute. In the light of this decision, the new 1923 California enactment ended abortively with the governor never signing it into law.

The 1921 legislation eventually met the same fate. In 1927 the United States Supreme Court handed down another key decision which invalidated a statute of the Territory of Hawaii.[92] The statute regulated the operation of foreign language schools, the certification of teachers, and the content of instructional materials in the same manner as the 1921 California legislation did. Indeed, the California law had been modeled on the Hawaiian one. The Supreme Court declared the Hawaiian statute unconstitutional in its entirety, thereby nullifying the corresponding laws of California and other states. As a result, Japanese language institutes could hire any teacher, use any textbook, and set any classroom schedule. The only restriction was that they were not allowed to open during the hours when the public schools were in session. From this point in time, Japanese immigrants were free to run their language institutes in any way they saw fit.

Quest for Naturalization Rights

As a part of their long and bitter struggle, Japanese immigrants sought the right of naturalization through the landmark 1922 Takao Ozawa case. Early naturalization statutes, barring Asians from acquiring American citizenship, formed the legal framework of the Ozawa case.[93] In 1790 Congress restricted the right of naturalization to an alien who was a "free white person." Subsequent enactments, legislated during the course of the nineteenth century, all contained this racial condition which defined an alien's general eligibility for admission into citizenship. In 1870 Congress created a second racial category. It made "aliens of African nativity and persons of African descent" also eligible. Both the white and black categories of eligibility were embedded in section 2169 of Title XXX of the Revised Federal Statutes of 1875. The Act of June 29, 1906 standardized naturalization requirements and procedures. Directly bearing on the Ozawa case, this legislation regulated nonracial requirements, but did not rescind the preceding racial limitations of section 2169. Thus only two types of aliens, namely, persons of white and black descent, were eligible to become American citizens when Ozawa Takao filed for naturalization in 1914.

Despite this racial restriction, the ineligibility of the Japanese was not a foregone conclusion in a strict legal sense. Though the Japanese definitely were not of African descent, the question of whether they might be classified as so-called free white persons remained an open one. This racial category was not defined precisely. What was meant by *free*? And, more significantly, what was meant by *white*? Was the category inclusive or exclusive? Could the Japanese be classified, not as mongolian, but as caucasian? Neither Congressional legislation nor any United States Supreme Court decision provided unequivocal answers to such key questions. The fate of the Chinese offered a clue but no definitive answers. Congress made the Chinese inadmissible into citizenship by the Chinese Exclusion Act of 1882, but the act made no mention of the Japanese. Due to the ambiguous meaning of a free white person, some lower federal courts issued naturalization papers to a number of Japanese. According to the 1910 census, some 420 were naturalized.[94] One of the first was Kaneko Shinsei, a resident of Riverside, California, who received his preliminary papers in 1892. Obtaining his final papers in 1896, Kaneko exercised his American citizenship by voting and serving as a juror. He even had an American passport issued to him with which he travelled abroad.[95] In 1906, in conjunction with the passage of the Act of 1906, the United States Attorney General ordered federal courts to cease issuing naturalization papers to Japanese applicants, which ended the practice that permitted the handful to become naturalized. Yet this administrative measure did not answer the legal questions regarding the eligibility of the Japanese under existing naturalization statutes because it did not have the weight of a judicial ruling.

The anti-Japanese exclusion movement first brought the question of naturalization rights into prominence. In October 1906 the San Francisco School Board resolved to segregate Japanese pupils in the San Francisco public schools. The Japanese government lodged a vigorous protest with the American government and precipitated an international crisis. In response to the crisis, President Theodore Roosevelt in his annual message to Congress on December 3 denounced the board's action as "a wicked absurdity."[96] While lauding the Japanese people to placate the Japanese government and public opinion in Japan, he recommended legislation to grant the Japanese in the United States the right of naturalization. Roosevelt probably never had any real intent of following through on his recommendation. But regardless of whether he did or not, his recommendation to Congress drew public attention to the question of naturalization rights for Japanese immigrants.

Japanese diplomats were aware of the ambiguous status of the Japanese immigrants. Even before Roosevelt's message to Congress, Consul Uchida Sadatsuchi of New York City noted in the spring of 1906 that the Supreme Court had yet to rule on the eligibility of the Japanese under existing naturalization statutes. Only lower court decisions and administrative interpretations barred them from naturalization. Although Uchida favored naturalization rights for the immigrants, he felt that "it was advisable to defer the solution to this question until an opportune time arrives."[97] Japanese Ambassador Aoki Shūzō believed that such a moment had arrived with the school crisis. Accordingly, independently of instructions from the Foreign Ministry, he broached the subject of naturalization with Secretary of State Elihu Root in late October. Shown a draft of Roosevelt's message to Congress, Aoki reported optimistically to Tokyo that the Roosevelt administration was disposed to granting Japanese the right.[98] Acknowledging that its acquisition would be "a basic solution to the immigration issue," Foreign Minister Hayashi Tadasu on November 18 thereupon ordered Aoki to explore the matter further with Secretary of State Root.[99]

Diplomatic efforts to negotiate the right of naturalization were short-lived. In early January 1907 Foreign Minister Hayashi instructed Ambassador Aoki to ascertain how the American government intended to solve the school and naturalization issues. Queried by Aoki about naturalization, Secretary of State Root refused flatly to consider it, contending that a bill of the kind recommended by President Roosevelt could not be introduced in time for Congressional action.[100] Undeterred by this rebuff, the Foreign Ministry laid down the condition that, upon satisfactory solution of the school issue, it would be willing to negotiate the curtailment of Japanese immigration in exchange for the right of naturalization. The American side never accepted the condition. Both Secretary of State Root and American Ambassador Luke E. Wright in Tokyo persisted in refusing adamantly to discuss naturalization. Confronted by this unyielding stance, Foreign Minister Hayashi conveyed to Ambassador Aoki on February 23 that "I consider naturalization impossible at this juncture."[101] Aoki had reached an identical conclusion. On the very next day, he reported that "the present juncture is most unsuitable for effecting any favorable legislation."[102] Judging any further pursuit of the matter to be futile, no matter how the immigration issue might be settled, the Foreign Ministry dropped the naturalization issue altogether.

Japanese immigrants also considered the naturalization question. As early as 1903, Negoro Motoyuki, a student at the University of California, analyzed the unclear legal status of the Japanese.[103] Kawasaki Minotarō, editor of the *Nichibei Shimbun,* also recognized the ambiguous status of the Japanese immigrants. To make the Japanese clearly admissible into citizenship, he proposed in July 1905 that the Japanese government negotiate naturalization rights directly with the American government.[104] When President Roosevelt's message to Congress was publicized, the *Shin Sekai* heralded his recommendation with great elation.[105] This newspaper later published an extensive article on the naturalization question by Miyakawa Masuji.[106] A practicing attorney in San Francisco, Miyakawa was among the handful of Japanese who had acquired American citizenship. Congress amended immigration statutes in February 1907, authorizing the President to halt the migration of Japanese laborers from the Hawaiian Islands. The day after the Congressional action, and as the Foreign Ministry was trying to negotiate naturalization rights, the Japanese Association of Washington wired Foreign Minister Hayashi and appealed to him to seek the right of naturalization in exchange for any immigration restrictions.[107] In April Takahashi Tetsuo submitted a formal petition to Ambassador Aoki on behalf of the association in which he stated that "the acquisition of naturalization rights would undercut the arguments for exclusion."[108] Immigrant leaders in San Francisco acted similarly. They dispatched Noda Otosaburō to Washington, D.C. to impress upon

Ambassador Aoki "the urgency of acquiring naturalization rights."[109] In June Kawakami Kiyoshi published an article entitled "The Naturalization of Japanese" in the *North American Review* in which he argued for naturalization rights for professionals, merchants, and farmers.[110]

This initial interest subsided as suddenly as it had surfaced. During the negotiation of the Gentlemen's Agreement of 1907–8, Japanese diplomats did not raise the naturalization issue. Neither did they bring it up in later talks to conclude the 1911 United States-Japan Treaty of Commerce and Navigation. For their part, immigrant leaders did not advocate the acquisition of naturalization rights persistently. In January 1909 the naturalization question appeared on the agenda of the Japanese Association of America's first conference with affiliated local associations. No specific course of action was adopted. Japanese association leaders simply referred it to a study committee where it languished from want of action. Some individuals were even critical of immigrant leaders who favored naturalization rights. Ōtsuka Zenjirō, a conservative reporter for the *Sōkō Shimbun* of San Francisco, felt that "naturalization is an act which reflects a lack of Japanese patriotism."[111] In his opinion, any Japanese who favored it was betraying his native country, Japan.

The 1913 California Alien Land Law revived the interest of the Japanese immigrants in naturalization rights. Since the law singled out aliens ineligible to citizenship, it was natural for them to turn to this old question. For if they had the right of naturalization, the alien land law would not be applicable to them. Reflecting this renewed interest, an intense, widespread discussion of the entire question arose within immigrant society. The immigrant press analyzed it in great depth during the spring and summer of 1913. Most newspapers championed the idea of seeking naturalization rights. The *Nichibei Shimbun* was at the forefront. The newspaper granted that "Japanese diplomats and other prominent persons say we should wait until an opportune time comes," but avowed that "we cannot agree with the position of waiting for that moment."[112] Admittedly, seeking the right would require time and careful study. But concluding that its acquisition would be "the basic solution" to the alien land law, the *Nichibei Shimbun* dismissed a policy of stoic inaction and called upon immigrant leaders to initiate a long-term drive to secure the right of naturalization.

This editorial stance of the *Nichibei Shimbun* was in keeping with Abiko Kyūtarō's advocacy of permanent settlement. Abiko did not place much stock in the ability of Japanese diplomats or visiting prominent Japanese to solve the problems Japanese immigrants faced. He believed that the only ones capable of solving the problems were the immigrants themselves, and the only sure and lasting way of solving them was for the immigrants to become independent and self-reliant. When the 1913 Alien Land Law was enacted, the *Nichibei Shimbun* warned the immigrants "not to waver" in their determination to settle down because of the new law. At the same time, it began to stress the need to nurture "a spirit of independence and self-reliance." Because of a deep-seated "sense of dependency," the immigrants had depended too much upon others to solve their problems for them. Rooted in Abiko's vision of permanent residency, the real meaning and challenge of being a Japanese in the United States was to shed this old sense of dependency.

Consequently, from 1914 the *Nichibei Shimbun* advised the immigrants not to depend upon the Japanese government. A 1914 editorial stated this position boldly. Partially entitled "Let's Not Rely Upon the Homeland Government," it declared that "unless we become self-reliant and not dependent upon others, we will never be able to build a solid foundation here."[113] A 1915 editorial said: "Don't be dependent; stand self-reliant and independent."[114] The 1916 New Year's edition proclaimed:

> We . . . must reorient ourselves. We must become independent and self-reliant. We must resolve to solve all problems which lie in our path by ourselves. With such a resolution, we must exert ourselves and struggle on to shape our own future.[115]

By launching a campaign to acquire the right of naturalization for themselves, according to the *Nichibei Shimbun,* Japanese immigrants would be exercising their independence and self-reliance.

Other immigrant newspapers, organizations, and individuals joined in supporting the idea of seeking the right of naturalization. Using identical language, the *Shin Sekai* interpreted "the acquisition of naturalization rights" as "the basic solution" to the alien land law.[116] Headquartered in San Francisco with most immigrant Christian churches under its jurisdiction, the Japanese Interdenominational Board of Missions endorsed the idea.[117] Superintendent Uchida Kōyū, head of the Buddhist Mission of America, also endorsed the idea.[118] As editor of the *Hokubei Nōhō,* Chiba Toyoji actually proposed a legal test case to determine whether or not the Japanese had the right of naturalization under existing statutes.[119] Immediately after the enactment of the 1913 Alien Land Law, individuals in San Francisco favoring naturalization founded the *Shiminken Kakutoku Kisei Dōshikai* (Society for Promoting the Acquisition of Citizenship), the name of the body denoting the purpose to which it was dedicated.[120] Addressing the general American public, Kawakami Kiyoshi wrote that "the only salvation of the Japanese lies in their admission into citizenship" and reiterated his belief that the Japanese should be allowed to naturalize.[121] Of all the immigrant newspapers, the *Taihoku Nippō* of Seattle dissented conspicuously. Opposed to any campaign to seek the right, it believed that such a quest was foreordained to fail because it would arouse more anti-Japanese hostility.[122]

The Japanese Association of America and its affiliated locals also favored naturalization. Just as the California state legislature was about to enact the land bill, Japanese association leaders met in April at an emergency conference.[123] The naturalization question was a major agenda item, and the deliberation on this subject mirrored the ongoing discussion within immigrant society. No delegate disputed that naturalization presented a fundamental solution to the pending land bill. No one, moreover, objected to seeking the right. Accepting the desirability of the goal, the delegates debated the means of achieving it. As a result of the proceedings, a 15-man committee was appointed and empowered to explore all possible countermeasures to the land bill, including the acquisition of the right of naturalization. The 1906 school imbroglio generated a sudden, brief interest in naturalization. The California Alien Land Law of 1913 resuscitated the interest permanently, producing a wide consensus among immigrant leaders that they should embark on actually seeking the right.

Immigrant leaders considered three alternative ways of obtaining the right.[124] The first was through diplomatic channels. They would ask the Japanese government to conclude a special convention with the American government granting the right. During the San Francisco school crisis, the Foreign Ministry had offered to curtail labor immigration in exchange for naturalization rights, only to have abandoned this condition in the face of stiff American opposition. This first alternative required the Foreign Ministry to reevaluate its negative assessment of the prospect of negotiating naturalization rights. The second way was to lobby for direct Congressional legislation. Immigrant leaders would campaign for a law specifically admitting the Japanese into citizenship. A leading proponent of this alternative was Masukawa Takeji of New York City who addressed immigrant groups up and down the Pacific Coast in the summer of 1913 to marshal support for it. Realistically, the prospect for such a piece of legislation was dim, if not nil, in the light of American public opinion. That left a third alternative. Immigrant leaders would seek the right of naturalization through litigation. To get a final judicial ruling regarding Japanese eligibility under existing statutes, they would take a naturalization test case to the Supreme Court. This last option had an attractive quality. It did not hinge on either the initiative of Japanese diplomats or the state of American public opinion. Japanese immigrants themselves were in a position to pursue it.

Leading up eventually to the Ozawa case, two important events occurred after the emergency conference of the Japanese Association of America and its affiliated locals. First, the newly appointed 15-man committee sent two representatives to Washington, D.C. to confer with the Japanese ambassador, Chinda Sutemi. The two emissaries were Abiko Kyūtarō and Ushijima Kinji. To counteract the adverse effects of the exclusion movement, Japanese association leaders decided to renew their "campaign of education" to enlighten the American public about Japan and Japanese immigrants as well as to educate the immigrants about the United States. Beyond seeking the right of naturalization, they deemed such a broad educational campaign necessary in order to foster a favorable climate of opinion. The two men were entrusted with a three-fold mission: to outline the campaign to Ambassador Chinda, to inform him of the condition of the immigrants in California, and to elicit from him the Foreign Ministry's stand on naturalization.

Abiko and Ushijima met with Ambassador Chinda in mid-June 1913 as he was protesting the enactment of the alien land law. Chinda submitted his first protest note to Secretary of State William Jennings Bryan on May 9; in it, he said nothing about naturalization. Eight days later Foreign Minister Makino Shinken instructed him to feel Bryan out on the subject.[125] Chinda did so immediately, and Bryan declined emphatically to consider it, as Secretary of State Elihu Root had in 1907.[126] In his second protest note of June 4, Chinda described the ineligibility of the Japanese as "mortifying to the Government and people of Japan" because it had been manipulated to restrict the Japanese immigrants' "civil" right in regard to land tenure. As long as the "distinction" had been "employed in relations to rights of [a] purely political nature," he stated, his government had "had no occasion to approach the Government of the United States on the subject."[127] Conceding naturalization was a domestic matter, Chinda couched his reference to it in these oblique terms. Having been rebuffed by Bryan, he never insisted on negotiating naturalization rights.

Chinda was awaiting a reply to his second protest note from Bryan when he received Abiko and Ushijima. Informed by them of the Japanese associations' plan to conduct an educational campaign, Chinda heartily endorsed it. As to naturalization rights, according to the two emissaries, Chinda stated that, in principle, his government favored it, but the American public was not ready to accept it. Rather than precipitately seeking the right, the groundwork of changing public opinion had to be done beforehand.[128] Chinda indicated the reluctance of his government to force the issue, a position which other Japanese diplomats would reiterate later. On July 16 Secretary of State Bryan answered Chinda's second note. Surmising that Chinda did not have instructions "to press the matter," Bryan ignored the subject of naturalization altogether.[129] A week later Foreign Minister Makino instructed Chinda to shelve the naturalization issue.[130] In the judgment of Japanese diplomats, the diplomatic possibility of negotiating naturalization rights was not present. For them the time was still inopportune, as it had been in 1907, making it evident to immigrant leaders that they could not count on the Japanese government to take the initiative.

The founding of the Pacific Coast Japanese Association Deliberative Council was the other event of importance. At the emergency April 1913 conference, Japanese association leaders also adopted a proposal to establish a broader national organization, embracing at least all Japanese immigrants on the Pacific Coast and in the adjacent western states. To implement this proposal, a preliminary meeting in San Francisco was held in November 1913. Then, in July 1914, representatives from Seattle, Portland, San Francisco, and Vancouver, Canada convened in Portland to form the council. As it was organized, the council was not a new organization. It was a higher coordinating organ of the existing central bodies to which all local Japanese associations were affiliated. Its purpose was to solve problems held in common by all the associations. From 1914 the council convened at least once a year. Inasmuch as the naturalization problem was shared by all Japanese immigrants in the United States, it assumed responsibility for solving it. At its inception, indeed, the council adopted a resolution that read:

> Whereas, recognizing the present urgency of solving the naturalization question, be it hereby resolved that a test case be instituted at an appropriate time in pursuit of the just legal goal of acquiring the right of naturalization for the Japanese.[131]

In order to go to court, the council had to find an ideal test case, both in a political and legal sense. That case proved to be that of Ozawa Takao which originated in Hawaii. His was unquestionably ideal in a political sense. Born June 15, 1875, Ozawa was a native of Kanagawa Prefecture who landed in San Francisco as a young student in 1894. Working as a school-boy, he attended various schools and graduated from Berkeley High School in Berkeley, California. He then studied at the University of California for three years until 1906, after which he discontinued his studies and moved to Honolulu where he settled down. He worked for an American company and had outstanding references to his moral character from his associates. He was married with two children. To argue his own case, Ozawa authored two legal briefs. Vouching for his own personal character, he unabashedly wrote in one of them:

I neither drink liquor of any kind, nor smoke, nor play cards, nor gamble, nor associate with any improper persons. My honesty and my industriousness are well known among my Japanese and American acquaintances and friends; and I am always trying my best to conduct myself according to the Golden Rule. So I have all [the] confidence in myself that as far as my character is concerned, I am second to none.

Attesting to his undivided allegiance to the United States, he continued:

In name, General Benedict Arnold was an American, but at heart he was a traitor. In name, I am not an American, but at heart I am a true American. I set forth the following facts that will sufficiently prove this. (1) I did not report my name, my marriage, or the names of my children to the Japanese Consulate in Honolulu; notwithstanding all Japanese subjects are requested to do so. These matters were reported to the American government. (2) I do not have any connection with any Japanese churches or schools, or any Japanese organizations here or elsewhere. (3) I am sending my children to an American church and American school in place of a Japanese one. (4) Most of the time I use the American (English) language at home, so that my children cannot speak the Japanese language. (5) I educated myself in American schools for nearly eleven years by supporting myself. (6) I have lived continuously within the United States for over twenty-eight years. (7) I chose as my wife one educated in American schools . . . instead of one educated in Japan. (8) I have steadily prepared to return the kindness which our Uncle Sam has extended to me . . . so it is my honest hope to do something good to the United States before I bid a farewell to this world.[132]

In sum, Ozawa was a paragon of an assimilated Japanese immigrant, a living refutation of the allegation of Japanese unassimilability. He could speak, read, and write English; he sent his children to American institutions and spoke English with them at home; he had no ties to the Japanese community and Japanese government; he was married to an American-educated woman; and his character was beyond reproach. Immigrant leaders were able to support him without fear his case would fail by virtue of the elementary political fact that Ozawa was not assimilated. From this perspective, he was an excellent candidate to be the central figure in a naturalization test case.

Legally, his case was also ideal. Ozawa fulfilled all the nonracial requirements for naturalization set by the Act of 1906. According to this statute, an applicant had to file a petition of intent to naturalize at least two years prior to formal application. Ozawa filed for naturalization on October 16, 1914, and he had filed his petition of intent on August 1, 1902 in Alameda County, California. He satisfied the five-year continuous residency requirement. He had lived in the United States and Hawaii for more than twenty years. His personal character and English fluency needless to say met the requirements related to moral fitness and knowledge of the English language. Fully qualified in terms of the Act of 1906, his case was impeccable from a legal point of view.

Ozawa was unsuccessful at the lower court level. After his petition to naturalize was rejected, he took his case to the United States District Court for the Territory of Hawaii. On March 25, 1916 Judge Charles F. Clemons rendered his decision in these words:

> The court finds that the petitioner is not qualified under Revised Statutes, section 2169, and must therefore deny his petition; and it is so ordered, in spite of the finding hereby made that he has fully established the allegation of his petition, and, except as to the requirements of section 2169, is in every way eminently qualified under the statutes to become an American citizen.[133]

Translated into ordinary language, classified as a member of the mongolian race, Ozawa was excluded by the racial restrictions of section 2169, and therefore ineligible to citizenship. Notwithstanding his obvious qualifications, he was not a free white person, which alone disqualified him. Ozawa filed an appeal that was granted on September 26, 1916, and his case then passed on to the Ninth Circuit Court of Appeals in San Francisco. Without handing down a decision, the appellate court referred the case to the Supreme Court on May 31,

1917.[134] Up to the point of his appeal, Ozawa was on his own in contesting the denial of his petition to naturalize. Save for a few close friends and associates, he did not have the support of any organized Japanese immigrant group. When he appealed to the Ninth Circuit Court, his case drew the notice of Japanese immigrant leaders on the Pacific Coast. Just as they were looking for an ideal test case, it suddenly loomed before them.

The Pacific Coast Japanese Association Deliberative Council first discussed the Ozawa case in August 1916.[135] Kanzaki Kiichi, general secretary of the Japanese Association of America, presented a report on it. With a possible test case in mind, the council voted to obtain the court transcript from Honolulu. Kanzaki agreed to solicit the legal opinions of the counsels to the Japanese Association of America and to circulate all information, including copies of the transcript, to the other central bodies. In the meantime the council resolved not to publicize the case before it had a chance to study it fully. In April 1915 Consul Numano Yasutarō of San Francisco had requested instructions from the Foreign Ministry on any test case. Foreign Minister Katō Takaaki ordered him "to take steps to prevent the Japanese within your jurisdiction from undertaking a test case campaign."[136] This order was in keeping with the Foreign Ministry's view, stated by Ambassador Chinda in 1913, that the time was inappropriate to pursue any course of action in the matter of naturalization. Consul Moroi Rokurō of Honolulu even tried to persuade Ozawa to withdraw his appeal.[137] Aware of the Japanese government's attitude, the council understandably held back publicity until it reached a final decision on the case.

The immigrant press covered the Ozawa case widely in the summer of 1917. Before the Ninth Circuit Court referred it to the Supreme Court, the *Nichibei Shimbun* editorialized that "the Japanese are considered aliens ineligible to citizenship . . . because we are presumed to be an inferior race" which was "an insulting treatment." Since ineligibility was at the heart of "discriminatory legislation," the Ozawa case "warranted as much support as possible."[138] Expecting the Ninth Circuit Court to rule on it, the newspaper was startled by the court's action. Notwithstanding its own reservations, however, the *Nichibei Shimbun* urged everyone to cooperate and pull behind Ozawa.[139] Like it or not, Ozawa had become the representative of all Japanese immigrants. The *Shin Sekai* and the *Rafu Shimpō* of Los Angeles concurred with the *Nichibei Shimbun*.[140] The Ozawa case was no longer a private legal battle. Passed on to the Supreme Court, the decision at this level would affect every Japanese in the United States. All three newspapers urged the Pacific Coast Japanese Association Deliberative Council, scheduled to convene in July, to assume the leadership on behalf of the immigrants and support the case.

The council met for two days in July in Los Angeles. Upon weighing carefully the implications, it voted unanimously to support Ozawa Takao. To carry out the decision, a four-man naturalization committee was appointed, composed of one representative from each central body (except Canada) and headed by Yamaoka Ototaka of Seattle.[141] This new committee went to work quickly. In mid-August Yamaoka, along with other immigrant leaders, conferred with Viscount Ishii Kikujirō in San Francisco. Ishii had just arrived as Ambassador Extraordinary and Plenipotentiary, leading a special Japanese diplomatic mission to Washington, D.C. to negotiate affairs relating to China. Taking advantage of Ishii's timely presence, a petition was submitted to him which asked for, among other things, assistance from the Japanese government in the Ozawa case. On Ishii's way back to Japan in November, Yamaoka conferred with him again. At the time of this second meeting, Ishii requested the naturalization committee to suspend its support of the Ozawa case. According to Yamaoka, Ishii said:

> All eminent persons in the executive branch of the American government and in every political party and faction believe that the Japanese should be allowed to naturalize as a matter of justice and humaneness. But public opinion at large is not ready, so no one will come out and take a public stand on the question. Thus it is better to postpone the case until the right time comes.[142]

Reiterating the Japanese government's long-held negative assessment of the naturalization situation, Ishii's remarks left no room for any doubt—the Foreign Ministry was unalterably opposed to the Ozawa case. The committee could not bank on any help from the Japanese government.

In 1918 the committee prepared to support Ozawa. In April Yamaoka placed Ishii Kikujirō's request before the committee as a formal resolution to withdraw its support of the Ozawa case. The committee summarily rejected this resolution.[143] Electing to proceed with the case, the committee retained David L. Withington, Ozawa's attorney, but as principal counsel selected George W. Wickersham, onetime United States Attorney General. Subsequently, Yamaoka travelled to Honolulu where he spoke directly with Ozawa and his attorney. In late 1917 Ozawa had been asked by Horikoshi Zenjūrō, a New York City businessman, and by Ishii himself, to defer his appeal.[144] A foe of litigation, Horikoshi returned to Japan at the end of that year. Stopping off in Honolulu en route, he tried to convince Ozawa to discontinue his appeal. With the same objective in mind, Ishii talked with him on his own return voyage to Japan. Ozawa turned a deaf ear to their appeal. When Yamaoka consulted with him, he categorically said that he would neither postpone nor withdraw his case under any circumstance, even in the "face of death."[145] In June the committee settled on final terms with George W. Wickersham for his legal service. All necessary preparations seemingly had been completed.

Concurrent events proved otherwise. These preparations were made in the middle of a new debate over the merits of the Ozawa case. The *Nichibei Shimbun* set off the debate by doing an abrupt turnabout. Beginning with an editorial in January 1918, it predicted inevitable defeat in the case since "public opinion greatly influences the judiciary." The wisest policy was "to promote a favorable public opinion first," and then to seek naturalization rights through "legislation" instead of litigation.[146] In March the newspaper raised a concrete legal objection to the Ozawa case, citing a Supreme Court decision in the Antonio Morena case.[147] Handed down on January 7, 1918, this decision involved the time lapse between the filing of a petition of intent and of a petition to naturalize. The Act of 1906 stipulated that an applicant had to file the latter at least two years but no more than seven years after filing the former. The court upheld the constitutionality of this procedural requirement in the Morena case.[148] Ozawa filed his petition of intent on August 1, 1902 and his petition to naturalize on October 16, 1914. Twelve years separated the two filings, five more than the allotted maximum of seven years. The *Nichibei Shimbun* still favored the quest for naturalization rights, but interpreted this unforeseen snag as a compelling reason to forego the Ozawa case.

A polemical debate over the case then ensued. The *Nichibei Shimbun* forcefully recommended postponement or withdrawal of the case prior to the April meeting of the naturalization committee. Once the committee decided to proceed with the case, it assailed the decision as "utterly regrettable," going so far as to condemn it as "arbitrary" and "undemocratic," and accusing the committee of exercising unauthorized power.[149] In May the newspaper opened its columns to opponents of the case and printed many anti-Ozawa articles in order to rally the opposition. The *Shin Sekai* took up the cause of the opposite side. Contrary to the accusation of improper conduct, according to its opinion, the naturalization committee was duly appointed and acted within prescribed authority, and the Morena decision had not changed the merits of the Ozawa case. Charging the *Nichibei Shimbun* with "inconsistency" and "undue pessimism," the *Shin Sekai* also allocated space to the immigrant public and published innumerable pro-Ozawa articles.[150] It even sponsored a public forum on naturalization in early May. And to prove the immigrant press supported the Ozawa case, it reprinted editorials from many other newspapers.[151] In the Sacramento area, the *Ōfu Nippō* claimed that the majority of the Japanese there were inclined towards postponing the case, while the *Kakushū Jiji* of Denver advocated going ahead with it.[152] The *Rafu Shimpō* took the *Nichibei Shimbun* severely to task for reversing its position, and lined up solidly behind the *Shin Sekai.*[153]

The Supreme Court did not take up the Ozawa case in 1918 or 1919. A political factor intervened and played a greater role than the decision in the Morena case. In June 1918 Secretary of State Robert Lansing asked Solicitor General John W. Davis to postpone the court's hearing of the case until the termination of World War I. Since the outbreak of the war, Japan had sided with Great Britain against Germany. Davis complied with Lansing's request out of consideration for Japan's contribution to the allied war effort and her sensitivity to the naturalization issue.[154] Japan's participation in the 1919 Versailles Peace Conference probably figured in this political decision as well. Japan brought three major issues to the conference table, one of which was a racial equality clause which she wanted inserted into the League of Nations Covenant.[155] An unfavorable decision to the Japanese side in the Ozawa case would have caused Japan to lose face in the eyes of the world which might have hardened her bargaining posture on this and other issues.

In December 1919 Wickersham advised Yamaoka to begin a search for a second case.[156] The Morena decision did affect the Ozawa case. Ozawa had not satisfied the procedural requirement regulating the time interval between the filing of a petition of intent and of a petition to naturalize. Wickersham feared the case might be declared moot by the Supreme Court on this simple technicality. With Yamaoka carrying the main burden in the Pacific Northwest, the naturalization committee examined possible cases throughout 1920. Meanwhile, Californians passed an initiative measure in November which amended the 1913 Alien Land Law. This amendment prohibited aliens ineligible to citizenship to purchase or lease agricultural land, to hold stocks in agricultural landholding companies, to transfer or sell agricultural land to each other, and disqualified them from being appointed as guardians of minors who had title to such land. Written to plug up the loopholes of the earlier legislation, this measure had the undisguised aim of driving Japanese immigrants out of California agriculture. The California electorate passed the initiative by an overwhelming margin of over two to one. This ominous new development, together with a new alien land law enacted by the state of Washington in March 1921, made the search for a second case at once more pressing.

Thus the naturalization committee itself instituted another case in May 1921. On behalf of the committee, Corwin S. Shank, a Seattle attorney, in cooperation with George W. Wickersham, brought the case of Yamashita Takuji and Kono Hyōsaburō before the Washington State Supreme Court.[157] The essence of this case was simple. In 1902 both Yamashita and Kono had been naturalized in Pierce County, Washington. Forming a real estate company, they filed articles of incorporation on May 14, 1921, with the Secretary of State. His office refused to accept the articles on the grounds that the two men had not been naturalized legally and were therefore unable to form such a company under the laws of the state. Yamashita and Kono applied promptly for a writ of mandate with the State Supreme Court in order to compel the Secretary of State to accept the articles of incorporation. The court declined to issue the writ at which point the two men appealed to the United States Supreme Court. The naturalization committee initiated this case as the companion to the Ozawa case because it was the shortest, and hence fastest, way of reaching the high tribunal.[158] Though the legal details differed, it nonetheless required the Supreme Court to rule on the question of Japanese eligibility under existing naturalization statutes.

All preparations were complete at last, but another political factor prevented the court from hearing the Ozawa case in the fall of 1921. In the winter of 1921–22, the Washington Conference on Arms Limitation was held. Fearful of Japan's growing naval power, the United States and Great Britain called the conference to persuade Japan to agree to limit her naval forces in order to preserve their own naval superiority in the Pacific. An unfavorable decision to the Japanese side in the Ozawa case, it was feared again, would cause Japan to lose face and might cause her to be less willing to agree to any proposal to limit her naval power in the Pacific.[159] Thus the Supreme Court again postponed hearing the Ozawa case. In this way, the long-sought high court ruling on this naturalization test case was delayed for still another year.

The Supreme Court finally took up the Ozawa case in 1922. Despite Wickersham's apprehension, the court heard the case and ruled that Ozawa Takao was ineligible to citizenship. Judged to be neither a free white person nor an African by birth or descent, he did not have the right of naturalization as a mongolian.[160] The court decided the Yamashita and Kono case in accordance with its ruling in the Ozawa case. In general, the immigrant press expressed controlled anger but little surprise at the decision. The leading champion of the Ozawa case, the *Shin Sekai*, commented indignantly: "The slim hope that we had entertained . . . has been shattered completely." "We are not surprised," it continued, "for we have been treated for a long time as if we did not have the right in fact."[161] The *Ōfu Nippō* deplored the decision as an expression of "racial prejudice" at odds with the "original founding spirit of the nation," but saw no purpose in becoming "irate."[162] The *Rafu Shimpō* interpreted it with a touch of irony. Since it did "not believe whites are the superior race," in one sense, it was "delighted" that the high tribunal "did not find the Japanese to be free white persons."[163] The *Taihoku Nippō* voiced a lack of astonishment, asserting that it had not expected any other decision.[164] The *Nichibei Shimbun* stated that the "expected decision has been handed down as expected," but felt no need for "pessimism" or "indignation."[165] In his capacity as head of the naturalization committee, Yamaoka Ototaka decried the decision as a "national humiliation" that cast the Japanese people in a humiliating light, but concluded that the Ozawa case had had the merit at least of clarifying, once and for all, the ineligibility of the Japanese.[166] The Supreme Court decision left not a shadow of doubt. By upholding their ineligibility, the high court guaranteed that the powerless political status of Japanese immigrants would remain unchanged.

Alien Land Law Litigation

In addition to the naturalization test case, Japanese immigrants also brought several key land test cases to court to contest the constitutionality of the alien land laws of the states of California and Washington. Of all anti-Japanese enactments, Japanese immigrants perceived the alien land laws enacted by various western states as a fundamental "bread-and-butter" issue. To the immigrants, these laws were literally "a matter of life-and-death" (*shikatsu mondai*) because they threatened to undermine their very livelihood. In California, the 1920 amendment to the 1913 Alien Land Law threatened to destroy the economic foundation of Japanese immigrant society. Japanese farmers had started at the bottom of California agriculture as laborers and had worked their way up to become farmers. The 1913 law had had enough loopholes in it, so that it had not been an insurmountable obstacle to the growth of Japanese agriculture. The 1920 amendment was designed to drive the Japanese out of farming, and Japanese farmers now faced the real prospect of being reduced again to farm laborers. Thus Japanese immigrant leaders and farmers in California did not hesitate to take their fight into court.

In 1921 Japanese farmers in California faced a bleak future. Tenant farmers whose leases were due to expire had very few options open to them. One option seemed to offer a measure of hope. Such farmers thought that they would be able to continue farming through so-called cropping contracts. Based on a distinction between an employment agreement and a lease, they would become employees of landowners under such contracts. In exchange for cultivating and harvesting crops, they would be paid by landowners either with a set share or in cash, with the amount determined by the total value of the harvest crop. Since the 1920 Alien Land Law prohibited lease agreements, if cropping contracts were drawn up carefully, they seemed the best way of approximating a share-lease agreement without violating the 1920 law.[167] Matsumoto Ryōsaku, managing director of the Japanese Agricultural Association, estimated that of the approximately 300,000 acres leased as of November 1921, the leases on 90,000 acres were due to expire.[168] The overall outlook for all Japanese farmers looked pessimistic. Agricultural prices had plummeted as the postwar years witnessed a sharp contraction in demand for agricultural commodities. Landowners had raised rents during the wartime boom years, but had not lowered them in the postwar period. In sum, Japanese farmers in California faced not only the stringent 1920 Alien Land Law, but also looked at a declining state of agriculture.

At the beginning of the legal battle, the Japanese immigrants of northern and southern California went to court independently under the separate leadership of the Japanese Association of America and the Central Japanese Association of Southern California. As the battle unfolded, however, the two central bodies joined forces to make their land litigation a coordinated struggle of all Japanese immigrants in California. Japanese immigrants brought four types of test cases into court: the first dealt with the legality of cropping contracts; three others challenged the prohibition against the leasing of land, the appointment of guardians, and the holding of stocks in landholding companies. The litigation on cropping contracts and leasing commenced first.

The legal status of cropping contracts was unclear. Were they prohibited by the 1920 Alien Land Law? The answer hinged on whether or not an employment agreement was interpreted as giving a Japanese farmer legal possession and enjoyment of agricultural land. State Attorney U.S. Webb did not assume a public position on this question until the summer of 1921. Because he did not, Japanese tenant farmers whose leases were due to expire felt that they had the option of switching to such contracts in order to continue farming. In July 1921 Webb suddenly announced that he considered cropping contracts illegal. He interpreted them as being like lease agreements because they would give employees rights identical to those granted to tenant farmers.[169] In late September Webb amplified on his views:

> It would seem that an alien placed in possession of lands under such an agreement would have such rights in the land as are given by the usual form of leasing. Such arrangements seek to accomplish what the statute prohibits without incurring its penalties.[170]

This interpretation placed in doubt the one option Japanese tenant farmers thought they had and prompted them to act immediately. Under the auspices of the Japanese Agricultural Association, the farmers of northern California convened two emergency meetings on September 2 and October 10 to discuss what actions they should undertake.[171] Reflecting the urgency of the moment, these meetings were held right during the harvest season. Chiba Toyoji, Matsumoto Ryōsaku's predecessor as managing director of the Japanese Agricultural Association, attended both meetings. He reported that the majority of the assembled farmers favored contesting the 1920 Alien Land Law. Prepared to die in America, these farmers were resolved to fight in court to the bitter end. A minority of farmers favored withdrawing from California and moving to less hostile states; a few even looked at Mexico and South America as alternative places outside of the United States to which the farmers might consider moving. One farmer, Awaya Manei of Fresno, expressed his utter disgust with the situation in California. To him, the racial discrimination against the Japanese was intolerable. As a result, he announced that he was pulling out of California immediately and relocating to Manchuria.[172] Chiba himself abandoned California. He desired, in his words, ''to go to a place where Japanese national power had influence.''[173] That place proved to be Dairen, Manchuria where he resettled and continued working as an agricultural expert.

On October 11, the day after the second meeting, the Japanese Association of America and its affiliated local associations convened their own emergency conference.[174] The Agricultural Association had solicited the assistance of the Japanese Association of America. Association leaders responded by forming a land litigation committee. To finance the cost of court litigation, they allocated a budget of $25,000, half to be collected from Japanese farmers and the balance from other Japanese immigrants. Two days later, this newly established land litigation committee had a bill of complaint filed in Santa Clara County on October 13. Seeking a temporary injunction against the 1920 Alien Land Law, the complaint was filed on behalf of J.J. O'Brien and J. Inouye who claimed they wanted to enter into a cropping contract. Most of the share leases expiring in 1921 were in northern California. In the light of State Attorney Webb's interpretation regarding cropping contracts, it was natural for Japanese farmers and immigrant leaders of northern California to consider the question of the legality of such contracts as the one demanding immediate clarification.

On the other hand, the leaders of the Central Japanese Association of Southern California deemed the ban on leasing more crucial. In August, they had formed their own land litigation committee with a projected budget of $20,000.[175]. On October 18 this committee had a bill of complaint filed on behalf of Porterfield and Mizuno. Also asking for a preliminary injunction, this bill claimed that Porterfield, an American owner of 80 acres of land in Los Angeles County, desired to lease his land to Mizuno. To contest the constitutionality of the prohibition against the leasing of land, Japanese association leaders of southern California decided to use their case as a test case.

Subsequently, the two central bodies cooperated to pursue commonly agreed upon goals. On November 5 the representatives of the two land litigation committees met and formed a joint committee whose decisions were to be binding on both central bodies.[176] In addition, both central bodies were to share the cost of all legal expenses. In anticipation of going to the United States Supreme Court, the Japanese Association of America assumed the responsibility of finding an appropriate lawyer to handle all appeals. In January 1922 the joint committee engaged Louis Marshall on the recommendation of the Japanese Association of America.[177] The need for an attorney for the appeal process had become necessary by the outcome of the two initial cases. The Japanese side lost in the Porterfield and Mizuno case. On

December 19 the court upheld the 1920 Alien Land Law's ban on leasing. On the other hand, the O'Brien and Inouye case ended in a momentary victory for Japanese farmers. The court ruled on December 20 that cropping contracts did not violate the 1920 Alien Land Law. This decision revived the hope of all tenant farmers, enabling those whose leases had expired to continue farming under such contracts. Both decisions were appealed, the first by the Japanese side and the second by the State of California.

At the beginning of 1922, the joint committee made decisions relating to two additional cases. Having lost the leasing test case, it decided to challenge the prohibition against the buying and selling of stocks in landholding companies. On February 7 the committee had the Frick and Satow case brought before the Federal District Court in San Francisco. Again asking for a preliminary injuction, the bill of complaint stated that Raymond L. Frick wished to sell to Satō Nobutada twenty-eight shares of capital stock in the Merced Farm Company, an agricultural landholding company. On May 23, 1922 the court ruled that such a transaction was prohibited by the 1920 Alien Land Law. Having lost again, the Japanese side appealed this decision, too.

The second case, involving Yano Hayao and the guardianship issue, began in October 1920. Prior to his case, a number of guardianship cases had been decided in court, but none of them had ever been appealed.[178] Yano had purchased fifteen acreas of land in Butte County before the 1920 Alien Land Law and placed the deed in the name of his minor daughter. On October 23, 1920, he filed a petition to be appointed as her guardian to administer her estate. The presiding judge denied the petition on the grounds that Yano had placed the deed in his daughter's name in order to evade the 1913 Alien Land Law. The state, then, instituted escheat proceedings, so Yano's attorney appealed the lower court ruling to the California State Supreme Court. The joint committee supported Yano at the State Supreme Court level. The court rendered its decision in May 1, 1922. Ruling the state could deny a petition of guardianship only on the basis of proven incompetency, it overturned the lower court ruling and ordered Yano appointed as the guardian of his daughter's estate. This meant that the State Supreme Court had indirectly invalidated that section of the 1920 Alien Land Law prohibiting the appointment of aliens ineligible to citizenship as guardians of minors who had title to agricultural land.

This first round of legal battles engendered optimism among Japanese immigrants. They believed that they could get "justice" through the American court system. The *Nichibei Shimbun* editorialized that it "expected final victory" in the cropping contract and leasing test cases at the United States Supreme Court level.[179] It applauded the State Supreme Court decision in the Yano case as "just" and expressed great satisfaction that Japanese immigrants had been able to defend their constitutional rights.[180] The case demonstrated the value of the immigrants being self-reliant and independent, for it enabled them to obtain a partial solution of their legal problems on their own initiative through the legal system. The Yano decision caused the *Shin Sekai* to reaffirm its faith in the United States. "Justice still exists in America," it said.[181] By the spring of 1923, the three key tests cases on cropping contracts, leasing, and stockholding were ready to be argued before the United States Supreme Court. In March the *Nichibei Shimbun* confidently stated "all preparations have been made." "Although it is hard to predict whether we will win or lose," it still said, "we are generally optimistic."[182]

Six months prior to the Supreme Court decisions, the California legislature strengthened the 1920 Alien Land Law. The 1920 law did not prohibit cropping contracts explicitly. To correct the oversight and to counter the decision in the O'Brien and Inouye case, the legislature amended the 1920 law, broadening its restrictive provisions to include the usage, cultivation, and occupancy of agricultural land for beneficial purposes. This amendment made it impossible to draw up employment agreements which granted Japanese farmers such rights as were contained in share-leases. The lower court ruling in the Yano case moved the legislature to act, too. It added a new section to the California Code of Civil Procedure. This section prohibited the appointment of aliens ineligible to citizenship, or of companies the majority of whose members or stockholders were such aliens, to act as guardians of any estate that included real property. From the Japanese farmers' point of view, these new enactments made the test cases pending before the United States Supreme Court all the more important; it was now imperative that the court hand down decisions favorable to their side.

But such decisions never came to pass. The Supreme Court ruled against the Japanese side in every test case, exactly a year after ruling that Japanese immigrants were ineligible to citizenship in the landmark Ozawa Takao case. On November 12, 1923, the court upheld the constitutionality of the prohibition against the leasing of land. Before ruling in the Porterfield and Mizuno case, the court first ruled on another test case which originated in the state of Washington. Embodying all the features of the 1920 California Alien Land Law, Washington had enacted its own Alien Land Law in March 1921, with one essential difference. Instead of the distinction between an alien eligible to citizenship and an alien ineligible to citizenship, the Washington legislature made the distinction between an alien who had "in good faith declared his intention to become a citizen" and an alien who had not. This broader distinction appeared on the surface not to discriminate against the Japanese. For any European immigrant who had not filed a petition of intent to naturalize was subject to the law. But the law automatically applied to the Japanese (and other Asians) because they were unable, unlike European immigrants, to file a petition of intent to naturalize. While appearing nondiscriminatory, the law in fact was aimed squarely at aliens who were ineligible to citizenship.

The Northwest American Japanese Association of Seattle acted more quickly than its California counterparts. In June 1921 it challenged the Washington alien land law prohibition against leasing in the Terrace and Nakatsuka case. The Seattle central body lost at the lower court level, but immediately appealed the case to the Supreme Court.[183] The Supreme Court upheld the lower court ruling in the Terrace and Nakatsuka case and applied its decision to the Porterfield and Mizuno case. A week later, on November 19, the court overturned the lower court ruling in the O'Brien and Inouye Case and affirmed the same in the Frick and Satow case. Finding the Washington and California State Alien Land Laws in violation of neither the constitution nor the 1911 U.S.–Japan Treaty of Commerce, the high tribunal upheld the prohibition against the leasing of agricultural land, the purchasing of stocks in land companies, and even cropping contracts. In this way, the two-year legal battle ended in total defeat for Japanese immigrants.

All Japanese immigrants were stunned by the defeat. The prevailing belief had been that they would not lose every case. If they lost the leasing test cases, they expected to fare better in the others. And if by chance they lost the Frick and Satow case, they were confident that the Supreme Court would not deny them the right to enter into cropping contracts. In reporting on the effects of the decisions, the San Francisco consul observed:

> The land law decisions have dealt a severe blow to Japanese immigrants, spiritually as well as materially. . . . Previously, they had won a favorable decision . . . on cropping contracts. As lease agreements expired, the majority switched to these contracts. Nearly everyone anticipated victory in this case. Just at the point when they firmly believed that

they could solve all their land law problems through cropping contracts, the case ended in failure. The sense of despair it aroused is hard to imagine.[184]

Every Japanese immigrant newspaper expressed a mixture of disbelief, dismay, and disillusionment. Having had an optimistic outlook, the *Nichibei Shimbun* said:

> The defeat . . . in the cropping contract and corporation stock test cases was wholly unexpected, taking not only our newspaper staff but also Japanese in general by surprise. No, not just the Japanese, it also took not a few Americans by surprise. As far as we know, even the American legal profession was taken aback since the defeat of the state in these two cases was expected.[185]

When the *Shin Sekai* learned of the November 12 decisions, it still retained "a slim hope" that the high court would rule favorably on cropping contracts.[186] Hearing of the November 19 decisions, it flatly said "there is nothing more to say." Convoluted legal arguments now were meaningless. Japanese immigrants had "fallen to a lot worse than Mexicans, Armenians, Poles, and Negroes."[187]

The *Rafu Shimpō* described the grave consequences of the failure in litigation in southern California:

> The extreme dejected spirits of the Japanese . . . cannot be concealed. Some people are thinking of returning to Japan. Some are seeking safe havens outside the state or country. Some are planning to change occupations despite lack of experience. Each person is planning according to their personal situation. And this is not limited to the farmers who bear the brunt of the failure in litigation. The number does not stop with them. Businessmen who deal in agricultural produce and many merchants who have had farmers as their main customers have also been affected drastically.[188]

In the Pacific Northwest, the *Taihoku Nippō* summarized the legal battle in a major editorial:

> People believed that even if anti-Japanese land laws were enacted, they would be probably unconstitutional; if they were taken to the Supreme Court, we would be permitted to lease land at least; barring that, we would surely be able to farm under cropping contracts. Not only Japanese farmers, not only leaders of the Japanese associations, but also many Americans in the legal profession and Japanese government officials thought in this way. But, alas, the Supreme Court has overturned the decision of the Federal District Court in California, ruling that we cannot enter into cropping contracts without violating the California

law. The Supreme Court decisions—our last ray of hope—have determined unequivocally that we do not have the right to purchase, lease,
or transfer agricultural land, that we cannot enter into cropping contracts, and that we cannot own stocks in landholding companies.[189]

This editorial concluded that the decisions had caused "a great panic"
among Japanese immigrants. The *Taihoku Nippō* equated the situation
of the Japanese immigrants to that of the *eta* or pariah caste in Japan.
Both were subject to severe discriminatory treatment.[190]

The strong Japanese immigrant reaction to the Supreme Court decisions was understandable in view of their far-reaching consequences.
Tenant farming, of any kind, was no longer possible. If a tenant
farmer wanted to continue in agriculture, he had no choice but to
continue as a laborer. Otherwise, he would have to leave agriculture
altogether. In a word, the worst Japanese fear became a reality. By
upholding the constitutionality of the alien land laws, the Supreme
Court decisions had destroyed the economic foundation of Japanese
immigrant society.

The Japanese Association of America and the Central Japanese Association of Southern California both convened emergency meetings
with their affiliated locals after the Supreme Court decision. Association leaders realized that they had to comply with the decisions. To
make sure Japanese farmers understood them, they explained the sole
option open to those farmers who had had share-leases and cropping
contracts. That option was to continue in agriculture as wage-earners
through employment agreements which provided neither a share of
the crop nor a cash remuneration relative to its value.[191] In January
1924 State Attorney General Webb conferred with county district
attorneys to solicit their cooperation in the enforcement of the Alien
Land Law. At this time, Webb announced his policy. He would en-
force the Supreme Court decisions fully, except that existing cropping
contracts would be allowed through the 1924 harvest season. Thereafter, he would not allow cropping contracts at all.

Japanese statistics from 1920 to 1925 indicate the drastic effects of
Webb's enforcement policy. The statistics on Japanese acreage holdings are as follows:[192]

JAPANESE AGRICULTURAL LANDHOLDINGS, 1920, 1922, 1925

Year	Owned	Cash-Lease	Share-Lease	Contract	Total
1920	74,769	192,150	121,000	70,137	458,056
1922	50,542	104,228	175,883		330,653
1925	41,898	76,397		189,671	307,966

The total acreage dropped from the 1920 peak of 458,056 acres to 330,653 in 1922, and to 307,966, the lowest level, by 1925. The leased acreage plummeted from the 1920 total of 313,150 acres to 76,397 acres by 1925, the latter figure reflecting the full enforcement of the Alien Land Law after 1924. The owned acreage fell from the 1920 high of 74,769 acres to 41,898 acres by 1925. The 1925 contract acreage of 189,671 include the acreage of former tenant farmers who continued in agriculture as managers or foremen of farms. In 1918 there had been 7,973 farmers. By 1929 this figure dipped to 4,591.[193]

The loss of owned acreage was caused by the inability of Japanese farmers to make outstanding payments. As exemplified by Abiko Kyūtarō and the Yamato Colony in 1914, this was an old problem which resurfaced in an acute form. During the wartime boom years, Japanese farmers had purchased additional land. Encountering the sudden postwar slump, these farmers could not meet their payments. The Yokohama Specie Bank adhered to its policy of not lending money to Japanese immigrants. The Sumitomo Bank, which established a San Francisco branch in 1917, had the same policy. The postwar financial dilemma of Japanese farmers was compounded by the uncertainties generated by the 1920 Alien Land Law. Given the precarious status of Japanese farmers, American banks refused to provide loans, even when the farmers were willing to put up their land as collateral.[194]

The Japanese Association of America surveyed the landholdings of Japanese farmers in northern California. Of the land purchased prior to 1920, there were still 14,753 acres with an unpaid balance of $2,080,195 as of May 1924.[195] The bulk of this acreage was concentrated in Fresno and its vicinity and consisted of 7,601 acres with $1,705,450 outstanding. Of this unpaid balance, $646,705.50 were due in 1924 and 1925. To save this land from being foreclosed, the Japanese Association of America submitted a petition to the Foreign Ministry in order to seek assistance. The 1920 Alien Land Law made it imperative to preserve existing landholdings. The petition asked Tokyo to intercede on behalf of Japanese immigrants and to pressure the Yokohama Specie Bank to change its no-loan policy. The Yokohama Specie Bank and the Sumitomo Bank, according to the petition, held over 80 percent of all immigrant savings.[196]

Simultaneously, the Japanese Association of America submitted a loan application to the San Francisco branch of the Yokohama Specie Bank.[197] The central body requested that a loan division be opened within the San Francisco branch and asked the division to grant a long-term loan of $646,000. As collateral for the loan, the application stated that Central California Japanese farmers would put up their land, estimated as having a market value of $3,875,199. To make sure that its petition to Tokyo would receive serious consideration, the Japanese Association of America dispatched General Secretary Takimoto Tamezō to Tokyo to negotiate directly with the Foreign Ministry and the Yokohama Specie Bank. While in Japan, Takimoto also sought the assistance of Shibusawa Eiichi, a prominent financier-banker who was knowledgeable about Japanese immigrants in the United States.[198]

All of these efforts produced a small concession from the Yokohama Specie Bank. The bank agreed to offer limited loans. The head office instructed the San Francisco branch in December 1924 that it could consider loans on an individual basis on three strict conditions.[199] No collateral could violate the California Bank Act which prohibited commercial banks from loaning money on second mortgages. This first condition meant that Japanese farmers had to put up collateral other than their land which had first mortgages on them. This in itself severely reduced loan possibilities. The second and third conditions were straightforward. In considering loans, the San Francisco branch had to take into account the total balance of debts on farming equipment extending beyond 1925 and had to be assured of repayment within a reasonable time period.

Japanese farmers never had had access to adequate bank loans over the years. The two small banks, the Nippon Bank of Sacramento and the Industrial Bank of Fresno, the sole surviving immigrant banks, both disappeared in the 1920s. The Industrial Bank was purchased in 1923 by the Valley Bank of Fresno, and the Nippon Bank was sold to the Sumitomo Bank in 1925.[200] The concession granted by the Yokohama Specie Bank did not rescue Japanese farmers who owed payments. By 1926 the San Francisco branch had lent only $101,800, a small fraction of the $646,705 initially requested, to farmers in the Fresno area; 622 acres were affected.[201] Thus the loss of acreage in owned land was caused by the lack of sufficient loans available to Japanese farmers, which made it impossible for them to make payments on land they purchased before the 1920 Alien Land Law went into effect.

The law had other negative effects. Except for landowning Japanese farmers, all Japanese farmers had a dim future once it was enforced fully from the fall of 1924. As a last exercise in futility, the Central Japanese Association of Southern California supported two so-called bonus test cases in the summer of 1924.[202] This litigation was based on the not-so-subtle distinction between a cropping contract and an employment agreement with a bonus. Cropping contracts had been a way of approximating share-leases; bonus contracts were a way of approximating cropping contracts. In a cropping contract, the payment to an employee of a share, or of a cash percentage of the crop, was the sole remuneration. In a bonus contract, this payment was in the form of a bonus on top of wages. In December 1924 the California State Supreme Court ruled that bonus contracts were cropping contracts in disguise, and therefore illegal too. In anticipation of this decision, the Japanese Association of America did not support this litigation. The Central Japanese Association of Southern California, however, backed the bonus test cases as a last legal straw in the faint hope of preventing Japanese tenant farmers from being reduced to agricultural laborers.

With the total failure in litigation, some ways of getting around the 1920 Alien Land Law had to be devised from 1925. Japanese farmers devised three methods with varying degrees of effectiveness.[203] One method was the so-called middleman arrangement. Obtaining the help of an American citizen, a Japanese farmer had the person lease land for him. The lessee was the nominal farmer who never cultivated the land. The Japanese did the actual farming and assumed the entire financial burden of operating the farm. To avoid prosecution for violating the alien land law, the middleman hired the Japanese as his manager or foreman in an employment agreement. The actual farmer carried out all business transaction in the operation of the farm in the name of the lessee. Two separate but parallel accounts were kept, one covering the transaction between the middleman and the farmer and another between the middleman and the lessor. In return for the service rendered by the middleman, the farmer paid a "middleman fee." The fee varied from place to place and depended on the agreement between the two parties. It could be a flat sum of money, a set percentage of the farmer's net profit, or so many dollars per acre leased. In 1926 the flat fee was $50 to $70 in Florin, the percentage of net profit was 5 percent in Hollister, and the fee per acre leased was $3.00 in Stockton.

This middleman arrangement had its drawbacks. First, it was premised on the existence of mutual trust. The two parties had to have a clear understanding which they both honored. If the middleman tried to exact more money than the initially agreed upon fee, the farmer found himself in a vulnerable position. Beholden to the middleman for his livelihood, he could not dismiss him lightly. When the middleman was an adult Nisei who was related by blood or an offspring of a friend or associate, no problems arose. But this arrangement was rare because there were only a handful of adult Nisei. The overwhelming majority of Nisei born in the continental United States were still children. In fact, most of the adult Nisei in California were born in Hawaii and therefore had no real close ties with local Japanese communities. Some of these Nisei blackmailed Issei farmers to force them to pay higher middleman fees. This underhanded "squeeze" was by no means practiced only by Nisei middlemen, but was employed by non-Japanese middlemen as well. Japanese farmers called these unscrupulous middlemen "parasites." Secondly, whether the middleman was a Nisei or not, if he died suddenly, the farmer had another serious problem. For if the deceased middleman left no one to fulfill his obligations, the farmer stood to lose his entire investment in the operation of the farm. Because of these drawbacks, Japanese farmers did not consider the middleman arrangement as the safest method of farming.

Not all Japanese communities used it. In 1926 Japanese farmers in Courtland continued to farm 11,882 acres under various arrangements. More than half of this total, 6,005 acres, consisted of land farmed in the name of Nisei. Of this figure, 850 acres were leased for cash, 2,880 acres for share, and 700 acres were farmed under contract. The balance of 1,575 acres consisted of land on which Japanese were hired as actual foremen. On the other hand, in Walnut Grove—just down the delta from Courtland—the figures were remarkably different. Out of 10,753 acres cultivated by 61 Japanese farmers in 1926, only 350 acres were farmed by three farmers using the name of Nisei. Thirty-eight farmers were actual foremen on 8,470 acres of the total acreage. The remaining 20 farmers cultivated 1,933 acres under verbal agreements with landowners.

In a verbal agreement, rather than use a middleman, a Japanese farmer entered into two separate, direct agreements with a landowner, one public and another private. The landowner hired the Japanese as a foremen on his farm. The terms of employment were written into a public agreement which the landowner could show to local law enforcement officers whenever the need arose. Based on an unwritten, private understanding, and in contrast to the public agreement, the Japanese cultivated the landowner's land as a cash or share tenant. To maintain the public facade that the Japanese was an employee, the two parties kept two different accounts parallel to the two agreements and similar to the accounting in the middleman arrangement. In general, landowners who had profited from leasing land to Japanese farmers had opposed the 1920 measure. To continue their profitable relationship, some landowners were amenable to verbal agreements.

The prevalence of verbal agreements was tied to two key factors. First, there had to be mutual trust between the two parties. If a landowner violated his verbal agreement, the farmer had no legal recourse. Given the inherent risks involved, no Japanese farmer was apt to enter into a verbal agreement unless he was reasonably certain that the landowner could be trusted. Secondly, even where mutual trust existed, a landowner was unlikely to enter into a verbal agreement if the local district attorney was a zealous enforcer of the Alien Land Law. The influence of landowners in local county politics was decisive. If landowners were able to influence local law enforcement officers to overlook verbal agreements, they had no fear of prosecution. Otherwise, they were reluctant to enter into such agreements. For Japanese farmers, verbal agreements were not always satisfactory nor everywhere possible.

Japanese farmers also employed a third method of farming. This was to have land companies lease land for them. In 1926 there were an estimated 415 Japanese-related land companies, of which 400 had been incorporated prior to the 1920 Alien Land Law. Almost all of the companies were located in northern and central California. Japanese farmers in this part of the state had the legal advice of Albert H. Eliot and Guy C. Calden, legal counsel of the Japanese Association of America, and 142 of the land companies had some ties with their law firm. There were two types of land companies. One was formed for personal profit; the other was organized for the welfare of a group of Japanese farmers. Stocks were issued, in either case, to American friends or Nisei who had nothing to do with the operation of the companies.

The Lodi Corporation was an example of the second type. In 1926 this company leased 1,026 acres in the Lodi area. Managed by the local Japanese Association, it operated for the benefit of local Japanese farmers. When a Japanese knew of a landowner who was willing to lease land, the person asked the company to become the lessee. Once the company checked the economic feasibility of farming the land, it leased the land for him. The company, then, hired the same person as a foreman on paper. The "foreman" farmed the land as if he had signed the lease himself. The company and the actual farmer had their own private agreement. The farmer put up his own capital to operate the farm. As in the middleman arrangement, instead of doing business in his own name, he had the company transact it in its name. To compensate the company for its service, the farmer paid 5 percent of his annual rental for cash leases and 5 percent of his net earnings for share leases. This income enabled the company to pay taxes and cover its administrative overhead. The secretary of the Japanese Association of Lodi managed the company's day-to-day affairs. He negotiated with landowners on behalf of all local farmers and handled all business transactions. Because this method of farming also demanded two separate accounting books, he recorded all transactions with the farmers in one set and with the landowners in another. In 1926 29 Japanese farmed under the auspices of the Lodi Corporation.

This third method was the safest way of farming. Assuming companies were managed efficiently, Japanese farmers had a sense of security. With stocks in the hands of American friends or Nisei, the companies were organized and operated for their benefit. They eliminated the problem of middlemen making exorbitant demands and the fear of landowners breaking verbal agreements. As long as books were maintained and taxes paid, neither the farmers nor the land companies could be prosecuted for conspiring to evade the Alien Land Law. Landowners were safe from prosecution, too. They dealt openly with land companies which were legal. What transpired between the companies and Japanese farmers did not implicate them in any way. As far as the law was concerned, they had signed legal lease agreements.

There are no precise figures for every Japanese farming community on the acreage farmed through the middleman arrangement, verbal agreement, and land companies. The impression is that there were extreme variations from one community to another. The use of Nisei middlemen predominated in Courtland. This practice later increased in every community, as many of the Nisei born in the continental United States reached adulthood during the 1930s. No land companies operated in Courtland, Walnut Grove, or Isleton, while the Lodi Corporation played an important role in the Lodi area. Verbal agreements were widespread in the Hanford and Salinas areas. Of course no method precluded any other, so the three alternative methods of farming may have co-existed in other locales. Had the methods not been devised, the harsh impact of the 1920 Alien Land Law on Japanese farmers would have been much greater.

The failure in land litigation had one final effect. It caused Japanese immigrants to entertain the idea of leaving California, and even the country. Japanese consuls first considered the idea of dispersing Japanese immigrants as a solution to the whole exclusion question. In July 1920 New York Consul Kumazaki Yasushi recommended that the

Foreign Ministry ought to consider scattering the Japanese population of California throughout the United States.[204] He attributed the resurgence of anti-Japanese agitation in California to the high Japanese concentration in the state. Short of the complete withdrawal of all Japanese immigrants from the United States, he believed that the next best solution was a policy of dispersal. Mindful of the economic cost of moving out of California, Kumazaki realized that the Foreign Ministry would have to provide financial assistance to Japanese immigrants if it adopted his recommendation. San Francisco Consul Ota Tamekichi and Los Angeles Consul Ōyama Ujirō both endorsed Kumazaki's idea of dispersal.[205] The Foreign Ministry, however, never acted on the idea.

Japanese immigrants toyed with the idea, too, but they did not give it serious consideration until the land litigation had failed. At the 1924 meeting of the Pacific Coast Japanese Association Deliberative Council, held in April, the idea appeared on the agenda as a resolution to investigate conditions in other states.[206] The delegates passed this resolution with the possible future migration of Japanese farmers in mind. In the fall the Japanese Association of America sent Matsumoto Manroku, an agricultural expert, to survey the American south on behalf of the council. His task was to ascertain if there were areas in this region of the United States where Japanese farmers might be able to farm. According to General Secretary Takimoto Tamezō, 50 persons had left California on their own during the summer to resettle in other states, mainly in Utah and Colorado.[207] In his opinion, Japanese farmers should migrate only after careful planning, and in groups. Studies of the agricultural prospects, the attitudes toward Japanese, and the likelihood of anti-Japanese agitation arising in other states had to be conducted beforehand. In November 1924 the Japanese Association of America published Matsumoto's formal report, in which he concluded that Georgia, particularly its delta region, and Florida offered the best possibility for Japanese farmers who desired to farm in another state.[208] The Japanese Association of America also dispatched other agricultural experts to survey Nevada, Utah, Colorado, and a few other states. In 1926 it published its findings, which concluded that Utah and Colorado offered distinct possibilities, too.[209]

Some Japanese immigrants considered leaving the country. A few people in southern California viewed Mexico as a prospective new immigrant land. In the spring of 1924, those interested in Mexico formed a study group to explore the possibilities of migration. The *Rafu Shimpō* editorialized that Mexico was "close to ideal," but cautioned future migrants of the necessity of taking capital to the country.[210] The Central Japanese Association of Southern California dispatched the head of its Agricultural Section, Dobayashi Motomu, to conduct a survey of Mexico for the benefit of future migrants. Of all persons who wrote about Mexico, Fujioka Shirō wrote the most favorably. A newspaperman with the *Rafu Shimpō,* he toured Mexico in 1925. In all of his writings, he depicted the country as a "pro-Japanese nation." Compared to the discriminatory treatment to which Japanese immigrants were subjected in the United States, Japanese immigrants were treated much better in Mexico—they were able to purchase and lease land, they could become naturalized Mexican citizens, and they could freely intermarry with Mexican women. Fujioka met a few Japanese immigrants who actually had moved to Mexico. One person had resettled in a small town where, Fujioka reported, he was able to establish himself as a wealthy, landowning merchant who commanded the respect of the local populace.[211] In 1927 and 1928 two books devoted to Japanese immigration to Mexico appeared, and Matsumoto Ryōsaku, onetime managing director of the Japanese Agricultural Association, wrote a preface for one of them.[212] These books projected Mexico as an ideal new immigrant land with a small population, vast tracts of undeveloped land, and an abundance of natural sources. In 1931 Fujioka himself published an immigration guide to Mexico.[213]

A handful of Japanese immigrants looked at other countries besides Mexico. A few viewed South America, especially Brazil, as a possible area to which they might migrate. In the summer of 1924, Nagata Shigeshi, head of the *Rikkōkai,* proposed to resettle Japanese immigrants in Brazil, where he was planning to establish a Japanese agricultural colony. His scheme called for Japanese immigrants in the United States to contribute capital to his Brazilian enterprise.[214] The *Rikkōkai,* of course, had helped many indigent student-laborers to immigrate to this country at the turn of the century. A few immigrants looked at Manchuria as another alternative. Such individuals were aware of the example of Chiba Toyoji and Awaya Manei, the two men who had earlier pulled out of California and resettled in Manchuria. Ironically, these two men had become Japanese colonialists. Those who wanted to follow in their footsteps believed that agriculture in Manchuria offered a unique opportunity to Japanese immigrant farmers to apply the modern American farming techniques they had learned in the United States.

Generally, Japanese immigrant newspapers were cautious in their editorial stance. If Japanese immigrants migrated in large numbers to other states, the *Nichibei Shimbun* was afraid that they would arouse anti-Japanese agitation. After all, such agitation had not surfaced in California itself until after the Japanese population had increased noticeably. The newspaper predicted that the same phenomenon would recur in states as yet unpopulated by Japanese immigrants if they appeared suddenly and in conspicuous numbers. Thus migration to another state was not a solution to the predicament of Japanese farmers.[215] Admittedly, Mexico had "almost unlimited natural resources" and offered "a great future prospect." But if anyone was planning to migrate there, he had to make adequate preparations and take enough capital in order to insure success. No one could hope to achieve success starting from scratch as a manual laborer.[216] The *Nichibei Shimbun* even argued against Japanese farmers leaving central California and migrating to southern California in search of new farming opportunities. It was better for them to remain in central California and make the best of a difficult situation.[217] Like the *Nichibei Shimbun,* the *Shin Sekai* adopted an editorial policy of warning Japanese immigrants against making any hasty decision. For if they moved to other states, there was no guarantee that they could improve their lot. In fact, anti-Japanese agitation, in all likelihood, would arise no matter where they relocated themselves. Japanese farmers in California were in a tough bind, but they had "no choice but to acquiesce to the current situation."[218] Mexico and South America seemed to offer an alternative, but not a really viable one. For without careful planning and sufficient capital to invest, migration to Mexico was unthinkable.[219]

Despite all the talk of leaving California, the majority of Japanese immigrants remained in the state. They already had too much invested in California in terms of time and money to pull up stakes and leave abruptly. But the very fact that they entertained the idea of leaving the state and country indicates the baneful effects of the 1920 Alien Land Law. It undermined the economic foundation of Japanese immigrant society in agriculture. That the full enforcement of the law did not produce a mass exodus from California in no way diminished its oppressiveness.

VII

The 1924 Immigration Act

Japanese immigrants interpreted the enactment of the 1924 Immigration Act as the culminating act of rejection by the United States. Enacted in the spring of 1924, this restrictive legislation was designed to control the racial composition of the American population. It regulated all immigration to the United States by setting an annual ceiling on immigration and by establishing a quota system based upon national origins. To ensure the predominance of the so-called Nordic race, the quota system heavily favored the countries of western and northern Eruope. It allotted to them large annual quotas, while giving eastern and southern European countries much smaller quotas. In terms of immigration from Asia, the 1924 Immigration Act stopped it entirely by an exclusionary clause that prohibited the admission of any alien ineligible to citizenship as an immigrant. Inasmuch as the Supreme Court had ruled the Japanese ineligible in the Ozawa case, this exclusionary clause automatically applied to the Japanese. In this way, the 1924 Immigration Act nullified the Gentlemen's Agreement of 1907–8 and abruptly terminated all Japanese immigration.

As Congress was enacting the 1924 Immigration Act, some uncertainty surrounded the exclusionary clause. Japanese Ambassador Hanihara Masanao protested the clause as being discriminatory against Japan. In an April 10 letter to Secretary of State Charles E. Hughes, Hanihara said that the clause singled out the Japanese people as "unworthy and undesirable." He pointed out that Congress had extended the Chinese Exclusion Act indefinitely in 1902 and had designated most of Asia in 1917 as barred zones from which no immigration was allowed. In view of this fact, and the public statements made by anti-Japanese exclusionists, Hanihara could not help but believe that those who supported the clause, notwithstanding their frequent denials, had only the Japanese in mind. In his opinion, there was no need for its inclusion because the Gentlemen's Agreement, faithfully honored by the Japanese government, had effectively limited Japanese immigration. The inclusion of the exclusionary clause by Congress would have "grave consequences," Hanihara warned, "upon the otherwise happy and mutually advantageous relations between" Japan and the United States.[1]

Out of deference to Japanese national sensibilities, Secretary of State Hughes tried to persuade Congress to drop the exclusionary clause altogether. When he was unsuccessful, he tried to secure a period of grace during which it would not be in effect, giving him time to negotiate a new immigration treaty which would be satisfactory to both Japan and the United States. With this in mind, Hughes sought March 1, 1925 as the effective date of the clause. To Hanihara's great shock, Senator Henry Cabot Lodge interpreted his usage of the phrase "grave consequences" as a "veiled threat" against the American government, and in mid-April Congress swiftly enacted the 1924 Immigration Act with the exclusionary clause included. President Calvin Coolidge signed the act on May 26 and it became effective on July 1, 1924. From this date, no alien ineligible to citizenship was to be admitted as an immigrant.

Japanese immigrants reacted to the 1924 Immigration Act in a number of ways. During the spring months, a number of immigrants endeavored to beat the deadline. The Gentlemen's Agreement remained in force until June 30. Under its terms, Japanese immigrants still were able to send for their wives, children, and parents, and still could return to Japan themselves and reenter the United States as long as they did so before July 1. But immigrant bachelors did not have the option of summoning picture-brides because the Japanese government had ceased issuing passports to such brides back in 1920. In April the *Nichibei Shimbun* urged single men to return to Japan to get married.[2] Some bachelors who had the economic means scurried back to find brides at this time. In order to expedite their return to the United States, the Foreign Ministry waived its regulation requiring wives to be entered in their husbands' family registry for six months to qualify for passports. This increased the possibility of such men being able to reenter the United States with their spouses before July 1. The number of immigrant men who actually married in Japan at this time was small. The San Francisco consul estimated that only about 442 brides entered the United States through the San Francisco immigration station during the months of May and June.[3]

Other Japanese immigrants sent for their children and/or parents at this time, too. Many had intended to summon them before the spring of 1924, but had procrastinated for one reason or another. Faced with a now or never situation, they finally acted decisively and sent for them. Still other Japanese immigrants who happened to be visiting Japan applied for immediate return passage to the United States. Under normal circumstances, returnees did not have to worry about rushing back because Foreign Ministry regulations permitted them to stay in Japan up to three years without forfeiting the right to return. With the June 30 deadline looming, however, all returnees were forced to make a sudden choice. They either had to cut short their visit, or face being barred from American shores permanently.

The June 30 deadline created a problem at ports of embarkation in Japan. Shipping lines were suddenly flooded with reservation requests. The demand for tickets exceeded the limited passenger space on ships making the trans-Pacific run. Prospective passengers converged upon Kobe and Yokohama in the hope of assuring themselves passage tickets or at least a spot on waiting lists. At the beginning of June, the Foreign Ministry estimated upwards of 1,500 to 2,500 people might be unable to obtain passage due to the limited number of ships scheduled to sail for the Hawaiian Islands and the continental United States.[4] Given the real possibility of missing the deadline, many people petitioned the Japanese government for assistance and requested that additional ships be made available promptly.[5] The Foreign Ministry solicited the cooperation of Japanese shipping lines to alleviate the problem. As a result, the Nihon Yūsen Kaisha, the Ōsaka Shōsen Kaisha, and the Tōyō Kisen Kaisha each agreed to place one additional ship in service on the trans-Pacific crossing during the month of June. In return, they were allowed to raise their passage rates by 50 percent.

The exact number of persons stranded at ports of embarkation is unknown. The Governor of Hyōgo Prefecture reported that sixteen ships bound for Hawaii and the United States sailed from Kobe in May and June, carrying a total of 2,694 passengers.[6] However, 679 people were left behind, among them a few who had failed to pass the required physical examination.[7] The Governor of Kanagawa Prefecture reported that 2,308 passengers sailed from Yokohama in June. The last ship bound for the United States from Yokohama was the *President Jackson* which departed on June 17. Unable to obtain accommodations on this ship, 22 persons were left stranded in Yokohama.[8] Whatever the actual total was, those who had the misfortune of being stranded at ports of embarkation became the victims of the 1924 Immigration Act. They were separated permanently from their families, with reunion only possible if their relatives decided to abandon the United States and return to Japan.

Emotional reaction to the 1924 Immigration Act was very widespread and intense in Japan. Nationalistic mass rallies were held throughout the country to protest its enactment. Japanese protesters designated July 1 as a so-called *Kokujokubi* or "National Humiliation Day" because, in their opinion, the Japanese people had been insulted by being singled out for exclusion. American-educated intellectuals reacted very strongly. Nitobe Inazō, a John Hopkins University graduate, vowed never to set foot on American soil again until after the 1924 Immigration Act was revised to remove its exclusionary clause. As an Amherst graduate and leading Christian intellectual, Uchimura Kanzō went much further. He appealed to his countrymen, not only not to visit the United States, but also to refrain from using American products, receiving American aid, reading material written by Americans, and attending American churches. Harvard-educated Kaneko Kentarō, president of the America-Japan Society, resigned his post in protest.[9]

Japanese immigrants protested the 1924 Immigration Act in a more subdued manner. No mass protest rallies were held in the United States, but Japanese immigrant newspapers uniformly interpreted its enactment as a manifestation of white supremacy. In Los Angeles, the *Rafu Shimpō* advised all Japanese immigrants "to remain calm" and "avoid unnecessary indignation." Arousing more "ill-feeling" would serve no useful purpose. According to this newspaper, Japan had not suffered humiliation alone—the United States had humiliated herself in the eyes of the world. By excluding the Japanese people, she had betrayed her own ideals, dishonored her best tradition, and revealed her own weakness to all. If a future "cataclysmic racial strife" should erupt, the United States had to assume responsibility for it. For she herself had "planted the seeds" by "branding" the Japanese people with "a stamp of inferiority."[10]

Other immigrant newspapers voiced stronger opinions. The *Taihoku Nippō* interpreted the 1924 Immigration Act in racial terms, too. By enacting it, the United States had "planted the seeds of a racial war" in which the white race would be pitted against the colored races.[11] To describe its own reaction, the Seattle newspaper used the term *gashin shōtan*.[12] Of Chinese classical origin, this term harked back in modern Japan to the Sino-Japanese War of 1894–95. Japanese newspapers first used it after the war when Japan was forced by Germany, France, and Russia to return the Liaotung Peninsula to China. Known as the Triple Intervention, this event provoked an outpouring of Japanese national indignation because Japan had been denied the fruits of her victory. *Gashin shōtan* counseled patience to the Japanese people. They had to strengthen themselves in order to seek ultimate revenge against Germany, France, and Russia in the future. By the same token, Japanese immigrants had to cultivate their own strength in the face of the 1924 Immigration Act in order to compel Americans to acknowledge the true worth of the Japanese people and to make them pay the respect they owed to Japan.

The *Shin Sekai* also interpreted the 1924 Immigration Act in strict racial terms. By treating the Japanese as "an inferior people," it had thrown down the gauntlet of "a racial struggle" between "the yellow and white races." In order to rise to the challenge, Japanese immigrants had to demonstrate the true character of the Japanese people by competing successfully with the white race, intellectually, physically, and morally.[13] The *Shin Sekai* ridiculed any Japanese person who scoffed at the designation of July 1 as a National Humiliation Day. "Anyone who remains in a toilet long enough will not be able to smell the foul odor," it said. "Anyone who works as a menial servant long enough will develop a servile mentality." And "anyone who does not consider a national humiliation a national humiliation has lost all of his sensibility."[14] In point of fact, Japanese immigrants in the United States were "treated just like *burakumin* in a humiliating way."[15]

This analogy to the despised outcaste group in Japan was not by happenstance. In 1922 leaders of this group established the *Suiheisha* and launched a national campaign to fight discrimination. The *Suihei* movement, as it came to be called, received wide press coverage which brought Japanese national attention to the plight of the *burakumin* or members of this outcaste group. The *Taihoku Nippō* likewise equated the treatment of Japanese immigrants in the United States to that of the *burakumin* in Japan. Ironically, however, this newspaper perceived no connection between the *burakumin*'s struggle for equality in Japan with that of the Japanese immigrants in America. Some *burakumin* felt that no Japanese had a right to protest the treatment of Japanese immigrants abroad because the Japanese themselves discriminated against *burakumin,* Koreans, and Chinese in Japan. Only if the Japanese treated all minority groups equally would they ever be justified in criticizing the United States. The *Taihoku Nippō* repudiated this line of reasoning. Japan had been insulted by the United States, plain and simple. Consequently, regardless of how minority groups were treated in Japan, all Japanese had the right to protest the American treatment of Japanese immigrants.[16]

Japanese immigrants themselves of course were not free of prejudice. Aware of what had happened to Chinese immigrants in the nineteenth century, Japanese immigrant leaders had always dreaded the thought of Japanese exclusion. During the course of the Japanese exclusion movement, the leaders repeatedly said, ''We are afraid that we will be excluded as the Chinese have been.'' Since they themselves had a low opinion of the Chinese people, this was not a pleasant thought to entertain. For their part, anti-Japanese exclusionists always linked Japanese immigration to the past ''evils'' of Chinese immigration. To counteract this negative association, Japanese immigrant leaders did everything possible to disassociate Japanese immigrants from their Chinese counterparts. In the end, however, all of their attempts at disassociation went for naught. For the Japanese people, stigmatized as an equally inferior and undesirable race, were excluded in an identical manner. Japanese immigrant leaders, then, reached the inevitable conclusion that, ''We have been excluded just like the Chinese,'' which expressed a realization that what they had dreaded for so long had become a horrible reality.

Japanese immigrant leaders believed in the superiority of the Japanese people. In 1913 five prominent leaders—Ushijima Kinji, Fujihira Junzō, Abiko Kyūtarō, Ikeda Goroku, and Kawakami Kiyoshi—addressed a revealing letter to Ambassador Chinda Sutemi. Fujihira headed the San Francisco branch of the Yokohama Specie Bank, while Ikeda was the publisher of the *Shin Sekai.* In discussing two immigration bills before Congress, these five men presented their opinion regarding a provision prohibiting the admission of any alien ineligible to citizenship. They wrote:

Of the ten or more immigration bills which have been introduced into Congress, the two most important ones are the Dillingham Bill in the Senate and the Burnett Bill in the House. Both bills contain a provision prohibiting the admission of aliens ineligible to citizenship under existing naturalization statutes. This provision has the objective of excluding Japanese and other Orientals. Among the countries of the Orient, there are those which still cannot claim to rank among the advanced, civilized world powers. That these lesser nations will be treated differentially by American immigration laws is understandable. But since Japan already ranks among the advanced, civilized nations, it is unfair for her to be treated as an inferior country.[17]

This letter expressed the ingrained prejudice of Japanese immigrant leaders. Countries like China and Korea were "inferior nations," in their opinion, whose subjects were unworthy of equal treatment. If the United States elected to discriminate against the people of such nations, that was understandable as well as acceptable. But Japan and her subjects were different. Japan was the equal of the western powers, and therefore her subjects deserved to be, indeed demanded to be, treated equally. Above all else, Japanese immigrant leaders wanted Japanese immigrants to be treated as European immigrants were. They conceded that the American government had the right to regulate immigration. They only wanted Japanese immigration to be placed on the same footing as European immigration. In terms of the 1924 Immigration Act, they wanted Japan placed under the quota system as European nations were. Thus Japanese immigrant leaders felt doubly affronted by the 1924 Immigration Act because it ranked the Japanese, not as the equal of Europeans, but on the same low level as previously excluded Asian people, the very people whom they themselves judged to be inferior.

An anti-Japanese incident which occurred shortly after July 1 reinforced the Japanese immigrant reaction to the 1924 Immigration Act. This took place on the night of July 22 in the town of Hopland in Mendocino County. On that night at 10:00 P.M., approximately 30 white youths armed with rifles, shotguns, and pistols surrounded a bunkhouse where eight Japanese laborers were lodged. These laborers had arrived in Hopland to work at a fruit packinghouse. The bunkhouse was situated behind the home of Wada Kumekusu, a local Japanese labor contractor. The white youths randomly fired their weapons and hit both the bunkhouse and Wada's home. Fortunately, no one was injured. Wada himself was not at home. He was at another packinghouse where he had other laborers employed. The white youths never tried to break into the bunkhouse or home. Apparently, they simply wanted to drive away the eight laborers by intimidation. They posted a "Get Rid of Japs" sign with a Klu Klux Klan emblem before they left, and the Japanese laborers fled from Hopland as soon as the white youths disappeared. The immigrant press interpreted this incident as another manifestation of white supremacy.[18]

Other acts of physical threat and violence had preceded this Hopland incident. Similar expulsions occurred in Delano, Los Angeles, and Porterville in 1922. The most publicized one occurred in Turlock in Stanislaus County. On the night of July 19, 1921, shortly after midnight, approximately 50–60 white men, armed with clubs, some with firearms, surrounded the Iwata Store where 18 Japanese workers had bunked down for the night. The white men first knocked on the door. When the Japanese refused to open it, they forced themselves in and then woke up all 18 Japanese workers. Ordering the workers outside, they placed eight on a Japanese-operated truck and commanded the Japanese driver to take them to Stockton. The remaining ten workers were loaded on another waiting truck and driven to Keyes, an adjacent town five miles north of Turlock. There the white men transferred them to a railroad freight car and warned them never to come back to Turlock at the risk of being lynched. This event was repeated twice in the course of the night. Returning to Turlock, the same white men raided another Japanese bunkhouse. They rounded up an additional 20 laborers in like manner and again dumped them off at Keyes. Meanwhile, another group of 50–60 white men went to three Japanese farms on the outskirts of Turlock. There they dragged out 20 laborers who had been hired by local Japanese farmers. These laborers were also taken to Keyes and warned never to return.[19] Taken together, the Hopland, Turlock, and other incidents reinforced the Japanese immigrants' reading of the 1924 Immigration Act. To them, the act came to symbolize not only their legal rejection by the United States, but also their persecution by lawless white elements.

All local Japanese consuls agreed that the 1924 Immigration Act had a pronounced psychological impact on Japanese immigrants. San Francisco Consul Ōyama Ujirō observed ''a deep sense of dejection among ordinary Japanese residents.''[20] Practically-speaking, Japanese immigrant bachelors, numbering well over 20,000, lost the most since they were now deprived of the opportunity of getting married in Japan and returning with their wives. A Portland consulate staff member reported that the negative psychological effect was great precisely because the 1924 Immigration Act ''placed the Japanese into the same category as the Chinese had been.''[21] Seattle Consul Ōhashi Tadaichi reported that the immigrants within his jurisdiction ''felt bitter and inceasingly resentful of the United States.''[22] Los Angeles Consul Wakasugi Kaname noted that many immigrants no longer perceived a future for themselves in the United States, and so he predicted that the number of Japanese residents would decrease in the coming years.[23] Consul Wakasugi also reported that two oldtime Issei, Kino Tamino-suke and Suda Kōgorō, formed an Awareness Group (*Kakuseidan*) in Los Angeles. The purpose of this group was to commemorate July 1, 1924, as a National Humiliation Day. In keeping with the meaning of *gashin shōtan*, both men favored developing the strengths and abilities of the Japanese people, so that one day Japan would be able to erase the stigma of inferiority with which Americans had branded the Japanese. The Awareness Group sold commemorative badges, with the proceeds earmarked for the erection of a July 1 memorial tower in Japan.[24]

The 1924 Immigration Act also affected the Japanese immigrants' view of their children, the Nisei. Immigrant leaders had begun to shift their attention from the Issei to the Nisei before its enactment. Under an editorial policy established by Abiko Kyūtarō, the *Nichibei Shimbun* changed its own emphasis from January 1924.[25] Attaching much greater importance to the Nisei generation, this newspaper began to declare repeatedly that the future of the Japanese in the United States lay with the Nisei. The Issei were already entering old age; the Nisei were about to come of age. Denied the right of naturalization, the Issei were aliens ineligible to citizenship without a real future in this country; the Nisei were American citizens with a potential bright future. The Issei now had to adopt the Nisei's future as their own. To enable the Nisei to realize their full potential as American citizens, the *Nichibei Shimbun* upheld the view that the Issei had a moral obligation and duty to support the Nisei in every way possible. Abiko envisioned the Nisei playing a pivotal role in future Japanese-American relations. Being Japanese by descent but American by birth and education, the Nisei were ideally suited to become a future bridge of understanding between the two nations to dispel the ignorance which had been, in Abiko's opinion, the fundamental cause of the exclusion movement.

The future of the Nisei in the United States, however, was not at all assured. Japanese immigrants could not rule out the possibility of their children being stripped of their American citizenship. In 1920 Senator James D. Phelan had first proposed a constitutional amendment denying American citizenship to any American-born person whose parents were ineligible to citizenship. In 1922 Congress enacted the Cable Act which directly affected Nisei women. Any Nisei woman who married an alien ineligible to citizenship lost her American citizenship by virtue of her marriage. In December 1923 Congress considered resolutions which reformulated Phelan's original constitutional amendment making the denial of American citizenship also retroactive to any person whose parents were both ineligible to citizenship. Next to the termination of all Japanese immigration, anti-Japanese exclusionists had had the goal of stripping the Nisei of their American citizenship. Any constitutional amendment of course required the approval of two-thirds of Congress and three-fourths of all state legislatures. For Japanese immigrants, although it was bad enough to be aliens ineligible to citizenship, it was something they could somehow live with. But the thought of their own children becoming aliens ineligible to citizenship was another matter. That would have been outrageous! Fortunately, the exclusionists were unable to marshal sufficient political support to deprive the Nisei of their American citizenship, but Japanese immigrant leaders were always alert to the possibility.

In the final analysis, the 1924 Immigration Act signified the complete failure of the Japanese immigrants' struggle against exclusion. The Supreme Court had upheld their ineligibility to citizenship as well as the constitutionality of the alien land laws. In retrospect, Japanese immigrants realized that all of their efforts to adapt themselves to American society and to demonstrate their assimilability had been in vain. The *Taihoku Nippō* described the sense of impasse reached by the immigrants. As the coordinating organ of all Japanese associations, the Pacific Coast Japanese Association Deliberative Council had been at the forefront of the anti-exclusion struggle. Now the situation of the council was tantamount to "picking up nails out of burnt ruins." Being too brittle, burnt nails are useless. This reference to picking up such nails was a metaphor for the psychological state of hopelessness and dejection into which Japanese immigrants had fallen. Japanese immigrants "have only one hope left," the *Taihoku Nippō* said, "and that is the maturation of our American-born children."[26]

Thus Japanese immigrants came to attach extra significance to the American-born generation. They transfered their hopes and aspirations onto the Nisei generation. The Issei could not escape the liability of being aliens ineligible to citizenship; the Nisei were American citizens who, in theory, had all the rights and privileges that came with their American citizenship. Since the Issei no longer perceived any real future for themselves, the Nisei's future, however precarious it appeared in 1924, suddenly loomed all-important to them. The future of the Japanese in the United States now depended on how their children would grow up and fare in their own native land. The anti-Japanese exclusion movement left an enduring legacy of bitterness and resentment in the hearts of Japanese immigrants. That legacy was mitigated partially by the hope that the Nisei would eventually vindicate the Japanese people in a brighter future.

Notes

Note: JARP = Japanese American Research Project Collection
JFMAD = Japanese Foreign Ministry Archival Documents
SBZSME = Shakai Bunko, *Zaibei Shakaishugisha Museifushugisha Enkaku*
UMWJ = *United Mine Workers' Journal*

Chapter II

1. Compiled from *Nihon Teikoku Tōkei Nenkan* (Tokyo, 1882–91).
2. Ibid.
3. Tomita Gentarō and Ōwada Yakichi, *Beikoku-yuki Hitori Annai: Ichimei Sōkō Jijō* (Yokohama, 1886), p. 36.
4. Akamine Seichirō, *Beikoku Ima Fushingi* (Tokyo, 1886), p. 21.
5. Ishida Kumatarō and Shūyū Sanjin, pseud., *Kitare, Nihonjin* (Tokyo, 1887), pp. 32–33.
6. "Nihon to Beikoku: Sōkō Dekaseginin no Mondai," *Kokumin no Tomo*, 23 (June 1, 1888), pp. 10–14, and "Tokubetsu Kisho," ibid., 24 (June 15, 1888), pp. 14–17. *See also Ozaki Gakudō Zenshū* (Tokyo, 1955), III, pp. 343–56.
7. *Japan Weekly Mail*, March 8, 1890.
8. Compiled from *Nihon Teikoku Tōkei Nenkan* (Tokyo, 1892–1901).

9. Carmen Blacker, *The Japanese Enlightenment: A Study of the Writings of Fukuzawa Yukichi* (Cambridge, 1964), pp. 7–8.

10. See Fukuzawa's editorials reprinted in *Fukuzawa Yukichi Zenshū* (Tokyo, 1960), IX, pp. 328–33, pp. 442–44, pp. 455–60, and X, pp. 464–69.

11. Kojō Yutaka, *Inoue Kakugorō-kun Ryakuden* (Tokyo, 1919), pp. 51–52.

12. Ibid., pp. 52–53.

13. Toshio Yoshimura, *George Shima: Potato King and Lover of Chinese Classics* (Fukushima, 1981), pp. 32–33. See also Fujioka Shirō, *Ayumi no Ato* (Los Angeles, 1957), pp. 467–68.

14. Wakayama-ken, *Wakayama-ken Iminshi* (Wakayama, 1957), pp. 148–56.

15. Ishida, *Kitare, Nihonjin,* p. 29.

16. Mutō Sanji, *Beikoku Ijūron* (Tokyo, 1887). For Mutō's life in America, see his recollection in *Mutō Sanji Zenshū* (Tokyo, 1963), I, pp. 23–42, and Irimajiri Yoshinaga, *Mutō Sanji* (Tokyo, 1964), pp. 27–30.

17. Imaizumi Genkichi, *Senku Kyūjūnen: Miyama Kan'ichi to Sono Jidai* (Kamakura, 1942), pp. 156–82.

18. Katayama Sen, *Jiden* (Tokyo, 1954), p. 124. For an English biography of Katayama, see Hyman Kublin, *Asian Revolutionary: The Life of Sen Katayama* (Princeton, 1964).

19. Nihon Rikkōkai, *Rikkōkai Sōritsu Gojūnenshi* (Tokyo, 1946).

20. Gotaro Ogawa, ed., *Conscription System in Japan* (New York, 1921).

21. Kikuchi Kunisaku, *Chōhei Kihi no Kenkyū* (Tokyo, 1977), pp. 176–277.

22. Nobutaka Ike, *The Beginnings of Political Democracy in Japan* (Baltimore, 1950); Robert A. Scalapino, *Democracy and the Party Movement in Prewar Japan* (Berkeley, 1953); and Roger W. Bowen, *Rebellion and Democracy in Meiji Japan* (Berkeley, 1980).

23. Ebihara Hachirō, "Sōkō Nihonjin Aikoku Dōmei Shimatsu," *Meiji Bunka Kenkyū,* 2 (1934), pp. 98–117, and Arai Katsuhiro and Tamura Norio, "Jiyū Minkenki ni Okeru Sōkō Wangan Chiku no Katsudō," *Tōkyō Keizai Daigaku Jimbun Shizen Kagaku Ronshū,* 65 (1983), pp. 75–136.

24. [Fumikura Heisaburō], comp., "Fukuinkai Enkaku Shiryō Shoki no Bu" (San Francisco, 1935), n.p.

25. Inasawa Ken'ichi et al., *Zaibei Nihonjin Chōrō Kyōkai Rekishi* (San Francisco, 1912). For a biography of Ernest A. Sturge, see *Sutōji Zenshū* (Tokyo, 1935), III.

26. Methodist Episcopal Church, *Minutes of the California Conference,* 32nd Session, September 10–15, 1884, p. 35.

27. Ibid., 36th Session, September 5–10, 1888, p. 48.

28. Ibid., 42nd Session, September 13–18, 1894, p. 67.

29. Of the League members, only Ishizuka Masatsugu and Hirota Zenrō remained in the United States. Hirota converted to Christianity and became a Methodist minister. Ishizuka lived a forlorn life as a laborer

who never married. For Ishizuka's life, see Irokawa Daikichi, *Shinpen Meiji Seishinshi* (Tokyo, 1973), pp. 122–80. Among the emigrés, Baba Tatsui died in Philadelphia in 1888. He had landed in San Francisco in 1886, but traveled to the East Coast. See N. Hagihara, "Baba Tatsui: An Early Japanese Liberal," *Far Eastern Affairs*, 3 (1963), pp. 121–43, and Eugene Soviak, "The Case of Baba Tatsui," *Monumenta Nipponica*, XVIII (1963), pp. 191–235.

30. Ebihara, "Sōkō Nihonjin Aikoku Dōmei Shimatsu," pp. 111–12.

31. For the founding of the *Shin Sekai*, see "Soejima-ō to Shin Sekai," *Shin Sekai*, June 15, 1909, and Soejima Hachirō, "Arishi Hi no Omokage: Shin Sekai Hakkan Tōji Ikanaru Dōki de Imareta," ibid., May 20, 1923. See also *Sutōji Zenshu*, III, pp. 69–70. For the general beginnings of the immigrant press, I have relied mainly on Ebihara Hachirō, *Kaigai Hōji Shimbun Zasshi Shi* (Tokyo, 1936), pp. 107–211. Other useful sources are Kono Hideo, "Sōkō no Hōji Shimbun," *Meiji Bunka*, 6:1 (1930), pp. 11–16; Takada Kikuo, "Sōkō de Hakkō Sareta Hōjishi 'Aikoku' no Kotodomo," *Meiji Bunka Kenkyū*, 6 (1935), pp. 153–59; Zaibei Nihonjinkai, *Zaibei Nihonjin Shi* (San Francisco, 1940), pp. 505–14; Robert E. Park, *The Immigrant Press and Its Control* (New York, 1922), pp. 280–86; and Shakuma, "Rekishi Inmetsu no Tan," pts. 52–54 (1922) in Oka Shigeki Papers, Japanese American Research Project Collection (hereafter JARP). The last source consists of ninety-seven articles on the early history of Japanese immigrants, published in the *Nichibei Shimbun*. The author was Washizu Bunzō who was an immigrant himself. Shakuma was his pen name.

32. Shakuma, "Rekishi Inmetsu no Tan," pt. 52.

33. Ibid., pt. 53.

34. Yone Noguchi, "Some Stories of My Western Life," *The Fortnight Review*, DLXVI, New Series (February 2, 1914), pp. 265–66.

35. Mutsu Munemitsu to Ōkuma Shigenobu, June 7, 1888, JARP, Japanese Foreign Ministry Archival Documents (hereafter JFMAD), reel 1. Mutsu was en route to Washington, D.C., to assume his new post.

36. Tomita and Ōwada, *Beikoku-yuki Hitori Annai*, pp. 61–64, and Ishida, *Kitare, Nihonjin*, pp. 147–49.

37. Cited in Imaizumi, *Senku Kyūjūnen: Miyama Kan'ichi to Sono Jidai*, p. 145.

38. Shakuma, "Rekishi Inmetsu no Tan," pt. 22.

39. Ibid.

40. Ozaki, "Nihon to Beikoku: Sōkō Dekaseginin no Mondai."

41. Mutsu to Ōkuma, June 7, 1888.

42. Keieisei, pseud., *Beikoku Kugaku Jikki* (Tokyo, 1911), p. 12.

43. Noguchi, "Some Stories of My Western Life," p. 268.

44. Yoshio Markino, "My Experiences in San Francisco," *McClure's Magazine*, 36:1 (November 1910), p. 109.

45. Keieisei, *Beikoku Kugaku Jikki*, p. 60.
46. Shimizu Tsuruzaburō, *Beikoku Rōdō Benran* (San Francisco, 1902), pp. 21–25.
47. Tomita and Ōwada, *Beikoku-yuki Hitori Annai*, pp. 45–46.
48. Chinda Sutemi to Hayashi Kaoru, July 3, 1893, and enclosures, *Nihon Gaikō Bunsho, 1893* (Tokyo, 1952), XXVI, pp. 734–40.
49. *Catalogue of Hopkins Academy*, 1888/1889 and 1891/1892.
50. *Bakurei Gakusō* (Berkeley, 1907), I, pp. 28–29, and Leland Stanford Junior University, *Register* 1891–1900.
51. Compiled from Superintendent of Immigration, *Annual Report* (Washington, D.C., 1892–1900).
52. Compiled from *Nihon Teikoku Tōkei Nenkan* (Tokyo, 1881–1901).
53. U.S. Census Office, *Twelfth Census of the United States, 1900, Population, Part I* (Washington, D.C., 1901), cxxiii, p. 492.
54. *Nihon Teikoku Tōkei Nenkan* (Tokyo, 1901), pp. 69–70.
55. Kawakita Shunsuke to Asada [Tokunori], January 21, 1890, JARP, JFMAD, reel 1.
56. Chinda to Aoki Shūzō, March 10, 1891, *Nihon Gaikō Bunsho, 1891* (Tokyo, 1952), XXIV, p. 462.
57. Mutsu Hirokichi to Komura Jutarō, August 11, 1898, Asian American Studies Center, JFMAD, reel 6 (hereafter AASC, JFMAD).
58. Sugimura Tokashi to Aoki, May 8, 1890, JARP, JFMAD, reel 1.
59. Chinda to Hayashi, July 30, 1891, enclosure, Fujita Yoshirō to Chinda, July 22, 1891, *Nihon Gaikō Bunsho, 1891* (Tokyo, 1952), XXIV, p. 500.
60. Shakuma, "Rekishi Inmetsu no Tan," pt. 4. *See also* Rokki Jihōsha, *Sanchūbu to Nihonjin* (Salt Lake City, 1925), p. 75.
61. Saitō Miki to Komura, April 2, 1897, AASC, JFMAD, reel 6. Takeuchi Kōjirō, *Beikoku Seihokubu Nihon Iminshi* (Seattle, 1929), p. 33, estimates that as many as 600 prostitutes were in Seattle in 1895.
62. Yamazaki Tomoko, *Sandakan Hachiban Shōkan* (Tokyo, 1972); Irie Toraji, *Hōjin Kaigai Hattenshi* (Tokyo, 1938), I, pp. 231–36; and Mori Katsumi, *Jinshin Baibai—Kaigai Dekasegijo* (Tokyo, 1960). Even though white slavery in Japan was outlawed in 1872, it was never stamped out fully.
63. Takeuchi, *Beikoku Seihokubu Nihon Iminshi*, p. 33.
64. Itō Kazuo, *Hokubei Hyakunen Sakura* (Seattle, 1969), pp. 893–94.
65. Chinda to Hayashi, January 16, 1892, *Nihon Gaikō Bunsho, 1892* (Tokyo, 1952), XXV, pp. 683–84.
66. Chinda to Hayashi, February 4, 1892, ibid., pp. 684–85.
67. Chinda to Enomoto Takeaki, September 3, 1891, JARP, JFMAD, reel 1.
68. Chinda to Aoki, May 20, 1890, ibid.
69. Chinda to Enomoto, July 30, 1891, ibid.

70. Shakuma, "Rekishi Inmetsu no Tan," pt. 6.
71. Heigan, "Nijūhachinenkan no Yo ga Kaikō," *Shin Sekai,* September 8, 1931. Like the series by Washizu Bunzō, this source consists of newspaper articles (100 in all) on the early history of Japanese immigrants. The author is Ninomiya Risaku. Heigan was his pen name.
72. Oka Shigeki, "Arabya Oyae Shusse Monogatari," *Amerika Shimbun,* February 12, 26, and March 5, 1938. A slightly different version of what happened to Yamada Waka can be found in Takeuchi, *Beikoku Seihokubu Nihon Iminshi,* pp. 486–89. A heavily fictionalized account is Yamazaki Tomoko, *Ameyuki-san no Uta* (Tokyo, 1978). For a brief description of Yamada's life in the Chinese Mission, *see* Woman's Occidental Board of Foreign Missions, *31st Annual Report* (San Francisco, 1904), p. 57.
73. Chinda to Hayashi, July 30, 1891, enclosure, Fujita to Chinda, July 22, 1891.
74. A. Inwood to Chinda, January 25, 1892, JARP, JFMAD, reel 1.
75. *Okina Kyūin Zenshū* (Toyama, 1972), II, p. 374.
76. San Francisco *Daily Report,* May 4, 1892.
77. Chinda to Hayashi, July 30, 1891, enclosure, Fujita to Chinda, July 22, 1891.
78. *Shin Sekai,* February 26–March 1, 5, 1900. For an example of a woman passed from one pimp to another, *see* the affidavit of a Japanese prostitute in U.S. Congress, Senate, *Reports of the Immigration Commission,* 61st Cong., 3rd sess., doc. 753 (Washington, D.C., 1911), pp. 109–10.
79. Seattle *Post Intelligencer,* February 15, April 19, 1891.
80. San Francisco *Bulletin,* January 11, 1890.
81. San Francisco *Examiner,* February, 18, 1891.
82. San Francisco *Bulletin,* May 4, 1891.
83. San Francisco *Daily Report,* May 19, 1891.
84. San Francisco *Examiner,* April 28, 1891.
85. San Francisco *Bulletin,* May 4, 1892.
86. San Francisco *Call,* May 4, 1892.
87. San Francisco *Daily Report,* May 4, 1892.
88. Chinda to Aoki, March 10, 1891.
89. Ibid.
90. Okabe Nagatsune to Chinda, April 8, 1891, *Nihon Gaikō Bunsho, 1891* (Tokyo, 1952), XXIV, p. 463. Okabe also instructed Chinda to cooperate with the local police and the Society for the Suppression of Vice to stamp out Japanese prostitution in the city. Okabe issued similar instructions to the Vancouver consul.
91. Kawakita to Aoki, June 11, 1889, enclosure, Ozawa Eizō to Kawakita, June 6, 1889, JARP, JFMAD, reel 1. Ozawa was the secretary of the Gospel Society.

92. Chinda to Okabe, June 13, 1891, enclosure, "Fuseigyō Fujoshi Torai Kinshi Seigan," May 16, 1891, ibid.
93. Hilary Conroy, *The Japanese Frontier in Hawaii, 1868–1898* (Berkeley, 1953).
94. Unless otherwise noted, all statistics are drawn from the recent studies by Kodama Masaaki who has used Foreign Ministry sources. *See,* for example, Kodama Masaaki, "Setonai Chiiki no Kanyaku Imin," in Gotō Yō'ichi, ed., *Setonai-kai no Chiiki no Shiteki Tenkai* (Tokyo, 1978), pp. 325–60. Conroy based his statistics on Hawaii Bureau of Immigration sources. The differences are only slight.
95. Yukiko Irwin and Hilary Conroy, "Robert Walker Irwin & Systematic Immigration to Hawaii," in Hilary Conroy and T. Scott Miyakawa, eds., *East Across the Pacific* (Santa Barbara, 1972), pp. 40–55. *See also* Shimaoka Hiroshi, "Hawai 'Kanyaku Imin' to Robāto Uōka Āuin," *Ōsaka Gakuin Daigaku Gaikokugo Ronshū,* 5 (1978), pp. 129–49; "Hawai 'Kanyaku Imin Seido Āuin Shisutemu' to Sono Hōkai," ibid., 6 (1978), pp. 68–89; and "Hawai Kanyaku Imin 'Dai-Ikkai Sen' no Keii," ibid., 8 (1980), pp. 109–29.
96. Andō Tarō to Aoki, April 29, 1886, and Andō to Aoki, July 8, 1886, reprinted in Hiroshima-ken, *Hiroshima Kenshi: Kindai-Gendai Shiryō-hen* (Hiroshima, 1976), III, pp. 95–101.
97. Ishikawa Tomonori, "Hiroshima-ken Nanbu Kuchita-son Keiyaku Imin no Shakai Chirigakuteki Kōsatsu," *Shigaku Kenkyū,* 99 (1967), pp. 33–52.
98. Kodama Masaaki, "Dekasegi Imin no Jittai: Hiroshima-ken Aki-gun Hesaka-son wo Sozai to Shite," *Hiroshima-shi Kōbunshokan Kiyō,* 3 (1980), pp. 31–53.
99. Ishikawa Tomonori, "Hiroshima Wangan Jigozen-son Keiyaku Imin no Shakai Chirigakuteki Kōsatsu," *Jinbun Chiri,* 19:1 (1967), pp. 75–91.
100. Hiroshima-ken, *Hiroshima Kenshi: Kindai* (Hiroshima, 1980), I, pp. 418–29.
101. Ibid., pp. 462–88.
102. Kodama, "Dekasegi Imin no Jittai."
103. Yamaguchi-ken Ōshima-gun Tōwa-chō, *Tōwa Chōshi* (Tōwa, 1982), p. 444.
104. Kuka Chōshi Henshū Iinkai, *Yamaguchi-ken Kuka Chōshi* (Kuka, 1954), p. 275.
105. Doi Yatarō, *Yamaguchi-ken Ōshima-gun Hawai Iminshi* (Tokuyama, 1980), p. 17.
106. Ibid.
107. Ibid., p. 20.
108. Kuka Chōshi Henshū Iinkai, *Yamaguchi-ken Kuka Chōshi,* pp. 280–81.
109. Ibid., p. 282.

110. Hiroshima-ken, *Hiroshima-kenshi: Kindai-Gendai Shiryō-hen*, III, pp. 103–104.
111. Irie Toraji, *Hōjin Kaigai Hattenshi* (Tokyo, 1938), I, pp. 95–96.
112. Kodama, "Setonai Chiiki no Kanyaku Imin," p. 330.
113. Ishikawa, "Hiroshima Wangan Jigozen-son Keiyaku Imin no Shakai Chirigakuteki Kōsatsu," p. 85.
114. Hiroshima-ken, *Hiroshima Kenshi: Kindai*, p. 1001.
115. Sugimura Tokashi to Governor Kokura, December 10, 1902, enclosure no. 2, Okabe Saburō to Sugimura Tokashi, November 22, 1902, in *Nihon Gaikō Bunsho, 1902* (Tokyo, 1957), XLIV, p. 828.
116. Irie, *Hōjin Kaigai Hattenshi*, I, pp. 120–42; Kodama Masaaki, "Shoki Imingaisha no Imin Boshū to Sono Jittai: Hiroshima-ken no Gōshū Kuinsurando Keiyaku Imin wo Sozai ni," *Hiroshima Kenshi Kenkyū*, 3 (1978), pp. 20–44; Ishikawa Tomonori, "Fuiji Shotō ni Okeru Nihonjin Keiyaku Imin (1894–1895) ni Tsuite—Hiroshina-ken Imin wo Rei to Shite," *Ijū Kenkyū*, 14 (1977), pp. 55–79; and Kobayashi Tadao, *Nyū Karedonia-tō no Nihonjin Keiyaku Imin no Rekishi* (Tokyo, 1977).
117. Irie, *Hōjin Kaigai Hattenshi*, I, pp. 109–10.
118. Ibid., pp. 113–19, and *Nihon Gaikō Bunsho, 1894* (Tokyo, 1952), XXIX, pp. 976–94.
119. Ishikawa Tomonori, "Nihon Shutsu Iminshi ni Okeru Imingaisha to Keiyaku Imin ni Tsuite," *Ryūkyū Daigaku Hōbun Gakubu Kiyō Shakai-hen*, 14 (1970), p. 24, and Kodama Masaaki, "Imingaisha no Jittai," in Hiroshima Shigaku Kenkyūkai, *Shigaku Kenkyū Gojūshūnen Kinen Ronsō, Nihon-hen*, (Okayama, 1980), p. 461.
120. Ishikawa, "Nihon Shutsu Iminshi ni Okeru Imingaisha to Keiyaku Imin ni Tsuite," p. 24.
121. Kodama, "Imingaisha no Jittai," p. 461.
122. Kodama, "Shoki Imingaisha no Imin Boshū to Sono Jittai."
123. Kodama Masaaki, "Imingaisha ni Tsuite no Ichi Kōsatsu—Kaigai Tokō Kabushiki Kaisha wo Chūshin ni," *Geibi Chihōshi Kenkyū*, 128 (1980), pp. 12–25.
124. An announcement of the establishment of the Nichibei Yōtatsusha appeared in *Ajiya*, 62 (October 1892), pp. 19–20.
125. Shakuma, "Rekishi Inmetsu no Tan," pts. 27–28.
126. Chinda to Mutsu, September 27, 1892, enclosure, "Tanaka Tadashichi Gushinsho," September 15, 1892, JARP, JFMAD, reel 8.
127. Rokki Jihōsha, *Sanchūbu to Nihonjin*, p. 78. Takahashi Kanji, *Imin no Chichi: Katsunuma Tomizō Sensei Den* (Honolulu, 1953), p. 7, notes that Katsunuma worked for Tanaka's office, but mistakenly states that the office was located in Salt Lake City.
128. Kodama, "Imingaisha ni Tsuite no Ichi Kōsatsu," pp. 12–13.
129. Ibid., pp. 16–17.
130. Ibid., p. 20.

131. The United Japanese Society of Hawaii, *A History of Japanese in Hawaii* (Honolulu, 1971), pp. 142–43. Sugawara and Hinata belonged to a Seiyūkai faction headed by Hoshi Tōru. Besides the Hiroshima Kaigai Tokō Company, Hoshi's group was involved with two other large emigration companies, the Kumamoto Emigration Company and the Morioka Emigration Company. For Hoshi's role in these companies and in Hawaiian affairs, *see* Ariizumi Sadao, *Hoshi Tōru* (Tokyo, 1983), pp. 217–47.

132. Sassa Hiroshi, "Imingaisha to Chihō Seitō," *Kokushikan Daigaku Bungakubu Jimbun Gakkai Kiyō,* 15 (1983), pp. 61–80.

133. Compiled from *Annual Report of the Superintendent of Immigration* (Washington, D.C., 1892–1901).

134. Compiled from ibid., 1902–8. For the figures on the laborers who migrated from the Hawaiian Islands, *see* U.S. Department of Commerce and Labor, *Bulletin of the Bureau of Labor,* 66 (1906), p. 378, and 94 (1911), p. 724. These bulletins include the third and fourth reports of the Hawaii Commissioner of Labor.

135. Aoki to Takahira [Kogorō], August 2, 1900, *Nihon Gaikō Bunsho, 1900* (Tokyo, 1956), XXXIII, p. 461. *See also* Irie, *Hōjin Kaigai Hattenshi,* I, pp. 315–17.

136. Komura to Keishi Sōkan et al., June 9, 1902, *Nihon Gaikō Bunsho, 1902* (Tokyo, 1957), XLIV, p. 699.

137. Compiled from *Nihon Teikoku Tōkei Nenkan* (Tokyo, 1902–1908). This passport total is less than the total admissions to the United States in the corresponding period. The difference is explained in part by the fact that many persons who received passports for Canada entered the United States via that country.

138. The United Japanese Society of Hawaii, *A History of the Japanese in Hawaii,* p. 111, pp. 287–96.

139. For the anti-Japanese exclusion movement, *see* Roger Daniels, *The Politics of Prejudice* (New York, 1968).

140. D. W. Stevens to Gōzō Tateno, October 12, 1891, *Nihon Gaikō Bunsho, 1891* (Tokyo, 1952), XXIV, pp. 511–13.

141. Enomoto to Kaku Fuken Chiji, April 26, 1892, *Nihon Gaikō Bunsho, 1892* (Tokyo, 1952), XXV, pp. 695–96.

142. Chinda to Aoki, May 7, 1891, enclosure no. 2, *Nihon Gaikō Bunsho, 1891* (Tokyo, 1952), XXIV, pp. 480–87.

143. Nishi to Keishi Sōkan et al., February 2, 1898, *Nihon Gaikō Bunsho, 1898* (Tokyo, 1954), XXXI:2, pp. 629–30.

144. Komura to Keishi Sōkan et al., March 29, 1898, ibid., pp. 631–32.

145. Abe to Keishi Sōkan et al., August 3, 1898, ibid., p. 624.

146. Gaimushō, Tsūshōkyoku, *Imin Toriatsukainin ni Yoru Imin no Enkaku* (Tokyo, 1910), pp. 95–102.

Chapter III

1. Rokki Jihōsha, *Sanchūbu to Nihonjin*, pp. 80–82.
2. Ibid., p. 83. William H. Remington had a letter of recommendation from the general traffic manager of the Oregon Short Line to the president of the Northern Pacific. See S. W. Eccles to C. S. Mellen, October 14, 1897, NP File 271, Archives and Manuscript Division, Minnesota Historical Society (unless otherwise noted, hereafter all letters relating to the Northern Pacific and the Great Northern cited below are from this depository).
3. Ōtsuka Shun'ichi, *Takoma Nihonjin Hattenshi* (Tacoma, 1917), p. 14. Both William H. Remington and Kumamoto Hifumi are shadowy figures. Remington at one time was associated with another contracting firm, the Remington, Johnson and Company of Salt Lake City. A native of Fukuoka Prefecture, Kumamoto arrived around 1888 and was able to speak fluent English. See Katō Toshirō, *Zaibei Dōhō Hattenshi* (Tokyo, 1908), p. 182.
4. Sometani Nariaki to Tsuzuki Keiroku, April 18, 1899, enclosure, "Sōkō Ihoku Taiheiyō ni Soi Gasshūkoku ni Zaijū Suru Nihon Imin no Genjō," JARP, JFMAD, reel 2.
5. Takeuchi, *Beikoku Seihokubu Nihon Iminshi*, pp. 290–91.
6. Ibid.
7. The best biographical account of Ban Shinzaburō is contained in the New Year's edition of the *Taihoku Nippō*, January 1, 1915. Ban presented his own account of his business activities in Ban Shinzaburō, "Yo wa Beikoku nite Yonsen Dōhō to Tomo ni Sūko no Tetsudō wo Fusetsu Shitari," *Jitsugyō no Nihon*, 12:16 (August 1909), pp. 1158–60. Two early stories of his success appeared in Manrisei, pseud., "Nihonjin no Kaigai no Seikōsha—Ukeoigyō Ban Shinzaburō-shi," *Jitsugyō no Nihon*, 7:12 (June 1904), pp. 921–23, and Ōfu Inshi, pseud., *Zaibei Seikō no Nihonjin* (Tokyo, 1904), pp. 137–56. See also Barbara Yasui, "The Nikkei in Oregon, 1834–1940," *Oregon Historical Quarterly*, LXXVI (1975), pp. 225–57.
8. Shakuma, "Rekishi Inmetsu no Tan," pt. 27.
9. Ibid.
10. *Shin Sekai*, May 2, June 2, 1900.
11. Rokki Jihōsha, *Sanchūbu to Nihonjin*, pp. 163–65; Morino Kenkichi, "Hokubei no Tankō Rōdō," *Amerika*, 11:1 (January 1907), pp. 8–9; Morino Kenkichi, "Nichibei Kangyōsha no Jigyō Seiseki," ibid., 11:2 (February 1907), pp. 76–77; Yamamura Shirō, "Abiko Kyūtarō wo Oboete," August 3, 1956, Oka Papers; and Kuroishi Seisaku, "Abiko Kyūtarō-Ō," n.d., ibid.
12. Rokki Jihōsha, *Sanchūbu to Nihonjin*, pp. 105–6.

13. Suzuki Rokusuke et al., *Intāmaunten Dōhō Hattatsushi* (Denver, 1909), p. 50.

14. Abiko Kyūtarō, "Hokubei ni Okeru Nihon Imin Mondai," *Tōkyō Keizai Zasshi* 1470 (December 19, 1908), p. 1113.

15. For biographical accounts of Abiko Kyūtarō, *see* Yokoyama Gennosuke, *Kaigai Katsudō no Nihonjin* (Tokyo, 1906), pp. 13–18; Uekatasei, pseud., "Zaibei Seikō Nihonjin no Hyōron—Abiko Kyūtarō-kun," *Amerika*, 10:11 (November 1906), pp. 793–94; Yamamura, "Abiko Kyūtarō wo Oboete; Yamano Masatarō, "Senpai Abiko-san," n.d. Oka Papers; Konno Toyoji, "Senken no Akari Arishi Kaitakusha: Abiko Kyūtarō-shi wo Keibo," September 1955, ibid.; Chiba Toyoji, "Chiba Toyoji Ikō" (Dairen, 1944), I, pp. 205–6; Fujioka, *Ayumi no Ato*, pp. 472–82; *Okina Kyūin Zenshū* (Toyama, 1972), III, pp. 227–36; and Oka Seizō, "Abiko Kyūtarō Den," *Hokubei Mainichi*, May 8–10, 13–16, June 13–14, 17–19, 26–28, July 2–3, 8–9, August 23, 26–30, 1980.

16. The other shareholders were: Minabe Umetarō, Minejima Giichi, Terazawa Rokunosuke, Akimoto Masanori, and Hatanaka Rokurō.

17. *Taihoku Nippō*, January 1, 1915.

18. Haraguchi Kiyoshi, *Jiyū Minken Shizuoka Jiken* (Tokyo, 1984), and Terasaki Osamu, "Suzuki Ototaka Shōden," in Tezuka Yutaka, *Kindai Nihonshi no Shin Kenkyū* (Tokyo, 1983), II, pp. 58–111. Yamaoka Ototaka was born as Suzuki Ototaka.

19. Shakuma, "Rekishi Inmetsu no Tan," pt. 27.

20. Saitō Miki to Komura, April 22, 1898, *Nihon Gaikō Bunsho, 1898* (Tokyo, 1954), XXXI:2, p. 28.

21. Saitō Miki to Komura, May 13, 1898, ibid., pp. 29–32.

22. Narita [Gorō] to Sugimura [Tokashi], March 12, 1900, *Nihon Gaikō Bunsho, 1900* (Tokyo, 1956), XXXIII, pp. 407–08, and Ōura [Yasutake] to Sugimura, March 16, 1900, enclosures, ibid., pp. 408–13.

23. Aoki to Keishi Sōkan et al., April 28, 1900, ibid., pp. 439–40.

24. Aoki to Keishi Sōkan, May 4, 1900, ibid., p. 446.

25. *Shizuoka Minyū Shimbun*, December 6–29, 1900, January 5–June 28, 1901. For examples of forged passports, *see* Narita to Aoki, June 5, 1900, enclosure, "Torishirabe-sho," and Narita to Aoki, July 16, 1900, enclosure, "Tetsuzuki-sho," JARP, JFMAD, reel 10. *See also* Terasaki, "Suzuki Ototaka Shōden," pp. 92–107.

26. Ueno Kisaburō to Komura, August 25, 1902, enclosure, "Beikoku ni Imin Suru Hompōjin Tokō Torishimari ni Kan Suru Seigan," November 25, 1901, JARP, JFMAD, reel 10. With reports of individual contractors appended, the petition was submitted to the San Francisco Consul on July 10, 1902.

27. Saitō to Komura, June 22, 1905, January 24, 1907, JARP, JFMAD, reel 12.

28. Saitō to Komura, May 28, 1902, enclosure, Alex. Center to H. Hack-field and Co., n.d., ibid.
29. U.S. Department of Commerce and Labor, *Bulletin of the Bureau of Labor,* 47 (1903), p. 761 and pp. 836–37.
30. Matsubara Kazuo to Saionji Kimmochi, April 18, 1906, enclosures, JARP, JFMAD, reel 12. The enclosures consist of clippings of ads placed in the local Japanese-language newspapers by mainland recruiting agents.
31. Ibid.
32. Saitō to Takahira, January 26, 1905, ibid.
33. W.H. Remington to H.J. Horn, May 12 and July 21, 1905, NP File 147.
34. Saitō to Komura, April 26, 1905, JARP, JFMAD, reel 12.
35. George T. Slade to L.W. Hill, February 28, 1906, GN File 4000, and C. T. Takahashi to F. W. Gilbert, April 6, 1906.
36. Matsubara to Saionji, March 16 and April 18, 1906, JARP, JFMAD, reel 12.
37. Ueno to Komura, June 5, 1902, ibid.
38. Ueno to Komura, July 15, 30, 1902, ibid.
39. Saitō to Chinda, April 2, 1903, ibid.
40. Okabe Saburō to Komura, March 16, 1903, ibid.
41. Okabe Saburō to Komura, enclosure, "Notice to Emigrants Intending to Go to the Mainland of the United States," March 16, 1903, ibid.
42. Saitō to Komura, December 2, 1903, ibid.
43. Saitō to Takahira, September 13, 1904, ibid.
44. Saitō to Chinda, April 22, 1905, enclosure, F.K. Swanzy to Saitō, April 18, 1905, ibid.
45. Saitō to Komura, April 26, 1905, ibid.
46. Daniels, *The Politics of Prejudice,* pp. 16–45.
47. Irie, *Hōjin Kaigai Hattenshi,* I, pp. 518–19.
48. Hokubei Okinawa Kurabu, *Hokubei Okinawajin Shi* (Los Angeles, 1981), pp. 56–58.
49. For the Japanese immigration to Mexico, *see also* Nishimukai Yoshiaki, "Shoki no Mekishiko Imin no Kōsatsu," *Nanbei Kenkyū,* 15 (1970), pp. 31–44; Okinawa-ken, *Okinawa Kenshi: Imin* (Naha, 1974), VII, pp. 315–25; and María Elena Ota Mishima, *Siete Migraciones Japonesas en México, 1890–1978* (Mexico, D.F., 1982), pp. 51–62.
50. Abiko to Hayashi, February 15, 1907, *Nihon Gaikō Bunsho, 1907* (Tokyo, 1961), XL:3, pp. 331–32.
51. Minami Kashū Dōhō Taikai to Hayashi, February 20, 1907, ibid., p. 343.
52. Aiba Tsuneji to Hayashi, March 25, 1907, enclosure, "Chinjōsho," March 12, 1907, ibid., pp. 381–86.
53. Matsubara to Hayashi, April 21, 1907, ibid., pp. 399–402.

54. Hisamizu Saburō to Hayashi, April 29, 1907, and enclosure, "Kashū Nihonjinkai Chinjōsho," April 1907, JARP, JFMAD, reel 7.

55. Yamaoka's activities in Japan are covered by numerous reports submitted by different government agencies to the Foreign Ministry. See JARP, JFMAD, reel 4.

56. U.S. Immigration Commission, *Immigrants in Industries, Part 25: Japanese and Other Immigrant Races in the Pacific Coast and Rocky Mountain States* (Washington, D.C., 1911), XXIII, p. 33.

57. Chinda to Mutsu, September 27, 1892, enclosure.

58. Sometani to Tsuzuki, April 18, 1899.

59. Ōtsuka, *Takoma Nihonjin Hattenshi,* p. 14.

60. Neither the Great Northern nor the Northern Pacific charged any tariff for such shipments at the beginning. In 1902 the rate was ½ cent per ton per mile, and from 1904 it was raised to 1 cent per ton per mile. As a concession to the contractors, these rates were cheaper than the going tariff.

61. Chinda to Mutsu, September 27, 1892, enclosure.

62. Rokki Jihōsha, *Sanchūbu to Nihonjin,* p. 82.

63. Kawamura Tetsutarō, *Saikin Katsudō Hokubei Jigyō Annai* (Tokyo, 1906), p. 83.

64. Rokki Jihōsha, *Sanchūbu to Nihonjin,* p. 84.

65. Gilbert to D. Boyle et al., March 14, 1906.

66. Elliott to D[aniel] Willard, March 29, 1906, and April 7, 1906, NP File 271.

67. Takahashi to Gilbert, April 6, 1906.

68. Takahashi to Gilbert, August 7, 1906.

69. Takahashi to Gilbert, April 6, 1906.

70. Takahashi to Horn, March 26, 1907.

71. U.S. Immigration Commission, *Immigrants in Industries,* XXV, pp. 279–92.

72. Morino Kenkichi, "Hokubei no Tankō Rōdō," *Amerika,* 11:1 (January 1907), pp. 8–9.

73. For early Japanese accounts of Alaska cannery work, *see* Matsumoto Yoshitoshi, "Kyokuhoku Ensei Arasuka Shake Kanzume no Ukeoi Jigyō," *Tobei Zasshi,* 10:11 (November 1906), pp. 781–83; Kawamura Yūchō, pseud., "Arasuka no Rōdō," *Amerika,* 11:2 (February 1907), pp. 71–72; Kawamura, *Saikin Katsudō Hokubei Jigyō Annai,* pp. 115–21; Kanai Shigeo and Itō Banshō, pseud., *Hokubei no Nihonjin* (San Francisco, 1909), pp. 63–66.

74. U.S. Immigration Commission, *Immigrants in Industries,* XXIII, p. 50.

75. Itō, *Hokubei Hyakunen Sakura,* pp. 457–58.

76. Lloyd H. Fisher, *The Harvest Labor Market in California* (Cambridge, 1953), pp. 20–41.

77. For example, *see* Kawamura, *Saikin Katsudō Hokubei Jigyō Annai*, p. 141.
78. *Shin Sekai*, August 15, 1906.
79. Ibid., September 26, 1906.
80. Ibid., September 16, 1907.
81. Ibid., September 9, 1906.
82. Ibid., February 4, 1900.
83. Ibid., June 9, August 11, 1908.
84. Washizu, Rekishi Inmetsu no Tan," pt. 17.
85. *Shin Sekai*, October 17, 1900.
86. Yoshimura Daijirō, *To-Bei Seigyō no Tebiki* (Osaka, 1903), p. 120.
87. *Shin Sekai*, September 1, 1908.
88. Sacramento Betsuin, "Kakochō, 1900–1902."
89. Mizutani Bangaku, pseud., *Hokubei Aichi Kenjinshi* (Sacramento, 1920), pp. 451–55.
90. "California, Number of Japanese Deaths by Causes, 1906–1913, in JARP, JFMAD, reel 57.
91. Kiyoshi K. Kawakami, *Asia At The Door* (New York, 1914), pp. 116–17.
92. Fresno *Morning Republican*, June 10, 1908.
93. Gaimushō, *Nihon Gaikō Bunsho: Tai-Bei Imin Mondai Keika Gaiyō* (Tokyo, 1972), p. 210.
94. Shimizu, *Beikoku Rōdō Benran*, pp. 261–62.
95. *Shin Sekai*, June 12, 1908.
96. *Nichibei Shimbun*, August 20, 1913.
97. Sashihara Hideo, "Zaibei Dōhō to Hanzai," *Beikoku Bukkyō*, February 1, March 1, and April 1, 1914.
98. Stewart Culin, "The Gambling Games of the Chinese in America," *Publications of the University of Pennsylvania, Philology, Literature and Archeology*, 1:4 (1891), pp. 1–17.
99. Shin Sekai Shimbunsha, *Panama Taiheiyō Bankoku Dai-Hakurankai* (San Francisco, 1912), appendix, "Zaibei Nihonjin Jūsho Seimei Roku," pp. 16–20, 53–54, 84–85, 123, 128–29.
100. Woman's Occidental Board of Foreign Missions, *26th Annual Report* (San Francisco, 1899), p. 85.
101. *Nihon Gaikō Bunsho: Tai-Bei Imin Mondai Keika Gaiyō* (Tokyo, 1972), p. 213.
102. *Shin Sekai*, June 8, 1914.

Chapter IV

1. Nimura Kazuo, "Shokkō Giyūkai to Kashū Nihonjin Kutsukō Dōmeikai," in Rōdō Undōshi Kenkyūkai, *Reimeiki Nihon Rōdō Undō no Saikentō* (Tokyo, 1979), pp. 116–49.

2. Hyman Kublin, "Takano Fusataro: A Study in Early Japanese Trades-Unionism," American Philosophical Society, *Proceedings*, 103:4 (1959), pp. 571–83; Ōshima Kiyoshi, "Rōdō Kumiai Undō no Sōshisha: Takano Fusatarō," *Ōhara Shakai Mondai Kenkyūjo Shiryōshitsuhō*, 106 (January 1965), pp. 1–15, 124 (October 1966), pp. 1–12, and 136 (April 1968), pp. 1–13; and Tachikawa Kenji, "Takano Fusatarō: Zaibei Taiken wo Chūshin to Shite," *Shirin*, 65 (1982), pp. 433–62.

3. Sumiya Mikio, "Takano Fusatarō to Rōdō Undō—Gompers to no Kankei wo Chūshin ni," *Keizaigaku Ronshū*, 29:1 (1963), pp. 63–82.

4. U.S. Immigration Commission, *Immigrants in Industries*, XXIII, pp. 197–200; Kashū Nihonjin Kutsukō Dōmeikai, *Kashū Nihonjin Kutsukō Dōmeikai Enkaku no Gaiyō* (San Francisco, 1917); Shakuma, "Rekishi Inmetsu no Tan," pts. 31–32; Nimura, "Shokkō Giyūkai to Kashū Nihonjin Kutsukō Dōmeikai."

5. Nihonjin Kutsukō Dōmeikai, *Nihonjin Kutsukō Dōmeikai Kiyaku Oyobi Saisoku* (San Francisco, 1904).

6. For the account of the Oxnard Strike, I have relied heavily upon Tomas Almaguer, "Class, Race, and Capitalist Development: The Social Transformation of a Southern California County, 1848–1903," Ph.D. dissertation, University of California, Berkeley, 1979, pp. 262–309, and Tomas Almaguer, "Racial Domination and Class Conflict in Capitalist Agriculture: The Oxnard Sugar Beet Workers' Strike of 1903," *Labor History*, XXV (1984), pp. 325–50. *See also* Philip Foner, *History of the Labor Movement in the United States* (New York, 1973), III, pp. 276–78.

7. For Inose Inosuke's background, *see* Ōfu Inshi, pseud., *Zaibei Seikō no Nihonjin*, pp. 156–68.

8. Oakland Tribune, April 21, 1903.

9. Almaguer, "Racial Domination and Class Conflict in Capitalist Agriculture," p. 345.

10. Ibid., p. 347.

11. American Federation of Labor, *Proceedings* (1893), p. 73.

12. Ibid. (1901), p. 22.

13. Ibid. (1904), p. 100.

14. Augusta H. Pio, "Exclude Japanese Labor," *American Federationist* (May 1905), pp. 274–76.

15. Samuel Gompers, *Seventy Years of Life and Labour* (New York, 1967), II, p. 59.

16. F. Tekano (sic), "Labor Movement in Japan," *American Federationist* (October 1894), pp. 163–66.

17. Fusataro Takano, "Labor Problem in Japan," ibid. (September 1896), pp. 133–35.

18. "Our Organizer in Japan," ibid. (June 1897), pp. 77–78.

19. Fusataro Takano, "New Trade-Union in Japan," ibid. (February 1898), pp. 272–73, and *Coast Seamen's Journal*, February 2, 1898.
20. Fusataro Takano, "A Remarkable Strike in Japan," *American Federationist* (September 1897), pp. 144–45, and *Coast Seamen's Journal*, September 1, 1897; "Prospects of the Japanese Labor Movement," *American Federationist* (November 1897), pp. 210–11; "Japanese Printers' Wages," *Coast Seamen's Journal*, October 27, 1897; "Female Labor in Japan," *American Federationist* (December 1897), pp. 231–32, and *Coast Seamen's Journal*, December 1, 1897; "Proposed Factory Act in Japan," *American Federationist* (January 1898), pp. 250–52, and *Coast Seamen's Journal*, January 12, 1898; "Experience of a Labor Agitator in Japan," *American Federationist* (March 1898), pp. 3–5, and *Coast Seamen's Journal*, March 2, 1898; "Strikes in Japan," *American Federationist* (April 1898), pp. 31–32, and *Coast Seamen's Journal*, March 30, 1898; "Great Railway Strike in Japan," *American Federationist* (May 1898), pp. 48–50, and *Coast Seamen's Journal*, May 4, 1898; "Labor Notes From Japan," *American Federationist* (August 1898), pp. 118–19, and *Coast Seamen's Journal*, August 3, 1898; "The Life Condition of Japanese Workers," *American Federationist* (September 1898), pp. 133–35, and *Coast Seamen's Journal*, September 14, 1898; "Street-Car Service in Tokio," *American Federationist* (October 1898), pp. 155–57, and *Coast Seamen's Journal*, October 12, 1898; "Japanese Farmers," *American Federationist* (November 1898), pp. 174–75; and *Coast Seamen's Journal*, November 30, 1898; "Factory Legislation in Japan," *American Federationist* (December 1898), pp. 200–1, and *Coast Seamen's Journal*, December 21, 1898; and "Japan Factory Legislation," *American Federationist* (January 1899), p. 216.
21. Ibid., (September 1905), p. 636.
22. Hyman Kublin, "The Origins of Japanese Socialist Tradition," *Journal of Politics*, 14 (1952), pp. 257–80.
23. Hyman Kublin, "The Japanese Socialists and the Russo-Japanese War," *Journal of Modern History*, 22 (1950), pp. 322–29.
24. Itoya Toshio, *Daigyaku Jiken* (Tokyo, 1970), and F. G. Notehelfer, *Kotoku Shusui: A Portrait of a Japanese Radical* (Cambridge, 1971), pp. 152–200.
25. Sumiya Mikio, *Katayama Sen: Kindai Nihon no Shisōka* (Tokyo, 1960), p. 137. Katayama published three other guides to America: *Zoku Tobei Annai* (Tokyo, 1902), *Shin Tobei* (Tokyo, 1904), and *Tobei no Hiketsu* (Tokyo, 1906).
26. The best summary of the activities of the immigrant socialists and anarchists is by Matsuo Shōichi, "Meiji Makki ni Okeru Zaibei Nihonjin Shakaishugi Museifushugi Undō Shōshi," in Shakai Bunko, *Zaibei Shakaishugisha Museifushugisha Enkaku* (Tokyo, 1964), pp. 17–29 (hereafter cited as *SBZSME*).

27. Iwasa Sakutarō, "Zaibei Undōshi Banashi," in *SBZSME*, p. 525.
28. Hippolyte Havel, "Kotoku's Correspondence with Albert Johnson," *Mother Earth*, 6:6 (1911), pp. 182–83.
29. Shiota Shōbei, *Kōtoku Shūsui no Nikki to Shokan* (Tokyo, 1965), p. 216.
30. Ibid., p. 223.
31. *SBZSME*, pp. 104–7.
32. Iwasa Sakutarō, "Beikoku Yori," *Hikari*, 18 (1906), p. 7, and Oakland *Socialist Voice*, June 16, 1906.
33. Kuramochi Zensaburō, "Shakai Kakumeitō Okoru," *Hikari*, 17 (1906), p. 7, and *Nichibei Shimbun*, June 23, 1906.
34. Hyman Weintraub, *Andrew Furuseth: Emancipator of the Seamen* (Berkeley, 1959), pp. 112–13.
35. Quoted by Philip Foner, *History of the Labor Movement in the United States* (New York, 1964), III, p. 270.
36. Oakland *Socialist Voice*, December 8, 1906.
37. Ira Kipnis, *The American Socialist Movement, 1897–1912* (New York, 1952), p. 277.
38. Oakland *Socialist Voice*, December 8, 1906.
39. Kipnis, *The American Socialist Movement*, p. 280.
40. Abe Isoo, *Hokubei no Shin Nippon* (Tokyo, 1905), p. 76.
41. Oakland *Socialist Voice*, January 19, 1907.
42. Ibid.
43. Ibid., March 16, 1907.
44. *SBZSME*, p. 462.
45. San Francisco *Chronicle*, December 30, 1906; San Francisco *Examiner*, December 30, 1906; San Francisco *Call*, December 30, 1906; and Berkeley *Daily Gazette*, December 31, 1906.
46. *SBZSME*, p. 467.
47. Ibid., pp. 178–89.
48. It is difficult to determine the exact membership. Conflicting figures range from 2,000 to 4,000 members. It is hard to believe that 4,000 out of an approximate 5,000 migratory labor force could be organized in one short harvest season. I have therefore elected the lower figure of 2,000.
49. *SBZSME*, p. 213.
50. *Shin Sekai*, June 9, 1908.
51. *SBZSME*, pp. 230–31.
52. Ibid., pp. 233–34.
53. Ibid., pp. 248–54.
54. Union Pacific Coal Company, *History of the Union Pacific Coal Mines, 1868–1940* (Omaha, 1940), pp. 13–15, and George B. Pryde, "The Union Pacific Coal Company, 1868 to August 1952," *Annals of Wyoming*, 25 (1953), pp. 191–205.
55. Compiled from Wyoming State Coal Mine Inspector, *Annual Report of*

the State Coal Mine Inspector, District No. 1, December 31, 1907, pp. 26–32.

56. Ibid.
57. James Morgan, "Union Movement in Wyoming," *Wyoming Labor Journal*, August 31, 1917, and Erma A. Fletcher, "A History of the Labor Movement in Wyoming," M.A. thesis, University of Wyoming, 1945.
58. Broncho Bill to editor, *United Mine Workers' Journal*, April 9, 1903 (hereafter cited as *UMWJ*). This miner later identified himself as Anderson F. Barnett.
59. Anderson F. Barnett to editor, *UMWJ*, May 14, 1903.
60. Ibid.
61. Barnett to editor, *UMWJ*, June 11, 1903.
62. J.W. Trul to editor, *UMWJ*, September 10, 1903.
63. Wyoming *Tribune*, May 23, 1907.
64. *UMWJ*, June 6, 1907.
65. Rock Springs *Miner*, June 1, 1907; Cheyenne *Daily Leader*, June 2, 1907.
66. Walter R. Ingalls, ed., *The Mineral Industry: Its Statistics, Technology and Trade During 1907* (New York, 1908), p. 210.
67. Joseph M. Gowaskie, "From Conflict to Cooperation: John Mitchell and Bituminous Coal Operators, 1898–1908," *The Historian*, XXXVIII (1976), pp. 669–88. *See also* Elsie Glick, *John Mitchell* (New York, 1929), and John Mitchell, *Organized Labor: Its Problems, Purposes and Ideals* (Philadelphia, 1903), especially pp. 186–94.
68. John Mitchell to William D. Ryan, June 6, 1907, in John Mitchell Papers.
69. Mitchell to Harry N. Taylor, June 10, 1907, Mitchell Papers.
70. After the conclusion of the Omaha conference, Mitchell wrote to Hart and said: "I received the copy of the agreement made between the representatives of the Union Pacific and the Central Coal and Coke Companies and the United Mine Workers of America and am very well satisfied with the terms arranged." Mitchell to John J. Hart, June 10, 1907, Mitchell Papers. That Mitchell cooperated with Hart is evidenced clearly in a later exchange of letters. Hart informed Mitchell that "things are going along pretty nicely at all our mines I am glad to say, except the men are not as enthusiastic about working every day as I'd like to see them." Mitchell advised him: "In the matter of the men remaining away from work, permit me to suggest, in a personal way, that you put your foot down firmly upon that practice. It is better to stop it in its inception. After a while the men will probably claim that it is established condition and any interferences with it would be an infringement upon their contract rights." See Hart to Mitchell, n.d., and Mitchell to Hart, November 30, 1907, Mitchell Papers.

71. *UMWJ,* June 27, 1907.
72. Wyoming *Tribune,* June 14, July 9, 1907.
73. Numano Yasutarō to Komuro Jutarō, August 21, 1909, enclosure, "Waiomingu-shū ni Okeru Nihon Kōfu to Rēboru Yunyon," JF-MAD JARP, reel 7; Rokki Jihōsha, *Sanchūbu to Nihonjin,* pp. 101–5; Kāru Yoneda, *Zaibei Nihonjin Rōdōsha no Rekishi* (Tokyo, 1967), p. 51.
74. United Mine Workers of America, *Minutes of the International Executive Board,* June 28, 1907.
75. Rocky Mountain *News,* July 11, 1907.
76. Denver *Post,* July 11, 1907.
77. Wyoming *Tribune,* July 11, 1907.
78. Cheyenne *Daily Leader,* July 11, 1907.
79. *UMWJ,* July 25, 1907.
80. Numano to Komura, August 21, 1909, enclosure, C. Condow et al to Mitchell, July 24, 1907. Condow is an alternative romanization of Kondō.
81. Numano to Komura, August 21, 1909. Since a copy of the original agreement is unavailable, the exact year is unknown.
82. United Mine Workers of America, *Minutes of the Fifteenth Annual Convention, January 18–27, 1904,* p. 151.
83. United Mine Workers of America, *Minutes of the Thirteenth Annual Convention, January 20–29, 1902,* p. 49.
84. *UMWJ,* March 3, 1904. Even after Mitchell stepped down from the UMWA presidency, he continued to uphold this view as a member of the AFL executive committee. When he argued for regulation of immigration in general, he always placed Asian immigration in a special undesirable category. In April 1909 he said: " . . . The trades unions and the workingmen of America would like to regulate immigration without prejudice against anyone except it be the Asiatics. The workingmen of America are opposed to an Asiatic workingman coming here." Transcript of Address before the American Academy of Political and Social Science, Philadelphia, April 17, 1909, Mitchell Papers. Later he elucidated upon the reasons: "The American wage-earner, be he native or immigrant, entertains no prejudice against his fellow from other lands; but, as self-preservation is the first law of nature, our workmen believe and contend that their labor should be protected against the competition of an induced immigration comprised largely of men whose standards and ideals are lower than our own. The demand for the exclusion of Asiatics . . . is based solely upon the fact that, as a race, their standard of living is extremely low and their assimilation by Americans impossible." John Mitchell, "Protect the Workman," *The Outlook,* September 11, 1909, 67; and John Mitchell, *Organized Labor,* pp. 176–85; and John Mitchell, *The Wage Earner and His Problems* (Washington, D.C., 1913), pp. 27–41.

85. *UMWJ,* November 21, 1901.
86. *UMWJ,* December 6, 1906.
87. Numano to Komura, August 21, 1909, enclosure, Mitchell to Condow et al., August 8, 1907. The contractors eventually stayed on as interpreters as a result of John Mitchell's concession. The contractors-turned-interpreters handled all the affairs of the Japanese miners relating to the union and the coal operators. The miners paid the interpreters a monthly "translation fee" of a dollar in exchange for this service. Interviews, Ota Noboru, November 11, 1977, and Ōno Shōgorō, November 12, 1977, Rock Springs, Wyoming. Mr. Ōno entered the service of the Union Pacific Coal Company in 1905 and retired after World War II.
88. For the complete text of the agreement, *see* Rock Springs *Miner,* August 17, 1907. For excerpts, *see UMWJ,* August 15, 1907.
89. *UMWJ,* August 15, 1907.
90. Union Pacific Coal Company, *History of the Union Pacific Coal Miners, 1868–1940,* xli.
91. Ibid., xii.
92. Rokki Jihōsha, *Sanchūbu to Nihonjin,* pp. 104–5.
93. Eugene O. Porter, "The Colorado Strike of 1913—An Interpretation," *Historian,* XII (1949), pp. 3–27; George S. McGovern and Leonard F. Guttridge, *The Great Coalfield War* (Boston, 1972); Billie B. Jensen, "Woodrow Wilson's Intervention in the Coal Strike of 1914," *Labor History,* XV (1974), pp. 66–77.
94. McGovern and Guttridge, *The Great Coalfield War,* pp. 51–52. *See also* George G. Suggs, Jr., "The Colorado Coal Miners' Strike, 1903–1904: A Prelude to Ludlow?" *Journal of the West,* 12:1 (1973), pp. 36–52, and George G. Suggs, Jr., "Militant Western Labor Confronts the Hostile State: A Case Study," *Western Historical Quarterly,* 2:4 (1971), pp. 385–400.
95. Suzuki, *Intāmaunten Dōhō Hattatsushi,* pp. 446–51.
96. U.S. Immigration Commission, *Immigrants in Industries,* XXV, pp. 257–70.
97. *Kororado Shimbun,* September 23, October 10, 1913.
98. Ibid., May 5, 1914.
99. Ibid., May 4, 1914.
100. Ibid.; *Nichibei Shimbun,* May 13–14, 1914; McGovern and Guttridge, *The Great Coalfield War,* pp. 263–64; and George P. West, *Report on the Colorado Strike* (Washington, D.C., 1915), p. 135. For Louis Tikas and Greek immigrant miners, *see* Zeese Papanikolas, *Buried Unsung: Louis Tikas and the Ludlow Massacre* (Salt Lake City, 1982).
101. *Kororado Shimbun,* May 7, 1914.
102. Ibid., June 13, 1914.
103. Ibid., January 23, 1915.

104. Ibid., January 28, 1915.
105. Philip Taft, *Labor Politics American Style: The California State Federation of Labor* (Cambridge, Mass., 1968), pp. 170–74, and Mary A.M. Burki, "Paul Scharrenberg: White Shirt Sailor," Ph.D. dissertation, University of Rochester, 1971, p. 81.
106. Sandra C. Taylor, *Advocate of Understanding: Sidney Gulick and the Search for Peace with Japan* (Kent, 1984).
107. The Federal Council of the Churches of Christ in America, *Report of the Christian Embassy to Japan, April 30, 1915*, p. 42. *See also* The Federal Council of the Churches of Christ in America, *Annual Report For The Year 1915* (New York, 1916), p. 172.
108. Sidney L. Gulick to Keishirō Matsui, February 2, 1915. Unless otherwise noted, all correspondence and Japanese government dispatches cited below are from Uyehara, Cecil H., *Checklist of Archives in the Japanese Ministry of Foreign Affairs, Tokyo, 1868–1945*, Washington, D.C.: U.S. Library of Congress, 1954, MT Series, reel 743.
109. San Francisco *Bulletin*, January 13, 1915. Frederick W. Ely wrote a regular column covering labor affairs in this daily.
110. See Sōdōmei Gojūnenshi Kankō Iinkai, *Sōdōmei Gojūnenshi* (Tokyo, 1964), I, p. 134; Shibusawa Masahide, *Taiheiyō ni Kakeru Hashi: Shibusawa Eiichi no Shōgai* (Tokyo, 1970), pp. 279–80; and Stephen S. Large, *The Rise of Labor in Japan: The Yuaikai, 1912–1919* (Tokyo, 1972), pp. 59–60. These works draw upon the opinions of Suzuki Bunji and Shibusawa Eiichi who credited Gulick with the original idea. *See* Suzuki Bunji, *Rōdō Undō Nijūnen* (Tokyo, 1931), pp. 110–11, and Shibusawa Eiichi, "Rōdōsha Shokun," *Rōdō Oyobi Sangyō*, 47 (July 1915), pp. 8–12. Paul Scharrenberg himself neither took credit for the idea nor denied originating it. *See* Paul Scharrenberg, "The Attitude of Organized Labor Towards the Japanese," *Annals of the American Academy of Political and Social Science: Present-Day Immigration With Special Reference to the Japanese*, 93:182 (1921), pp. 34–38, and Paul Scharrenberg, "History of the First Half Century of the California State Federation of Labor," MSS, n.d., 79–81, Scharrenberg Collection, Bancroft Library, University of California, Berkeley. Neither Philip Taft nor Mary A.M. Burki treats the question of who first proposed the idea.
111. Matsui to Gulick, February 4, 1915.
112. Numano Yasutarō to Katō Takaaki, January 14, 1915.
113. Katō to Numano, February 9, 1915.
114. For the founding of the Yūaikai and its formative years, *see* Sōdōmei Gojūnenshi Kankō Iinkai, *Sōdōmei Gojūnenshi*, pp. 43–121; Large, *The Rise of Labor in Japan*, pp. 11–57; and Matsuo Takayoshi, *Taishō Demokurashi no Kenkyū* (Tokyo, 1966), pp. 138–235.
115. For Suzuki's personal background, *see* Sōdōmei Gojūnenshi Kankō Iinkai, *Sōdōmei Gojūnenshi*, pp. 59–67; Large, *The Rise of Labor in Japan*,

pp. 11–57; and Matsuo, *Taishō Demokurashi no Kenkyū*, pp. 138–59. *See also* the recent essays by Yoshida Chiyo, "Suzuki Bunji ni Kansuru Ichi Kenkyū—Oitachi to Haikei," *Nihon Rōdō Kyōkai Zasshi*, 200/201 (1975), pp. 103–14; "Suzuki Bunji no Shōgai: Miyagi no Rōdō Undō wo Chūshin to Shite," ibid., 19:2 (1977), pp. 62–72; and "Seinen Jidai no Suzuki Bunji," *Mita Gakkai Zasshi*, 70:6 (1977), pp. 674–85. For Reverend Clay MacCauley's influence on Suzuki, *see* Matsui Shichirō, "Kurei Makkōrei no Shōgai to Shisō—Sono Yūaikai to no Kankei," *Keizai Keiri Ronsō*, 7:3 (December 1972), pp. 66–85.

116. Shibusawa, *Taiheiyō ni Kakeru Hashi*, especially pp. 167–436, and Kyugoro Obata, *An Interpretation of the Life of Viscount Shibusawa* (Tokyo, 1939), pp. 167–235.

117. Gulick to Matsui, February 10, 1915, and Suzuki, *Rōdō Undō Nijūnen*, p. 111.

118. The Federal Council of the Churches of Christ in America, *Report of the Christian Embassy to Japan, April 30, 1915*, p. 25.

119. Katō to Numano, February 27, 1915.

120. Numano to Katō, April 9, 1915.

121. Ibid.

122. Gulick to Suzuki, April 7, 1915. A Japanese translation of this letter appeared in *Rōdō Oyobi Sangyō*, 46 (June 1915), p. 41.

123. Gulick to Shibusawa, April 7, 1915.

124. Shibusawa, *Taiheiyō ni Kakeru Hashi*, pp. 280–281.

125. Matsui to Shibusawa, May 1, 1915.

126. Katō to Shibusawa, May 8, 1915. Of Suzuki's projected travel expenses of 2,000 yen, Shibusawa contributed 500 yen. Shibusawa to Sakata Jūjirō, June 1, 1915.

127. Suzuki Bunji, "Tobei Tsūshin," *Rōdō Oyobi Sangyō*, 50 (October 1915), pp. 2–10. The San Francisco commercial and labor presses covered Suzuki's arrival and initial activities. *See*, for example, San Francisco *Bulletin*, July 6, 20, August 28, 1915, and *Labor Clarion*, September 3, 10, 1915. The Japanese immigrant press gave him extensive coverage. *See Shin Sekai*, August 6, 7, 9, 14, 16, 19, 20, and September 6, 1915, and the *Nichibei Shimbun* on the corresponding dates.

128. William T. Bonsor, "Abuse of Courtesy?" *Labor Clarion*, July 30, 1915.

129. California State Federation of Labor, *Proceedings of the Sixteenth Annual Convention, October 4 to 8, 1915*, 11.

130. Ibid., 13–14.

131. Suzuki Bunji, "Kashū Rōdō Taikai Shusseki no Ki," *Rōdō Oyobi Sangyō*, 52 (December 1915), pp. 8–14.

132. California State Federation of Labor, *Proceedings of the Sixteenth Annual Convention, October 4 to 8, 1915*, p. 35.

133. Suzuki, "Kashū Rōdō Taikai Shusseki no Ki." Suzuki later expounded

on the economic reason. *See* Suzuki Bunji, "Beikoku no Rōdōsha," in Nihon Imin Kyōkai, *Saikin Ishokumin Kenkyū* (Tokyo, 1917), pp. 474–506.

134. Yoshimatsu Sadaya reported that Mutō Chōzō, a Japanese who accompanied them to the convention, got along marvelously with German-American delegates. A close friend of Suzuki, Mutō was en route back to Japan after studying in Germany and England. His ability to converse in German made him popular among such delegates. Yoshimatsu Sadaya, "Rōdō Taikai Zakkan," *Rōdō Oyobi Sangyō*, 52 (December 1915), pp. 15–20.

135. American Federation of Labor, *Report of Proceedings of the Thirty-Fifth Annual Convention, November 8 to 22, 1915*, p. 233.

136. Suzuki Bunji, "Beikoku Rōdō Taikai Shusseki no Ki," *Rōdō Oyobi Sangyō*, 54 (February 1916), pp. 12–16.

137. Numano to Ishii Kikujirō, December 21, 1915.

138. *Shin Sekai*, December 13, 1915, and Suzuki Bunji, "Zaibei Nihon Rōdō Dōmeikai Seiritsu," *Rōdō Oyobi Sangyō*, 54 (February 1916), pp. 17–18.

139. Kublin, *Asian Revolutionary: The Life of Sen Katayama*, pp. 213–34.

140. Numano to Ishii, January 5, 1916.

141. Katayama Sen Tanjō Hyakunen Kinenkai, *Katayama Sen Chosakushū* (Tokyo, 1960), II, pp. 316–17.

142. Oka Shigeki, "Katayama Sen to Amerika," *Kaizō* (July 1951), pp. 77–83.

143. James D. Phelan to Scharrenberg, October 14, 1915.

144. Scharrenberg to Phelan, October 15, 1915.

145. California State Federation of Labor, Press Release, January 31, 1916.

146. *Coast Seamen's Journal*, December 22, 1915.

147. Franklin Hichborn, *Story of the Session of the California Legislature of 1915* (San Francisco, 1916), pp. 231–32.

148. Frederick W. Ely to Shibusawa, August 21, 1916.

149. Ishii to Hanihara Masanao, August 19, 1916.

150. Hanihara to Ishii, August 22, 1916.

151. California State Federation of Labor, *Proceedings of the Seventeenth Annual Convention, October 2 to 6, 1916*, p. 17.

152. Ibid., 41–42.

153. Ibid., 16.

154. *Labor Clarion*, August 4, 11, 18, 1916. See also *Shin Sekai*, August 3, 5, 6, 8, 9, 1916.

155. California State Federation of Labor, *Proceedings of the Seventeenth Annual Convention*, p. 16. In August Ely had noted that the Japanese workers and employment agencies were "highly commended by trade unionists for their action." Ely to Shibusawa, August 21, 1916.

156. California State Federation of Labor, *Proceedings of the Seventeenth Annual Convention*, p. 19.

157. San Francisco *Examiner*, October 5, 1916. During the strike of San Francisco culinary workers, Hugo Ernst had praised the Japanese for having been "loyal to the labor movement." *Labor Clarion*, August 18, 1916.

158. San Francisco *Bulletin*, October 5, 1916.

159. California State Federation of Labor, *Proceedings of the Seventeenth Annual Convention*, p. 36.

160. Ibid., p. 37. For another abbreviated account, *see* Taft, *Labor Politics American Style*, pp. 172–74.

161. Suzuki Bunji, "Rōdō Taikai Shusseki no Ki," *Rōdō Oyobi Sangyō*, 65 (January 1917), pp. 2–11.

162. Ibid. *See also Shin Sekai*, October 9, 17–20, 1916.

163. *Shin Sekai*, November 17, 1916.

164. San Francisco *Bulletin*, October 21, 1916.

165. Hanihara to Honno Ichirō, December 1, 1916.

166. American Federation of Labor, *Report of Proceedings of the Thirty-Sixth Annual Convention, November 13 to 25, 1916*, p. 191.

167. Ibid.

168. Satō Aimaro to Honno, November 25, 1916.

169. Suzuki Bunji, "Shimei wo Hatashite Kaeru—Beikoku Rōdō Taikai Shusseki Hōkoku," *Rōdō Oyobi Sangyō*, 67 (March 1917), pp. 2–11.

170. California State Federation of Labor, *Proceedings of the Eighteenth Annual Convention, October 1 to 6, 1917*, p. 77.

171. Alexander Saxton, *The Indispensable Enemy: Labor and the Anti-Chinese Movement in California* (Berkeley and Los Angeles, 1971).

172. Burki, "Paul Scharrenberg: White Shirt Sailor," pp. 162–73.

173. Paul Scharrenberg, "Transcript of Taped Recorded Interviews for the Bancroft Library, May–August, 1954," p. 62.

174. Paul Scharrenberg, "The Japanese in Hawaii," *American Federationist*, 29:10 (1922), p. 742.

175. Paul Scharrenberg, "Vital Issues Before State Labor Movement," *Organized Labor*, September 1, 1928, p. 5. Scharrenberg was not above conjuring up the yellow peril image. As late as 1945, he reminded William Green, AFL president, that "if it had not been for the vision, the determination and the perseverance of the American Federation of Labor there would have been a *million* instead of a hundred thousand Japanese in this country (emphasis added)." Scharrenberg to William Green, March 1, 1945, Scharrenberg Collection, Bancroft Library. This remark was made in conjunction with the anticipated release of Japanese-Americans from American concentration camps and their return to the Pacific Coast.

NOTES

176. K. K. Kawakami, *Japan in World Politics* (New York, 1917), p. 88.
177. Ibid., p. 96.
178. *Heimin,* 12 (August 1917).

Chapter V

1. Abiko Kyūtarō, "Hokubei ni Okeru Nihon Imin Mondai," *Tōkyō Keizai Zasshi,* 1470 (December 19, 1908), pp. 9–11, and 1471, (December 26, 1908), pp. 9–11, and Abiko Kyūtarō, "Hainichi Mondai no Shinsō Oyobi Sono Shōrai," *Taiyō,* 15:5 (1909), pp. 60–67.
2. Abiko Kyūtarō, "Genka no Kyōgu ni Shosuru Zairyū Dōhō no Kakugo," *Hokubei Nōhō,* 2:1 (1911), pp. 11–14, and Abiko Kyūtarō, "Zaibei Dōhō Toku ni Shūkyōka ni Nozomu," *Shin Tenchi,* 2:6 (1911), pp. 5–8.
3. Yamamura, "Abiko Kyūtarō wo Oboete," August 3, 1956, Oka Papers; Yamano, "Senpai Abiko-san," n.d., ibid; Konno, "Senken no Akari Arishi Kaitakusha: Abiko Kyūtarō-shi wo Keibo," September, 1955, ibid; Fujioka, *Ayumi no Ato,* pp. 472–82; and *Okina Kyūin Zenshū,* III, pp. 227–36.
4. Kashū Nihonjin Chūō Nōkai, *Rōnō Konshinkai Kinen* (San Francisco, 1909).
5. *Hokubei Nōhō,* 2:1 (1911), p. 6.
6. Abiko, "Hainichi Mondai no Shinsō Oyobi Sono Shōrai."
7. For Abiko's thinking regarding the establishment of the Yamato Colony, *see* Abiko Kyūtarō, "Shakkan Moshikomisho," February 10, 1914, JARP, JFMAD, reel 17; Shakuma, "Rekishi Inmetsu no Tan," pts. 93–96; Oka Seizō, "Abiko Kyūtarō Den," *Hokubei Mainichi,* May 13–16, 1980; Fujioka, *Ayumi no Ato,* pp. 472–77; and Yamano, "Senpai Abiko-san." For a history of the colony, *see* Kesa Noda, *Yamato Colony, 1906–1960* (Livingston-Merced, 1981).
8. Zaibei Nihonjinkai, *Zaibei Nihonjinshi,* pp. 813–14.
9. U.S. Census Office, *Twelfth Census of the United States, 1900* (Washington, D.C., 1902), pt. I: *Agriculture,* cxviii.
10. Ueno Kisaburō to Komura Jutarō, April 30, 1902, enclosure no. 2, *Nihon Gaikō Bunsho, 1902* (Tokyo, 1957), XLIV, pp. 697–99.
11. U.S. Bureau of the Census, *Chinese and Japanese in the United States, 1910* (Washington, D.C., 1914), Bul. 127, p. 44.
12. *Nichibei Nenkan,* no. 3, San Francisco, 1907, pp. 104–5; no. 4, 1908, pp. 102–3; no. 5, 1909, appendix no. 1, pp. 1–2; no. 6, 1910, pp. 87–88; no. 7, 1911, pp. 130–31; no. 8, 1912, pp. 100–1; no. 9, 1913, pp. 107–8; and no. 10, 1914, pp. 120–21. These figures do not always add up correctly, but the margin of error is small.

13. *Nichibei Nenkan,* no. 6, 1910, pp. 64–78, and Ōfu Nippōsha, *Sakuramento Heigen Nihonjin Taisei Ichiran Dai-Ni* (Sacramento, 1909), pp. 44–46.
14. *Nichibei Nenkan,* no. 6, 1910, p. 80.
15. Ibid., p. 73.
16. Ibid., p. 71.
17. U.S. Immigration Commission, *Immigrants in Industries,* XXIV, pp. 303–5.
18. Ibid., pp. 306–7.
19. *Nichibei Shimbun,* April 26, 1913.
20. See the documents relating to Yokoi Hideyoshi and others in JARP, JFMAD, reel no. 17.
21. Numano Yasutarō to Katō Takaaki, October 14, 1914, JARP, JFMAD, reel 57. This report is based on a comprehensive consular listing of all landholdings as of the end of 1913. A detailed list of individual owners and their acreage is appended to it. The total owned acreage of 29,735 acres is higher than the *Nichibei Nenkan* figure of 26,707 for 1913. The 1914 *Nichibei Nenkan* total was 31,828 acres, but the newspaper noted that this increase was in part attributable to omissions in the 1913 total. The 1913 consular total is doubtless more accurate. The data below on the number of landholding companies are drawn from this report too.
22. Abiko, "Shakkan Moshikomisho," February 10, 1914.
23. Zaibei Nihonjinkai, *Zaibei Nihonjinshi,* p. 278.
24. California State Superintendent of Banks, *First Annual Report* (Sacramento, 1910), pp. 535–38.
25. See, for example, Ivan H. Light, *Ethnic Enterprise in America: Business and Welfare Among Chinese, Japanese, and Blacks* (Berkeley, 1972), pp. 27–30.
26. Chiba Toyoji, "Zairyū Dōhō Nōgyō Kinyū Mondai," *Hokubei Nōhō,* 2:5 (1911), pp. 1–3.
27. Numano to Makino Shinken, November 1, 1913, JARP, JFMAD, reel 17.
28. Numano to Katō, April 27, 1914, ibid.
29. The 1914 and 1918 figures are drawn from *Nichibei Nenkan,* no. 11, 1915, 123–24, and no. 12, 1918, 5–6. The 1920 data are from Eliot G. Mears, *Resident Orientals on the American Pacific Coast* (Chicago, 1928), p. 255. Mears used the statistics of the Japanese Association of America in his study. The 1920 U.S. Census recorded a total acreage of only 361,276 acres. Since the census figures are much lower than Japanese statistics, I have relied upon Mears.
30. There is no statistical breakdown of the acreage purchased in the name of Nisei children.
31. Chiba Toyoji, "Kashū Tochihō no Dageki Eikyō Ippan," *Kashū Chūō Nōkai Geppō,* 2:12 (1917), pp. 1–3.
32. *Nichibei Nenkan,* no. 12, 1918, pp. 7–8.

33. Chinda Sutemi to Okabe Nagatsune, June 13, 1891, enclosure, "Dai-Nipponjinkai Kisoku," JARP, JFMAD, reel 1.

34. Daniels, *The Politics of Prejudice*, pp. 21–22.

35. Zaibei Nihonjin Kyōgikai Chūōbu, *Dai-Ikkai Oyobi Nikai Hōkokusho* (San Francisco, 1902).

36. Tōga Yo'ichi, *Nichibei Kankei Zai-Beikoku Nihonjin Hatten Shiyō* (Oakland, 1927), pp. 127–32.

37. Thomas J. O'Brien to Hayashi Tadasu, November 26, 1907, *Nihon Gaikō Bunsho: Tai-Bei Imin Mondai Keika Gaiyō Fuzokusho*, pp. 47–52.

38. Hayashi to O'Brien, February 18, 1908, ibid., pp. 84–94.

39. Independent of the Foreign Ministry, Takahashi Sakuei, a professor of international law at Tokyo University, appeared in San Francisco, exactly at the time Koike assumed his new post, in order to secure reports on the immigrant socialists and anarchists. For the record, however, he arrived in the United States to study the immigration question. From two informants Takahashi obtained secret reports which ended up in the hands of Yamagata Aritomo, elder statesman of the ruling Meiji oligarchy, who wanted to topple the Saionji Cabinet for being too lenient on political radicals. See Ōhara Kei, "Takahashi Sakuei Kyōju Ate Koike Chōzō Tatsumi Tetsuo no Tegami," *Tōkyō Keidai Gakkaishi*, 29/30 (1960), pp. 395–424; Ōhara Kei, "Genrō Yamagata Aritomo e no Shokan," ibid., 39 (1963), pp. 157–97; and Takahashi Sakuei, *Nichibei no Shin Kankei* (Tokyo, 1910), pp. 321–31.

40. *Shin Sekai*, January 16, 1908.

41. Zaibei Nihonjinkai, *Zaibei Nihonjinkai Hōkokusho* (San Francisco, 1909–10), no. 1, pp. 2–3, and no. 2, p. 4.

42. *Hōrei Zensho*, 5 (Tokyo, 1909), pp. 171–72.

43. Hayashi to O'Brien, February 23, 1908, *Nihon Gaikō Bunsho: Tai-Bei Imon Mondai Keika Gaiyō Fuzokusho*, p. 105.

44. Nagai Matsuzō to Chinda, June 17, 1902, enclosure, "Geisai no Shikaku," JARP, JFMAD, reel 3.

45. The immigrant press is full of examples. See "Asahaka na Kekkon," *Taihoku Nippō*, April 25, 26, 28–30, and May 1–3, 1913, and "Kiyū Komogomo Itaru Dōhō no Shashin Kekkon," *Nichibei Shimbun*, April 15–17, 1914.

46. Fujita Kiyuko, "'Zairyū Fujin ni Atau' wo Yomite," *Shin Sekai*, September 8–10, 1912.

47. "Watashi no Kokuhaku," *Shin Sekai*, April 9, 13, 16, 17, 19, 1914. See also *Taihoku Nippō*, April 13, 16, 18, 22, 23, 1914.

48. *Shin Sekai*, December 29, 1909.

49. *Nichibei Shimbun*, September 12, 1912.

50. *Shin Sekai*, April 17, 18, May 3, 1908.

51. *Taihoku Nippō*, June 16–17, 1914.

52. *Nichibei Shimbun*, July 2, 15, 1913.

53. Ibid., February 17–19, 1916.
54. Ibid., October 11, 1916.
55. *Shin Sekai,* August 15–16, 1916, and Zaibei Nihonjinkai, *Shin To-Bei Fujin no Shiori* (San Francisco, 1919).
56. Zaibei Nihonjinkai, *Zaibei Nihonjinkai Nenpō* (San Francisco, 1917), pp. 5–6.
57. Hokubei Nihonjinkai to Aidaho Nihonjinkai, September 25, 1923, in Seibu Aidaho-shū Nihonjinkai Ta no Nihonjinkai Yori Juryō Shita Shinsho, January, 1921–December, 1928, JARP.
58. Japanese Association of Watsonville to Nihonjinkai, October 12, 1923, ibid.
59. Kawai Michiko, "Fujin no Me ni Eizuru Tokō Fujin," *Nihon Imin Kyōkai Hōkoku* (Tokyo, 1917), no. 14, pp. 31–50.
60. Ota [Tamekichi] to Uchida [Yasuya], October 5, 1919, *Nihon Gaikō Bunsho, 1919* (Tokyo, 1970), I, p. 69. Consul Matsunaga Naokichi of Seattle and Consul Ōyama Ujirō of Los Angeles made the same recommendation. *See* Matsunaga to Uchida, October 11, 1919, and Ōyama to Uchida, October 11, 1919, ibid., pp. 70–71. After consulting with State Department officials, Ambassador Shidehara Kijūrō followed suit in November. *See* Shidehara to Uchida, November 24, 1919, ibid., pp. 81–83.
61. San Francisco *Call,* October 31, 1919.
62. *Nichibei Shimbun,* July 20, August 8, 14, 1915.
63. Ota to Uchida, November 20, 1919, *Nihon Gaikō Bunsho, 1919,* I, p. 78. Under an editorial policy laid down by Abiko, the *Nichibei Shimbun* lashed out at the Japanese Association of America and Consul Ota in daily editorials. *Nichibei Shimbun,* November 1–29, December 1, 1919; *Okina Kyūin Zenshū,* III, pp. 230–31; and Akashi Junzō, "Abiko-shi no Inshō: Shashin Kekkon Kinshi Jiken no Kioku," 1956, Oka Papers. During the picture-bride controversy, Okina was the Oakland correspondent of the *Nichibei Shimbun.* Akashi was an employee of the newspaper from 1917 to 1921.
64. *Taihoku Nippō,* November 4, 1919, and *Rafu Shimpo,* November 4–7, 1919.
65. Ota to Uchida, December 2, 1919, *Nihon Gaikō Bunsho, 1919,* I, p. 96.
66. Uchida to Shidehara, December 6, 1919, ibid., pp. 101–2.

Chapter VI

1. Zaibei Nihonjinkai, *Zaibei Nihonjinkai Hōkokusho,* no. 1 (San Francisco, 1909), 13–14, no. 5 (San Francisco, 1913), pp. 14–16, and no. 6. (San Francisco, 1914), pp. 10–11.
2. *Nichibei Shimbun,* March 13, 1915, and Zaibei Nihonjinkai, *Zaibei Nihonjinkai Hōkokusho,* no. 8 (San Francisco, 1916), 9–10.

3. *Shin Sekai,* June 26, 1918.
4. Ibid., August 23, 1918.
5. Ibid., July 14, 1918.
6. Ibuka Seiko, ed., *Nihon Minzoku no Sekaiteki Bōchō* (Tokyo, 1933), pp. 415–52, and Yamamuro Buho, *Kobayashi Masasuke Den* (Tokyo, 1963), pp. 111–23.
7. Zaibei Nihonjinkai, *Zaibei Nihonjinkai Hōkokusho,* no. 7 (San Francisco, 1915).
8. Ōhashi Kanzō, *Hokubei Kashū Sutakuton Dōhōshi* (Stockton, 1937), pp. 94–99, pp. 141–42.
9. *Shin Sekai,* November 12, 19, 1911.
10. Ibid., November 25, 1911.
11. Ibid., November 21, 1911.
12. Ibid., December 8, 1911.
13. Ibid., December 29, 1911.
14. Ibid., February 15–16, 1912.
15. Ibid., March 13–14, 1912. Published by Doi Uchizō, this newspaper was the *Chūka Jihō* (The Japanese Times of Central California). The editor was Wakao Kyonan. As a result of this incident, 7 persons were arrested and charged with assault and battery, and 32 were charged with disturbing the peace. *Shin Sekai,* March 17, 1913, and Fresno *Morning Republican,* March 15, 1913.
16. Kuyama Yasushi, *Kindai Nihon to Kirisutokyō, Meiji-hen* (Tokyo, 1962), pp. 201–04.
17. Ibid., pp. 270–75.
18. *Shin Sekai,* April 1–2, 1912.
19. Ibid., April 2, 1912.
20. Itō Banshō, pseud., *Fukei Jiken no Shinsō* (Fresno, 1912), p. 87.
21. SBZSME, pp. 311–84, and Ohara Kei, " 'Daigyaku Jiken' no Kokusaiteki Eikyō," *Shisō,* 471 (1963), pp. 62–73.
22. Tōga Yo'ichi, *Nichibei Kankei Zai-Beikoku Nihonjin Hatten Shiyō,* p. 102. Sakon sympathized with the farmers near the Ashio Copper Mine in Tochigi Prefecture who had suffered from the sulfuric gas discharged by the mine. Just two months prior to his first controversial article, an incident relating to the mines had occurred. In December 1901 Tanaka Shōzō unsuccessfully attempted to petition the Emperor directly to bring the plight of the farmers to his attention. Kōtoku Shūsui had drafted the petition. *See* Itoya Toshio, *Kōtoku Shūsui Kenkyū* (Tokyo, 1967), pp. 143–49.
23. *Nichibei Shimbun,* April 3, 1913. This issue marked the fourteenth anniversary of the *Nichibei Shimbun.*
24. Ibid., September 27, 1912, January 1, 1913.
25. Chinda to Mutsu, September 27, 1892, enclosure, "Tanaka Tadashichi Gushinsho," September 15, 1892.

26. Zaibei Nihonjinkai, *Zaibei Nihonjinkai Kaihō Meishi Shōtai Hōkokusho* (San Francisco, 1912), Rinjigō.
27. Among these prominent Japanese were Gotō Shimpei, Shibusawa Eiichi, Takekoshi Yosaburō, Takahashi Sakue, and Kaneko Kentarō. *See, for example, Nichibei Shimbun,* January 1, 1913.
28. Otis Gibson, *The Chinese in America* (Cincinatti, 1877), pp. 111–12.
29. Ibid., p. 124.
30. Ibid., p. 126.
31. Sidney L. Gulick, *The American Japanese Problem* (New York, 1914), p. 114.
32. Ibid., p. 117.
33. Sidney L. Gulick, *American Democracy and Asiatic Citizenship* (New York, 1918), p. 216.
34. Miyazaki Kohachirō, "Dōka to Dendōdan," *Shin Tenchi,* 3:6 (1912), p. 2.
35. For Kawakami's personal recollection of his early socialist days and his departure from Japan, *see* Kawakami Kiyoshi, *Beisō Tatakawaba?* (Tokyo, 1949), p. 210–31.
36. Kiyoshi Kawakami, *Asia at the Door,* pp. 62–64.
37. Ibid., p. 66.
38. Ibid., p. 70.
39. Sidney L. Gulick, *Evolution of the Japanese* (New York, 1903), p. 77.
40. Bettensei, pseud., "Sōkō no Yōmagai," *Ajiya* (January 25, 1892), p. 20. The writer was Nakasawa Setsu.
41. *Aikoku,* April 29, 1892.
42. Fukuzawa Yukichi, "Datsuaron," in *Fukuzawa Yukichi Zenshū,* X, pp. 238–40.
43. San Francisco *Bulletin,* May 4, 1892.
44. [Bukyo] Arata, "Japanese Students: One of Them Pleads Their Case," Oakland *Enquirer,* June 18, 1892.
45. Kawakami, *Asia at the Door,* p. 79.
46. Ibid., pp. 78–79.
47. Information regarding Ichihashi's early life has been pieced together from several sources: Yamato Ichihashi Papers, Stanford University; the Japanese family registry of Ichihashi Hiromasa; and *Fukuinkai Enkaku Shiryō, Sanki no Bu (C), October 1895–December 1897,* JARP.
48. Yamato Ichihashi, *Japanese Immigration: Its Status in California* (San Francisco, 1913), p. 44.
49. Ichihashi to Numano, December 28, 1915, Uyehara, *Checklist of Archives of the Japanese Ministry of Foreign Affairs, Tokyo, 1868–1945,* MT Series, reel no. 746.
50. U.S. Congress, House of Representatives, Committee on Immigration and Naturalization, *Hearings on Japanese Immigration,* Part 2: Stockton,

Angel Island, and San Francisco, July 15–17, 19–20, 1920, 66th Congress, 2nd Session, Washington, D.C., 1921, pp. 680–81, p. 688.

51. Taiheiyō Engan Nihonjinkai Kyōgikai, "Gijiroku," June 14–17, 1919.

52. U.S. Congress, House of Representatives, Committee on Immigration and Naturalization, *Hearings on Japanese Immigration*, 702.

53. Japanese Association of America, "Memorial Addressed to President Woodrow Wilson," September 18, 1919.

54. U.S. Congress, House of Representatives, Committee on Immigration and Naturalization, *Hearings on Japanese Immigration*, p. 704.

55. Satō Tsutau, *Beika ni Okeru Dai-Nisei no Kyōiku* (Vancouver, 1932), pp. 1–2.

56. *Shin Sekai*, May 13, 1908.

57. Mikiko, "Jido no Kannen ni Tsukite," *Beikoku Bukkyō*, 9:9 (1908), pp. 15–17.

58. Zaibei Nihonjinkai, *Zaibei Nihonjinkai Hōkokusho*, no. 1 (San Francisco, 1909), p. 14.

59. *Shin Sekai*, August 12, 28, 1908.

60. *Shin Sekai*, January 13, 1910.

61. Zaibei Nihonjinkai, *Zaibei Nihonjinkai Hōkokusho*, no 3 (San Francisco, 1911), p. 10.

62. For a summary of Nagai's speech, *see Shin Tenchi*, 1:2 (1910), pp. 5–6.

63. Tōga Yo'ichi (Sankei), "Jido Kyōiku to Dōhō no Kakugo," *Shin Tenchi*, 1:5 (1910) pp. 12–13; Kannansei, pseud., "Kyōiku Sagen," *Beikoku Bukkyō*, 11:8 (1910), pp. 7–9; and *Shin Sekai*, July 27, August 7, 19–21, September 4, 11, 18, 1910. *See also* Satō, *Beika ni Okeru Dai-Nisei no Kyōiku*, pp. 18–38.

64. *Shin Sekai*, July 29, 31, 1910, August 26, 1911.

65. Hokka Nihongo Gakuen Kyōkai, *Beikoku Kashū Nihongo Gakuen Enkakushi* (San Francisco, 1930), pp. 36–37.

66. *Shin Sekai*, April 7, 1912.

67. This is the official Meiji government translation of the Rescript on Education.

68. Herbert Passin, *Society and Education in Japan* (New York, 1967), and Karasawa Tomitarō, *Kyokasho no Rekishi* (Tokyo, 1956).

69. Hokka Nihongo Gakuen Kyōkai, *Beikoku Kashū Nihongo Gakuen Enkakushi*, pp. 27–28.

70. Ibid., p. 43.

71. *Shin Sekai*, June 26, 1913.

72. Ibid., June 24, 1913.

73. Taiheiyō Engan Nihonjinkai Kyōgikai, "Gijiroku," July 15–16, 1914. The petition was printed in Nihon Imin Kyōkai, *Nihon Imin Kyōkai Hōkokusho*, 6 (1916), pp. 25–31.

74. "Nijū Kokuseki Mondai no Kaiketsu," *Nihon Imin Kyōkai Hōkokusho*, 7 (1916), pp. 27–28.

75. Daniels, *The Politics of Prejudice,* p. 85.
76. Taiheiyō Engan Nihonjinkai Kyōgikai, "Gijiroku," February 23–25 and June 24–26, 1920.
77. Ibid., July 18–21, 1921.
78. Reflecting the youthfulness of the Nisei generation, the members of the American Loyalty League were 15 years old or older. The majority of the 80 persons who participated in founding the League were in their mid-teens. *Shin Sekai,* March 29-April 1, 1923.
79. Zaibei Nihonjinkai, *Shussei Todoki Oyobi Kokuseki Ridatsu no Shiori* (San Francisco, 1922).
80. Taiheiyō Engan Nihonjinkai Kyōgikai, "Gijiroku," July 18–21, 1921, and May 24–26, 1922.
81. Hokka Nihongo Gakuen Kyōkai, *Beikoku Kashū Nihongo Gakuen Enkakushi,* pp. 9–10, and Tamezo Takimoto, "The Japanese Language Schools," March 1923, JARP, JFMAD, reel 43.
82. Nanka Kyōikukai, *Dai-Nisei no Kyōiku* (Los Angeles, 1926), p. 14.
83. Hokka Nihongo Gakuen Kyōkai, *Beikoku Kashū Nihongo Gakuen Enkakushi,* p. 102.
84. S[ukeo] Kitasawa, "Report on the Japanese Language School," ca. 1922, JARP, JFMAD, reel 43.
85. Takimoto Tamezō, "Nihongo Gakuen ni Kansuru Hōkokusho," ca. 1922, JARP, JFMAD, reel 42.
86. Oakland *Tribune,* October 25–31, 1920.
87. Yoshi S. Kuno to Dr. [Benjamin Ide] Wheeler, March 7, 1921, Yoshi S. Kuno Papers, Bancroft Library, University of California.
88. Yoshi S. Kuno to Sam H. Cohn, October 2, 1921, ibid.
89. Takimoto, "Nihongo Gakuen ni Kansuru Hōkokusho."
90. To be studied at a rate of two volumes per year, this new sixteen-volume series was for an eight-year course of study.
91. *Meyer v. Nebraska,* 262 U.S. 390 (1923).
92. *Farrington v. Tokushige,* 273 U.S. 284 (1927). For the background of this case and the litigation process, see Hawai Hōchisha, Hawai no Nihongo Gakkō ni Kansuru Shiso Oyobi Futai Jiken (Honolulu, 1927), and Hawai Hōchisha, *Nihongo Gakkō Shōso Jūshūnen Kinenshi* (Honolulu, 1937).
93. For details of the legal background, see Mears, *Resident Orientals on the American Pacific Coast,* pp. 96–118; Raymond L. Buell, "Some Legal Aspects of the Japanese Question," *American Journal of International Law,* XVII (1923), pp. 29–49; and Milton R. Konvitz, *The Alien and the Asiatic in American Law* (Ithaca, 1946), pp. 79–116. For the briefs of the Ozawa case, see San Francisco Consulate General of Japan, *Documental History of Law Cases Affecting Japanese in the United States, 1916–1924* (San Francisco, 1925), I, pp. 1–120, and JARP, JFMAD, reel 39.

94. United States Bureau of the Census, *Chinese and Japanese in the United States, 1910,* (Washington, D.C., 1914), Bul. 127, pp. 10–11.
95. Fujioka, *Minzoku Hatten no Senkusha,* pp. 107–9.
96. Daniels, *The Politics of Prejudice,* p. 39. Daniels interprets Roosevelt's message as "chiefly for Japanese consumption" which Roosevelt made "in order to have an advanced position from which to retreat in his dealings with California."
97. Uchida Sadatsuchi to Hayashi Tadasu, May 31, 1906, *Nihon Gaikō Bunsho, 1906* (Tokyo, 1959), II, p. 400.
98. Aoki Shūzō to Hayashi, November 1, 10, 1906, ibid., pp. 454–55, p. 477.
99. Hayashi to Aoki, November 18, 1906, ibid., p. 499.
100. Aoki to Hayashi, January 10, 1907, *Nihon Gaikō Bunsho, 1907* (Tokyo, 1961), III, p. 269.
101. Hayashi to Aoki, February 23, 1907, ibid., p. 345.
102. Aoki to Hayashi, February 24, 1907, ibid., p. 346. This brief diplomatic effort to negotiate naturalization rights is also covered within the broader context of the school and immigration issues by Raymond Esthus, *Theodore Roosevelt and Japan* (Seattle, 1966), pp. 128–95; and Charles E. Neu, *An Uncertain Friendship: Theodore Roosevelt and Japan, 1906–1909* (Cambridge, Mass., 1967), pp. 52–88.
103. Negoro Motoyuki, "Beikoku ni Okeru Nihonjin no Shiminken," *Nihonjin,* 196 (October 1903), pp. 28–31.
104. Kawasaki Minotarō, "Zaibei Nihonjin no Kikaken," *Taiyō,* 11:10 (July 1905), pp. 74–80.
105. *Shin Sekai,* December 6, 1906.
106. Ibid., January 12, 1907.
107. Shatoru Nihonjinkai to Hayashi, February 19, 1907, *Nihon Gaikō Bunsho, 1907,* III, p. 333.
108. Hisamizu Saburō to Hayashi, April 29, 1907, enclosure, "Kashū Nihonjinkai Chinjōsho," April 1907, JARP, JFMAD, reel 7. This petition is appended to Takahashi Sakuei, *Nichibei no Shin Kankei,* pp. 350–74.
109. Matsubara Kazuo to Hayashi, April 21, 1907, *Nihon Gaikō Bunsho, 1907,* III, pp. 401–2.
110. K. K. Kawakami, "The Naturalization of Japanese," *North American Review,* 185 (June 21, 1907), pp. 394–402.
111. Ōtsuka Sokumei, "Kashū Imonron," *Nihon Oyobi Nihonjin,* 463 (July 1907), pp. 17–21.
112. *Nichibei Shimbun,* March 28, 30, April 15, 16, 1913.
113. Ibid., July 14, 1914.
114. Ibid., December 17, 1915.
115. Ibid., January 1, 1916.
116. *Shin Sekai,* March 8, April 7, May 14, 31, and June 2, 1913.

117. *Shin Tenchi,* 4:5 (1913), p. 1.

118. *Beikoku Bukkyō,* 14:5 (1913), p. 1. Superintendent Uchida also published his opinions in support of the idea in the immigrant press. See *Nichibei Shimbun,* April 27, 29, 1913.

119. Chiba Toyoji, *Hainichi Mondai Kōgai* (San Francisco, 1913), pp. 110–26.

120. Shiminken Kakutoku Kisei Dōshikai, *Nichibei Mondai ni Taisuru Wagato no Shuchō* (San Francisco, 1913).

121. Kiyoshi K. Kawakami, "How California Treats the Japanese," *The Independent,* 74 (May 8, 1913), p. 1022, and Kiyoshi K. Kawakami, *Asia at the Door,* pp. 87–89.

122. *Taihoku Nippō,* June 16–18, 20, 21, 23–28, 1913.

123. *Shin Sekai,* April 30–May 1, 1913.

124. *Nichibei Shimbun,* April 16, 1913; *Shin Sekai,* May 24, 1913; Chiba, *Hainichi Mondai Kōgai,* pp. 119–25; and proceedings of the Japanese Association of America and its affiliated local associations published in the *Shin Sekai,* April 30–May 1, 1913.

125. Makino Shinken to Chinda Sutemi, May 17, 1913, *Nihon Gaikō Bunsho, 1913* (Tokyo, 1965), III, pp. 211–12.

126. Chinda to Makino, May 18, 1913, ibid., pp. 214–15. *See also* Paolo E. Coletta, "'The Most Thankless Task': Bryan and the California Alien Land Legislation," *Pacific Historical Review,* XXXVI (1967), pp. 163–87.

127. Chinda to William Jennings Bryan, June 4, 1913, *Nihon Gaikō Bunsho, 1913,* III, pp. 262–63. This protest note and others can also be found in U.S. Department of State, *Papers Relating to the Foreign Relations of the United States, 1912/1913* (Washington, D.C., 1920), pp. 629–53.

128. *Shin Sekai,* June 30, August 18, 1913.

129. Bryan to Chinda, July 16, 1913, *Nihon Gaikō Bunsho, 1913,* III, p. 295.

130. Makino to Chinda, July 23, 1913, ibid., pp. 323–24.

131. Taiheiyō Engan Nihonjinkai Kyōgikai, "Gijiroku," July 15–16, 1914.

132. Takao Ozawa, "Naturalization of a Japanese Subject," undated brief, JARP, JFMAD, reel 39.

133. San Francisco Consulate General, *Documental History of Law Cases Affecting Japanese in the United States, 1916–1924,* I, pp. 8–9.

134. The Ninth Circuit Court asked the Supreme Court to rule basically on two legal questions: First, was the Act of 1906 complete in itself or limited by section 2169 of the Revised Federal Statutes which restricted eligibility to free white persons and persons of African descent? Secondly, if the Act of 1906 was so limited, then were the Japanese eligible under this restriction?

135. Taiheiyō Engan Nihonjinkai Kyōgikai, "Gijiroku," August 12–14, 1916.

136. Nihon Gaimushō, "Ozawa Takao Kika Sosho Jiken . . . ni Kansuru

Ken," December 1919, JARP, JFMAD, reel 39. This document summarizes the Foreign Ministry's position on the Ozawa case.

137. Ibid.
138. *Nichibei Shimbun,* May 30, 1917.
139. Ibid., June 1, 4, 26, and July 11, 1917.
140. *Shin Sekai,* June 2, 3, 1917, and *Rafu Shimpō,* June 3, July 3, 1917.
141. Taiheiyō Engan Nihonjinkai Kyōgikai, "Gijiroku," July 26–27, 1917.
142. Ibid., July 1–3, 1918.
143. Ibid.
144. *Nichibei Shimbun,* January 31, 1918, and Nihon Gaimushō, "Ozawa Takao Kika Sosho Jiken . . . ni Kansuru Ken," December 1919.
145. *Shin Sekai,* May 7, 1918.
146. *Nichibei Shimbun,* January 1, 8, 1918.
147. Ibid., March 7, 1918.
148. *United States v. Morena,* 38 Sup. Ct. 151 (1918).
149. *Nichibei Shimbun,* April 15, 18, 20, 1918.
150. *Shin Sekai,* April 11, 12, 14, and May, 1918. Hardly a day passed without a pro-Ozawa article in the month of May.
151. Ibid., May 12–14, 1918. The editorials were from the *Ōshū Nippō* of Portland, the *Hokubei Hōchi* and *Rafu Asahi* of Los Angeles, the *Taimusu* of Stockton, the *Nippu Jiji* of Honolulu, and the *Hokubei Jiji* of Seattle.
152. *Ōfu Nippō,* May 9, 1918, and *Kakushū Jiji,* May 15, 16, 1918.
153. *Rafu Shimpō,* May 12, 1918.
154. M. Browning Carrott, "Prejudice Goes to Court—The Japanese and the Supreme Court in the 1920s," *California History,* 62:2 (1983), p. 126.
155. The other two issues were Japan's claim to former German rights in Shantung Province and control over the Micronesian Islands.
156. Taiheiyō Engan Nihonjinkai Kyōgikai, "Gijiroku," June 24–26, 1920. See also Beikoku Seihokubu Renraku Nihonjinkai, *Kaimu Oyobi Kaikei Hōkoku, August 20, 1920–February 28, 1921* (Seattle, 1921), pp. 22–23.
157. For the briefs of the Yamashita and Kono cases, see San Francisco Consulate General, *Documental History of Law Cases Affecting Japanese in the United States, 1916–1924,* I, pp. 121–175.
158. Taiheiyō Engan Nihonjinkai Kyōgikai, "Gijiroku," July 18–21, 1921. See also Beikoku Seihokubu Renraku Nihonjinkai, *Kaimu Hōkoku, March 1–August 31, 1921* (Seattle, 1921), pp. 78–82.
159. Carrott, "Prejudice Goes to Court," p. 126.
160. In terms of the legal questions raised by the Ninth Circuit Court, the Supreme Court ruled that section 2169 of the Revised Federal Statutes limited the Act of 1906 and that Ozawa was excluded by the racial restrictions of that section.
161. *Shin Sekai,* November 14, 1922.

162. *Ōfu Nippō*, November 18, 1922.
163. *Rafu Shimpō*, November 15–17, 1922.
164. *Taihoku Nippō*, November 14, 1922.
165. *Nichibei Shimbun*, November 14, 15, 1922.
166. Taiheiyō Engan Nihonjinkai Kyōgikai, "Gijiroku," July 10–12, 1923.
167. Matsumoto Ryōsaku and Satō Nobutada, "Kashū Nihonjin Nōgyōsha no Jitsujō," November 1921, JARP, JFMAD, reel 52. This report was submitted by the Japanese Agricultural Association to the Japanese Embassy.
168. Ibid.
169. Sacramento *Bee*, July 8, 1921. Webb made this July announcement in conjunction with the authorization of county grand juries to investigate violations of the alien land law.
170. Ibid., September 22, 1921. In August the Stockton Chamber of Commerce had asked Webb about cropping contracts on behalf of local landowners. If landowners agreed to pay Japanese farmers $1.50 per 100 lbs. of onion, $5.00 per ton for sugar beets, and 1½ cents per lb. for asparagus in exchange for the cultivation and harvest of these crops under employment agreements, would the landowners violate the 1920 Alien Land Law?
171. Matsumoto and Satō, "Kashū Nihonjin Nōgyōsha no Jitsujō," and *Shin Sekai*, September 3, and October 11, 1921.
172. Chiba Toyoji, "Chiba Toyoji Ikō," II, pp. 610–12. For Awaya Manei's life in Manchuria, *see* Minami Manshū Kyōikukai, *Manshū Shotō Gakkō Shūshin Kunwa Shiryō* (Dairen, 1927), I, pp. 196–215.
173. Chiba, "Chiba Toyoji Ikō," II, p. 616.
174. *Shin Sekai*, October 12, 13, 1921.
175. Fujioka Shirō, *Beikoku Chūō Nihonjinkai Shi* (Los Angeles, 1940), p. 99.
176. Ibid., pp. 102–3, and Ōyama Ujirō to Uchida Yasuya, November 5, 1921, JARP, JFMAD, reel 52.
177. Ōyama to Uchida, January 24, 1924, ibid. A partner in the Guggenheimer, Untermeyer & Marshall firm of New York, Marshall was an expert on constitutional law with experience in arguing cases before the Supreme Court.
178. For these cases, *see* San Francisco Consulate General, *Documental History of Law Cases Affecting Japanese in the United States, 1916–1924*, II, pp. 913–1013.
179. *Nichibei Shimbun*, January 16, 1922.
180. Ibid., May 3, 1922.
181. *Shin Sekai*, May 9, 1922.
182. *Nichibei Shimbun*, March 23, 1923.
183. Beikoku Seihokubu Renraku Nihonjinkai, *Kaimu Hōkoku, March 1, 1921–August 31, 1921*, (Seattle, 1921).

184. Ōyama Ujirō, "Gasshūkoku Daishinin no Kashū Tochihō Hanketsu no Eikyō Gaikyō," February 26, 1924, JARP, JFMAD, reel 53.
185. *Nichibei Shimbun,* November 21, 1923.
186. *Shin Sekai,* November 13, 1923.
187. Ibid., November 20, 1923.
188. *Rafu Shimpō,* November 27, 1923.
189. *Taihoku Nippō,* November 28, 1923.
190. Ibid., December 4, 1923.
191. *Shin Sekai,* December 1, 2, 1923, and Fujioka, *Minzoku Hatten no Senkusha,* pp. 128–33. A number of tenant farmers renewed their leases for three years just before the 1920 Alien Land Law became effective on December 9. These leases all expired in December 1923.
192. Mears, *Resident Orientals on the American Pacific Coast,* p. 255. The Foreign Ministry published slightly different statistics for 1922, recording 51,000 owned acres, 152,000 leased acres, and 145,000 contract acres for a total of 348,000 acres. See Gaimushō Tsūshōkyoku Iminka, *Kashū Oyobi Kashū Tochihō Sosho Keika Gaiyō* (Tokyo, 1923), p. 27. These figures do not change the substance of the argument, however.
193. Zaibei Nihonjinkai, *Zaibei Nihonjinshi,* p. 195.
194. Ōyama to Shidehara Kijūrō, September 26, 1924, JARP, JFMAD, reel 53. Consul Ōyama sympathized with the plight of Japanese farmers and felt that it was absurd of the Yokohama Specie Bank not to lend them money.
195. Zaibei Nihonjinkai, "Chūka Chihō Tochi Shoyūsha Hogo ni Kansuru Seigan Riyūsho, September 1924, JARP, JFMAD, reel 53.
196. Ibid.
197. Ōyama to Shidehara, September 26, 1924, ibid.
198. Shibusawa Eiichi Denki Shiryō Kankōkai, *Shibusawa Eiichi Denki Shiryō* (Tokyo, 1960), XXXIII, pp. 405–16.
199. Ichinomiya Reitarō to Kojima Kuta, December 20, 1924, JARP, JFMAD, reel 53.
200. California State Superintendent of Banks, *Fourteenth Annual Report* (Sacramento, 1923), p. 211, and *Sixteenth Annual Report* (Sacramento, 1925), p. 719.
201. Zai-Sōkō Nihon Teikoku Sō-Ryōjikan, "Hompōjin Nōkōsha no Jōkyō ni Kansuru Chōsa Hōkokusho," September 1926, Part I, JARP, JFMAD, reel 24.
202. These were the Noji and Makimoto cases. For the legal details, *see* San Francisco Consulate General, *Documental History of Law Cases Affecting Japanese in the United States, 1916–1924,* II, pp. 795–816. For the activities of the Central Japanese Association of Southern California, *see* Nanka Chūō Nihonjinkai, *Taishō Jūsan Nendo Nenpō* (Los Angeles, 1925).
203. The primary source for this section is a comprehensive report on Japanese farmers of northern California compiled by the Japanese Consulate

of San Francisco. Divided into two parts, the report is entitled "Hompōjin Nōkōsha no Jōkyō ni Kansuru Chōsa Hōkokusho," September 1926, Part I, and October 1926, Part II. An unpublished summary is entitled "Ippan Hōjin Nōgyō Gaikan," October 1926, while the published version has the same title and publication date. Part I is in JARP, JFMAD, reel 24; part II and the unpublished and published summary are in *Hompōjin no Kaigai Nōgyō Kankei Zakken,* Showa Series, Japanese Foreign Ministry, Diplomatic Records Office, Tokyo. This report surveyed how Japanese farmers resisted the 1920 Alien Land Law through middlemen, verbal agreements, and land companies. All statistics cited here are drawn from it. The report offers the best insight into how Japanese farmers mitigated the harsh effects of the law. Thus far the principal source of information on this subject has been the short comments elicited from a few Japanese farmers by interviewers who worked for Edward K. Strong. *See* Edward K. Strong, *Japanese in California,* (Stanford, 1933), pp. 103–4.

204. Kumazaki Yasushi to Uchida, July 22, 1920, JARP, JFMAD, reel 33.
205. Ota Tamekichi to Uchida, July 24, 1920, and Ōyama to Uchida, July 30, 1920, ibid.
206. Taiheiyō Engan Nihonjinkai Kyōgikai, "Gijiroku," April 9–11, 1924.
207. Takimoto Tamezō, "Gojin no Jūyō Mondai, Fuzoku Shorui Dai-Nigo: Beikoku Taiheiyō Engan Igai no Nōkōchi Chōsa ni Kansuru Ken," August 15, 1924, JARP, JFMAD, reel 53.
208. Zaibei Nihonjinkai, *Shūgai Shisatsu Hōkoku* (San Francisco, 1924).
209. Zaibei Nihonjinkai, *Shūgai Nōkōchi Chōsa Hōkoku* (San Francisco, 1926).
210. *Rafu Shimpō,* April 22, 1924.
211. Fujioka, *Minzoku Hatten no Senkusha,* pp. 167–227.
212. Ryū Hatsutarō, *Sekai Muhi no Shinnichikoku: Dai-Hōko Mekishiko* (Mexico City, 1927), and Yoshiyama Kitoku, *Chūmoku Subeki Mekishiko* (Tokyo, 1928). Matsumoto wrote his preface in the second book.
213. Fujioka Shirō, *Hokubei Mekishiko Imin no Shiori* (Tokyo, 1931).
214. Nagata Shigeshi, "Zaibei Nihonjin ni Atauru Sho," *Rikkō Sekai* (June 1924), pp. 1–25.
215. *Nichibei Shimbun,* January 30, 1924.
216. Ibid., May 20, 1924, January 7, 1925.
217. Ibid., November 13, 1924.
218. *Shin Sekai,* February 18, 1924.
219. Ibid., April 22, 1924.

Chapter VII

1. Hanihara Masao to Charles E. Hughes, April 10, 1924, *Nihon Gaikō Bunsho: Tai-Bei Imin Mondai Keika Gaiyō Fuzokusho,* p. 751.
2. *Nichibei Shimbun,* April 17, 1924.

3. Ōyama Ujirō to Hanihara Masanao, July 10, 1924, JARP, JFMAD, reel 51.
4. Matsui Keishirō to Hanihara, June 6, 1924, ibid.
5. For example, see Hiratsuka Hiroyoshi to Matsui Keishirō and Fujimura Yoshirō, June 4, 1924, enclosure, "Chinjōsho," June 2, 1924, ibid. This petition was addressed to Foreign Minister Matsui and Communication Minister Fujimura and submitted through Hyōgo Prefectural Governor Hiratsuka by prospective passengers who were waiting anxiously for possible openings on ships bound for the United States from Kobe.
6. Hiratsuka to Wakatsuki Reijirō et al., June 26, 1924, ibid.
7. Yasukochi Asakichi to Gaimushō Tsūshōkyokuchō, June 24, 1924, ibid.
8. Ibid., June 19, 1924, ibid.
9. Lee A. Makela, "Japanese Attitudes Towards the United States Immigration Act of 1924," Ph.D. dissertation, Stanford University, 1972; John R. Stemen, "The Diplomacy of the Immigration Issue," Ph.D. dissertation, Indiana University, 1960, pp. 228–71; Yoshida Tadao, Kokujoku (Tokyo, 1983); and Iino Masako, "Beikoku ni Okeru Hainichi Undō to Senkyūhyaku Nijūyonen Iminhō Seitei Katei," Tsudajuku Daigaku Kiyō, no. 10 (1978), pp. 1–41.
10. Rafu Shimpō, April 20, May 8, 28, 29, 1924.
11. Taihoku Nippō, May 3, 1924.
12. Ibid., June 3, 1914.
13. Shin Sekai, May 21, 23, 1924.
14. Ibid., July 3, 1924.
15. Ibid., April 19, 1924.
16. Taihoku Nippō, June 28, 1924.
17. Ikeda Goroku et al. to Chinda Sutemi, December 21, 1913, Nihon Gaikō Bunsho, 1914 (Tokyo, 1965), I, pp. 246–49.
18. Shin Sekai, July 25–31, 1924.
19. Yuji Ichioka, "The 1921 Turlock Incident," in Emma Gee, ed., Counterpoint, Los Angeles, 1976, pp. 195–99.
20. Ōyama to Shidehara, August 3, 1924, Nihon Gaikō Bunsho, 1924 (Tokyo, 1980), I, pp. 218–19.
21. Okamoto to Shidehara, August 7, 1924, ibid., pp. 220–21.
22. Ōhashi to Shidehara, August 9, 1924, ibid., p. 221.
23. Wakasugi to Shidehara, Augst 6, 1924, ibid., pp. 219–20.
24. Wakasugi to Shidehara, November 7, 1924, and enclosure, "Kakuseidan Shuisho," July 1924, JARP, JFMAD, reel 35.
25. Nichibei Shimbun, January 1, 1924.
26. Taihoku Nippō, May 7, 1924.

Bibliography

What follows is a select list of primary and secondary sources; see the notes for a full citation of sources. This study is based mainly upon the primary sources in the Japanese American Research Project (JARP) Collection deposited at the University Research Library of UCLA. This collection consists of Japanese language source materials pertaining to Japanese immigration and Japanese immigrants in the United States, and is the richest collection of its kind in the continental United States. The JARP Collection includes an invaluable microfilm series of Japanese Foreign Ministry archival documents on Japanese immigration history. Consisting of embassy and consular reports filed to Tokyo, and numerous attached documents, this series was indispensable for this study. The *Nihon Gaikō Bunsho*—or the published series of Japanese Foreign Ministry papers relating to foreign affairs—and the U.S. Library of Congress microfilm series of Foreign Ministry archival documents were also indispensable. Another microfilm series of Foreign Ministry documents on Japanese immigration—a series deposited at the Asian American Studies Center at UCLA, but not found in the JARP Collection, the *Nihon Gaikō Bunsho*, or the U.S. Library of Congress—was important to this study, too.

Besides Foreign Ministry archival documents, Japanese immigrant newspapers and periodicals were important primary sources. For this study the following newspapers were used: *Shin Sekai* (New World Daily), 1899–1900, 1906–25; *Nichibei Shimbun* (Japanese American News), 1905, 1912–19, 1922–25; *Rafu Shimpō* (Los Angeles Japanese Daily), 1914–24; *Taihoku Nippō* (Great Northern Daily), 1911–24; *Ōfu Nippō* (Sacramento Japanese Daily),

1909-23; *Kororado Shimbun* (Colorado Shimbun), 1911-17; and *Kakushū Jiji* (Colorado Times), 1917-24. The *Nichibei Shimbun* published the most useful yearbook, *Nichibei Nenkan* (Japanese American Yearbook), from 1905 to 1918. Of the many periodicals, the following were most helpful: *Shin Tenchi*, 1910-17, monthly organ of the Japanese International Board of Missions; *Beikoku Bukkyō*, 1901-18, monthly organ of the Buddhist Mission of America; *Hokubei Nōhō*, 1910-11, an agricultural monthly published by Noda Otosaburō; and *Kashū Chūō Nōkai Geppō*, 1916-18, monthly bulletin of the Japanese Agricultural Association of California. The records of the Great Northern and Northern Pacific Railroad Companies deposited at the Minnesota Historical Society were invaluable for examining Japanese railroad labor contracting. Other primary sources, books, dissertations, and articles published by and about Japanese immigrants which were useful to this study are listed below:

Other Primary Sources, Books, and Dissertations

ABE ISOO. *Hokubei no Shin Nippon.* Tokyo: Hakubunkan, 1905.

AKAMINE SEICHIRŌ. *Beikoku Ima Fushingi.* Tokyo: Jitsugakukai Eigakkō, 1886.

ALMAGUER, TOMAS. "Class, Race, and Capitalist Development: The Social Transformation of a Southern California County, 1848-1903." Ph.D. dissertation. University of California, Berkeley, 1979.

ARIIZUMI SADAO. *Hoshi Tōru.* Tokyo: Asahi Shimbunsha, 1983.

ARRINGTON, LEONARD J. *Beet Sugar in the West: A History of the Utah-Idaho Sugar Company, 1891-1966.* Seattle: University of Washington Press, 1966.

AYASAWA, IWAO F. *A History of Labor in Modern Japan.* Honolulu: East-West Center Press, 1966.

BAILEY, THOMAS A. *Theodore Roosevelt and the Japanese-American Crises.* Stanford: Stanford University Press, 1934.

BEIKOKU SEIHOKUBU RENRAKU NIHONJINKAI, *Kaimu Hōkoku, March 1-August 31, 1921,* Seattle: Beikoku Seihokubu Renraku Nihonjinkai, 1921.

———*Kaimu Hōkoku, September 1, 1921-February 28, 1922.* Seattle: Beikoku Seihokubu Renraku Nihonjinkai, 1922.

———*Kaimu Hōkokusho, March 1, 1922-July 31, 1922.* Seattle: Beikoku Seihokubu Renraku Nihonjinkai, 1922.

———*Kaimu Oyobi Kaikei Hōkoku, August 20, 1920-February 28, 1921.* Seattle: Beikoku Seihokubu Renraku Nihonjinkai, 1921.

BLACKER, CARMEN. *The Japanese Enlightenment: A Study of the Writings of Fukuzawa Yukichi.* Cambridge: Cambridge University Press, 1964.

BODDY, E. MANCHESTER. *Japanese in America.* Los Angeles: E. Manchester Boddy, 1921.

BOWEN, ROGER W. *Rebellion and Democracy in Meiji Japan.* Berkeley: University of California Press, 1980.

BURKI, MARY A.M. "Paul Scharrenberg: White Shirt Sailor" Ph.D. dissertation. University of Rochester, 1971.

CHIBA TOYOJI. "Chiba Toyoji Ikō." Dairen: unpublished, 1944. 2 vols.

———*Hainichi Mondai Kōgai.* San Francisco: Nichibeisha, 1913.

CONROY, HILARY, and MIYAKAWA, T. SCOTT. *East Across the Pacific.* Santa Barbara: Clio Press, 1972.

CONROY, HILARY. *The Japanese Frontier in Hawaii, 1868–1898.* Berkeley: University of California Press, 1953.

COOLIDGE, MARY R. *Chinese Immigration.* New York: Holt, 1909.

CROSS, IRA B. *A History of the Labor Movement in California.* Berkeley: University of California Press, 1935.

DANIELS, ROGER. *The Politics of Prejudice.* New York: Atheneum, 1968.

DOI YATARŌ. *Yamaguchi-ken Ōshima-gun Hawai Iminshi.* Tokuyama: Matsuno Shoten, 1980.

DUBOFSKY, MELVYN. *We Shall Be All: A History of the Industrial Workers of the World.* Chicago: Quadrangle Books, 1969.

EBIHARA HACHIRŌ. *Kaigai Hōji Shimbun Zasshi Shi.* Tokyo: Gakuji Shoin, 1936.

ESTHUS, RAYMOND. *Theodore Roosevelt and Japan.* Seattle: University of Washington Press, 1966.

FISHER, LLOYD H. *The Harvest Labor Market in California.* Cambridge: Harvard University Press, 1953.

FLETCHER, ERMA A. "A History of the Labor Movement in Wyoming." M.A. thesis. University of Wyoming, 1945.

FONER, PHILIP. *History of the Labor Movement in the United States.* New York: International Publishers, 1947–82. 6 vols.

FRANKS, JOEL S. "Boot and Shoemakers in Nineteenth Century San Francisco, 1860–1892: A Study in Class, Culture, Ethnicity, and Popular Protest in an Industrializing Community." Ph.D. dissertation. University of California, Irvine, 1983.

FUJII SEI. *Nōka no Tame ni.* Los Angeles: Komatsu Yoshimoto, 1924.

FUJIOKA SHIRŌ. *Ayumi no Ato.* Los Angeles: Ayumi no Ato Kankō Kōenkai, 1957.

———. *Beikoku Chūō Nihonjinkai Shi.* Los Angeles: Beikoku Chūō Nihonjinkai, 1940.

——— *Hokubei Mekishiko Imin no Shiori.* Tokyo: Dōbunsha, 1931.

——— *Minzoku Hatten no Senkusha.* Tokyo: Dōbunsha, 1927.

Fukuzawa Yukichi Zenshū. Tokyo: Iwanami Shoten, 1960. IX-X.

[FUMIKURA HEISABURŌ], comp. "Fukuinkai Enkaku Shiryō." San Francisco, 1935.

GAIMUSHŌ, TSŪSHŌKYOKU. *Imin Toriatsukainin ni Yoru Imin no Enkaku.* Tokyo: Gaimushō, 1910.

——*Nihon Gaikō Bunsho, 1891–1924.* Tokyo: Gamushō, 1952–1980.

——*Nihon Gaikō Bunsho: Tai-Bei Imin Mondai Keika Gaiyō.* Tokyo: Gaimushō, 1972.

——*Nihon Gaikō Bunsho: Tai-Bei Imin Mondai Keika Gaiyō Fuzokusho,* Tokyo: Gaimushō, 1972.

GEE, EMMA, ed. *Counterpoint.* Los Angeles: UCLA, Asian American Studies Center, 1976.

GIBSON, OTIS. *The Chinese in America.* Cincinatti: Hitchcock & Walden, 1877.

GLUCK, ELSIE. *John Mitchell.* New York: John Day, 1929.

GULICK, SIDNEY L. *American Democracy and Asiatic Citizenship.* New York: Charles Scribner's Sons, 1918.

——. *The American Japanese Problem.* New York: Charles Scribner's Sons, 1914.

——. *Evolution of the Japanese.* New York: Fleming H. Revell, 1903.

GOMPERS, SAMUEL. *Seventy Years of Life and Labour.* New York: E. P. Dutton, 1925. 2 vols.

GOTŌ YŌ'ICHI. *Setonai-kai no Chiiki no Shiteki Tenkai.* Tokyo: Fukutake Shoten, 1978.

HARAGUCHI KIYOSHI. *Jiyū Minken Shizuoka Jiken.* Tokyo: San'ichi Shobō, 1984.

HATA, DONALD T., Jr. *" 'Undesirables': Early Immigrants and the Anti-Japanese Movement in San Francisco, 1892–1893."* New York: Arno Press, 1978.

HICHBORN, FRANKLIN. *Story of the Session of the California Legislature of 1915.* San Francisco: James H. Barry, 1916.

HIROSHIMA-KEN. *Hiroshima Kenshi, Kindai.* Hiroshima: Hiroshima-ken, 1980 and 1982. 2 vols.

——. *Hiroshima Kenshi, Kindai Gendai Shiryō-hen.* Hiroshima: Hiroshima-ken, 1976. III.

HOKKA NIHONGO GAKUEN KYŌKAI. *Beikoku Kashū Nihongo Gakuen Enkakushi.* San Francisco: Hokka Nihongo Gakuen Kyōkai, 1930.

HOKUBEI OKINAWA KURABU. *Hokubei Okinawajinshi.* Los Angeles: Hokubei Okinawa Kurabu, 1981.

IBUKA SEIKO, ed. *Nihon Minzoku no Sekaiteki Bōchō: Kobayashi Masasuke Ronbunshū.* Tokyo: Keigansha, 1933.

ICHIHASHI, YAMATO. *Japanese Immigration: Its Status in California.* San Francisco: Japanese Association of America, 1913.

——. *Japanese in the United States.* Stanford: University Press, 1932.

ICHIOKA, YUJI, et al., comp. *A Buried Past: An Annotated Bibliography of the Japanese American Research Project Collection.* Berkeley and Los Angeles: University of California Press, 1974.

IKE, NOBUTAKA. *The Beginnings of Political Democracy in Japan.* Baltimore: John Hopkins University Press, 1950.

IMAIZUMI GENKICHI. *Senku Kyūjūnen: Miyama Kan'ichi to Sono Jidai.* Kamakura: Mikunisha, 1942.

INASAWA KEN'ICHI et al. *Zaibei Nihonjin Chōrō Kyōkai Rekishi.* San Francisco, 1912.

INGALLS, WALTER R., ed. *The Mineral Industry: Its Statistics, Technology and Trade During 1907.* New York: Hill Publishing, 1908.

IRIE TORAJI, *Hōjin Kaigai Hattenshi.* Tokyo: Imin Mondai Kenkyūkai, 1938. 2 vols.

IRIMAJIRI, YOSHINAGA. *Mutō Sanji.* Tokyo: Yoshikawa Kōbunkan, 1964.

IRIYE, AKIRA. *Pacific Estrangement.* Cambridge: Harvard University Press, 1972.

IROKAWA DAIKICHI. *Shinpen Meiji Seishinshi.* Tokyo: Chūō Kōronsha, 1973.

ISHIDA KUMATARŌ and SHŪYŪ SANJIN, pseud. *Kitare, Nihonjin.* Tokyo: privately printed, 1887.

ITŌ BANSHŌ, pseud. *Fukei Jiken no Shinsō.* Fresno: Shinjūsha, 1912.

ITŌ KAZUO. *Hokubei Hyakunen Sakura.* Seattle: Hokubei Hyakunen Sakura Jikkō Iinkai, 1969.

———*Zoku Hokubei Hyakunen Sakura.* Seattle: Hokubei Hyakunen Sakura Jikkō Iinkai, 1972.

ITOYA TOSHIO. *Daigyaku Jiken.* Tokyo: San'ichi Shobō, 1970.

———*Kōtoku Shūsui Kenkyū.* Tokyo: Aoki Shoten, 1967.

KACHI, TERUKO O. *The Treaty of 1911 and the Immigration and Alien Land Law Issue Between the United States and Japan, 1911–1913.* New York: Arno Press, 1978.

KAJIMA MORINOSUKE. *Nihon Gaikōshi.* Tokyo: Kajima Kenkyūjo Shuppankai, 1971. XIII.

KAMEI SHUNSUKE. *Jiyū no Seichi—Nihonjin to Amerika.* Tokyo: Kenkyūsha Shuppan, 1978.

KANAI SHIGEO and ITŌ BANSHŌ, pseud. *Hokubei no Nihonjin.* San Francisco: Kanai Tsūyaku Jimusho, 1909.

KANZAKI KIYOSHI. *Kakumei Densetsu: Bakuretsu no Kan.* Tokyo: Chūō Kōronsha, 1960.

———*Kakumei Densetsu: Tennō Ansatsu no Kan.* Tokyo: Chūō Kōronsha, 1960.

KARASAWA TOMITARŌ. *Kyokasho no Rekishi.* Tokyo: Sōbunsha, 1956.

KASHŪ NIHONJIN CHŪŌ NŌKAI. *Rōnō Konshinkai Kinen.* San Francisco: Kashū Nihonjin Chūō Nōkai, 1909.

KASHŪ NIHONJIN KUTSUKŌ DŌMEIKAI. *Kashū Nihonjin Kutsukō Dōmeikai Enkaku no Gaiyō.* San Francisco: Kashū Nihonjin Kutsukō Dōmeikai, 1917.

KATAYAMA SEN. *Jiden.* Tokyo: Iwanami Shoten, 1954.

———*The Labor Movement in Japan.* Chicago: C. H. Kerr, 1918.

——*Shin Tobei*. Tokyo: Tobei Kyōkai, 1904.

——*Tobei no Hiketsu*. Tokyo: Tobei Kyōkai, 1906.

——*Zoku Tobei Annai*. Tokyo: Tobei Kyōkai, 1902.

KATAYAMA SEN TANJŌ HYAKUNEN KINENKAI. *Katayama Sen Chosakushū*, Tokyo: Katayama Sen Tanjō Hyakunen Kinenkai, 1960. II.

KATŌ TOSHIRŌ. *Zaibei Dōhō Hattenshi*. Tokyo: Hakubunkan, 1908.

KAWAKAMI, KIYOSHI K. *Asia at the Door*. New York: Fleming H. Revell, 1914.

——*Beisō Tatakawaba?* Tokyo: Nichibei Tsūshinsha, 1949.

——*Japan and World Peace*. New York: Macmillan, 1919.

——*Japan in World Politics*. New York: Macmillan, 1919.

——*The Real Japanese Question*. New York: Macmillan, 1921.

KAWAMURA TETSUTARŌ. *Saikin Katsudō Hokubei Jigyō Annai*. Tokyo: Hakubunkan, 1906.

KAWASHIMA ISAMI. *Nichibei Gaikōshi*. San Francisco: Hatae Minoru, 1932.

KEIEISEI, pseud. *Beikoku Kugaku Jikki*. Tokyo: Naigai Shuppan Kyōkai, 1911.

KIKUCHI KUNISAKU. *Chōkei Kihi no Kenkyū*. Tokyo: Rippū Shobō, 1977.

KINMOUTH, EARL H. *The Self-Made Man in Meiji Japanese Thought*. Berkeley and Los Angeles: University of California Press, 1981.

KIPNIS, IRA. *The American Socialist Movement, 1897–1912*. New York: Columbia University Press, 1952.

KOBAYASHI TADAO. *Nyū Karedonia-tō no Nihonjin: Keiyaku Imin no Rekishi*. Tokyo: Karucha Shuppansha, 1977.

KOJŌ YUTAKA. *Inoue Kakugorō-kun Ryakuden*. Tokyo: Inoue Kakugorō-kun Kōrō Hyōshōkai, 1919.

KONVITZ, MILTON R. *The Alien and the Asiatic in American Law*. Ithaca: Cornell University Press, 1946.

Kōtoku Shūsui Zenshū. Tokyo: Meiji Bunken, 1968, VI.

KUBLIN, HYMAN. *Asian Revolutionary: The Life of Sen Katayama*. Princeton: Princeton University Press, 1964.

KUKA CHŌSHI HENSHŪ IINKAI. *Yamaguchi-ken Kuka Chōshi*. Kuka: Kuka Chōshi Henshū Iinkai, 1954.

KUYAMA YASUSHI. *Kindai Nihon to Kirisutokyō*. Nishinomiya: Kirisutokyō Gakuto Kyōdaidan, 1962, Meiji-hen.

LARGE, STEPHEN S. *The Rise of Labor in Japan: The Yuaikai, 1912–1919*. Tokyo: Sophia University, 1972.

LIGHT, IVAN H. *Ethnic Enterprise in America: Business and Welfare Among Chinese, Japanese, and Blacks*. Berkeley and Los Angeles: University of California Press, 1972.

MAKELA, LEE A. "Japanese Attitudes Towards the United States Immigration Act of 1924." Ph.D. dissertation. Stanford University, 1972.

MATSUO TAKAYOSHI. *Taishō Demokurashi no Kenkyū*. Tokyo: Aoki Shoten, 1966.

McGOVERN, GEORGE S., and GUTTRIDGE, LEONARD F. *The Great Coalfield War.* Boston: Houghton Mifflin, 1972.

MEARS, ELIOT G. *Resident Orientals on the American Pacific Coast.* Chicago: University of Chicago Press, 1928.

MILLIS, H. A. *The Japanese Problem in the United States.* New York: Macmillan, 1915.

MINAMI MANSHŪ KYŌIKUKAI. *Manshū Shotō Gakkō Shūshin Kunwa Shiryō.* Dairen: Minami Manshū Kyōikukai, 1927. I.

MISHIMA, MARÍA ELENA OTA. *Siete Migraciones Japonesas en México, 1890–1978.* México, D.F.: El Colegio de México, 1982.

MITCHELL, JOHN. *Organized Labor: Its Problems, Purposes and Ideals.* Philadelphia: American Book & Bible House, 1903.

——*The Wage Earner and His Problems.* Washington, D.C.: P.S. Ridsdale, 1913.

MIZUTANI BANGAKU, pseud. *Hokubei Aichi Kenjinshi.* Sacramento: Aichi Kenjinkai, 1920.

MODELL, JOHN. *The Economics and Politics of Racial Accomodation: The Japanese of Los Angeles, 1900–1942.* Urbana: University of Illinois Press, 1977.

MORI KATSUMI. *Jinshin Baibai—Kaigai Dekasegijo.* Tokyo: Shibundo, 1960.

MORIYAMA, ALAN T. *Imingaisha: Japanese Emigration Companies and Hawaii.* Honolulu: University of Hawaii Press, 1985.

MURAI KŌ. *Zaibei Nihonjin Sangyō Sōran.* Los Angeles: Beikoku Sangyō Nipposha, 1940.

MURAYAMA, YUZO. "The Economic History of Japanese Immigration to the Pacific Northwest: 1890–1920." Ph.D. dissertation. University of Washington, 1982.

MUTŌ SANJI. *Beikoku Ijūron.* Tokyo: Maruzen Shokan, 1887.

Mutō Sanji Zenshū. Tokyo: Shinjūsha, 1963. I.

NAGAI MATSUZŌ. *Nichibei Bunka Kōshōshi.* Tokyo: Yōyōsha, 1955, V.

NANKA KYŌIKUKAI. *Dai-Nisei no Kyōiku.* Los Angeles: Nanka Kyōikukai, 1926.

NANKA NIKKEIJIN SHŌGYŌ KAIGISHO. *Minami Kashū Nihonjin Shichijūnenshi.* Los Angeles: Nanka Nikkeijin Shōgyō Kaigisho, 1960.

——*Minami Kashū Nihonjinshi.* Los Angeles: Nanka Nikkeijin Shōgyō Kaigisho, 1956.

NEU, CHARLES E. *An Uncertain Friendship: Theodore Roosevelt and Japan, 1906–1909.* Cambridge: Harvard University Press, 1967.

NIHON IMIN KYŌKAI. *Nihon Imin Kyōkai Hōkokusho.* no. 2–16, Tokyo, 1915–1919.

——*Saikin Ishokumin Kenkyū.* Tokyo: Tōyōsha, 1917.

NIHON RIKKŌKAI. *Nihon Rikkōkai Sōritsu Gojūnenshi.* Tokyo: Rikkōkai, 1946.

Nihon Teikoku Tōkei Nenkan, 1882–1908.

NIHONJIN KUTSUKŌ DŌMEIKAI. *Nihonjin Kutsukō Dōmeikai Kiyaku Oyobi Saisoku*. San Francisco: Nihonjin Kutsukō Dōmeikai, 1904.

NODA, KESA. *Yamato Colony, 1906–1960*. Livingston-Merced: Livingston-Merced JACL Chapter, 1981.

NOTEHELFER, F. G. *Kotoku Shusui: A Portrait of a Japanese Radical*. Cambridge: Cambridge University Press, 1971.

OBATA, KYUGORO. *An Interpretation of the Life of Viscount Shibusawa*. Tokyo: Shibusawa Seien-O Kinenkai, 1939.

ŌFU INSHI, pseud. *Zaibei Seikō no Nihonjin*. Tokyo: Hōbunkan, 1904.

ŌFU NIPPŌSHA. *Sakuramento Heigen Nihonjin Taisei Ichiran Dai-Ni*. Sacramento: Ōfu Nippōsha, 1909.

OGAWA, GOTARO. *Conscription System in Japan*. New York: Oxford University Press, 1921.

ŌHASHI KANZŌ. *Hokubei Kashū Sutakuton Dōhōshi*. Stockton: Su-shi Nihonjinkai, 1937.

OKA NAOKI. *Sokoku wo Teki to Shite*. Tokyo: Meiji Bunken, 1965.

OKAMOTO SHIRŌ, ed. *Jūdai Naru Kekka*. Tokyo: Minyūsha, 1924.

Okina Kyūin Zenshū. Toyama: Okina Kyūin Zenshū Kankōkai, 1971–1973, 10 vols.

OKINAWA-KEN. *Okinawa Kenshi: Imin*. Naha: Okinawa-ken, 1974, VII.

ŌTSUKA SHUN'ICHI. *Takoma Nihonjin Hattenshi*. Tacoma: Takoma Jihōsha, 1917.

ŌTSUKA ZENJIRŌ. *Hishakaishugi*. Tokyo: Ōtsuka Zenjirō, 1911.

ŌYAMA UJIRŌ. *Taiheiyō no Higan*. Tokyo: Hōchi Shimbunsha, 1925.

Ozaki Gakudō Zenshū. Tokyo: Kōronsha, 1955, III.

PAPANIKOLAS, ZEESE. *Buried Unsung: Louis Tikas and the Ludlow Massacre*. Salt Lake City: University of Utah Press, 1982.

PARK, ROBERT E. *The Immigrant Press and Its Control*. New York: Harper & Bros., 1922.

PASSIN, HERBERT. *Society and Education in Japan*. New York: Columbia University Press, 1965.

RAYBACK, JOSEPH G. *A History of American Labor*. New York: The Free Press, 1966.

ROKKI JIHŌSHA. *Sanchūbu to Nihonjin*. Salt Lake City: Rokki Jihōsha, 1925.

RYŪ HATSUTARŌ. *Sekai Muhi no Shinnichikoku: Dai-Hōko Mekishiko*. Mexico City: Kōshinsha, 1927.

SACRAMENTO BETSUIN. "Kakochō, 1900–1902."

SAN FRANCISCO CONSULATE GENERAL OF JAPAN. *Documental History of Law Cases Affecting Japanese in the United States, 1916–1924*. San Francisco: San Francisco Consulate General of Japan, 1925, 2 vols.

SANDMEYER, ELMER C. *The Anti-Chinese Movement in California*. Urbana: University of Illinois Press, 1939.

SATŌ TSUTAU. *Beika ni Okeru Dai-Nisei no Kyōiku*. Vancouver, Can.: Jikyōdō, 1932.

SAXTON, ALEXANDER. *The Indispensable Enemy: Labor and the Anti-Chinese Movement in California.* Berkeley and Los Angeles: University of California Press, 1971.

SCALAPINO, ROBERT A. *Democracy and the Party Movement in Prewar Japan.* Berkeley: University of California Press, 1953.

———*The Early Japanese Labor Movement.* Berkeley: Center for Japanese Studies, Japan Research Monograph, no. 5, 1983.

SHAKAI BUNKO. *Zaibei Shakaishugisha Museifushugisha Enkaku.* Tokyo: Kashiwa Shobō, 1964, I.

———*Shakaishugisha Museifushugisha Jimbutsu Kenkyū Shiryō.* Tokyo: Kashiwa, 1964, VII–VIII.

SHANNON, DAVID A. *The Socialist Party of America.* Chicago: Quadrangle Books, 1967.

SHIBUSAWA MASAHIDE. *Taiheiyō ni Kakeru Hashi: Shibusawa Eiichi no Shōgai.* Tokyo: Yomiuri Shimbunsha, 1970.

SHIBUSAWA SEIEN KINEN ZAIDAN RYŪMONSHA. *Shibusawa Eiichi Denki Shiryō.* Tokyo: Shibusawa Eiichi Denki Shiryō Kankōkai, 1955–1964. XXXI–XXXV, XXXIX–XL.

SHIMANUKI HYŌDAYŪ. *Rikkōkai to wa Nanzo ya.* Tokyo: Keiseisha, 1911.

———*Shin Tobeihō.* Tokyo: Hakubunkan, 1911.

———*Saikin Tobeisaku.* Tokyo: Nihon Rikkōkai, 1904.

———*Tobei Annai.* Tokyo: Chūyōdō, 1901.

SHIMINKEN KAKUTOKU KISEI DŌSHIKAI. *Nichibei Mondai ni Taisuru Wagato no Shuchō.* San Francisco: Shiminken Kakutoku Kisei Dōshikai, 1913.

SHIMIZU TSURUZABURŌ. *Beikoku Rōdō Benran.* Tokyo: privately printed, 1902.

SHIOTA SHŌBEI. *Kōtoku Shūsui no Nikki to Shokan.* Tokyo: Miraisha, 1965.

SHIZUOKA-KEN MINKEN HYAKUNEN JIKKŌ IINKAI. *Dokyumento Shizuoka-ken no Minken.* Tokyo: San'ichi Shobō, 1984.

SŌDŌMEI GOJŪNENSHI KANKŌ IINKAI. *Sōdōmei Gojūnenshi.* Tokyo: Sōdōmei, 1964, I.

STEMEN, JOHN R. "The Diplomacy of the Immigration Issue." Ph.D. dissertation. Indiana University, 1960.

STRONG, EDWARD K. *Japanese in California.* Stanford: Stanford University Press, 1933.

SUEHIRO SHIGEO. *Hokubei no Nihonjin.* Tokyo: Nishōdō, 1915.

SUMIYA MIKIO. *Katayama Sen: Kindai Nihon no Shisōka.* Tokyo: Tōkyō Daigaku Shuppankai, 1960.

Sutōji Zenshū, Tokyo: Sutōji Zenshū Kankōkai, 1934–1935, 4 vols.

SUZUKI BUNJI. *Nihon no Rōdō Mondai.* Tokyo: Kaigai Shokumin Gakkō Shuppanbu, 1919.

———*Rōdō Undō Nijūnen.* Tokyo: Ichigensha, 1931.

SUZUKI ROKUSUKE et al, *Intāmaunten Dōhō Hattatsushi.* Denver: Denba Shimpōsha, 1910.

TAFT, PHILIP. *Labor Politics American Style: The California State Federation of Labor.* Cambridge: Harvard University Press, 1968.
——*The A.F. of L. in the Time of Gompers.* New York: Harper, 1957.
TAIHEIYŌ ENGAN NIHONJINKAI KYŌGIKAI, "Gijiroku," 1914–1925.
TAKAHASHI KANJI. *Imin no Chichi: Katsunuma Tomizō Sensei Den.* Honolulu: Suda Bunkichi, 1953.
TAKAHASHI SAKUEI. *Nichibei no Shin Kankei.* Tokyo: Shimizu Shoten, 1910.
TAKEUCHI KŌJIRŌ. *Beikoku Seihokubu Nihon Iminshi.* Seattle: Taihoku Nippōsha, 1929.
TAYLOR, SANDRA C. *Advocate of Understanding: Sidney Gulick and the Search for Peace with Japan.* Kent, Ohio: Kent State University Press, 1984.
TEZUKA YUTAKA. *Kindai Nihonshi no Shin Kenkyū.* Tokyo: Keiō Tsūshin, 1983, II.
TŌGA YO'ICHI. *Nichibei Kankei Zai-Beikoku Nihonjin Hatten Shiyō.* Oakland: Beikoku Seisho Kyōkai Nihonjinbu, 1927.
TOMITA GENTARŌ and ŌWADA YAKICHI. *Beikoku-yuki Hitori Annai: Ichimei Sōkō Jijō,* Yokohama: Kaiinsha, 1886.
TOTTEN, GEORGE O. *The Social Democratic Movement in Prewar Japan.* New Haven: Yale University Press, 1966.
TSURUTANI HISASHI. *Amerika Seibu Kaitaku to Nihonjin.* Tokyo: Nihon Hōsō Shuppan Kyōkai, 1977.
Union Pacific Coal Company. *History of the Union Pacific Coal Mines, 1868–1940,* Omaha, Neb.: The Colonial Press, [1940].
United Japanese Society of Hawaii. *A History of Japanese in Hawaii.* Honolulu: United Japanese Society of Hawaii, 1971.
U.S. Bureau of the Census. *Chinese and Japanese in the United States, 1910.* Washington, D.C.: GPO, 1914, Bul. 127.
U.S. Commission on Industrial Relations. *Final Report and Testimony: The Colorado Coal Miners' Strike.* Washington, D.C.: GPO. 1916.
U.S. Congress, House Committee on Immigration and Naturalization. *Hearings on Japanese Immigration.* Parts 1–4, 1920. Washington, D.C.: GPO, 1921.
U.S. Congress, House Committee on Mines and Mining. *Conditions in the Coal Mines of Colorado.* Parts 1–4. Washington, D.C.: GPO, 1914.
U.S. Department of Commerce and Labor. *Bulletin of the Bureau of Labor.* 47 (1903), 66 (1906), and 94 (1911).
U.S. Immigration Commission. *Immigrants in Industries: Part 25: Japanese and Other Immigrant Races in the Pacific Coast and Rocky Mountain States.* Washington, D.C.: GPO, 1911, XXIII–XXV.
U.S. Superintendent of Immigration. *Annual Reports, 1890–1908.* Washington, D.C.: GPO, 1891–1909.
UYEHARA, CECIL H. *Checklist of Archives in the Japanese Ministry of Foreign Affairs, Tokyo, 1868–1945.* Washington, D.C.: Library of Congress, 1954.

WAKATSUKI YASUO. *Hainichi no Rekishi.* Tokyo: Chūkō Shinsho, 1972.

WAKAYAMA-KEN. *Wakayama-ken Iminshi.* [Wakayama-shi]: Wakayama-ken, 1957.

WARE, NORMAN J. *The Labor Movement in the United States, 1860–1895.* New York: Vintage Books, n.d.

WASHIZU [BUNZŌ] SHAKUMA. *Zaibei Nihonjin Shikan.* Los Angeles: Rafu Shimpōsha, 1930.

WATANABE KANJIRŌ. *Kaigai Dekasegi Annai.* Tokyo: Naigai Shuppan Kyōkai, 1902.

WEINTRAUB, HYMAN. *Andrew Furuseth: Emancipator of the Seamen.* Berkeley: University of California Press, 1959.

WEST, GEORGE P. *Report on the Colorado Strike.* Washington, D.C., U.S. Commission on Industrial Relations, 1915.

YAGASAKI, NORITAKA. "Ethnic Cooperativism and Immigrant Agriculture: A Study of Japanese Floriculture and Truck Farming in California." Ph.D. dissertation, University of California, Berkeley, 1982.

YAMAGUCHI-KEN ŌSHIMA-GUN TŌWA-CHŌ. *Tōwa Chōsi.* Tōwa: Tōwa-chō, 1982.

YAMANAKA CHŪJI. *Funtō no Dai-Issen.* Tokyo: privately printed, 1925.

YAMANE GO'ICHI. *Saikin Tobei Annai.* Tokyo: Tobei Zasshisha, 1906.

YAMAZAKI TOMOKO. *Ameyuki-san no Uta.* Tokyo: Bungei Shunjū, 1978.

——*Sandakan Hachiban Shōkan.* Tokyo: Chikuma Shobō, 1972.

YOKOYAMA GENNOSUKE. *Kaigai Katsudō no Nihonjin.* Tokyo: Shōkadō, 1906.

YONEDA KĀRU. *Zaibei Nihonjin Rōdōsha no Rekishi.* Tokyo: Shin Nihon Shuppan, 1967.

YOSHIDA TADAO. *Kokujoku.* Tokyo: Keizai Ōraisha, 1983.

YOSHIMURA DAIJIRŌ. *Dokuritsu Jikyū Hokubei Yūgaku Annai.* Osaka: Okashima Shoten, 1903.

——*Seinen no Tobei.* Tokyo: Chūyōdō, 1902.

——*Tobei Seigyō no Tebiki.* Osaka: Okashima Shoten, 1903.

YOSHIMURA, TOSHIO. *George Shima: Potato King and Lover of Chinese Classics.* Fukushima: Oseido, 1981.

YOSHIYAMA KITOKU. *Chūmoku Subeki Mekishiko.* Tokyo: Nichiboku Kenkyūsha, 1928.

ZAIBEI NIHONJIN KYŌGIKAI CHŪŌBU. *Dai-Ikkai Oyobi Nikai Hōkokusho.* San Francisco: Zaibei Nihonjin Kyōgikai Chūōbu, 1902.

ZAIBEI NIHONJINKAI. *Shin Tobei Fujin no Shiori.* San Francisco: Zaibei Nihonjinkai, 1919.

——*Shūgai Nōkōchi Chōsa Hōkoku.* San Francisco: Zaibei Nihonjinkai, 1926.

——*Shūgai Shisatsu Hōkoku.* San Francisco: Zaibei Nihonjinkai, 1924.

——*Shussei Todoki Oyobi Kokuseki Ridatsu no Shiori.* San Francisco: Zaibei Nihonjinkai, 1922.

——*Zaibei Nihonjinkai Hōkokusho.* San Francisco: Zaibei Nihonjinkai, 1909–1918, no. 1–10.
——*Zaibei Nihonjinkai Kaihō Meishi Shōtai Hōkokusho.* San Francisco: Zaibei Nihonjinkai, 1912, Rinjigō.
——*Zaibei Nihonjinkai Nenpō.* San Francisco, Zaibei Nihonjinkai, 1917.
——*Zaibei Nihonjinshi.* San Francisco, Zaibei Nihonjinkai, 1940.

Articles

ABIKO KYŪTARŌ. "Genka no Kyōgu ni Shosuru Zairyū Dōhō no Kakugo." *Hokubei Nōhō* 2:1 (1911), 11–14.
——"Hainichi Mondai no Shinsō Oyobi Sono Shōrai." *Taiyō* 15:5 (1909), 60–67.
——"Hokubei ni Okeru Nihon Imin Mondai." *Tōkyō Keizai Zasshi* 1470 (December 19, 1908), 9–11 and 1471 (December 26, 1908), 9–11.
——"Zaibei Dōhō Toku ni Shūkyōka ni Nozomu." *Shin Tenchi* 2:6 (1911), 5–8.
ALMAGUER, TOMAS. "Racial Domination and Class Conflict in Capitalist Agriculture: The Oxnard Sugar Beet Workers' Strike of 1903." *Labor History* XXV (1984), 325–50.
ARAI KATSUHIRO, and TAMURA NORIO. "Jiyū Minkenki ni Okeru Sōkō Wangan Chiku no Katsudō." *Tōkyō Keizai Daigaku Jimbun Shizen Kagaku Ronshū* 65 (1983), 75–136.
BAN SHINZABURŌ. "Yo wa Beikoku nite Yonsen Dōhō to Tomo ni Sūko no Tetsudō wo Fusetsu Shitari." *Jitsugyō no Nihon* 12:16 (1909), 1158–60.
BUELL, RAYMOND L. "Some Legal Aspects of the Japanese Question." *American Journal of International Law* XVII (1923), 29–49.
CARROTT, M. BROWNING. "Prejudice Goes to Court—The Japanese and the Supreme Court in the 1920s." *California History* LXII (1983), 122–38.
COLETTA, PAOLO E. "'The Most Thankless Task': Bryan and the California Alien Land Legislation." *Pacific Historical Review* XXXVI (1967), 163–87.
CULIN, STEWART. "The Gambling Games of the Chinese in America." *Publications of the University of Pennsylvania, Philology, Literature and Archaeology* 1:4 (1891), 1–17.
DANIELS, ROGER. "The Japanese." In Higham, John, ed. *Ethnic Leadership in America.* Baltimore: Johns Hopkins University Press, 1978, 36–63.
——"Westerners from the East: Oriental Immigrants Reappraised." *Pacific Historical Review* XXXV (1966), 373–83.

EBIHARA HACHIRŌ. "Sōkō Nihonjin Aikoku Dōmei Shimatsu." *Meiji Bunka Kenkyū* 2 (1934), 98–117.

FERGUSON, EDWIN E. "The California Alien Land Law and the 14th Amendment." *California Law Review* XXXV (1947), 61–90.

GOWASKIE, JOSEPH M. "From Conflict to Cooperation: John Mitchell and Bituminous Coal Operators, 1898–1908." *Historian* XXXVIII (1976), 669–88.

HAGIHARA, N. "Baba Tatsui: An Early Japanese Liberal." *Far Eastern Affairs*, 3 (1963), 121–43.

HALLAGAN, WILLIAM S. "Labor Contracting in Turn-of-the-Century California Agriculture." *Journal of Economic History* 40 (1980), 757–76.

HAVEL, HIPPOLYTE. "Kotoku's Correspondence with Albert Johnson." *Mother Earth* 6:6 (1911), 180–84; 6:7 (1911), 207–9; 6:9 (1911), 282–86.

HIGGS, ROBERT. "Landless by Law: Japanese Immigrants in California Agriculture to 1941." *Journal of Economic History* 38 (1978), 205–25.

HIGGS, ROBERT. "The Wealth of Japanese Tenant Farmers in California, 1909." *Agricultural History* 53 (1979), 488–93.

HILL, HERBERT. "Anti-Oriental Agitation and the Rise of Working-Class Racism." *Society* X (1973), 43–54.

———"Racial Practices of Organized Labor." *New Politics* IV (1965), 26–46.

IINO MASAKO. "Beikoru Ni Okeru Hainichi Undō to Senkyūhyaku Nijūyonen Iminhō Seitei Katei," *Tsudajuku Daigaku Kiyō*, no. 10 (1978), 1–41.

IKE, NOBUTAKA. "Kotoku Denjiro: Advocate of Direct Action." *Far Eastern Quarterly* III (1944), 222–35.

ISHIKAWA TOMONORI. "Fuiji Shotō ni Okeru Nihonjin Keiyaku Imin ni Tsuite." *Ijū Kenkyū* 14 (1977), 55–79.

———"Hiroshima Wangan Jigozen-son Keiyaku Imin no Shakai Chirigakuteki Kōsatsu." *Jimbun Chiri* 19:1 (1967), 75–91.

———"Hiroshima-ken Nanbu Kuchita-son Keiyaku Imin no Shakai Chirigakuteki Kōsatsu." *Shigaku Kenkyū* 99 (1967), 33–52.

———"Nihon Shutsu Imin ni Okeru Imingaisha to Keiyaku Imin ni Tsuite." *Ryūkyū Daigaku Hōbun Gakubu Kiyō, Shakai-hen* 14 (1970), 19–46.

———"Setonai Chiiki Kara no (Shutsu) Imin." *Shigaku Kenkyū* 126 (1975), 54–71.

———"Yamaguchi-ken Ōshima-gun Kuka-son Shoki Hawai Keiyaku Imin no Shakai Chirigakuteki Kōsatsu." *Chiri Kagaku* 7 (1967), 25–37.

IWATA, MASAKAZU. "The Japanese Immigrants in California Agriculture." *Agricultural History* XXXVI (1962), 25–37.

JENSEN, BILLIE B. "Woodrow Wilson's Intervention in the Coal Strike of 1914." *Labor History* XV (1974), 66–77.

KAWAI MICHIKO. "Fujin no Me ni Eizuru Tokō Fujin." *Nihon Imin Kyōkai Hōkoku*, Tokyo, 1917, no. 14, 31–50.

KAWAKAMI, KIYOSHI K. "How California Treats the Japanese." *The Independent* 74 (May 8, 1913), 1019–22.

——"The Naturalization of Japanese." *North American Review* 185 (June 21, 1907), 394–402.

KAWAMURA [TETSUTARŌ] YŪCHŌ, pseud. "Arasuka no Rōdō." *Amerika* 11:2 (February 1907), 71–72.

KAWASAKI MINOTARŌ. "Zaibei Nihonjin no Kikaken." *Taiyō* 11:10 (1905), 74–80.

KODAMA MASAAKI. "Dekasegi Imin no Jittai: Hiroshima-ken Aki-gun Hesaka-son wo Sozai to Shite." *Hiroshima-shi Kōbun Shokan Kiyō* 3 (1980), 31–53.

——"Imingaisha ni Tsuite no Ichi Kōsatsu—Kaigai Tokō Kabushikigaisha wo Chūshin ni." *Geibi Chihōshi Kenkyū* 128 (1980), 12–25.

——"Imingaisha no Jittai." In Hiroshima Shigaku Kenkyūkai. *Shigaku Kenkyū Gojūshūnen Kinen Ronsō, Nihon-hen.* Okayama: Fukutake Shoten, 1980, 459–84.

——"Kanyaku Iminsū ni Tsuite." *Hiroshima Kenshi Kenkyū*, 7 (1982), 75–93.

——"Meijiki Amerika Gasshūkoku e no Nihonjin Imin." *Shakai Keizai Shigaku* 47:4 (1981), 423–50.

——"Shoki Imingaisha no Imin Boshū to Sono Jittai." *Hiroshima Kenshi Kenkyū* 3 (1978), 20–44.

KONO HIDEO. "Sōkō no Hōji Shimbun." *Meiji Bunka* 6:1 (1930), 11–16.

KUBLIN, HYMAN. "The Japanese Socialists and the Russo-Japanese War." *Journal of Modern History* 22 (1950), 322–39.

——"The Origins of Japanese Socialist Tradition." *Journal of Politics* 14 (1952), 257–80.

——"Takano Fusataro: A Study in Early Japanese Trades-Unionism." American Philosophical Society, *Proceedings*, 103:4 (1959), 571–83.

MANRISEI, pseud. "Nihonjin no Kaigai no Seikōsha—Ukeoigyo Ban Shinzaburō-shi." *Jitsugyō no Nihon* 7:12 (June 1904), 921–23.

MARKINO, YOSHIO. "My Experiences in San Francisco." *McClure's Magazine* 36:1 (November 1910), 107–12.

MASSON, JACK, and GUIMARY, DONALD. "Asian Labor Contractors in the Alaskan Canned Salmon Industry, 1880–1937," *Labor History* XXII (1981), 377–397.

MATSUMOTO YOSHITOSHI. "Kyohuhoku Ensei Arasuka Shake Kanzume no Ukeoi Jigyō." *Tobei Zasshi* 10:11 (November 1906), 781–83.

McGOVNEY, DUDLEY O. "The Anti-Japanese Land Laws of California and Ten Other States." *California Law Review* XXXV (1947), 7–60.

Methodist Episcopal Church, *Minutes of the California Conference*, 1884–1894.

MORGAN, JAMES. "Union Movement in Wyoming." *Wyoming Labor Journal* (August 31, 1917).

MORINO KENKICHI. "Hokubei no Tankō Rōdō." *Amerika* 11:1 (January 1907), 8–9.

———. "Nichibei Kangyōsha no Jigyō Seiseki." *Amerika* 11:2 (February 1907), 76–77.

MURAYAMA TAMOTSU. "Abiko Kyūtarō: Hainichi Iminhō to Tatakau." In Niigata Nippōsha. *Zoku Echigo ga Unda Nihonteki Jimbutsu.* Niigata: Niigata Nippōsha, 1965, 311–32.

MURAYAMA, YUZO. "Contractors, Collusion, and Competition: Japanese Immigrant Railroad Laborers in the Pacific Northwest, 1898–1911." *Explorations in Economic History* 21 (1984), 290–305.

NAGATA SHIGESHI. "Zaibei Nihonjin ni Atauru Sho." *Rikkō Sekai* (June 1924), 1–25.

NAGASAWA SETSU. "Sōkō no Yōmagai." *Ajiya,* 31 (January 25, 1892), 20–21; 32 (February 1, 1892), 17; 37 (May 2, 1892), 6–7; 38 (May 9, 1892), 17–18; and 39 (May 16, 1892), 19.

———. "Sōkō Oyobi Sono Kinbō ni Okeru Sanzen no Dōhō." *Ajiya* 29 (January 11, 1892), 3–4.

NEGORO MOTOYUKI. "Beikoku ni Okeru Nihonjin no Shiminken." *Nihonjin* 196 (October 1903), 28–31.

NIMURA KAZUO, "Shokkō Giyūkai to Kashū Nihonjin Kutsukō Dōmeikai." In Rōdō Undōshi Kenkyūkai. *Reimeiki Nihon Rōdō Undō no Saikentō.* Tokyo: Rōdō Junpōsha, 1979, 116–49.

NISHIMUKAI YOSHIAKI. "Shoki no Mekishiko Imin no Kōsatsu." *Nanbei Kenkyū* 15 (1970), 31–44.

NOGUCHI, YONE. "Some Stories of My Western Life." *The Fortnight Review* DLXVI, new series (February 2, 1914), 263–76.

ŌHARA KEI. "Takahashi Sakuei Kyōju Ate Koike Chōzō Tatsumi Tetsuo no Tegami." *Tōkyō Keidai Gakkaishi* 29/30 (1960), 395–424.

———. "Genrō Yamagata Aritomo e no Shokan." *Tōkyō Keidai Gakkaishi* 39 (1963), 157–97.

———. " 'Furesuno Rōdō Dōmeikai' ni Tsuite." In Fujibayashi Keizō Hakase Kanreki Kinen Ronbunshū Henshū Iinkai. *Rōdō Mondai no Gendaiteki Kadai.* Tokyo: Daiyamondosha, 1960, 25–45.

OKA SHIGEKI. "Arabya Oyae Shusse Monogatari." *Amerika Shimbun* (February 12, 26, March 5, 1938).

———. "Katayama Sen to Amerika." *Kaizō* (July 1951), 77–83.

ŌSHIMA KIYOSHI. "Rōdō Kumiai Undō no Sōshisha: Takano Fusatarō." *Ōhara Shakai Mondai Kenkyūjo Shiryōshitsuhō* 106 (January 1965), 1–15, 124 (October 1966), 1–12, and 136 (April 1968), 1–13.

ŌTSUKA [ZENJIRŌ] SOKUMEI, pseud. "Kashū Iminron." *Nihon Oyobi Nihonjin* 463 (July 1907), 17–21.

PAPANIKOLAS, HELEN Z. and KASAI, ALICE. "Japanese Life in Utah." In Papanikolas, Helen Z., ed. *The Peoples of Utah.* Salt Lake City: Utah State Historical Society, 1976, 333–62.

PORTER, EUGENE O. "The Colorado Strike of 1913—An Interpretation." *Historian* XII (1949), 3–27.

PRYDE, GEORGE B. "The Union Pacific Coal Company, 1868 to August 1952." *Annals of Wyoming* 25 (1953), 191–205.

SALOUTOS, THEODORE. "The Immigrant in Pacific Coast Agriculture, 1880–1940." *Agricultural History* 49 (1975), 182–201.

SASSA HIROSHI. "Imingaisha to Chihō Seitō." *Kokushikan Daigaku Bungakubu Jimbun Gakkai Kiyō* 15 (1983), 61–80.

SAXTON, ALEXANDER. "Race and the House of Labor." In Nash, Gary B. and Weiss, Richard. *The Great Fear: Race in the Mind of America.* New York: Holt, Rinehart and Winston, 1970, 98–120.

SCHARRENBERG, PAUL. "The Attitude of Organized Labor Towards the Japanese." *Annals of the American Academy of Political and Social Science: Present-Day Immigration with Special Reference to the Japanese* 93:182 (1921), 34–38.

——"The Japanese in Hawaii." *American Federationist* 29:10 (1922), 742–50.

——"Vital Issues Before State Labor Movement." *Organized Labor* (September 1, 1928).

SHIMAOKA HIROSHI. "Hawai Kanyaku Imin 'Dai-Ikkai' no Keii." *Ōsaka Gakuin Daigaku Gaikokugo Ronshū* 8 (1980), 109–29.

——"Hawai 'Kanyaku Imin' to Robāto Uōka Āuin." *Ōsaka Gakuin Daigaku Gaikokugo Ronshū* 5 (1978), 129–49.

——"Hawai 'Kanyaku Imin Seido Āuin Shisutemu' to Sono Hōkai." *Ōsaka Gakuin Daigaku Gaikokugo Ronshū* 6 (1978), 68–89.

SOVIAK, EUGENE. "The Case of Baba Tatsui." *Monumenta Nipponica* XVIII (1963), 191–235.

SUGGS, GEORGE G. Jr. "The Colorado Coal Miners' Strike, 1903–1904: A Prelude to Ludlow?" *Journal of the West* 12:1 (1973), 36–52.

——"Militant Western Labor Confronts the Hostile State: A Case Study." *Western Historical Quarterly* 2:4 (1971), 385–400.

SUMIYA MIKIO. "Takano Fusatarō to Rōdo Undō—Gompers to no Kankei wo Chūshin ni." *Keizaigaku Ronshū* 29:1 (1963), 63–82.

SUZUKI BUNJI. "Tobei Tsūshin." *Rōdō Oyobi Sangyō* 50 (October 1915), 2–10.

——"Kashū Rōdō Taikai Shusseki no Ki." *Rōdō Oyobi Sangyō* 52 (December 1915), 8–14.

——"Beikoku Rōdō Taikai Shusseki no Ki." *Rōdō Oyobi Sangyō* 54 (February 1916), 12–16.

——"Zaibei Nihon Rōdō Dōmeikai Seiritsu." *Rōdō Oyobi Sangyō* 54 (February 1916), 17–18.

——"Rōdō Taikai Shusseki no Ki." *Rōdō Oyobi Sangyō* 65 (January 1917), 2–11.

"Shimei wo Hatashite Kaeru—Beikoku Rōdō Taikai Shusseki Hōkoku." *Rōdō Oyobi Sangyō* 67 (March 1917), 2–11.

TACHIKAWA KENJI. "Takano Fusatarō: Zaibei Taiken wo Chūshin to Shite." *Shirin* 65 (1982), 433–62.

TAKADA KIKUO. "Sōkō de Hakkō Sareta Hōjishi 'Aikoku' no Kotodomo." *Meiji Bunka Kenkyū* 6 (1935), 153–59.

UEKATASEI, pseud. "Zaibei Seikō Nihonjin no Hyōron—Abiko Kyūtarō-kun." *Amerika* 10:11 (November 1906), 793–794.

WAKATSUKI YASUO. "Amerika Imin Tashutsu Chiku no Yōin Bunseki." *Tamagawa Daigaku Nōgakubu Kenkyū Hōkoku* 19 (1979), 104–23.

———"Japanese Emigration to the United States, 1866–1924." In Fleming, Donald, ed. *Perspectives in American History* XII (1979), 389–515.

[WASHIZU BUNZŌ] SHAKUMA, pseud. "Rekishi Inmetsu no Tan," pts. 1–97, 1922.

YASUI, BARBARA. "The Nikkei in Oregon, 1834–1940," *Oregon Historical Quarterly* LXXVI (1975), 225–257.

YOSHIDA CHIYO. "Suzuki Bunji ni Kansuru Ichi Kenkyū—Oitachi to Haikei." *Nihon Rōdō Kyōkai Zasshi* 200/201 (1975), 103–14.

———"Suzuki Bunji no Shōgai: Miyagi no Rōdō Undō wo Chūshin to Shite." *Nihon Rōdō Kyōkai Zasshi* 19:2 (1977), 62–72.

———"Seinen Jidai no Suzuki Bunji." *Mita Gakkai Zasshi* 70:6 (1977), 674–85.

Index

Abe Isoo, 102, 104–105, 131, 190
Abe Kumakichi, 81
Abe Toyoji, 205
Abiko Kyūtarō: founding the *Nichibei Shimbun*, 20–21; as labor contractor, 59–61; as advocate of permanent settlement, 146–50; loan application to Yokohama Specie Bank, 154–55; opposition to termination of picture-bride practice, 174–75; alleged link to Kōtoku Shūsui, 183–84; on naturalization issue, 214–15, 217–18, 249, 252
Adaptation and assimilation to American society, 185–96
Aikoku, 191
Akamine Seichirō, 11, 17
Alien land law litigation: origin of, 226–29; O'Brien and Inouye case, 229–32; Porterfield and Mizuno case, 229–32; Yano case, 230–31; Frick and Satow case, 230, 232; Terrace and Nakatsuka case, 232; Supreme Court decisions and impact, 232–43; bonus test cases, 236–37
Amano Sanji, 171
American Federation of Labor (AFL), 2–3, 91, 93, 99–102, 105–106, 128–30, 132–34, 137, 141–45
American Federationist, 100–101
American Land and Produce Company, 149

American Loyalty League, 206
American Railway Union (ARU), 114
American Socialist Party, 106–107
American Sugar Beet Company, 96–97
Ammons, Elias, 126
Andō Tarō, 41–42
Anti-Jap Laundry League, 133–34, 138–40
Anti-Japanese exclusion movement, 5–6, 52, 68–69; termination of labor migration from Hawaii, 69–72; enactment of alien land laws, 137, 153–56, 224–25; agitation against picture-brides, 173–75; agitation against and regulation of Japanese language schools, 204–10; Hopland and Turlock anti-Japanese incidents, 250–51. *See also* 1924 Immigration Act.
Aoki Shūzō. 212–13
Araeda Aiji, 171
Araeda Asako, 171
Arai Seikichi, 31
Arai Tatsuya, 204
Association of Japanese Language Institutes, 207
Astoria and Columbia River Railway, 58
Awaya Manei, 228, 242

Baba Kozaburō, 97
Bakersfield lèse-majesté affair of 1911, 180–85

311